THE SECESSIONIST IMPULSE

The Secessionist Impulse

Alabama and Mississippi in 1860

William L. Barney

Princeton University Press
Princeton, New Jersey

Copyright © 1974 by Princeton University Press

All Rights Reserved

LCC: 73–16769

ISBN: 0–691–04622–0

Library of Congress Cataloging in Publication Data will
be found on the last printed page of this book

Publication of this book has been aided by
the Andrew W. Mellon Foundation

This book has been composed in Linotype Times Roman

Printed in the United States of America
by Princeton University Press, Princeton, New Jersey

For

Elaine *in Every Way*

CONTENTS

MAPS AND TABLES

MAPS

TABLES

ix

THE historiography on the coming of the Civil War, far from being a surfeited field, is deficient in many areas. A notable omission has been the lack of an adequate interpretation for the divergent ideologies of Southern political parties in 1860. After the breakup of the national Democratic party at Charleston in April, 1860, it was clear that the Breckinridge Democrats were the political instrument of Southern discontent. They insisted upon congressional protection of slavery in the territories, agitated over the reopening of the African slave trade, demanded additional slave territory, and were to provide leadership for the secession movement. The Bell Whigs and Douglas Democrats were more content with the status quo and accepted secession only with great reluctance. This fundamental divergence in Southern politics has long been recognized, but too little attention has been focused on the social and economic factors which conditioned the stance and behavior of the parties. This study, a detailed analysis of politics and secession in Alabama and Mississippi, offers an interpretation of Southern political alignments in 1860 and rests heavily on both published and manuscript census returns.

A party's ideology is a social product and cannot be understood in isolation from the voting coalitions and leadership groups which comprise the party. For the presidential election of 1860 and the subsequent elections for delegates to secession conventions, the parties' main areas of voter support, their ideologies, and the socioeconomic characteristics of their politically active members are examined. Emphasis is also placed on the pervasive sense of crisis in the South and, in particular, on the siege mentality and near paranoia which gripped Alabama and Mississippi by the fall of 1860. A fear of abolitionist plots aimed at enticing slaves to revolt, an uneasiness over severe food shortages brought about by a devastating drought, urgent demands for action generated by vigilance committees and groups of minute men, and intense racial anxieties are indispensable factors in appreciating why secession took place, when and how it did, and why it received the tacit, if not explicit, approval of the citizenry. Alabama and Mississippi were the economic bastions of the cotton aristocracy of the deep South; politically they were viewed as the two states which, after South Carolina, would have to take the lead in secession. The governors of both states had taken an advanced position on Southern rights and neither their sense of honor nor political reputations would have remained untarnished by a retreat. As A. B. Moore of Alabama expressed it to his fellow governor in South Carolina, W. H. Gist, "a crisis is approaching where the utmost vigilance, prudence and foresight will be demanded of us—So. Carolina, Ala., & Miss. have assumed high ground, & I must —will not take a single step backwards." The son of the old fire-eater Robert Barnwell Rhett observed back in January, 1860:

As to uniting the *whole* South on any means of resistance worth a fig, the idea is as absurd as it is unnecessary. Alabama and Mississippi are the only states, besides ours, of which there is ground to expect action. Georgia can do nothing (for Stephens[,] Toombs[,] and Cobb), but would throw them overboard or drive them on, in the event of an issue by other states. Those I have mentioned are quite enough to break down the spoils Democracy and, on the election of a Black Republican, to dissolve the Union.[1]

[1] A. B. Moore to W. H. Gist, April 2, 1860, Governor A. B. Moore Correspondence, ADAH; R. B. Rhett, Jr., to William Porcher Miles, January 29, 1860, W. P. Miles Papers, SHC. Alexander Stephens, Robert Toombs, and Howell Cobb were noted for their leadership of the pro-Union faction in Georgia politics.

ACKNOWLEDGMENTS

OF THE intellectual and personal debts which I collected while working on this study, none was greater than the one owed to Professor James Shenton of Columbia University who provided the original inspiration and ideas which I tried to build upon. To Professor Shenton, as well as my graduate colleagues in his seminars at Columbia, I owe a special thanks for alerting me to both the possibilities and the enjoyment of research into the antebellum South.

The task of finding and collecting data was made immeasurably lighter by the assistance and courtesy of the directors and staffs at Duke University, the University of Alabama, the University of Mississippi, the Alabama and Mississippi Departments of Archives and History, the Library of Congress, and the Southern Historical Collection in Chapel Hill, North Carolina. All of these archivists, as well as numerous clerks in Alabama and Mississippi courthouses, were unusually cooperative in permitting me access to their manuscript and newspaper holdings.

For helping me see where ideas had to be sharpened and prose trimmed, I am particularly grateful to Professors James Shenton, Eric Foner, and John Garraty of Columbia. Miss R. Miriam Brokaw and Lewis Bateman of Princeton University Press have been more than patient in offering suggestions and improvements. To Professor Elizabeth Strasser of Trenton State College I am indebted for assistance in preparing the maps.

To my wife, Elaine, I can but express a debt of gratitude that can scarcely be repaid. As researcher, typist, and proofreader, she contributed much of her time and energy. But above all, by being herself, she provided me with the encouragement and assistance which was as indispensable as it was unspoken.

William L. Barney

February 27, 1973
Hopewell, N.J.

ABBREVIATIONS

JOURNALS

AgH	*Agricultural History*
AHQ	*Alabama Historical Quarterly*
AR	*Alabama Review*
AHR	*American Historical Review*
ASR	*American Sociological Review*
CWH	*Civil War History*
DBR	*DeBow's Review*
JEH	*Journal of Economic History*
JMH	*Journal of Mississippi History*
JNH	*Journal of Negro History*
JSH	*Journal of Southern History*
MVHR	*Mississippi Valley Historical Review*
NCHR	*North Carolina Historical Review*
PSQ	*Political Science Quarterly*
PMHS	*Publications of the Mississippi Historical Society*
SAQ	*South Atlantic Quarterly*
SWHQ	*Southwestern Historical Quarterly*
TAHS	*Transactions of the Alabama Historical Society*

MANUSCRIPTS

ADAH	Alabamba Department of Archives and History
DU	Duke University
LC	Library of Congress
MDAH	Mississippi Department of Archives and History
SHC	Southern Historical Collection: University of North Carolina
UA	University of Alabama

The spelling, punctuation, and syntax of all the quotations have been followed exactly as they appeared in the original.

THE SECESSIONIST IMPULSE

ONE

THE BELEAGUERED SOUTH

"WE stand committed to the South, but we stand more vitally committed to the cause of slavery," stressed L. W. Spratt of South Carolina in 1859. "It is, indeed, to be doubted whether the South have [sic] any cause apart from the institution which affects her."[1] Spratt was in the forefront of the effort to reopen the African slave trade, but his views on the fundamental importance of slavery amounted to a truism and were shared by nearly all Southerners. During the secession winter of 1860–61 the deep South decided that slavery could no longer be protected within a Union controlled by the Republican party and embarked on the gamble of independence. The impetus for secession had been building for a generation and the movement itself served as an outlet for the ambitions and anxieties of a beleaguered society prepared to accept the leadership of those who would take it down the road to revolution.

I

Southerners were susceptible to the bold, aggressive ideology of the secessionists because of the intense internal and external pressures exerted on their slave society during the 1850's. This decade traditionally has been viewed as one of the most prosperous in the antebellum South. The prices and production of cotton, the South's great staple, were both up over comparable figures for the 1840's, and crop production in 1859 set a record. The cotton kingdom was rounding out its contours by pushing into Florida, Arkansas, and the river valleys of eastern Texas. Promising starts in manufacturing and railroad construction augured well for the future. In the

[1] *DBR*, xxvii (1859), 208.

3

case of Mississippi, it has been argued that this very prosperity imparted to the state's leaders a confidence in their
ability to go it alone outside of the Union that was lacking in
the crisis a decade earlier over the Compromise of 1850.[2]
Despite the decided growth in the Southern economy, serious dislocations arose as a result of the oligarchic concentration of wealth. Within the cotton South approximately 40%
of the slaves, farm value, cotton output, and total agricultural wealth were controlled by the top 5% of the farming
population. Planters owned not only more land than their
agricultural neighbors but also more valuable land. Moreover,
this plutocratic stratification of landholdings was characteristic of all soil regions. The elitist pattern held throughout the
1850's with only a slight distribution shift in favor of the
upper middle classes at the relative expense of the richest and
poorest groups, especially in relation to slaves. Whereas in
1850 the lower half of farming families owned 8% of the
agricultural wealth, their share fell to 6% by 1860.[3] In a
study on Hancock County, Georgia, James Bonner found that
the planters were buying up the land of small farmers and
making it increasingly difficult for the smaller landholders to
enlarge their holdings or for the tenant farmers to acquire
any land at all. The result was an exodus of small farmers
from the county and increased farm tenancy for those who remained. The sheer economic power of the elite of the slaveholding class, those owning 50 or more slaves, was staggering.

[2] Robert R. Russel, *Economic Aspects of Southern Sectionalism,
1840–1861* (New York, 1960), 199–230; John Hebron Moore,
"Mississippi's Ante-Bellum Textile Industry," *JMH*, xvi (April, 1954),
81–98; Richard W. Griffin, "Cotton Manufacturing in Alabama to
1865," *AHQ* (Fall, 1956), 289–307; and John Hebron Moore, "Economic Conditions in Mississippi on the Eve of the Civil War," *JMH*,
xxii (July, 1960), 167–178.

[3] Gavin Wright, " 'Economic Democracy' and the Concentration
of Agricultural Wealth in the Cotton South, 1850–1860," *AgH*,
xliv (Jan., 1970), 63–93; Fabian Linden, "Economic Democracy in
the Slave South: An Appraisal of Some Recent Views," *JNH*, xxxi
(April, 1946), 140–189.

Comprising less than one-third of 1% of the total white population of Alabama (or about 2% of all the white families), this group owned 28.1% of the state's total wealth in 1860. The figures for the deep South as a whole were just as impressive: 24.5% of the total personal property and 28.7% of the total real property.[4]

When combined with the rising expectations and declining profits of the 1850's, this elitist domination led to political unrest. As the railroads pushed into new regions and lowered transportation and marketing costs, cotton production became potentially profitable for a growing number of Southerners. At the same time, however, the increased agricultural demand inflated slave prices beyond the means of those struggling to enter commercial agriculture. Land prices and the cost of supplies also rose. Cotton prices did not rise proportionately and consequently the average rates of return in agriculture, including profits from the sale of slaves and non-cotton surpluses, dropped by 25% from 1849 through 1859. Since cotton earnings depended more on large volume than high prices and since the cotton output per slave generally increased with the size of the holdings, the profits of the planters fell the least. But the smaller producers were hard pressed and by 1859 most were not earning the opportunity rate of 6% on their investments. For relief they began to demand cheaper slaves and more land.[5]

[4] James C. Bonner, "Profile of a Late Ante-Bellum Community," *AHR*, XLIX (July, 1944), 663–680; James Benson Sellers, *Slavery in Alabama* (University, Ala., 1964), 42; Joseph Karl Mann, "The Large Slaveholders of the Deep South," unpublished Ph.D. thesis (University of Texas, 1964), 177–178. Mann, who defined the deep South as Georgia, Alabama, Mississippi, and Louisiana, estimated that the land of the large planters was worth on the average 75% more per acre than other holdings in these states, 35.

[5] Ulrich B. Phillips, "The Economic Cost of Slave-Holding," *PSQ*, XX (June, 1905), 266; Charles S. Davis, *The Cotton Kingdom in Alabama* (Montgomery, 1939), 165, noted: "Between the years of 1855 and 1860 the price of provisions rose to a peak all out of proportion to the price of land and cotton." James D. Foust and Dale E. Swan, "Productivity and Profitability of Antebellum Slave Labor:

The political manifestations in the late 1850's of this economic discontent were the movement for the reopening of the African slave trade and the popularity of expansionism in the 1860 presidential campaign. These issues posed no threat to the oligarchic control of Southern politics since the South's wealth was hardly to be redistributed; more of it simply was to be created. The clamor over the slave trade began in South Carolina in 1854. From there it spread to most of the lower South and became a volatile issue in state legislatures and Southern commercial conventions. Although the movement in part was energized by a drive to enforce moral unity within the South on the slavery issue, partisan motives were undoubtedly paramount.[6]

What better way for a Southern radical to embitter sectional relations than to agitate an issue which to many Northerners represented the quintessence of the heinous qualities of slavery? Such political action, however, could be effective only because the demand for slaves had outstripped the supply. One thousand dollars, the average price in the late 1850's for an able field hand, was either beyond the means or too much of a capital risk for the typical nonslaveholder. This labor shortage could be alleviated, according to the proslavery traders, only by importing more slaves. A greater supply would meet the increasing demands of the cotton and sugar

A Micro-Approach," *AgH*, xliv (Jan., 1970), 46, 55, 57; Louis M. Hacker, *The Triumph of American Capitalism* (New York, 1940), 303. The relationship between reopening the slave trade and reaffirming the morality of slavery is handled by Ronald T. Takaki, *A Pro-Slavery Crusade* (New York, 1971).

6 W. J. Carnathan, "The Proposal to Reopen the African Slave Trade in the South, 1854–1860," *SAQ* (Oct. 1926), 410–429; Harvey Wish, "The Revival of the African Slave Trade in the United States, 1856–1860," *MVHR*, xxvii (March, 1941), 569–588; Russel, *Economic Aspects*, 216; Steven Channing, *Crisis of Fear, Secession in South Carolina* (New York, 1970), 149. In the nation as a whole prices increased by close to 10% during the 1850's. See U.S. Bureau of the Census, *Historical Statistics of the United States, Colonial Times to 1957* (Washington, 1960), 115.

states, allow more whites to buy, and provide a labor surplus for use in new areas. In addition, the security of slavery would be greatly strengthened since more Southerners would have a direct economic stake in the institution. Slave property would no longer be in danger of becoming the prerogative of the privileged few but would be democraticized among the masses.[7]

However, internal opposition within the South was sufficient to stymie the proslavery traders. The predominantly Whiggish opponents, after emphasizing that there was absolutely no chance of ever restoring the trade, insisted that the consequences of the trade would be socially and economically dangerous. If the small or nonslaveholder were to benefit, enough slaves would have to be imported to lower prices significantly. Such a huge influx would lessen the value of existing slaves, reduce the efficiency of the labor force, and lead to lower cotton prices by glutting the market. The only beneficiary would be Britain, the chief purchaser of Southern cotton. The present slaveholder would see the value of his property reduced. "It is abolitionism in its worst form; for if you can, under any plea of interest and good to the community, reduce the price of the slave one-half or one-third, you can abolish it altogether." Not only were the paternalistic sensibilities of the planters upset, but their fears over internal security were heightened. A fresh stock of barbarous and untutored slaves would necessitate harsher forms of discipline and foster a treacherous feeling of superiority in the present slaves. "The idea of leaving one's family, even for a day, amid a mass of barbarians—vicious, unruly, discontented, accustomed to the rule of force, speaking a different language, and never having learned to regard their master as their friend— would be revolting to human nature," grieved James Pettigrew of South Carolina.[8]

[7] *DBR*, xxiv (1858), 473–492; xxv (1858), 491–507; xxvii (1859), 205–213.

[8] *Ibid.*, xxiv (1858), 579–583; xxv (1858), 166–185; xxvi (1858), 293; xxvii (1859), 214–220.

The opponents of the trade were careful to pose as the real friends of the nonslaveholders. They noted that nine-tenths of this class were so poor that their only source of wealth was their labor. Additional slaves, by decreasing the value of all labor, would leave the bulk of Southerners even poorer. "We must keep up the wages of white labor or we will lose it," reasoned Senator Albert Gallatin Brown of Mississippi. "With more land to cultivate, then re-open the slave trade." The opposition cleverly denounced the contention that slavery must be strengthened by diffusing ownership as "a foul libel upon the citizens of the South to thus endorse what Greeley and Seward have been asserting so many years, that there is a class of poor white citizens in our midst inimical to our interests."[9]

But the most telling argument against the trade was the connection between the permanence of slavery and the maintenance of high slave prices. In the upper South agricultural slave labor had become unprofitable. Many Southerners suspected that emancipation had been stayed only by the profits reaped by the sale of surplus slaves to the lower South for use in the cotton fields. Lowering slave prices by supplying African imports would cut into the profit margin of the domestic slave trade and remove the incentive of the Virginia slaveholder in maintaining the institution. The result, it was predicted, would be abolition in Maryland, Delaware, and Virginia within ten to fifteen years.[10]

The African slave trade remained closed. The agitation over its reopening had served more to expose the basic contradictions besetting the Southern economy than to relieve the pressure on the small or nonslaveholder struggling to improve his status.

Land, the other prime economic indicator, was easier to acquire than slaves, but even here the pinch was being felt by the late 1850's. Flux and mobility were intrinsic to the slave economy. Planters invariably needed more land since, accord-

---

[9] *The Mississippi Democrat*, Oct. 2, 1858; DBR, XXIV (1858), 581.
[10] DBR, 580.

ing to DeBow, "they were every few years compelled to purchase land to supply the place of that which they had worn out." This land hunger, plus the oligarchic distribution of the means of production within the planting areas, resulted in a continuous cycle of migration. Nonslaveholders, unable to compete with the planters, were usually the first to leave. They staked out new territory and, if they had settled in an area with good soil and suitable market outlets, were soon followed by the planters determined to make a fresh start. Once the planters moved in, the greater efficiency of their large-scale operations gave them a decided competitive advantage over the smaller producers. They bought up land, consolidated their holdings, and forced the yeomanry to move on again. Ulrich B. Phillips summarized this stage: "When the land had become more completely occupied and opportunity restricted, an outflow would begin, and the smallest units would lead the exodus. Both flush times and hard times quickened this fluctuation of the total of units, merely hastening movements which were already in progress." Thus the cycle began anew.[11]

The South, as had much of the nation, had seemingly always been blessed with abundant land. The cotton-slave frontier had moved progressively from the Georgia-Carolina uplands in the early 1800's, to the river valleys and black belt regions of Alabama and Mississippi after the War of 1812, into the upland regions of the latter two states which had been opened by the Jacksonian Indian removal policy of the 1830's, and, after the Mexican War, had accelerated its expansion into eastern Texas and Arkansas. By 1860, for the

[11] Charles S. Sydnor, *Slavery in Mississippi* (Baton Rouge, 1966). 192; J.D.B. DeBow, *The Industrial Resources, Etc., of The Southern and Western States . . .* (New Orleans, 1852), Vol. II, 118; W. H. Yarbrough, *Economic Aspects of Slavery in Relation to Southern and Southwestern Migration* (Nashville, 1932), 95; Lewis C. Gray, "Economic Efficiency and Competitive Advantages of Slavery Under the Plantation System," *AgH,* IV (April, 1930), 31–47, Ulrich B. Phillips, "The Origin and Growth of the Southern Black Belts," *AHR,* XI (July, 1906), 798–816.

first time in more than fifty years, there was no sizeable virgin area of good cotton land left to entice slaveholders. There were certainly large tracts of land left in the slave South but the best of it had already been spoken for and was in the hands of a small elite.[12] Of the cotton land under cultivation, such a competent observer as Daniel Lee, editor of the *Southern Cultivator*, estimated in 1858 that 40% of it was exhausted. Mississippi, a relatively new agricultural region, was exhausting its soil at the rate of 3% a year.[13] *The Semi-Weekly Mississippian*, the leading Breckinridge organ in the state, sounded an ominous note when it warned:

> We have reached that period in our history where something must be done for progress, or our declension in resources of strength will be rapid and evident. We need not ask what will be the fate of those vast tracts of worn-out lands, now lying everywhere as useless as the bills of spurious and broken banks; but what will become of those on which we rely now, not merely for the articles of our export

[12] There can be no quarrel with Lewis Gray's observation of the large amounts of unexploited land in the South of 1860. Gray, *History of Agriculture in the Southern United States to 1860* (New York, 1941), Vol. II, 641–642. Where I must differ is in my insistence that the amount of land per se was not the crucial issue, but rather its social utilization, fertility, and availability to the society as a whole. Albert Gallatin Brown, one of the most successful politicians in the antebellum South, championed homestead legislation because, as he noted in 1852, "Our lands have all been picked and culled. . . ." He referred to public lands in the South as "the refuse tracts." M. W. Cluskey, ed., *Speeches, Messages, and Other Writings of the Hon. Albert G. Brown* . . . (Philadelphia, 1859), 195; Yarbrough, *Economic Aspects*, presents the case for soil exhaustion and land monopoly in the older regions serving as the twin catalysts of the South's constant expansion.

[13] Eugene D. Genovese, *The Political Economy of Slavery* (New York, 1965), 97, 98. Only massive applications of fertilizers have enabled the modern South to continue commercial agriculture. *Ibid.*, 98, 99. In the 1850's commercial fertilizers were too expensive to be used profitably on a large scale. L. Harper, Mississippi Geological Survey, *Preliminary Report on the Geology and Agriculture of the State of Mississippi* (Jackson, 1857), 24.

10

—cotton, etc., but for bread, the staff of life? They are rapidly falling into the condition of the former. . . . An improvident agriculture has already ruined millions of the best acres of our soil, and if persisted in, will ultimately turn the whole country into a wide, ruinous waste.

In lamenting "the painful signs of senility and decay" in Madison County, Alabama, Clement C. Clay spoke of "numerous farm houses, once the abode of industrious and intelligent freemen, now occupied by slaves, or tenantless, deserted and dilapidated fields, once fertile, now unfenced, abandoned, and covered with those evil harbingers, foxtail and broomsedge."[14]

The extent of soil erosion varied, of course, with the diligence of the cultivator, the lay of land, and the soil's freshness, chemical properties, and utilization. However, diminishing fertility was not a localized problem but was endemic to Southern agriculture. In Alabama and Mississippi, only the comparatively small number of planters on the alluvial soil of the Mississippi-Yazoo basin had few worries concerning soil exhaustion. Their soil was so rich and deep, and the region so flat, that even after the turn of the century erosion was only a minor problem. The majority of planters, those who farmed prairie and loam soils, were not so fortunate. The yellow loam lands of southern Madison and northern Hinds counties, Mississippi, were once ranked among the state's finest planting areas; by the late 1850's crop yields were down sharply and the land was being abandoned. Even the heavier prairie soils were being seriously depleted in the 1850's. Erosion was already prevalent in the rich prairies of eastern Mississippi in 1857 and the same was true in the more extensive prairie region of Alabama, the Black Belt. In the early 1880's the state geologist was surprised to find that cotton yields in this once very fertile region were the lowest of any in the state.[15]

[14] Jackson *Semi-Weekly Mississippian*, Aug. 10, 1860; *DBR*, xviii (1855), 727.

[15] Mississippi State Geological Survey, *Bulletin No. 14; Mississippi, Its Geology, Geography, Soil and Mineral Resources*, E. N. Lowe,

Soil exhaustion was a major problem in Alabama and Mississippi on the eve of the Civil War. By contributing to the shrinking supply of good farm land, it enhanced the popularity of expansionist designs for an agrarian population too long accustomed to believing that fresh lands could always be acquired.[16]

With so much of the cultivated areas in poor condition, and with large planters constantly on the lookout for fresh lands, the options for the small farmer were increasingly being circumscribed. Good, though not choice, farm land in the Chickasaw cession of northern Mississippi sold on an average from $1.89 to $2.25 per acre in the 1830's and 1840's; in the 1850's the average price was $6.92. Such a price was beyond the means of many of the land-hungry. The agent of a large land speculation in Mississippi told Olmsted that most of the poor people who had bought land on credit had defaulted. Only those working in a cotton factory had the income to meet the terms on the usual purchase of 160 acres at $2 to $3 per acre, payable in three years at 6% interest. The small farmer could turn to the vast pine barren stretches of southern Alabama and Mississippi, where land was cheap, but hardly

Director (Jackson, 1919), 285; Eugene W. Hilgard, Mississippi Geological Survey, *Report on the Geology and Agriculture of the State of Mississippi* (Jackson, 1860), 239, 332; Eugene Allen Smith, Geological Survey of Alabama, *Report for the Years 1881 and 1882. Embracing an Account of the Agricultural Features of the State* (Montgomery, 1883), 304. This region still led the state in cotton production because of the immense acreage planted in cotton. Smith placed the major blame for the low yields on the "improvident culture" and this soil-exhaustive, one-crop agriculture was just as prevalent in the 1850's. Davis, *Cotton Kingdom*, 173–178, found that most planters knew about soil conservation but seldom did anything about it. For a useful, but very brief, treatment of this entire problem, see William C. Bagley, *Soil Exhaustion and the Civil War* (Washington, 1942).

[16] Hilgard, *Report on the Geology of Mississippi*, 332, spoke of the yearning "for that utopian soil which never gives out, said to exist somewhere to the westward" as an impediment to agricultural reform in Mississippi.

10% of it was suitable for farming. The badly eroded lands of the older sections of Mississippi were going for $5 per acre; fresher lands from $10 to $20. In the entire state, improved farm acreage more than doubled in value during the 1850's.[17]

Whenever possible the small farmer flocked to any region that offered cheap farmable land. As a rule the emigrants sought an area, the soil and climate of which most resembled that which they had left behind. That the trek was becoming longer was shown by the fact that the plurality of emigrants from Georgia, Alabama, and Mississippi in the 1850's settled not in the neighboring state to the west but as far west as Texas. The average farmer could not afford the price of the better land in the older states, and where he was ensconced on desirable land, pressure from planters encouraged him to sell out. A comparison of land tenure in the northern tier of counties in Mississippi between 1850 and 1860 reveals the small farmer maintaining his share of the land only in the poor, hilly county of Tishomingo in the northeast highlands. In the more fertile soils of the brown loam and Delta sections to the west, landholdings were consolidated more rapidly, and, unlike Tishomingo, the number of farms dropped in the 1850's.[18] This trend toward larger units of production was characteristic of both Alabama and Mississippi. Thus, even a remote, hilly area such as Walker County in northern Ala-

---

[17] Bonner, "Profile," 675, found that the large planters were buying up unimproved land for ranging ground and as a reserve for future crop productions; Mary E. Young, *Redskins, Ruffleshirts, and Rednecks: Indian Allotments in Alabama and Mississippi, 1830–1860* (Norman, Okla., 1961), 136; Frederick Law Olmsted, *A Journey in the Back Country* (London, 1860), 328; DeBow, *Industrial Resources,* Vol. II, 108; Nollie W. Hickman, "Logging and Rafting Timber in South Mississippi, 1840–1910," *JMH,* XIX (July, 1957), 154; Sydnor, *Slavery in Mississippi,* 191.

[18] Frank L. Owsley, "The Pattern of Migration and Settlement on the Southern Frontier," *JSH,* XI (May, 1945), 147–176; Barnes F. Lathrop, *Migration Into East Texas, 1835–1860* (Austin, 1949), 56, 57; Young, *Redskins,* 130–136.

bama experienced a land boom when the Graduation Act of 1855 lowered the price of some federal land to 12½ ¢ per acre. A central belt of counties in Mississippi, stretching east from Jackson to the Alabama line, experienced phenomenal growth rates in the 1850's when the construction of the Vicksburg and Meridian Railroad opened up its land to commercial agriculture. For the most part, though, the small farmer could barely have held his own in the 1850's.[19]

Alabama and Mississippi were still growing on the eve of the Civil War: population, both free and slave, farm units, and agricultural production were all on the upswing. And yet, despite the greater than 50% increase in total farm acreage in both states, the total number of farmers and planters in each was *less* in 1860 than in 1850. The farmer accounted for about 2 out of every 3 employed in 1850; about 1 out of every 2 in 1860.[20] All the factors discussed above—the concentration of land holdings, soil exhaustion, competition for new land, and the contracting base of virgin land—combined to prevent the economy of these two "prosperous" states from supporting more farmers in 1860 than it had in 1850.

[19] The average number of acres per farm in Alabama increased from 289 to 346 between 1850 and 1860; in Mississippi the increase was from 309 to 370 acres; *Eighth Census of the United States, 1860: Agriculture* (Washington, 1864), 222; John M. Dombhart, *History of Walker County: Its Towns and Its People* (Thornton, Ark., 1937), 43.

[20] *Eighth Census: Agriculture*, 222, gives the farm acreage for 1850 and 1860. *The Seventh Census of The United States . . . ,* J.D.B. DeBow, Supt. (Washington, 1853), lists the farmers, planters, and total occupations for Ala. on 428, 429; for Miss., on 454, 455. The same data for 1860 will be found in *The Eighth Census: Population of the United States in 1860*, compiled by Joseph C. G. Kennedy (Washington, 1864), 11 for Ala.; for Miss., 273 It should be noted that the 1860 occupational listings include farm laborers, a group that was not separately enumerated in 1850. If, as is probable, some of the 1850 "farmers" were really farm laborers by the 1860 classification, my case is overstated. However, even if the two 1860 groups are lumped together, farmers were still increasing less than the population as a whole, and far less than the number of farms and farm acreage.

14

Many farmers undoubtedly migrated to Texas, beckoned by the lure of cheap land; others fell into farm tenancy or, worse yet, into the status of factory labor.[21]

Traditionally, the South had avoided through expansion the worst consequences of the internal economic stresses generated by plantation slavery. Expansion meant fresh land to replace that which had been exhausted, and new opportunities for those denied slaveholding status in the older regions. In theory, however, the economic necessity behind demands for more land and its frequent corollary of cheaper slave prices through fresh importations from Africa could have been met by a territorial restriction on slavery. Within little more than a generation, slaves would have doubled by natural increase, their value would decrease, and more whites would be able to afford them. Marginal and badly worn land could be made productive again with this cheap labor, agricultural reform would become profitable, and the pressure on rural resources would be relieved by drawing both whites and slaves into industry. Following the example of the North, the South would be able to free herself of a dependency upon ever more land by turning to industrialization and urbanization.

Most Southerners rejected this solution for their economic needs because they realized its utter incompatibility with their existing class and racial accommodations. Very few planters would have agreed to a political economy where the value of their slave property steadily depreciated or their monopolization of the South's sources of wealth and status aspirations was eroded by competing centers of power. With her resources tied up in land and slaves, the South would have required huge inputs of outside capital to finance any agricultural and industrial diversification program. Such external control invariably would undermine the slaveholders' patriarchal world. White industrial labor would be more

[21] Yarbrough, *Economic Aspects*, 99; Linden, "Economic Democracy," 179; Bonner, "Profile," 666.

likely to develop a class consciousness in conflict with the slaveholders' needs when the poorer whites worked in a factory, as opposed to living on the land tied to the planters by kinship, social gatherings, and economic dependence. Southern labor, deeply resentful of competition from skilled slaves, was already a nuisance to the planters.[22]

Above all, how would all those slaves be controlled in a South with fixed territorial limits? For decades expansion had enabled Southerners to evade the social and economic problems of coping with an ever-growing mass of blacks confined to a given geographic area. The spread of slavery, Southerners insisted, meant better care and lighter discipline for the blacks since they were continually being transferred to regions where their labor was more productive and their numbers were less crowded. As long as the option of adding slave territory was kept open, Southerners could delude themselves with the comforting belief that eventually slavery and its terrible racial dilemma could vanish, slowly and painlessly, by a diffusion of all the blacks out of the American South into the tropics of Central and South America. This projection of emancipation under socially safe conditions was not so much a viable policy as it was both a vague hope that someday the South would be all white and an indispensable outlet for anxieties over servile insurrections and the feared loss of white identity through amalgamation with the blacks. But if slavery were confined to its present limits, not only would this illusion be shattered but also the blacks would become unmanageable as a result of their sheer density. "Let them reflect upon the probable consequences of penning up the slaves within a narrow limit—their great increase in number

[22] However, poorly organized as it was, this white labor was not yet a real threat. "As long as Negro labor was available, the freedom of white workers to bargain collectively and take concerted action would be substantially curtailed." Richard B. Morris, "The Measure of Bondage in the Slave States," *MVHR*, xli (Sept., 1954), 229. For the severe limits imposed by the planters on industrialization and the class contradictions besetting any such program, see Genovese, *Political Economy*, 180–235.

—the lessened demand for their labor—the diminished inducement to good treatment—the war between the two races likely to spring up," pleaded Representative John Millson of Virginia in 1850 to his Northern colleagues in Congress. It was this image of the dangers awaiting slave society that led another Southern Congressman, E. Carrington Cable of Florida, to announce: "In contemplation of the future, we demand an *outlet* for our blacks, through which they may find their way to the equatorial regions, where, if you please, they may become free."[23]

By 1890 many estimated the South would have 10 million slaves. Unless she had acquired more territory in the meantime, she would be faced with a large surplus of slaves and the refusal of the North to accept any significant influx of blacks, free or slave. M. Tarver of Missouri cautioned that "long before the number reaches ten million the country will become so exhausted and occupied, that property in slaves must become of little or no value, unless some other than agricultural employment is found for them." But large concentrations of industrial slaves would be socially dangerous. They would be economically pitted against white mechanics and their training could raise their intellectual awareness to the point where they might start acting for themselves. James Hammond of South Carolina argued in 1849: "Whenever a slave is made a mechanic, he's more than half freed, and soon becomes, as we too well know, and all history attests, with rare exceptions, the most corrupt and turbulent of his class." Slave discipline would be weakened. Roger Pryor stressed that "it was not for our interest that our negroes should be so employed, because such employment would imply a certain degree of accomplishment and instruction, and gives the

[23] *Congressional Globe*, 31st Congress, 1st Session, Appendix, 189, 241. This social function of expansion has generally been overlooked by historians but it was an argument constantly resorted to by Southerners whenever slavery was threatened with confinement. The earliest examples of its use are pinpointed by Donald L. Robinson, *Slavery in the Structure of American Politics, 1765–1820* (New York, 1971), 410–411, 439–440.

negro an opportunity for brooding and meditation, and the fermentation of discontent."[24]

Not all Southerners shared these misgivings, particularly those who favored the restoration of the African slave trade or who were leery of the social consequences of employing white labor in factories. Nonetheless, the fears of the majority, in conjunction with the anti-industrial bias of many planters, limited the proportion of industrial slaves in 1860 to but 5% of the slave labor force. Despite their small numbers industrial or artisan slaves were still responsible for nearly all the leaders of the major slave revolts and were involved "almost exclusively" in the conspiracy of 1856. Similar disciplinary problems would arise if the slaves were shifted into the cities. The urban environment, by permitting the slave more freedom of movement and opportunities for personal initiative than was possible in a rural setting, weakened the bond of unquestioning dependence which tied the slave to the master.[25] If these bonds were ever broken, the stability of Southern society would be upset. Consequently, the skilled urban slave represented a grave threat to security: "The negro mechanic in town necessarily enjoys a latitude which cannot be allowed other negroes, either in town or country, and his influence over them, both by direct contact and example, is very disastrous to wholesome discipline."[26]

The social necessity of keeping the slaves ignorant and isolated in the countryside reinforced white racial attitudes which viewed blacks as incapable of anything more than unskilled slave labor. Emancipation was unthinkable. "All experience proves that the Negroes cannot be emancipated

[24] DeBow, *Industrial Resources*, Vol. II, iii; *DBR*, XVIII (1850), 518; *ibid.*, XXIV (1858), 581.

[25] Most industrial slaves were engaged in small scale rural enterprises where discipline was less of a problem than in cities and when capitalization could be minimized. Robert S. Starobin, *Industrial Slavery in the Old South* (New York, 1970). The decay of urban slavery is traced and explained by Richard C. Wade, *Slavery in the Cities, The South 1820–1860* (New York, 1964).

[26] *The Mississippi Democrat*, Jan. 21, 1860.

without bringing want, misery and barbarism upon them. It is clear, too, that these Negroes cannot be liberated without destroying the prosperity, happiness and political power of the Southern States. . . ." In this blending of Southern paternalism and social needs with pseudo-anthropology and a distorted reading of the results of abolition in the British West Indies, Dr. J. C. Nott of Mobile, a leading racial ethnologist, summarized the case against emancipation. On a more personal level, the mere thought of a horde of free blacks in their midst was enough to make Southerners (and most Northerners) cringe. The end of slavery would mean "the amalagamation of a superior with an inferior race . . . the destruction of our commerce—the butchery of our wives and daughters —the debauchery of our sons. . . ." Having ruled out freeing the blacks and convinced that their confinement would result in the destruction of slavery, Southerners turned to expansion as the solution for their impasse. "How are we to preserve the institution of slavery?" asked O. R. Singleton, a Democratic representative from Mississippi. "There is but one mode by which . . . it can be perpetuated for any considerable number of years. We may fail in that, but certainly it is the surest chance offered us to preserve it. The mode is by expansion, and that expansion must be in the direction of Mexico."[27]

Other Southerners, opting for different areas, might have quarreled with Singleton on specifics but not with his prescription for saving slavery. Resolutions demanding Cuba were passed by Democratic county conventions in the late 1850's, especially those in eastern Mississippi. Stressing that "slavery must go South if it goes at all," A. G. Brown and other exponents of the Southern version of Manifest Destiny dreamed of a glorious tropical empire. The South would have room for her surplus slaves, access to valuable minerals, a monopolization of the world's production of tropical goods, and a guarantee of continued control over international cotton

[27] *DBR*, x (1851), 329; *Clayton Banner*, April 23, 1860; *Congressional Globe*, 36th Congress, 1st Session, Appendix, 53.

19

markets. This expansionism was far more than just political rhetoric. After talking and boarding with common folk throughout the South, Olmsted observed that "Most of the citizens of the slave States appear to believe that the continuance of slavery depends upon the continued and rapid territorial dispersion of the slave-holding community."[28]

The spread of slavery, however, was apparently forever blocked by the external menace posed by the Republican party, the political manifestation of the Northern free-soil ideology. The rise in the political importance of antislavery sentiments from roughly 1830 to 1860 coincided with expanding industrialization in the Northeast and the growth of commercial farming based on family labor in the Old Northwest. By the 1850's rail transportation had linked the maturing economies of these two regions, and both were in substantial agreement on a program of tariffs, homesteads, internal improvements, and free soil.[29] Simultaneously, evangelical Protestantism with its message of individual regeneration and responsibility for sin exposed Northerners to the possibility of sweeping reforms through the extirpation of social evil. The Republicans fused the religious fervor of the abolitionists with the entrepreneurial drive of the rising middle classes into

[28] Percy Lee Rainwater, *Mississippi: Storm Center of Secession, 1856–1861* (Baton Rouge, 1938), 71–74; *The Mississippi Democrat*, May 28, July 16, 1859; *Mississippi Free Trader*, Aug. 20, 1860; Olmsted, *Journey*, 291.

[29] Direct economic ties between the Northeast and South had long been established. Based on the ability of Northern capitalists to market and manufacture cotton, these ties constituted a strong conservative bond. See Philip S. Foner, *Business and Slavery: The New York Merchants and the Irrepressible Conflict* (Chapel Hill, 1941) and Thomas H. O'Connor, *Lords of the Loom: The Cotton Whigs and the Coming of the Civil War* (New York, 1968). Although western trade with the South continued to increase in absolute figures during the 1850's, the flow of eastern manufactured goods for western foodstuffs had overshadowed this trade in the same decade and had much greater potential for the future. Douglas C. North, *The Economic Growth of the United States 1790–1860* (New York, 1966), 103.

an ideology which measured the outside world by the cherished Northern values of economic self-improvement, moral righteousness, and freedom. Although more conservative and suspicious of the reform impulse, Southerners shared many of these values, but their society was ultimately based on slavery, an institution which Northerners had come to stigmatize as an undemocratic and immoral threat to their self-interests and beliefs. By the terms of the Republican indictment, slavery made a mockery of Christianity, denigrated and drove out free labor by subjecting it to unpaid, compulsory slave competition, and subverted the civil liberties of all by supporting an arrogant elite of slaveholders who crushed all opposition to their hegemony.[30]

Friction was inevitable when the seaboard nation became a continental empire and both sections claimed the great prize of the federal territories. To protect free institutions and to undermine slavery, the Republicans insisted that the territories be reserved for free labor. They were convinced that slavery was such an inefficient labor system, requiring continuous large increments of virgin soil, that denying it fresh land would result in its certain extinction. "Let slavery be shut up absolutely within its present bounds, let the hope of its extension over a new tier of States stretching around the Gulf of Mexico, and covering Central America, be forever cut off, and the laws of political economy would determine the speedy abolition of slavery in the older States," proclaimed one Republican paper in 1860. Eventually the same laws would produce the same results in the newer cotton states. The Republicans claimed their policy was constitutional since Congress had complete sovereignty over the territories, a power which had been first exercised in the Ordinance of 1787, barring slavery from the Old Northwest. Another decided political

[30] Eric Foner, *Free Soil, Free Labor, Free Men: The Ideology of the Republican Party Before the Civil War* (New York, 1970), is indispensable. Also useful is the chapter on the American Civil War in Barrington Moore, Jr., *Social Origins of Dictatorship and Democracy* (Boston, 1966), 111–115.

21

asset of attacking slavery through restriction was the avoidance of the direct clash with Northern racism. Indeed, free soilism was popular with many white supremacists who desired no blacks at all in the territories.[31]

Northern blacks were deprived of their civil liberties and were the victims of humiliating Jim Crow legislation; their opportunities to attend public schools or to earn a living were severely limited. Some states excluded them completely. The chief difference between the Northern and the Southern racist was that the former frequently believed that slavery was morally wrong. There was no felt inconsistency between holding this belief and also maintaining that blacks were not quite equal to whites. Equal enough not to be enslaved, because that was barbaric and unchristian, but not sufficiently equal to share fully in social rights and the privileges of citizenship. Having accepted blacks as free but still unequal, the North could not understand why the South could not do the same or at least admit that slaveholders enjoyed privileges and powers which were anathema in an egalitarian society. Of course, the free states had a much smaller black population, and no class whose entire social position was predicated on the existence of slavery. Southerners responded that for them racial control was not an abstraction or a convenience but a matter of survival. They pointed out that in the North there were so few blacks that white society could safely afford to grant them quasi-freedom. But Southerners were positive that only the iron discipline of slavery could adequately protect themselves from physical and social inundation by large numbers of blacks.[32]

The Republicans were in the forefront of efforts to win decent treatment for blacks and their record on civil rights

[31] New York *Independent*, quoted in the New Orleans *Daily Delta*, Dec. 7, 1860; Eugene H. Berwanger, *The Frontier Against Slavery* (Urbana, 1967), *passim*.

[32] Leon F. Litwack, *North of Slavery* (Chicago, 1961), *passim; Congressional Globe*, 31st Congress, 1st Session, Appendix, 213, 361; Milledgeville (Ga.) *Southern Recorder*, Sept. 25, 1860.

22

was far more enlightened than that of Northern Democrats who had to appeal to a constituency of transplanted Southern yeomanry in the lower Midwest and poor urban immigrants who feared black economic competition. But by no means did they envision a biracial society committed to equality. Once the slaves were freed, the Republicans would have been content to allow the South to control the blacks through a rigorous caste system of serfdom and segregation. Rather than encouraging or even permitting a sizeable migration of freedmen into the North, where the antebellum proportion of blacks was under 2%, most Republicans would have preferred the South to join with them in a federally sponsored colonization of blacks in Central America.[33]

Despite the prevalent racial attitudes in the North, the South still found the Republican program completely unacceptable. The profits of the plantation, the hubris of the planter, and the racial phobias of all Southern whites who were all too well aware that the freed blacks would remain among them precluded any possibility of emancipation, or its political equivalent, the forced atrophy of slavery through encirclement.

Increasingly the South felt hemmed in and betrayed. They had been denied the opportunity to use their slaves in the gold mines of California and shut out of Kansas. Even with a sympathetic and Southern dominated Buchanan administration, their hopes for Cuba or a slice of Mexico had been thwarted. The apparent victories of the Kansas-Nebraska Act and the Dred Scott decision which theoretically opened up all the territories to slavery by overturning the restrictions of the Missouri Compromise had been for naught. "The truth is,"

[33] Foner, *Free Labor*, 261–300, provides a welcome corrective to the recent trend of overemphasizing Republican racism to the exclusion of their idealism, but V. Jacque Voegeli, *Free But Not Equal, The Midwest and the Negro during the Civil War* (Chicago, 1967), 95–112, establishes that once Republican colonization schemes failed, they turned to a policy of utilizing and confining the freedmen within the South rather than allowing any migration northward.

23

fumed S. D. Moore of Alabama, "I care not for constitutional rights, Supreme Court decisions, and laws of Congress, the South is excluded from the common territories of the Union. The right of expansion claimed to be a necessity of her continued existence, is practically and effectively denied the South." An embittered Richard K. Crallé, a close friend and biographer of Calhoun, wrote in 1857 that "*In the Union, our Institution must stop where it is. We shall, however, get some secretaries of the Treasury, of War in exchange for our rights* and our honor. . . ."[34]

Compounding this sense of helplessness was the knowledge that the South was ever more isolated in a world that was abandoning slavery. Cassius Marcellus Clay of Kentucky, one of the most caustic and persistent of antislavery critics, constantly reminded his fellow Southerners that "the great world *is* attacking slavery." The institution had once flourished throughout most of the Western Hemisphere but by 1860 Southerners shared slavery only with Cuba and Brazil. Southerners were shocked by John Brown's raid in 1859, which they interpreted as the boldest example yet of an escalating pattern of aggression directed against their society, but they felt terribly alone and vulnerable when wide segments of Northern public opinion hailed Brown as a martyr. But at the same time as the need for self-protection became critical, the South's political power was shrinking. Sectional parity had been lost in the Senate by 1850 and the South, conscious that the North was outgaining her in population and economic growth, feared that it would be but a matter of time before the free states had the votes to abolish slavery by a constitutional amendment.[35]

[34] *DBR*, xxviii (1860), 536; Richard K. Crallé to Robert M. T. Hunter, Oct. 24, 1857, "Correspondence of Robert M. T. Hunter, 1826–1876," ed. Charles H. Ambler, *American Historical Association Annual Report*, 1916, Vol. 2, 243–244. Filibustering in the Caribbean was one attempt to break out of this impasse.

[35] Cassius Marcellus Clay, *The Writings of Cassius Marcellus Clay: Including Speeches and Addresses* (New York, 1848),

To some degree the South had always been concerned over the safety of slavery within the Union, but she was not alarmed until the late 1840's when the Wilmot Proviso, by proposing to keep slavery out of the territories seized in the Mexican War, first raised the specter that the South would be consigned to a permanent minority position. In 1849 a young Georgia radical, Henry L. Benning, was worrying "that the Union by its *natural and ordinary* working is giving anti-slavery-ism such a preponderance in the Genl. Government, both by adding to the number of free states and diminishing the number of slave, that it (anti-slavery-ism) will be able soon to abolish slavery by act of Congress and then to execute the law."[36] As the presidential election of 1860 approached, the Union had added no more slave states and slavery in the border states seemed so moribund that many were predicting its slow death, perhaps within a generation.[37]

The mood of despair, the foreboding that the attempt to maintain both the Union and slavery "will only be to whet a knife for the throats of our families and slaves," convinced many that an aggressive, even belligerent, defense of Southern rights offered the best hope for the survival of slavery. For all the economic motives behind the struggle to reopen the African slave trade, much of the impetus derived from the belief that "the slave trade is almost the only possible measure, the last resource to arrest the decline of the South in the Union." Stocked with cheap slave labor, whites would leave the South

---

434; R. B. Rhett to John C. Calhoun, July 19, 1849, "Correspondence Addressed to John C. Calhoun, 1837–1849," ed. Chauncey S. Boucher and Robert P. Brooks, *Annual Report of the American Historical Association for the Year 1929*, 518.

[36] Henry L. Benning to Howell Cobb, July 1, 1849, "The Correspondence of Robert Toombs, A. H. Stephens, and Howell Cobb," ed. Ulrich B. Phillips, *American Historical Association Annual Report*, 1911, Vol. 2, 171.

[37] For this reason the cotton states mistrusted the upper South during all periods of political crisis. See the 1848 and 1849 letters in the "Calhoun Correspondence," 482, 495, 496.

in search of land and carry the slave gospel wherever they went.

> Give me free trade with Africa and they may have as many Wilmot provisos or (as much) Squatter Sovereignty as they please and all the Territories will be carved and admitted as Slave States. Send poor men from the South without Negroes (as we are now doing) to the Territories and they will vote to make free States—for Instance look at Indiana[,] Illinois[,] California[,] and Kansas, on the other hand meet the men of the abolition aid Society in the Territories with a cheap African—he will make slave States —make the Local Laws to protect his Negroes and your rights.[38]

Additional slaves would not only allow the South to expand and perhaps win back some free areas that it had lost but would prevent present slave areas from contracting. "I have long been satisfied of one fact: that while negroes are worth $1,200 each in the cotton, rice and sugar fields of the South, we will not only never have another slave State, but that the border States will soon be drained of their negroes and gradually abolitionized."[39]

II

The grievances and frustrations experienced by Southerners in the 1850's provided a breeding ground for secessionist ideas to take root. In order to exploit this opportunity, radical leaders in Alabama and Mississippi (and throughout most of the lower South) had to work within the structural context of a political economy which catered almost exclusively

[38] D. L. Yulee to John C. Calhoun, July 10, 1849, "Calhoun Correspondence," 516; Edward A. Pollard, *Black Diamonds Gathered in the Darkey Homes of the South* (New York, 1859), 52; John Cowden to Gov. Pettus, Sept. 23, 1860, Series E. Governors' Records, Vol. 49, Administration of Governor John J. Pettus: Correspondence for the year 1860, MDAH.

[39] *The Weekly Panola Star* (Miss.), April 26, 1860.

to the needs of rural slaveholders. They also had to satisfy, or at least neutralize, the masses of Southerners, the nonslaveholders.

The most noteworthy aspect of urbanism in the Cotton Kingdom was its relative insignificance. In 1860 only 5% of Alabama's population lived in urban areas and only 3% of Mississippi's. In sharp contrast, the urban population of New England in 1860 stood at 37% of the total, the Middle Atlantic states at 35%, and even the more recently settled Old Northwest and trans-Mississippi West at 14% and 13% respectively. The slave South as a whole was the least urbanized region in the country and, with the exception of a few port cities, consistently had lagged behind the North and West in urban growth. Moreover, as emphasized by Elkins and McKitrick, the lack of small towns was a defining characteristic which very early set apart the development of the Old Southwest from that of the Old Northwest. In Ohio, Indiana, and Illinois the small town, "the market center which had two hundred or more people and was struggling to become bigger," was the focal point of a whole range of activities in commerce, industry, and real estate whose success depended mainly upon the growth of the town. The enterprise and energy of the town, above all its need to grow and prosper, set the tone for country life and the tempo of political activity.[40]

The Old Southwest of Alabama and Mississippi never developed a vigorous town life and hence never had a politics that was oriented to town needs. "There was but a limited field for the display of energy in the towns," recalled H. S. Fulkerson of Mississippi. With little in the way of manufacturing interests to attract them, young men turned not to busi-

[40] Harold D. Woodman, *King Cotton and His Retainers: Financing and Marketing the Cotton Crop of the South, 1800–1925* (Lexington, Ky., 1968), 190; North, *Economic Growth*, 258. An urban area is defined by a minimum population of 2,500. Stanley Elkins and Eric McKitrick, "A Meaning for Turner's Frontier: Democracy in the Old Northwest," *PSQ*, LXIX (Sept., 1954), 341–347.

ness but to the legal profession and politics. By the early 1850's, at a conservative estimate, the Old Northwest had five to six times more towns per capita. The towns that did spring up in the deep South impressed visitors in the 1850's not with their hustle and booster spirit but rather with their lethargic air of dilapidated decay. "The houses are all poor and shabby, and have no shade to hide their tatters. . . . It had flourished once with the trade and traffic of four or five stores. Those were its 'palmy days.' Now it has only two stores— poor, low buildings; a tavern, dentist, doctor and shoemaker." Such was a Michigan school teacher's impression in 1858 of Satartia, Mississippi, the second largest town in the lush Delta county of Yazoo. Olmsted's description of the towns that he passed through in central Mississippi, save Jackson, the capital, as "forlorn, poverty-stricken collections of shops, groggeries, and lawyers' offices, mingled with unsightly and usually dilapidated dwelling-houses," was hardly more flattering.[41] Occasionally a sleepy little village, such as Washington, the one-time capital of Jeffersonian Mississippi, exuded an air of quiet beauty, but even to Mississippians, many of their county seats struck a note more funereal than bucolic.[42]

If it was not the shabbiness of town life that elicited comments from travelers, it was the complete absence of towns. Robert Russell, an Englishman traveling up the Alabama River by steamboat from Mobile to Montgomery in 1855, commented on the lack of villages, of signs of enterprise on

---

[41] H. S. Fulkerson, *Random Recollections of Early Days in Mississippi* (Baton Rouge, 1937), 144; Elkins and McKitrick, "Meaning for Turner's Frontier," 341–342; A. DePuy Van Buren, *Jottings of a Year's Sojourn in the South* (Battle Creek, Mich., 1859), 37; Olmsted, *Journey*, 159.

[42] Charles S. Sydnor, *A Gentleman of the Old Natchez Region, Benjamin L. C. Wailes* (Durham, 1938), 80. J.F.H. Claiborne, in his "Trip Through the Piney Woods," *PMHS*, IX (1906), 487–538, eloquently describes the quiet decay and stagnant quality of the county seats in the pines of southeastern Mississippi. Claiborne, writing in the early 1840's, noted that much of this region had lost farmers to the recently opened Indian lands of northern Mississippi.

his two-day trip. "In fact, the more fertile the land the more destitute is the country of villages and towns." Russell's observations were echoed in 1860 by J. W. Dorr, a member of the editorial department of the New Orleans *Crescent*. Of the rich cotton parish of Concordia, Louisiana, Dorr noted: "There is, literally, no other interest in Concordia but the agricultural. There is no town in the parish, and but three or four stores. . . ."[43]

Aside from providing a rudimentary political and judicial nexus centered around the courthouse and a market to facilitate the exchange of cotton for needed finished goods produced elsewhere, the town had few functions to perform in an area where agriculture was so dominant. The function of promoting its own growth, of attracting capital and men of talent, was largely denied it. This was the prerogative of the plantation, the social and economic embodiment of all that a Southerner could yearn for—land, slaves, and cotton, and the preeminence that accrued to their possessors. The ambitious, young Southerner looked not to the town, as his counterpart in the Old Northwest might have, but to the countryside. In 1860 an estimated 76% of the Southern free labor force was engaged in agriculture, as opposed to only 59% in the North and West.[44]

The attraction of the Southern town for native-born talent was so weak that much of its business and professional activity, as well as its skilled and semiskilled trades, was virtually abdicated to foreigners. With less than one in five of their number going into agriculture, the foreign immigrants gravitated to the towns where opportunity awaited and their skills were sorely needed. At least one town, Selma, Alabama, ac-

---

[43] Robert Russell, *North America, Its Agriculture and Climate* (Edinburgh, 1857), 289; quoted in Lewis E. Atherton, *The Southern Country Store, 1800–1860* (Baton Rouge, 1949), 19.

[44] Elkins and McKitrick, "A Meaning for Turner's Frontier: The Southwest Frontier and New England," *PSQ*, LXIX (Dec., 1954), 567–568; Bernard Mandel, *Labor: Free and Slave, Workingmen and the Anti-Slavery Movement in the United States* (New York, 1955), 14.

tively solicited immigrants with industrial and mechanical skills. Colonel Philip J. Weaver of Selma went to Germany around 1850 and returned with 300 immigrants. Although comprising less than 2½% of the total Mississippi population in 1860, foreigners dominated the commercial life of many towns, especially those strung along the Mississippi River. European immigrants were in the majority of all those engaged in commerce and trade in Port Gibson. Only two tradesmen were native Mississippians. Indeed, only 18.5% of all whites gainfully employed in Port Gibson were natives of the state. In the inland towns their younger age and much higher percentage of foreign and Northern-born distinguished storekeepers from farmers and planters. The more successful storekeepers, having put their savings into land and slaves, went into planting as soon as their resources permitted.[45]

At the crux of the overwhelmingly rural nature of the South was lack of purchasing power by the nonslaveholding white masses, which in turn was a result of the monopolization of the best lands, slave labor force, and income by an economic elite. Genovese, examining the size of the 1860 rural market in two Mississippi cotton counties, DeSoto and Marshall, found that one-third of the gross income was in the hands of 6% of the landowners. Only the very large planters, accounting for 10% of all landowners, spent more than $1,000 a year for food and supplies, and this sum included

---

[45] Herbert Weaver, "Foreigners in Ante-Bellum Towns of the Lower South," *JSH*, XIII (Feb., 1947), 67; Edward A. Evans, "A Study of Some Phases of Social and Economic Conditions of the Free Inhabitants of the Alabama Black Belt in 1860," unpublished master's essay (University of Alabama, 1940), 92; John Hardy, *Selma: Her Institutions and Her Men* (Selma, 1879), 42; Herbert Weaver, "Foreigners in Ante-Bellum Mississippi," *JMH*, XVI (July, 1954), 151–163; Harris Gaylord Warren, "People and Occupations in Port Gibson, 1860," *JMH*, X (April, 1948), 104–115. Atherton, *Southern Country Store*, 191, 203; William D. McCain, *The Story of Jackson: A History of the Capital of Mississippi, 1821–1951* (Jackson, 1953), Vol. I, 74; Daniel Robinson Hundley, *Social Relations in Our Southern States* (New York, 1860), 115.

purchases for their slaves. The average sum spent by slave-holders for supplies ranged from $30 to $35 per person; for nonslaveholders the average was $25. Perceptive travelers noticed this lack of consumer demand, especially in rural areas. Olmsted went to the heart of the problem when he noted that "their slavery system interposes to prevent the demand of commerce from having its legitimate effect upon the mass of people."[46]

The wealth of the South, stressed Olmsted, lay in cotton, and those with capital invested it in land and slaves to produce the staple for export markets. They soon monopolized the best land and the labor supply and hence the wealth of any given area. The planters alone derived any benefit from cotton production since the nonslaveholders, even if they spent all their earnings, could not create enough of a demand to warrant bringing in goods at a great cost. Only the planters could afford that. The nonslaveholders were likewise beholden to the planters for their schools, churches, and newspapers. General prosperity could be achieved only by enlarging and cheapening the local supply of the means of home comfort. In a free community, this was accomplished chiefly by the wages of labor, but in the South most of the labor force was composed of slaves who, of course, were not paid wages. The planters had the money but used it to create a demand either in imported luxury goods which were consumed by themselves and their families or in plantation supplies, such as bacon and corn, which were purchased in bulk from the West. Neither demand pulled the nonslaveholders into a market economy.[47]

Thus, the Southern economy presents an anomalous picture. On the one hand, an expanding and prosperous plantation agriculture dominated by an elite; on the other hand, the circumscribed, subsistence agriculture of the rural masses. The result was an economy which could sustain a more rapid

[16] North, *Economic Growth*, 130; Woodman, *King Cotton*, 193; Genovese, *Political Economy*, 168–169, Olmsted, *Journey*, 306.
[17] Olmsted, *Journey*, 306–311.

rate of growth in per capita income than the North between 1840 and 1860, but which could not generate any significant consumer demand.[48]

This is not to suggest that we should accept uncritically the abolitionist picture of a two-class Southern society which portrayed a small elite of wealthy, powerful planters controlling the slaves and lording it over a mass of degraded, impoverished nonslaveholders. Indeed, Southern society did have room for a middle class of relatively prosperous farmers and small slaveowners. However, it is the economic power and political influence of this class which is crucial, not its mere existence. The bulk of the nonslaveholders were subsistence farmers, not poor white "trash," but they were nonetheless isolated, uneducated, and denied a proportionate share of either political offices or economic control.[49] Above all, by having only a peripheral relationship to a market economy, they were locked into rural self-sufficiency.

Moreover, unless out on the hustings actively soliciting the vote of the nonslaveholders, Southern leaders readily admitted their concern over the economic assimilation of the nonslaveholders. One of the main arguments used in the largely futile compaign for greater manufacturing in the South was that industry would provide employment for the nonslaveholders and integrate them into the economy. In their present condition, occupying inferior land and scratching out but "a scanty subsistence," they had given up all hope of

---

[48] Stanley L. Engerman, "The Effects of Slavery Upon the Southern Economy: A Review of the Recent Debate," *Did Slavery Pay?*, ed. Hugh G. J. Aitken (Boston, 1971), 319, presents the latest effort to estimate per capita income by regions.

[49] Wright, " 'Economic Democracy,' " *passim*, argues convincingly that wealth was more concentrated in the cotton South than in the rural North. Although less than one-third of the white families in the cotton South owned slaves, the percentages of slaveholders in the cotton state legislatures in 1860 ranged from 54% in Texas to 82% in South Carolina. See Ralph A. Wooster, *The People in Power: Courthouse and Statehouse in the Lower South, 1850–1860* (Knoxville, 1969), 41.

advancement. As factory hands, they would earn a cash income, become useful citizens, and provide a market for the produce of the small agriculturists who remained behind in the countryside.[50]

The ineffective consumer demand in rural areas led both to a dearth of the locally oriented service industries and small businesses that were the base of a viable town life in the North and West and to a weak home market in foodstuffs.[51] There is no consensus on whether or not plantations were normally self-sufficient in food supplies.[52] However, the more fertile the district, the greater was the specialization in staple crop production. Percy Roberts, a Mississippi planter, credited no more than one in twenty of Delta planters with meeting their own needs of corn and meat. The three major food deficit regions of Alabama and Mississippi—the Mississippi and Tennessee River Valleys and the black belt of southern Alabama—all specialized in cotton production. They alleviated most of their food deficiencies with importations by cheap water transport from the farmers of the West and upper South, not with purchases from local farmers. The small farmers in the cotton belts were unable to take advantage of the plantation market because they practiced a less diversified agriculture than the planters and were more likely to be deficient in grain or meat. Some of the more prosperous yeomanry in the hill country undoubtedly found a market for their surplus food crops in the black belts, but the bulk of the agricultural population, the small- and non-slavehold-

[50] DeBow, *Industrial Resources*, Vol. II, 107–108.

[51] North, *Economic Growth*, 132; Sam Bowers Hilliard, "Hog Meat and Hoecake: A Geographical View of Food Supply in the Heart of the Old South, 1840–1860," unpublished Ph.D. thesis (University of Wisconsin, 1966), 35.

[52] The traditional view held that plantations, especially in the more recently developed Southwest, were not self-sufficient. See Sydnor, *Slavery in Mississippi*, 32–35, Davis, *Cotton Kingdom*, 167–168, and North, *Economic Growth*, 129. Robert E. Gallman challenges this interpretation in "Self-Sufficiency in the Cotton Economy of the Antebellum South," *AgH*, XLIV (Jan., 1970), 5–23.

ing farmers, lived by subsistence agriculture. "Farm economy meant a diversified, self-sufficient type of agriculture, where the money crops were subordinated to food crops, and where the labor was performed by the family or the family aided by a few slaves."[53]

The dominance of the plantation as an item of capitalization, producer of wealth, and source of consumer demand in the countryside, meant that the entire thrust of the Southern economy was directed to its needs. The transportation network, far from feeding burgeoning cities and factories, simply hastened the arrival of staple crops at the port cities of their debarkation. Nascent industrialization, centered in the textile industry, had no independent base of its own. Planters supplied the industrialists with much of their capital and were the market for the cheap cotton goods intended for slave use. Where towns did arise, it was in response to agricultural needs. The greatest of these needs in a region which was chronically deficient in liquid capital resources was credit —credit to finance the marketing of the staples and to purchase additional land, slaves, and plantation supplies before the proceeds of last year's crop were in. Factors in New Orleans and Mobile, acting as commission merchants and bankers, supplied credit to the planters of the Southwest in return for the exclusive right to market the planter's crop. Frequently they were also purchasing agents, meeting the planter's needs in both plantation necessities and luxury imports. Representing Northern and European capital, they could tap financial resources beyond the reach of most planters and local merchants.[54]

[53] *DBR*, xxv (1858), 390; Hilliard, "Hog Meat," 73, 140, 316, 363–364; Gallman, "Self-Sufficiency," 9–12; and Frank L. Owsley, *Plain Folk of the Old South* (Chicago, 1965), 135.

[54] Ulrich B. Phillips, "Transportation in the Antebellum South: An Economic Analysis," in *The Slave Economy of the Old South*, ed. Eugene D. Genovese (Baton Rouge, 1968), 153–167, and *ibid.*, "Railroads in the South," 168–175; Genovese, *Political Economy*, 180–208; A. H. Stone, "The Cotton Factorage System of the Southern States," *AHR*, xx (1915), 557–665; Ralph H. Haskins, "Planter and Cotton

Given its superior credit facilities, the factorage system had such a competitive advantage over interior towns in attracting the cotton trade and the patronage of the planter that it hindered the development of local markets.[55] Interior towns, on the fall line of rivers at the head of steamboat navigation or on bluffs above navigable rivers draining fertile plantation districts, were secondary centers of credit, catering to the smaller producers, and exchange points for goods produced elsewhere. With its merchants vying for the cotton trade and its many resident planters, the towns were clearly dependent upon the plantation.[56] The villages of the hinterland provided credit for the small farmers. The storekeeper accepted cotton in return for general merchandise and used the cotton as credit to meet his wholesale bills. No cotton, no credit was a rule in many local stores. The residents of these villages, which were often little more than a denser version of the countryside surrounding them, led a humdrum existence relieved only by the demands of the fall harvest or a political rally.[57]

Factor in the Old South: Some Areas of Friction," *AgH*, XXIX (1955), 1–14; Woodman, *King Cotton*, is very inclusive and is more sympathetic to the factor.

[55] Ulrich B. Phillips, *Life and Labor in the Old South* (Boston, 1963), 142; Atherton, *Southern Country Store*, 34. For the accusations in Natchez, a Mississippi river town, that the large planters contributed nothing to the town's prosperity and, worse yet, blocked the internal improvements that would enable the small planters to do more business in the town on a cash basis, see Paul W. Gates, *The Farmer's Age: Agriculture, 1815–1860* (New York, 1968), 134–135.

[56] Phillips, "Transportation," 157–158; Martha Boman, "A City in the Old South: Jackson, Mississippi, 1850–1860," *JMH*, XV (Jan., 1953), 1–32; Clanton W. Williams, "Conservatism in Old Montgomery, 1817–1861," *AR*, X (April, 1957), 96–110.

[57] Atherton, *Southern Country Store, passim*; T. H. Ball, *A Glance into the Great South-East, or, Clarke County, Alabama, and its Surroundings, From 1540–1877* (Grove Hill, Ala., 1882), 257; Frank L. and Harriet C. Owsley, "The Economic Basis of Society in the Late Ante-Bellum South," *JSH*, VI (Feb., 1940), 31; Phillips, "Historical Notes of Milledgeville, Ga.," *The Slave Economy*, 176; *Weekly Panola Star*, Aug. 23, 1860.

The economic power of the planter was sufficient to retard the urbanization of the South. But this power was only a part of a broader social context in which the planter was the social ideal. All Southerners, no matter what their occupation, aspired to planter status. As long as no competitive norms of social pre-eminence emerged, the planter's status was secure. This consideration, plus his special responsibility as maintainer of racial control, made most planters implicitly anti-urban. The small town presented no threat. T. N. Martin's recollection that Okolona "was found[ed] mainly by wealthy planters, as a convenient place for their comfort and pleasure in pastime and amusement" reminds us that planters enjoyed the amenities of town life. The town gave the planter an opportunity to show off his wealth by building fine homes and staffing them with house slaves.[58] Wealthy Lowndes County planters on the rich prairie lands west of Columbus, Mississippi, preferring to live in town in their "splendid residences," used the railroad to commute to their plantations. Genteel watering spas in the North and the newer resort towns in the South along the Mississippi coast were favorites of the gentry.[59]

A city though was a different story. The uneasiness experienced by B. L. C. Wailes, a Natchez planter, when he was jostled by a crowd in New York City, was not a personal idiosyncrasy. The problem, as Wailes' biographer, Charles Sydnor, makes clear, was that Wailes naturally felt uncomfortable among lower class Northerners since there was no

[58] Bonner, "Profile," provides some statistical measurement of the attraction of the planter ideal. T. N. Martin Manuscript, "Historical Sketch of Chickasaw County, And Also of the Towns of Houston and Okolona," 15, MDAH. Urban slaves, unless they had a skill which could return profits to the owner by the hiring out practice or through industrial contracts, were often an economic liability but a social necessity. See C. A. Rogers, *Incidents of Travel in the Southern States and Cuba* (New York, 1862), 249, and Olmsted, *Journey*, 421.

[59] *The Mississippi Democrat*, Sept. 3, 1859; William L. Lipscomb, *A History of Columbus, Mississippi, During the 19th Century* (Birmingham, 1909), 74.

36

class quite comparable to them in the lower South. Their lack of respect and rudeness left Wailes feeling more insecure than he had on the Arkansas frontier. This loss of deference was only one of the threats posed by the city. Slave discipline was difficult to maintain in the midst of the city's unique blend of diversity and mobility. The South never solved the problem of control and gradually allowed urban slavery to wither.[60]

The most unsettling of the nagging fears that the city instilled in the planter was the conviction that "every city was destined to be the seat of freesoilism."[61] The city harbored immigrants and the propertyless, two elements which an increasing body of Southern opinion came to identify with mass support of abolitionism in the North. In the words of George Fitzhugh, the most articulate Southern critic of the exploitive consequences of unrestrained Northern capitalism, "the bestowing upon men equality of rights, is but giving license to the strong to oppress the weak." Hence, "they [free laborers] are driven to cities to dwell in damp and crowded cellars, and thousands are even forced to lie in the open air. This accounts for the rapid growth of Northern cities." Pitted in merciless competition against the immigrants, that "torrent of pauperism, crime, agrarianism, and infidelity which Europe is pouring forth from her jails and alms houses on the already crowded North," Northern labor allegedly joined the immigrant as easy prey for radical ideas subversive to social order.[62] Although overdrawn, such an

[60] Sydnor, *B. L. C. Wailes*, 281–283. Presumably the urban poor of New Orleans and Mobile would also have frightened Wailes. Wade, *Slavery in the Cities, passim.*

[61] Quoted in Theodore R. Marmor, "Anti-Industrialism and the Old South: The Agrarian Perspective of John C. Calhoun," *New Perspectives on the American Past*, ed. Stanley N. Katz and Stanley I. Kutter (Boston, 1969), Vol. I, 503. Marmor stresses the green belt tendency of early Southern industry: placing factories in the countryside to avoid the morally corrupt city.

[62] *George Fitzhugh, Sociology for the South, or the Failure of Free Society* (Richmond, 1854), cited in *Slavery Defended: The Views*

analysis does reveal the Southern elite's perception that industrialization and urbanism, in short, the products of liberal Northern capitalism, would involve if allowed to take root in the South the creation of classes whose interests ultimately would undermine the social hegemony of the planter.[63]

III

Politics entertained the Southern masses and furnished them with a means of relieving their grievances without challenging the authority or power of the planters. The nonslaveholder found himself in the anomalous position of either being eulogized or damned. By his sheer numbers and voting strength, he could destroy slavery if he ever decided to strike out against a system that rendered him in the main economically superfluous. How to maintain his loyalty was a recurring problem for the slaveholder and a matter of the gravest concern. Clearly, homage had to be paid the nonslaveholder as the truest friend of the South, but, at the same time, any rumblings of discontent or support for a program or party at variance with the slaveholders' interests had to be denounced immediately.

The nonslaveholders fell into two main groups. The more prosperous owned land and comprised the yeomanry, practicing a subsistence agriculture. These farmers, along with a small group of urban tradesmen, were the slave South's

---

of the Old South, ed. Eric L. McKitrick (Englewood Cliffs, N.J., 1963), 38, 46, 47.

[63] Genovese, *Political Economy*, 157–173. There were pockets of pro-urban boosterism; see Lye W. Dorsett and Arthur H. Shaffer, "Was the Antebellum South Antiurban? A Suggestion," *JSH*, XXXVIII (Feb., 1972), 93–100, but the results were meager. And, as Genovese has shown in his study on Fitzhugh, *The World the Slaveholders Made* (New York, 1969), 202–206, urbanization would have to be on a small scale and would have posed no threat to the planter only if it were part of an autarkic pattern in which the South was far less dependent on export markets for her staples—a most unreasonable expectation.

middle class.[64] The less fortunate, owning no land, were the bottom rung of white society and totaled about 20% to 25% of all whites. Many of this group were found in the pine barrens, living off the forests by hunting, fishing, herding cattle and hogs, or tapping the pines for turpentine. Others, scattered throughout town and country, made up the skilled and unskilled labor pool.[65]

The economic prospects of the nonslaveholders, not bright to begin with, deteriorated as the slave economy matured. Competition for slave labor drove its price up beyond the means of those attempting to break into the system and provided the main impetus for the agitation over the reopening of the African slave trade. The price of land also rose sharply in the 1850's and the yeomanry, who already occupied inferior soils compared to the planters, were under pressure to sell out and move on. "The small farmers, that is to say, the mass of the white population, are fast disappearing," noted a country paper in the Mississippi Valley. Railroad promoters argued that only the promise of better marketing facilities could stem the tide of emigration from the mountains of Alabama to the cheap lands of Arkansas and Texas. The mobility of the nonslaveholders in Jefferson County, Mississippi, was tremendous. About 87% of the nonholders emigrated during the decade; the ratio among slaveholders varied inversely with the number of slaves held.[66]

For those who chose to remain, most avenues of advancement were closed. There was slight demand for white agricultural labor and that was seasonal. In addition, most whites held manual labor for another to be self-demeaning, work fit only for a slave. After migrating to California, a North Carolinian wrote back home that "it is different to a Slave State[;] here labour is dignified[,] everybody works. . . ."

[64] What is most significant about this class is its strikingly small share of Southern wealth. See Linden, "Economic Democracy," especially the tables on 159, 161 and 163.

[65] *Ibid.*, 144.

[66] Quoted in Olmsted, *Journey*, 330; Linden, "Economic Democracy," 179.

Skilled trades, such as blacksmithing and carpentry, carried no social stigma, but competition from trained slaves, hired out from one plantation to another, severely hindered their development. Olmsted mentioned a mechanic who, "saying he would starve before he helped a slave become a mechanic," indignantly refused an offer to use three slaves for six years in return for teaching them his trade. The towns had little industrial activity and attracted native talent only in the professions and politics. The dominance of commercial and trade life in the towns by immigrants indicated the disinterest in these fields by Southerners as much as any special drive of the foreign-born.[67]

Southern mores attached a preeminent importance to land ownership, and the dream of achieving or maintaining that status kept the whites in the countryside. The same factor deterred nonslaveholders from the industrial crafts. James Martin, a cotton manufacturer in Florence, Alabama, echoed the complaints of many industrialists in a public letter to DeBow. He referred to the "strange notion that our young men have, in believing that the training of the mind and hand to any kind of handicraft, causes them to lose cast[e] in society." This disinclination of ambitious young Southerners with property expectations to learn a trade, combined with the lack of incentives for them to do so, left the South with a shortage of mechanics. "Not so [in the] North. Capital there seeks labor, having only to pay interest instead of the full value of the laborer." Frankness would have required Martin to add that, weak as unions and the workers' bargaining position were in the North, they were still much stronger than in the South where the use or threat of slave labor crippled labor organizations. Southern whites who went into factory labor were of the poorest sort, scorned by a Mississippi

[67] J. H. Jones, "Evolution of Wilkinson County," *PMHS*, IX (1906), 84; speech of John D. Phelan in the *Montgomery Weekly Advertiser*, Dec. 19, 1860; Olmsted, *Journey*, 299, 180; Edward Davis to Charity A. Mangum, Feb., 1859, *The Papers of Willie Person Mangum*, ed. Henry T. Shanks (Raleigh, 1956), Vol. V.

industrialist as "the very dregs of society, and it may be in some instances worse than dregs." They were subject to intense controls and the overweening paternalism of the manufacturers.[68]

Common laborers, as a group, faced a host of coercive mechanisms. Indentured servitude, involuntary apprenticeship, compulsory labor for debtors, vagrants, the unemployed, and seamen were some of the devices by which, in the apt phrase of Richard B. Morris, the unskilled "stumbled into the quagmire of quasi-bondage." Construction work on internal improvements was so brutal and dangerous that one paper reported: "It has been stated by one who has navigated the lakes and rivers adjacent to New Orleans, that for every foot of canal from the city to the lake, a distance of about seven miles, the life of a foreigner was sacrificed." Natives shunned such hazardous work, especially in the summer months, and the deficit was made up by contracting for cargo ships of Irish immigrants, who were forced to accept such employment to pay their passage money.[69]

The plight of the nonslaveholders was noted by travelers and slaveholders alike. What struck outsiders was the extent to which nonslaveholders were maligned both by the planters above them and the slaves below them in the social hierarchy. The planter viewed his poorer neighbors as a nuisance and a threat to slave discipline. Prone to carry off the planter's cattle and ply his slaves with liquor, enticing them to steal from the plantation to pay for it, the poor were especially unwelcome in the black belts. A planter's son from the Yazoo area expressed this antipathy when he told Olmsted: "When I get to be representative, I'm going to have a law made that all such kind of men shall be took up by the State and sent to the penitentiary, to make 'em work and earn something to support their families." Other spokesmen for the slaveholders,

[68] *DBR*, xxiv (1858), 383, 385; J. M. Wesson to J. F. H. Claiborne, Aug. 11, 1858, J. F. H. Claiborne Papers, SHC.

[69] Morris, "Measure of Bondage," 223; *Semi-Weekly Mississippian*, May 29, 1860.

equally convinced of the economic uselessness of the bulk of the nonslaveholders, put forth more practical solutions for those "multitudes of men in our midst who have nothing to do. . . ." The planter was urged to invest in the still-to-be-exploited coal fields of northern Alabama and employ poor whites in his mines. Most ingenious was the plan of J. M. Wesson, a Mississippi industrialist, who would give the poor whites an economic stake in the perpetuation of slavery by employing them in the production of cheap textiles and shoes aimed at the plantation market. "When they become the manufacturer of the article consumed by the negro on the one hand, and the manufacturer of the article produced by the negro on the other, they are as exclusively identified with him as the owner is, for by him they both get their bread."[70]

These efforts at raising the productivity of the nonslaveholders while keeping them loyal to slavery met with but scant success because of the very narrow limits within which they had to operate. They had to have the support of the planters, whose primary interests were always in land and slaves, and, at the same time, they had to stop short of creating a large, educated labor force which might attack the planter's monopolization of wealth. The same considerations made free schools and better educational facilities suspect since they could undermine slavery's support among the poorer classes. "If the poor whites realized that slavery kept them poor, would they not vote it down?" asked a Carolina planter. Denigrated by the planters, the nonslaveholders were also subject to the scorn of their bitterest economic rivals, the slaves and lowly Irish, who disdainfully considered them lazy and shiftless. Perhaps the ultimate insult to this class was paid by Daniel R. Hundley, a patrician Southerner who penned an invaluable social commentary on the South of 1860. Hundley referred to the yeomanry, the most prosperous group of the

[70] Olmsted, *Journey*, 137; *Mobile Daily Advertiser*, July 20, 1860, "Letter from Talledega"; Wesson to Claiborne, Claiborne Papers, SHC.

nonslaveholders and the one with the most status, as "the industrious poor whites of the South."[71]

Traditionally the slaveholders had at their disposal a whole panoply of mutually enforcing devices by which to keep the nonslaveholders in line. Most effective of these was the substitution of race for class as the prime determinant of social and political behavior. The black was defined as the member of a permanently inferior race, socially useful only as a slave in the performance of menial labor under strict discipline. The white man, no matter how poor, was by definition socially superior to the black. In this scheme the slaveholder was the poor man's best friend. He not only directed and supervised slave labor into productive channels but also freed the whites from degrading common labor. "The line between menial and liberal labor is thus distinctly drawn, and the latter elevated and ennobled. Instead of an aristocracy of wealth, we have an aristocracy of race which elevates all white men with the true spirit of freedom, and a chivalry to maintain it at every sacrifice."[72] Appealing as it did to basic instincts of self-respect, this argument was a powerful one and was virtually unassailable as long as the poor feared the social and economic consequences of freeing the blacks more than the continued dominance of the slaveholder.

The nonslaveholder was in a very passive, dependent position vis-à-vis the planter. Not only did ties of kinship and regional patterns of family settlements mute class conflict, but planting as a way of life and success story had such prestige that it became "a regional way of thinking." When the yeo-

---

[71] Quoted in Edmund Kirke (pseudonym of J. R. Gilmore), *Among the Pines: or, South in Secession Time* (New York, 1862), 175; James Stirling, *Letters From the Slave States* (London, 1857), 266; Hundley, *Social Relations*, 195.

[72] Wilbert E. Moore and Robin M. Williams, "Stratification in the Ante-Bellum South," *ASR*, 7 (June, 1942), 343–351, W. O. Brown, "Role of the Poor Whites in Race Contacts of the South," *Social Forces*, 19 (Dec., 1940), 258–268; Vicksburg *Daily Evening Citizen*, Jan. 1, 1861.

manry gathered, they discussed slaves and cotton, not their farms and produce. Slaves easily outranked other forms of personal property and even real estate as both an investment and means of social advancement. A merchant-farmer in Alabama told a Yankee salesman that a merchant could expect on the average a 30% return on his capital investment, the planter only 8% to 12%. However, the merchant and other ambitious Southerners invested their profits in land and slaves. These could be exploited socially, the more so as one approached planter status. Any attack on slavery was also an attack on this social ideal; to decry slavery was to deny to those coveting planter status their most cherished ambition. Nonholders were also beholden to the planters in an economic sense. Many of them who grew cotton had it ginned by the planter. The price was not cheap. On Hugh Davis' plantation it amounted to one-fourteenth of the ginned cotton, all the cotton seed from the lint (for fertilizer and livestock feed), plus some cash or farm produce. In a larger context the nonslaveholders, deficient in the land, slaves, and copious credit essential to entering the market economy or directing political programs to meet their own needs, were economically extraneous.[73]

Ironically, the egalitarian flavor of Southern politics functioned to minimize discontent from below. In Alabama and Mississippi, the franchise was open to nearly all adult white males and there were no property qualifications for office-holding. Slaveholders had no special legal and political privileges and the poor were free to participate in the political process. The wealthy might grumble over belonging to an oppressed class, subject to a coarse and vulgar democracy,

[73] Edgar T. Thompson, "The Planter in the Pattern of Race Relations in the South," *Social Forces*, 19 (Dec., 1940), 245; Van Buren, *Jottings*, 9; Frederic Bancroft, *Slave-Trading in the Old South* (Baltimore, 1931), 343–350; F. N. Boney, ed., "Southern Sojourn: A Yankee Salesman in Ante-Bellum Alabama," *AR*, xx (April, 1967), 149; Weymouth T. Jordan, *Hugh Davis and his Alabama Plantation* (University, Ala., 1948), 134.

but any good politician knew that his success at the polls depended on how well he played the game of rhetorical obeisance to the needs and prejudices of the nonslaveholders. Thus, every Southern election acted as a catharsis for the common man's frustrations. Office seekers outdid themselves in denouncing their opponents' snobbishness or aristocratic tendencies. The wise politician already knew what Thomas Dabney, a wealthy Virginia planter who migrated to Mississippi in the mid-1830's, had to learn for himself. As related by his daughter, Susan Smedes,

> Thomas was misunderstood and misjudged by the people in Mississippi by whom he found himself surrounded. The plainer classes in Virginia, like those in England, from whom they were descended, recognized the difference between themselves and the higher classes, and did not aspire to social equality. But in Mississippi the tone was different. They resented anything like superiority in breeding.[74]

A political cartoon run by the Whig paper in Starkville, Mississippi, during an 1857 election for a state representative exemplifies the courting of the nonslaveholder. The Democrats and most of the planters supported Robert Muldrow, the incumbent and a large slaveholder. The minority Whigs, led by two wealthy and influential planters who were personal opponents of Muldrow, put up Samuel H. Daniel, a small farmer. The successful Whig campaign played up their man as the underdog friend of the yeomanry. Their cartoon at the start of the contest portrayed the candidates in the middle of a race: "Daniel was mounted on a mule, and Muldrow was seated in a two-horse buggy, a slave driving; Daniel was considerably behind Muldrow on the road marked 'To Jackson.' " Rare was the politician with the mental agility of a James L. Alcorn who could parry while on the stump his

[74] Sir Charles Lyell, *A Second Visit to the United States* (New York, 1849), Vol. 2, 163; Susan Dabney Smedes, *Memorials of a Southern Planter*, ed. Fletcher M. Green (New York, 1965), 53.

opponent's charge of being against the poor by the mere fact of his fashionable attire. Alcorn cleverly responded that he was showing his audience the same respect and deference he would show in church or in entertaining his best friends. More common was the admission of the Alabama candidate that he felt it was good politics to leave his horse at home and travel on foot while campaigning. Such a humble posture won votes. Even sending a daughter off to the city for a new Parisian gown and then allowing her to show it off in front of the home folks could be a serious political faux pas.[75]

The very intensity and prevalence of all this rhetorical demagoguery helped to keep the slaveholder in a safe position. The same piney woods farmer who pulled down his wealthy neighbor's fences or stole his cattle out of jealousy was bound to receive at least symbolic satisfaction from a political system that gave him the vote and produced politicians who would cater to his hatred and fear of the rich. An overly overt elitism would have been much more dangerous to the wealthy by denying antiplanter resentments and frustrations an outlet.

The control of the communications media by rabid proslavery spokesmen helped solidify entrenched interests. The press and the pulpit were centers of orthodoxy, preaching the virtues of slavery. They so ruthlessly filtered out any new ideas or reform ideologies in the least bit subversive to slaveholder hegemony that Clement Eaton has written eloquently of an intellectual blockade besetting the South in the three decades prior to secession. Rigid censorship was imposed on incoming mails and literature from the North. Itinerant peddlers and book and periodical agents were required to pay stiff, nearly prohibitive, license fees to the local authorities and faced heavy penalties for failing to comply. School commissioners also got into the act by refusing to hire Yankee

[75] Thomas B. Carroll, *Historical Sketches of Oktibbeha County* (Gulfport, Miss., 1931), 67; Charles J. Swift, unpublished typed manuscript of a biography of Alcorn, in James L. Alcorn and Family Papers, p. 12, MDAH; Lyell, *Second Visit*, 61–62.

teachers, claiming they were "wholly unsuitable for the training, teaching and governing [of] the youthful mind of the South."[76]

The high rate of illiteracy among the poor placed a premium on the oral communication of ideas. Revivalistic camp meetings and political barbecues were the chief sources for many of the average Southerner's values and conceptions of the outside world. They were primarily social occasions, a chance to get together with neighbors and combat the tedium of a hard, isolated existence. It was at these barbecues, and less formally during courthouse day gatherings, that the issues were explained and interpreted for the voters. The innate conservatism of such a dissemination of political ideas was admired by the aristocrat. A Natchez physician, William H. Holcombe, contrasted this arrangement with the socially unsettling system in the North. There, the masses were more literate, but this meant only that they could read, not reason. "Narrowminded, self-conceited, . . . they become a ready prey, by means of cheap newspapers, pamphlets and pressures, to the designing, the ambitious, and the unprincipled." This evil was exacerbated by the political power held by this ignorant multitude. Every politician must pander to their prejudices, but in the South proper balance was maintained. "The thoroughly ignorant in the South, gaining all their knowledge by oral communication, take their cue of opinion and conduct from their superiors in attainment. They are the most conservative people in the world, while the corresponding class in the North is the most radical."[77]

[76] Clement Eaton, *The Freedom-Of-Thought Struggle in the Old South* (New York, 1964), especially 335–353; *Natchez Daily Courier*, Aug. 18, 1860.

[77] In 1850 the reported illiteracy rate among Southern whites was 20%; in the Northwest the rate was 10%; in the Middle States 3%; and in New England 0.4%. See J. D. B. DeBow, *Compendium of the Seventh Census* (Washington, 1854), 153. Hundley, *Social Relations*, 201; William H. Holcombe Daily Journal, quoted in Donald M. Rawson, "Party Politics in Mississippi, 1850–1860," unpublished Ph.D. thesis (Vanderbilt University, 1964), 312–313.

All these restraints on the development of antislavery sentiments had worked very well, but by the late 1850's more slaveowners were becoming uneasy and fearful. Hinton Helper's *The Impending Crisis*, published in 1857, was a searing indictment of the pernicious effects of slavery upon nonslaveholders and accordingly was savagely denounced in the South. Some areas held book burnings. Helper's argument was symptomatic of a permanent problem—the continuing loyalty of the nonslaveholder to a social system whose rewards increasingly were being monopolized by the few. The potential for abolitionism in the upper South had long been recognized. Much of the land was too exhausted to support plantation agriculture. As the planter and his slaves moved out, Southerners worried that their place would be taken by Northern free laborers. These Northerners, set apart from the lazy Southern nonslaveholders by their "habits of industry and enterprise," would reclaim the land and win it over for free society. And, "it may be safely assumed that when the slaves have once progressed south, they will never return to the north again." These forebodings were echoed in the debates over the slave trade. Lower slave prices through an increased supply would give the South the cheap labor it needed to hold onto the border states and would lend more credence to the popular argument that every Southerner could ultimately hope to acquire slaves. This would cement the loyalty of that "large class of persons who have to make their own bread with their own hands" and hence now demand that slave labor be restricted to such fields as would not compete with themselves.[78]

As a panacea for Southern ills, the reopening of the African slave trade broke apart on its own contradictions and the specter of disgruntled nonslaveholders remained. It was a problem the South would still face if it seceded. D. H. Hamilton, the U. S. marshal in Charleston, pointedly asked the South Carolina Congressman, William P. Miles: ". . . think

[78] DeBow, *Industrial Resources*, Vol. II, 120; *DBR*, XXIV (1858), 487.

you that 360,000 Slaveholders will dictate terms for 3,000,-
000 of nonslaveholders at the South. I fear not, I mistrust our
own people more than I fear all of the efforts of the Abolitionists."[79]

Many slaveholders would not have fully agreed with Hamilton's misgivings, but, faced with pressures from all sides,
they found a program of Southern nationalism increasingly
attractive as a means of assuring home rule in both class and
racial matters. The leadership that they were prepared to follow was to push for Southern independence in 1860 unless
slavery was guaranteed further expansion within the Union.

[79] D. H. Hamilton to Miles, Feb. 2, 1860, Miles Papers, SHC.

THE STRUCTURE OF LEADERSHIP

THE dominance of the slaveholder and the subservience of town to country and of farm to plantation were manifested in the structure of political leadership. The men who articulated the issues and defined them for Southern society operated within organizations whose prime function was to protect and further the interests of slaveholders. "All that the master had was involved in the making and execution of laws," noted Thomas B. Carroll, a judge in postwar Mississippi and the son of an antebellum physician.

> The masters knew what legislation was necessary, and that only they or their dependents could and would frame and put into operation the needed statutes. They did not seek the emoluments of paltry office; on the contrary, they virtually hand-picked the men who were most available to represent the semi-feudal system on the board of police or in the principal county offices and in the State Legislature.[1]

The second great function of the party was to provide entry into the centers of power and wealth for those ambitious men intent on social and economic advancement. Their goal was land and slaves and politics could aid tremendously in their acquisition. The usual means of upward mobility for those who did not inherit wealth was the use of the legal profession as a springboard for establishing themselves in new communities. From law the more successful progressed to politics and eventually to the life of the gentry.

The career of Hugh Davis is illustrative in this regard. The Davis family encompassed all the mobility and drive associ-

[1] Thomas B. Carroll, *Historical Sketches of Oktibbeha County* (Gulfport, Miss., 1931), 100–101.

50

ated with the frontier. His grandfather, a Virginia planter, had moved to Kentucky in the 1780's, and Hugh's father, Nathaniel, moved on to Huntsville, Alabama, in 1817. All four sons were trained in the law and eventually migrated. At age 23 Hugh settled in Marion, Alabama. He practiced law from 1834 to 1852 and by 1840 had achieved sufficient status to marry into a socially prominent family. Service on various local committees appointed by the County Commissioners Court introduced Hugh to local politics and assured him an advantageous position from which to amass his wealth. His duties as County Solicitor, the attorney for the county's legal affairs, furnished him with firsthand knowledge of impending tax sales on land. In addition, as local representative of several Alabama banking and railroad establishments, he learned in detail of the economic opportunities available in his community. After gradually building up his landholdings in the 1840's, Hugh was ready by 1852 to retire from law and at the age of 41 begin the life of a planter. He had a small stock of eighteen slaves acquired piecemeal by purchase, in lieu of legal fees, and as gifts from his father and his wife's relatives. Though possessing little cash and encumbered with heavy debts on his land and slaves, Hugh had no difficulty in obtaining from Marion merchants the necessary credit to begin planting. He was deemed a good credit risk. He owned considerable property in and around Marion and had scattered holdings in Centerville and Montevallo. The prestige of his wife's name and the soundness of his legal reputation invested him with the respectability of a social class which merchants assumed would meet its obligations. Davis remained in debt for his first years as a planter, but a succession of good cotton crops, his cash staple, enabled him not only to pay his debts and achieve solvency but also to expand his plantation.[2]

The success pattern of Hugh Davis was probably typical of those who rose in the social hierarchy. Contemporaries usually specified the professions, especially law, as the stepping

[2] Weymouth T. Jordan, *Hugh Davis and His Alabama Plantation* (University, Ala., 1948), 7–16, 75, 114–116, and 129–130.

stone for the young and ambitious Southerners eager to advance rapidly. In the 1830's Ingraham observed:

> . . . no men grow old or gray in their profession if at all successful. As soon as the young lawyer acquires sufficient [capital] to purchase a few hundred acres of the rich alluvial lands, and a few slaves, he quits his profession at once, though perhaps just rising into eminence, and turns cotton planter. The bar at Natchez is composed, with but few exceptions, entirely of young men.

The economic pace was slower in the 1850's but the goal of professionals still remained planter status. After investing their profits in slaves, some law firms rented farm land if none other was available for sale. All surpluses were put into the endeavor, and, if all went well, the lawyers had both a nest egg and an operating plantation on which to retire.[3]

Lawyers who entered politics had all the advantages— ready access to information and the decision-making process, and an insider's knowledge of an area's economic possibilities—that Davis so skillfully exploited in his career. Political fanfare also gave the young lawyer a chance to make a name for himself. A Douglas physician, G. W. Files, identified this drive for political recognition as the hallmark of a radical, or Breckinridge, stance in politics. "The talking men in our county as elsewhere are mostly on the other side, for they are principally lawyers or ambitious young men, who take an ultra shoot [sic] because it gives notoriety and makes them talked about among the people." Lawyers, of course, were aware of these advantages and entered politics in great numbers. One editor commented resentfully on this trend by complaining that lawyers were monopolizing local offices. He accused the legal profession of becoming "a mere prepatory

[3] Joseph Holt Ingraham, *The South-West. By a Yankee* (New York, 1835), Vol. ii, 84–85. Ingraham was a school teacher from Maine who came South around 1830 to teach languages at Jefferson College near Natchez. Wirt Armistead Cate, *Lucius Q. C. Lamar: Secession and Reunion* (Chapel Hill, 1935), 42–43.

[sic] school for the training of politicians" and, as such, "a sort of aristocracy."[4] A compilation of biographical information on about one-third of the Alabama lower house elected in 1859 confirms the heavy preponderance of lawyers in politics. Over 70% of this sample launched their careers as lawyers. [5]

The lawyer-politicians who succeeded in politics were likely to be a confident, even swaggering lot. John J. Pettus, the fire-eating governor of Mississippi, was typical of those self-made men who rose from the ranks that Clement Eaton describes as the moving force of Southern politics in the 1850's. Trained in the law, he removed twice from his birthplace in Tennessee before he found solid opportunities in Kemper County, Mississippi. Combining the practice of law with the raising of cotton, he followed the South's best prescription for success. In 1843 he began a Democratic career in state politics that by 1859 carried him to the governor's chair. Pettus was an unpolished man who had carved his own fortune out of the undeveloped slave South that he knew as a young man. He rewarded this society with his undivided loyalty. William H. Russell, a British correspondent who visited Pettus early in the war, reported that he "believes that the society in which he lives is the highest development of civilized life." Russell was impressed with the raw power and

---

[4] *Mobile Daily Register*, June 1, 1860, Gainesville (Ala.) *Independent*, Dec. 15, 1860.

[5] Although many of these men no longer identified themselves as lawyers in the 1860 census, the fact remains that they had utilized law as an entry into politics. This explains the apparent inconsistency between my findings and those reported in Ralph A. Wooster, *The People in Power: Courthouse and Statehouse in the Lower South 1850–1860* (Knoxville, 1969), 35. Thomas M. Owen, *History of Alabama and Dictionary of Alabama* (Chicago, 1921), Vols. III and IV. These volumes contain short biographies of a surprisingly large number of prominent Alabamians. Owen was supplemented by William Garrett, *Reminiscences of Public Men in Alabama for Thirty Years* (Atlanta, 1872) and W. Brewer, *Alabama: Her History, Resources, War Record, and Public Men. From 1540 to 1872* (Montgomery, 1872).

53

energy of the man, who struck him as having never completely shed the trappings of the frontier. Unquestionably, Pettus had something of the backwoodsman about him, but "he was not ashamed of the fact when taunted with it during his election contest, but very rightly made the most of his independence and his hard work."[6] Here was a man, a social type, that a patrician Whig could never understand and the gulf between them separated the older wealth and complacency of the Whigs from the newer wealth and dynamism of the Democrats.

Party labels were taken seriously, as professions of faith, and the renunciation of one's party was an agonizing decision. "The feeling is an intensely strong one—the party name which a man has borne for twenty or thirty years, becomes part of his individuality. . . ." Politicians who did cross party lines were singled out with a special virulence by their erstwhile compatriots. A top Douglas steward in northern Mississippi, R. W. Flournoy, was castigated by the Breckinridge press in a wonderfully imaginative mixed metaphor. "He is the yellow flower of Douglasism, the mastodon of squatterism under the influence of whose fragrance, and, neath the weight of whose tread that insignificant mammoth, Southern Rights, holds its nose in terror and bends its trembling form in awe."[7]

In 1860 three parties jockeyed for power within the South —the Bell Whigs and the Breckinridge and Douglas Democrats. There were ideological differences between the Bell and Douglas forces, the most serious arising from the territorial issue of popular sovereignty, but they were united against the Breckinridge ultimatum on positive congressional protection

[6] Clement Eaton, *The Waning of the Old South Civilization* (Athens, Ga., 1968), 40; Robert W. Dubay, "John Jones Pettus: A Study in Secession," unpublished master's essay (University of Southern Mississippi, 1966); William Howard Russell, *My Diary North and South* (Boston, 1863), 300.

[7] William Kirkland to William M. Otey, Oct. 29, 1860, Wyche-Otey Papers, SHC; *Montgomery Weekly Mail*, quoted in the *Mobile Daily Advertiser*, May 6, 1860; Hayneville *Watchman*, July 13 and 20, 1860; *Prairie News*, quoted in the *Semi-Weekly Mississippian*, Aug. 24, 1860.

for slavery within the territories. In their opposition they sought to stake out a safe, middle ground for the South. Although the Breckinridge camp harbored a number of opponents of immediate secession, most of the extreme Southern rights men and the eventual secessionist leaders were Breckinridge Democrats.

The types of individuals attracted to each party provide a key to the contrasting partisan ideologies. The Bell party proudly accepted its description by friend and foe alike as a party of old men. Rationalizing that their age begat wisdom and conservatism, they treated it as a positive political asset. Support from old Whigs, Americans, and old Democratic Union men was heralded as the backbone of the party. Bell accounts of their state conventions portrayed the delegates as the solid and selfless citizenry—mature and reflective gentlemen, with deep roots in their communities and with the most at stake in the present crisis, not "mere politicians." Many of them had eschewed politics for years but now had joined the great fight to save the Union and the Constitution. Men of such character saw their program as twofold: to put down sectional agitators, North and South, and, on a nostalgic note, to restore the " 'good old times' " of the Republic.[8]

The party's self-image and solution to the sectional crisis suffered from obvious, fatal political defects. Successful projection of the party as belonging to the older, more conservative citizens deterred infusions of fresh new talent and left those with little to conserve, be it property or a secure social station, looking for a party with a more positive ideology. A letter writer to the *Canton Citizen* summarized the problem of age.

> The Democratic party takes pains to encourage recruits to its standards by opening up the way to promotion of the young and ambitious, while the Opposition, American or

[8] *Mobile Evening News*, Sept. 27; *Natchez Daily Courier*, June 27; *The Alabama Reporter*, May 31; *Mobile Daily Advertiser*, July 1; *Marion American*, quoted in the *Mobile Daily Advertiser*, June 1; Hayneville *Watchman*, quoted in *ibid.*, July 17, 1860.

Whig party, takes equal pains to keep the old standard bearers always prominently before the people and give no thought to the claims of young men. [The Democratic party, like the Methodists, swell their ranks by welcoming new, untutored recruits.] The Opposition, like the Episcopal Church, requires him to be first right in the faith, then to be well educated, and then to fill the place of someone who removed away, or had died, and at all times to be able to trace his succession from the early fathers.

A few Bell editors warned unavailingly that the party was in danger of becoming fossilized. Too many Whigs expected from politics the same deference to age, wealth, and social position that they had traditionally been accorded in their nonpolitical activities. When this deference was not forthcoming, many chose to ignore politics rather than alter their class conception of what politics should be. Gradually, the Whigs of the old Natchez region, in the words of Sydnor, "were metamorphosed from a political party into a social class, and the word 'Whig' came to denote little more than an aristocratic way of life."[9] It is no surprise then that the Whigs who comprised the vast majority of the Bell forces in 1860 looked to the past for their political inspiration, hoping for a restoration of old values and a return to tranquillity.

The Whigs delighted in depicting the Breckinridge politicians as the counter image of themselves. Youth, ambition, disaffection, fanaticism, and corruption—these were the qualities, claimed the Whig press, that distinguished their opponents. Although Breckinridge himself was considered a moderate, it was charged that he would, if ever elected, be dominated by his radical followers.[10] The Democrats must

[9] Quoted in *Weekly Vicksburg Whig*, June 27, 1860. The Whig party, "wherever it had power, possessed the suicidal policy of keeping a set of 'old fogies' in office perpetually, to the exclusion of young men of fine capacity and ability"; Canton *American Citizen*, June 16, 1860; Charles S. Sydnor, *A Gentleman of the Old Natchez Region, Benjamin L. C. Wailes* (Durham, 1938), 291.

[10] Gainesville *Independent*, April 14; *Weekly Vicksburg Whig*, May

always be radicals, reasoned John F. Bosworth of the Canton *American Citizen.* Dependent upon the vote of those with but a minimal stake in the community—naturalized foreigners, squatters, and the poor—they must cater to the low prejudices of these partisans to remain in power. Consequently, they exaggerated sectional differences for their political effect; they won votes from their land-hungry constituents by professing the need for more slave territory. The result was a party intent only on the spoils of office. The Democrats were ingrates and grasping parvenus, declaimed the *Weekly Vicksburg Whig.* Such men were incapable of appreciating the benefits of the Union and "because it does not foster them by bestowing place without requiring capacity, and conferring wealth without labor, regard our institutions as a failure." The crisis forced upon the South by Lincoln's election was blamed on reckless Breckinridge politicians. "Ambition[,] that predominant trait in the character of Southern politicians, has had much to do in bringing about this calamitous result. Unwilling to abide their time, our young aspiring politicians have been too much like the stripling, who wanted 'to marry *right now.*' "[11]

More caustic were privately circulated Whig appraisals. Mississippi's leaders were "intriguing demagogues and fanatics." Wailes characterized the opposition as violent, intemperate, even insane. No matter how moribund his party became, an old Whig like Wailes would never consider switching to the Democratic party. Many of its followers were utterly beneath him. Of the crowd at a political barbecue in 1857 near Natchez to honor General Quitman, he noted that a high percentage "consisted of foreigners from Natchez & the fag end

9, Aug. 1; *Natchez Daily Courier,* May 29, July 10, Aug. 16, 1860; *Speech of William C. Smedes, Esq.* . . . (Vicksburg, 1860), 9; William P. Gould Diary, Oct. 26, 1860, ADAH; Frank H. Heck, "John C. Breckinridge in the Crisis of 1860–1861," *JSH,* XXI (Aug., 1955), 316–346, confirms the moderation of Breckinridge himself.

[11] Canton *American Citizen,* June 2; *Weekly Vicksburg Whig,* Oct. 31; Tuscaloosa *Independent Monitor,* Nov. 16, 1860.

of democracy[,] not twenty men of promise or high respectability present." For Wailes, Democratic leaders were incompetents, their demands were too sectional, and their philosophy of government by universal manhood suffrage inevitably degenerated into demagoguery, the antithesis of rule by an upper class elite.[12]

Although resentful of the corruption charge, members of the Breckinridge party generally described themselves in the same terms used by their opponents in an attempt to discredit them. Emphasizing the positive side of the characteristics ascribed them by the opposition, they used them to political advantage. The party gladly admitted attracting a disproportionate share of the young and ambitious, and added that no other party in the South had ever been so popular with this class. They were fanatics, but only in their devotion to Southern rights. They were assuredly friends of the poor, and not out of a condescending aloofness or sycophantic courting of votes. The legitimate needs of the poor were recognized, especially their interest in the preservation of slavery. Honesty compelled the Breckinridge party to explain to the poor that the election of anyone except Breckinridge would doom slavery by denying it access to the territories. As to being "mere politicians," the party was proud of its political sensibilities and attention to electioneering details.[13]

The Breckinridge portrayal of the Bell forces did not differ substantially from the Whigs' own self-image. It was an easy image to deflate because of its air of slightly veiled pomposity and class-consciousness. The Douglas men, who described themselves in plantation regions as wealthy and conservative Democrats, were accused by the Breckinridge press in the Black Belt of being too popular among nonslaveholders, of creating a party that would be sympathetic to abolitionism.[14]

[12] Kenneth McKenzie to Duncan McLaurin, Jan. 1, 1860, Duncan McLaurin Papers, DU; B. L. C. Wailes Diary, Nov. 6, 1860, DU; quoted in Sydnor, *B. L. C. Wailes*, 293; *ibid.*, 291.

[13] *Semi-Weekly Mississippian*, Aug. 14, Oct. 9, 1860.

[14] For the self-identification of Douglas leaders with conservative

In northern Alabama, where the Douglas Democrats claimed to represent the yeomanry, the Breckinridge men relied on ingrained partisan attitudes to sharpen their attacks on the Douglasites. They were not true Democrats at all, it was charged, for old line Whigs and Know-Nothings gave them their support. Since the Whigs included the old Federalists and National Bank men who were the lifelong opponents of Andrew Jackson, the idol of the yeomanry, the Douglas party was smeared by association.[15]

The validity of these party impressions can be verified and given greater precision by identifying the 1860 politicians. These individuals, defined to include not only the prominent leaders but also the party workers and activists (my use of this term is meant to designate only involvement in politics, not a particularly radical brand of politics) on the local level, were identified from contemporary Alabama and Mississippi newspaper accounts. Correlation of manuscript census data with the individual party members provided a quantitative framework for isolating and measuring those socio-economic factors which characterized the politicians of the various parties.[16] To determine whether any correlations that emerged might have been a function of the level of leadership studied, the party structures of Alabama and Mississippi have been differentiated into those three groups who had major responsibility for party affairs on the state, county, and local levels.

The chain of command in state politics stretched from the party's central executive committee to the county chairmen, and rested upon the support of the party workers at the local level. This entire structure deserves the closest attention, for each layer rested upon the other. Moreover, it was at the state level that most of the pressure in Southern politics was gen-

---

planting interests, see the Gainesville *Independent*, July 21, 1860; for the charges of abolitionist tendencies, see the *Clayton Banner*, Sept. 6, and the Talladega *Democratic Watchtower*, July 11, 1860.

[15] *Florence Gazette*, May 30, July 25, 1860.

[16] For methodological details, see Appendix B.

erated. Constant scrutiny from their own party press forced all Democrats to toe a hard line on Southern rights. Jefferson Davis, the recognized leader of the Mississippi Democrats, found it necessary to mend his political fences as soon as he had returned home from a New England swing in the summer of 1858; he had been sharply criticized by his party for his conciliatory speeches during the trip. As the South took an increasingly intransigent stand on slavery, her leaders found service on the national level both distasteful and futile. L.Q.C. Lamar had hardly completed his first Congressional term before he was convinced that Southern men of talent could accomplish little for their section there. Wiley P. Harris spoke of his Congressional experience as "painfully disagreeable" and "a real torture." "I could not bring myself to think that I was doing the least good. The house was nothing more than a tumultuous popular assembly." Southerners complained that private interests treated representatives like pawns and constantly plied them for favors. By 1860 the Southern state machines demanded that congressional advice be ignored. "The course of the Southern Rights party in the South is simply to disregard Congressional counsels [as to unity and caution] and to move steadily on to the vindication of their rights."[17]

The central executive committees represented the greatest concentration of political power within the respective state party organizations. The committees in Alabama and Mississippi had specifically been empowered by their state conventions which had met in January, 1860, to call new state conventions in the event of a bolt at Charleston. The calls went out in the middle of May.

[17] Ralph Richardson, "Jefferson Davis, Sectional Democrat, 1858," *Antislavery and Disunion, 1858–1861*, ed. by J. Jeffrey Auer (New York, 1963), 51–70; Edward Mayes, *Lucius Q. C. Lamar: His Life, Times, and Speeches, 1825–1893* (Nashville, 1896), 76; "Autobiography of Wiley P. Harris," Dunbar Rowland, *Courts, Judges, and Lawyers of Mississippi, 1798–1935* (Jackson, 1935), 305, 309; *Mississippi Free Trader*, June 4, 1860.

II

With the exceptions of one nonslaveholder and one Virginian, the Alabama Breckinridge central committee was completely monopolized by slaveholding lawyers born in the Deep South.[18] Their median wealth of $62,000 revealed them as successful professionals, well-embarked on a planting career. A majority of the committee was under the age of forty-five and the median slaveholder was nineteen. Representation was weighted in favor of the southern cotton regions; Madison and Lauderdale were the only northern counties represented on the committee. The Bell committee involved a different type of leadership. Those born in the North and the upper South and employed as businessmen, planters, and editors were in the majority. Of the four lawyers on the committee only two were under forty-five, as contrasted with five Breckinridge lawyers in this age group. Surprisingly, the Bell members were less wealthy than their Breckinridge counterparts as is attested by their median property holdings of $25,-000 and median slaveholdings of eight. Mobile and the central hill counties of Shelby and Talladega were the only ones with committee representation from outside the planting districts. The two committees were distinguished not by any preponderance of age and wealth on the Bell side, but by the leadership positions in the Breckinridge camp held by young, successful lawyers.

County chairmen and presidents of local political clubs comprised the middle rung of the party structure. To the former fell the tasks of maintaining discipline, curbing dissent, and controlling county meetings; the latter concentrated on raising funds for campaign literature. The Breckinridge chairmen were at their best when word came down in May

[18] For the Breckinridge central committee see the Talladega *Democratic Watchtower*, June 13; for the Bell, the *Selma Weekly Reporter*, Aug. 1, 1860. Eight of the nine Breckinridge and eleven of the twelve Bell committeemen were located in the census. The Douglas committee was too small for a useful analysis.

that the Charleston bolters were to be supported and new slates of delegates drawn up for the state convention at Montgomery in June. Despite occasional charges from dissidents that the Charleston delegation had been instructed by a convention composed "of factionists and disunionists, who by application of the gag law and stocking [sic] of the cards had won the trick from the conservatives,"[19] the chairmen wheeled the local organizations into line. Serious defections, denying the authority of the executive committee to call a state convention and pledging to support whoever was nominated at the Baltimore convention of the National Democrats, were limited largely to northern Alabama. The defectors held their own meetings and chose their own delegates to a separate state convention in Montgomery which nominated delegates pledged to attend and support only the national convention in Baltimore, not the rival national convention in Richmond arranged by the Southerners who walked out at Charleston. The Bell chairmen had a more passive role to play. The Breckinridge party line on the issue of positive protection to slavery in the territories had already given them an issue to react against and, with the selection of the Bell-Everett ticket in early May, they had their candidate. On May 23 the *Selma Reporter* issued a call for a state convention of the Constitutional Union party to meet in Selma on June 27. Accordingly, nominating meetings for delegates were held in the middle of June.

The county leaders for the three major parties were identified and grouped according to the indices furnished by the manuscript census returns,[20] as shown in Table 1.

The relative dominance of youth among the Breckinridge leaders and of old age in both the Bell and Douglas groups is

[19] Greenville *Southern Messenger*, May 16, 1860.

[20] See Appendix B. Although I have attempted to maintain the distinction between the politicians and the voters, the readers should be cautioned here, as elsewhere, from drawing any generalizations about the voting population solely from the characteristics of those who were politically active.

TABLE 1

Alabama County Leaders

Party Membership by Age & Wealth

Age	Party	Under $25,000	$25,000–$49,999	$50,000 & Over	Total N	Total %
Under 40	Breck.	15%	6%	12.5%	16	33
	Bell	9	–	3	4	12
	Doug.	4	4	4	3	12.5
40–49	Breck.	15	4	6	12	25
	Bell	9	9	18	12	36
	Doug.	4	4	12.5	5	21
50 & Over	Breck.	10	12.5	19	20	42
	Bell	18	12	21	17	51
	Doug.	17	12.5	37.5	16	67

Summary of Wealth & Slaveholdings by Party

	Breck.	Bell	Doug.
Median Wealth	$36,250	$34,000	$65,500
% Slaveholders	90	88	87.5
Median Holding	19	18	39

SOURCES: The county leaders were those individuals identified in these newspaper accounts as party chairmen or political club presidents. The sample from the States' Rights Opposition party was too small for a useful analysis.

The figures for wealth in this and in subsequent tables are the sum of the real and personal property holdings listed under the names of those individuals (or their wives) found in the census returns. Occasional variations of $\pm 1\%$ in the addition of the columns in the tables are a result of rounding off. The N column refers to the base number of politicians found for each age category.

immediately apparent. Slaveholders virtually monopolized each set. The influence of planters (owners of 30 or more slaves) was about equal in the Douglas (33%) and Breckinridge (29%) samples, but decidedly weaker in the Bell group (18%). Young planters were typically Breckinridge

63

men; Douglas attracted the highest percentage of planters over the age of fifty. Rather surprisingly in light of the traditional interpretation, the smaller slaveholding farmers carried the most weight among the Bell leaders (21%) and the least among the Breckinridge (6%). However, the median age of these Bell farmers was 54, and their conservative politics reinforces the impression that the Breckinridge demands on expansion and Southern rights had little appeal for the older politicians.

Among the three sets lawyers were most prominent and town business elements the least in the Breckinridge sample, comprising 31% and 12.5% respectively of the whole; these figures were nearly reversed in the Bell set as the lawyers' influence dropped to 12% and the business groups' rose to 27%.[21] Those born outside the deep South[22] played the largest role in the Douglas sample and the smallest in the Breckinridge.

The broadest layer of the political structure embraced the party workers at the county level. These party activists were the convention delegates, committeemen, political club members, and editors whose labor and enthusiasm were essential to any successful political campaign. They raised funds, distributed campaign literature, imported outside speakers, planned the ever popular political barbecue, and generally touted their man. Many of them were also inspectors and returning officers at the polls on election day. The editors had the indispensable tasks of projecting their party's image, waging its rhetorical battles, and publicizing its candidates. Though relatively inexpensive to set up, newspapers required

[21] For the Douglasites the figures were 12% for the lawyers and 17% for business groups.

[22] As used here, the term deep South includes the entire slave South with the exceptions of Virginia, Maryland, and Delaware. This definition of the deep South, by including such border states as Kentucky and Missouri, is clearly an unorthodox one, but it has been utilized so as to isolate the oldest areas of the Upper South which served as a source of migration to newer regions.

party funds and business advertisements to be profitable. Usually edited by young men just beginning their political careers, all but a few papers had a partisan affiliation.[23] The successful, older editors became top party strategists.

In those Breckinridge counties (carried by a majority) where slaveholders comprised over half of the family units, samples of all four Alabama parties were found. The fourth party, the States' Rights Opposition (S.R.O.), was led by lawyers such as Thomas J. Judge, Samuel F. Rice, William P. Chilton, and Thomas H. Watts.[24] The party was primarily a group of disgruntled Whigs who had rejected the standard conservatism of their fellow Whigs. Limited to the cotton regions of southern Alabama, the mere existence of the party was further evidence of traditional Whiggism's bankruptcy. As the Democrats increasingly monopolized political power by insisting on a fervent defense of Southern rights, Whigs with political aspirations had little choice but to ape this successful ideology. In the gubernatorial election of 1859 the States' Rights Opposition Whigs backed a fire-eating Democrat, William F. Samford, against the incumbent, A. B. Moore. Charging that Moore supinely submitted to outrages such as Congress' refusal to admit Kansas under the Lecompton Constitution, Samford stood on the high grounds of Southern rights. "My complaint is that the Southern cause has not received the earnest, active, outspoken sympathy of our governor." The States' Rights Whigs' best chance to share

[23] Clement Eaton, *The Growth of Southern Civilization, 1790–1860* (New York, 1961), 265–266; Lewis E. Atherton, *The Southern Country Store, 1800–1860* (Baton Rouge, 1949), 199. Out of twenty Breckinridge editors in Alabama traced in the census returns, twelve were under forty; fourteen reported less than $10,000 in property holdings; ten were small slaveholders. A sample of fourteen Bell editors had similar characteristics. Twelve were under forty and twelve reported under $10,000 in property; only four, however, were slaveholders.

[24] Of these four, Watts was the only Bell supporter; the other three backed Breckinridge. Like the other three, however, Watts worked for immediate secession after Lincoln's election.

in the political spoils came with the nomination of Breckinridge. The party officially supported Breckinridge and its local organizations cooperated with the Democrats. In return the party demanded that the Breckinridge forces faithfully adhere to their own platform pronouncements on the territorial rights of the slaveholder.[25]

Old line Whigs, placing as always Unionism over Southernism, blasted their former party compatriots as greedy political renegades. Only the lust for office, it was charged, could explain such party apostasy. Loyal Whigs and Bell supporters were indignant at the Democratic claim that the Alabama convention of the States' Rights Opposition was the real opposition party in Alabama. "The so-called convention which met at Montgomery, and declared for Breckinridge, was a miserable conclave of disunionists and secessionists who ought to have been in the Democratic party long ago, as they have invariably caused the defeat of the Opposition by their ultraism."[26]

The party profiles by age-wealth patterns and the distribution of slaveholders by age and occupation are given in Table 2.

Another variable besides age which differentiated the partisan affiliation of the politically active farmers and planters was the greater commitment to cotton production and plantation agriculture by the Breckinridge politicians. In Marengo and Dallas counties the Breckinridge planters, both young and old, had larger plantations and produced on the average more than twice as much cotton as did their Bell counterparts. Except for the comparable size of landholdings, the pattern in Perry County was similar. Here, the younger Breckinridge farmers and planters were most involved in a commercially

[25] Lewy Dorman, *Party Politics in Alabama From 1850 Through 1860* (Montgomery, 1935), 137–153; quoted in George Petrie, "William F. Samford, Statesman and Man of Letters," *TAHS*, IV, 1904, 477; *Montgomery Weekly Mail*, July 3, 1860.

[26] Hayneville *Watchman*, July 13, 20, 1860; Canton *American Citizen*, July 14, 1860.

oriented agriculture. Both led their respective groups, when compared to Bell agriculturists, in cotton production and in the lowest ratio of corn to cotton output.[27]

There was a marked shift of the older, wealthier politicians away from Breckinridge in those high slaveholder density counties lost by him (see Table 3). Among slaveholders Breckinridge was most popular with the lawyers and the younger farmers and planters under the age of forty. Least prone to back him were the older planters. In Greene County, where a direct comparison of the planters was possible, the young Breckinridge planters were the leading cotton producers. The slaveowning town middle class supported all the parties about equally, but the nonholders exhibited a strong preference for Douglas. The Bell group led among natives of the Upper South (18%), the Douglas among the Northern and foreign-born combined (13%).

The party samples from Montgomery, as for other counties with a town in excess of 1,000 population, will be treated separately. This enables special attention to be focused on those political organizations with deeper roots in the town and prevents any distortion which might arise by combining such samples with those drawn from an overwhelmingly rural environment. All four parties were represented in Montgomery. The Breckinridge group was the youngest and was most popular among slaveholding lawyers and physicians. In contrast, more than half of the Bell supporters were businessmen and artisans.[28] Nonslaveholders' support for

[27] This conclusion and subsequent ones dealing with agriculture are based on the use of Schedule No. 4 of the census returns, which lists for each farm or plantation within a county its cash value, amount of improved and unimproved acreage, and crop and livestock production. Kit C. Carter, "A Critical Analysis of the Basis of Party Alignment in Lowndes County, Alabama, 1836–1860," unpublished master's essay (University of Alabama, 1961), 53, found in Lowndes that the Bell politicians produced much less cotton than the Breckinridge and States' Rights men.

[28] Thus, while 26% of the Breckinridge men were young slaveholding farmers, planters, and professionals, a mere 2% of the Bell group

67

TABLE 2

Politicians in Breckinridge, High Slaveholder Density Alabama Counties

Age	Party	Under $25,000	$25,000–$49,999	$50,000 & Over	Total N	%
		Party Membership by Age & Wealth				
Under 40	Breck.	30%	8%	13%	84	51
	Bell	21	7	7	31	35
	Doug.	23	3	10	11	35
	S. R. O.	17	13	10	21	41
40–49	Breck.	7	8	10	43	26
	Bell	17	4.5	10	28	31
	Doug.	10	10	16	11	35
	S. R. O.	8	4	13	13	25
50 & Over	Breck.	5	2	15	37	23
	Bell	10	12	11	30	34
	Doug.	3	3	23	9	29
	S. R. O.	11	6	17	18	34

Party Membership of Slaveholders by Age & Occupation[a]

Occupation	Party	Under 40	40–49	50 & Over	Total N	%
Planters	Breck.	11%	10%	11%	52	32
	Bell	3	8	13	22	25
	Doug.	10	16	19	14	45
	S. R. O.	10	8	17	18	35
Farmers	Breck.	10	7	4	34	21
	Bell	9	4	9	20	22
	Doug.	6	6	6	6	19
	S. R. O.	17	6	4	14	27
Lawyers	Breck.	12	3	1	27	16
	Bell	2	3	1	6	7
	Doug.	10	–	–	3	10
	S. R. O.	2	–	6	4	8
T. M. C.[b]	Breck.	2	1	1	7	4
	Bell	4	7	3	13	15
	Doug.	–	3	–	1	3
	S. R. O.	4	6	2	6	12

TABLE 2 (*continued*)

Summary of Wealth & Slaveholdings by Party

	Breck.	Bell	Doug.	S. R. O.
Median Wealth	$33,950	$25,800	$36,000	$42,950
% Slaveholders	82	83	87	94
Median Holding	27	21	31	25

SOURCES: Breck.—48 from Lowndes, 43-Marengo, 40-Perry, 26-Pickens, 7-Sumter; Bell—26 from Perry, 25-Marengo, 16-Lowndes, 16-Pickens, 6-Sumter; Doug.—22 from Sumter, 9-Lowndes; S. R. O.—52 from Lowndes.

[a] Only the major occupational categories of slaveholders have been tabulated. The percentages are based on the total party sample.

[b] Town Middle Class.

Douglas, the bulk of which came from the town middle class, was about twice that for any other party.[29] Slaveowning farmers comprised a majority in only one party, the States' Rights Opposition. The closest affinities among the parties were between the Breckinridge and States' Rights on the one hand, and the Bell and Douglas on the other. The first two were the wealthiest and had the highest percentage of large slaveholders; they drew most heavily on natives of the Deep South and young slaveholding farmers and planters. The latter two parties, relying more on those born in the North or abroad,[30] town business elements, and older wealth in general, were clearly not attracting the younger politicians committed to the land and its exploitation by slave labor.

The town of Selma serviced the agricultural needs of Dallas, a rich cotton county. The politicians, regardless of wealth, split along age lines; under forty typically for Breckinridge, over forty usually against. Characteristic of

---

fell into this category. However, 55% of the Bell politicians were engaged in business or the skilled trades, only 21% of the Breckinridge.

[29] Nonslaveholders comprised 39% of the Douglas group; their next largest role was 21% in the Breckinridge set.

[30] The Bell party led all four in Northern born with 20%; the Douglas led in foreign-born with 14%.

TABLE 3

Politicians in Anti-Breckinridge, High Slaveholder Density Alabama Counties

		Party Membership by Age & Wealth				
Age	*Party*	*Under $25,000*	*$25,000– $49,999*	*$50,000 & Over*	*Total* N	*Total* %
Under 40	Breck.	34%	13%	7%	68	54
	Bell	18	8	10	32	36
	Doug.	36	4	5	62	46
	S. R. O.	21	13	6	19	40
40–49	Breck.	11	5	9	31	25
	Bell	11	12	11	31	35
	Doug.	13	8	8	39	29
	S. R. O.	8.5	8.5	15	15	32
50 & Over	Breck.	12	5	5	27	21
	Bell	7	3	19	26	29
	Doug.	10	5	10	34	25
	S. R. O.	6	6	15	13	28

Summary of Wealth & Slaveholdings by Party

	Breck.	*Bell*	*Doug.*	*S. R. O.*
Median Wealth	$20,750	$33,450	$16,500	$34,560
% Slaveholders	82	86	71	94
Median Holding	13	25	19	29

SOURCES: Breck.—55 from Monroe, 52-Greene, 19-Macon; Bell—61 from Greene, 28-Limestone; Doug.—57 from Greene, 33-Chambers, 24-Macon, 21-Monroe; S. R. O.—47 from Macon.

Breckinridge's slaveholder adherents were the younger professionals and the large planters who owned more than fifty slaves.[31] The older, small slaveholding farmers and the over

[31] For example, slaveholding lawyers and physicians under forty years made up 27% of the Breckinridge sample, 3% of the Douglas, and only 2% of the Bell; if forty and over, the support of this group switched to 24% of the Douglas, 8% of the Bell, and only 2% of the Breckinridge sample.

forty professionals and businessmen gave Bell and Douglas solid support. The Breckinridge party had a slight edge over the Douglas in attracting nonslaveholders, 32% to 27%. Young businessmen, born in the Deep South, comprised the bulk of the former; young professionals and artisans, with a heavy sprinkling of Northern born, the latter. While 15% and 14% of the Douglas and Bell followers respectively were born in the North, none of the Breckinridge men was. Douglas also led among the foreign-born.

The contrasts between the two rival Democratic organizations were very sharp in Madison County, which included Huntsville, the hub of the Tennessee Valley. Although both parties were comparable in their median wealth, the young wealth backed Breckinridge, the old wealth Douglas. Higher percentages of planters under fifty and professionals of all ages distinguished the Breckinridge slaveholders. Smaller slaveholding farmers of all ages, planters over fifty, and older businessmen marked Douglas' slaveholder support. The Breckinridge planters were the largest cotton producers. Rounding out these party profiles was the attraction of native Virginians for Douglas and of nonslaveholding professionals for Breckinridge.[32] The small Bell sample of nineteen was dominated by merchants and businessmen and contained no large slaveholders.

The lines of party cleavages thus far uncovered held true in the medium slaveholder concentration counties, those where the ratio of slaveholders to families ranged from 25 to 49%. The data for the Breckinridge counties are summarized in Table 4.

Two factors distinguished the agricultural practices of the Breckinridge and States' Rights farmers and planters. They

[32] Six out of nine Breckinridge planters produced 100 or more bales of cotton; only three out of thirteen Douglas planters traced in the returns did so. Virginians comprised 31% of the Douglas sample, just 11% of the Breckinridge. The support of professionals (13% to 0%) accounted for the higher percentage of nonslaveholders in the Breckinridge set (21% to 8%).

TABLE 4

Politicians in Breckinridge,
Medium Slaveholder Density Alabama Counties

		Party Membership by Age & Wealth				
Age	*Party*	*Under* $25,000	$25,000– $49,999	$50,000 & Over	*Total* N	%
Under 40	Breck.	32%	11%	13%	98	56
	Bell	39	6	4	34	49
	Doug.	35	7	–	23	43
	S. R. O.	34	3	5	16	42
40–49	Breck.	11	5	10	46	26
	Bell	10	3	–	9	13
	Doug.	11	2	2	8	15
	S. R. O.	16	13	3	12	32
50 & Over	Breck.	7	4	6	31	18
	Bell	12	13	13	26	38
	Doug.	17	7	19	23	43
	S. R. O.	16	10	–	10	26

		Party Membership of Slaveholders by Age & Occupation				
Occupation	*Party*	*Under* 40	*40–49*	50 & Over	*Total* N	%
Planters	Breck.	8%	6%	6%	34	19
	Bell	4	–	16	14	20
	Doug.	–	–	18	10	18
	S. R. O.	5	–	3	3	8
Farmers	Breck.	15	7	5	48	27
	Bell	7	7	17	22	32
	Doug.	11	6	18	19	35
	S. R. O.	5	13	13	12	32
Lawyers	Breck.	11	5	2	31	18
	Bell	9	1	1	8	12
	Doug.	4	–	–	2	4
	S. R. O.	13	5	3	8	21
T. M. C.	Breck.	5	5	2	19	11
	Bell	9	–	1	7	10
	Doug.	4	4	1	5	9
	S. R. O.	8	5	3	6	16

72

TABLE 4 (*continued*)

Summary of Wealth & Slaveholdings by Party

	Breck.	Bell	Doug.	S. R. O.
Median Wealth	$24,275	$15,500	$15,500	$15,070
% Slaveholders	86	81	76	79
Median Holding	19	16	11	10

SOURCES: Breck.—62 from Barbour, 48-Russell, 40-Talladega, 25-Clarke; Bell—50 from Talladega, 19-Russell; Doug.—30 from Pike, 24-Clarke; S. R. O.—28 from Pike, 10-Russell.

either produced more cotton and less corn relative to the Douglas group, as was the case in Clarke and Pike, or they owned only about one half as much unimproved acreage, that is, land in reserve. This latter pattern was sharpest between the Breckinridge and Bell groups in Talladega.

Barbour and Tuscaloosa were two Breckinridge counties meriting special attention. The former was a hotbed of secessionist sentiment, and the Democratic leaders there were dubbed by Lewy Dorman as the Eufaula Regency, the "most consistent secessionists in the state during the fifties."[33] Slaveholding lawyers and lawyer-planters in their thirties or early forties almost completely dominated the eleven-man regency. The party as a whole attracted young wealth. The bulk of the slaveholders were under forty-five and evenly divided between farmers and planters, on the one hand, and lawyers and lawyer-planters on the other. Young lawyers dominated the 15% minority of nonslaveholding members.

Only a Bell organization was uncovered in Tuscaloosa, a county with excellent soil in its southeastern section, a fine trade outlet on the Black Warrior River, and two commercial centers on the river, Tuscaloosa and its smaller sister town of Northport. The business communities of these two towns provided the largest single contingent of Bell politicians, a 40% bloc about evenly divided between small slaveholders and nonholders. The countryside was poorly represented; slaveholding farmers, the majority of whom had not yet

[33] Dorman, *Party Politics*, 36.

achieved planter status, comprised just 23% of the sample.[34] Rooted in the towns, drawing upon Yankees and Virginians for one-fourth, and nonslaveholders for one-third of its membership, and with very little appeal for the larger slaveholders, the Bell party of Tuscaloosa had no use for a radical ideology tailored to rural needs.

In the anti-Breckinridge, medium slaveholder counties party samples were found in the southern, central, and northern areas of the state. The breakdown of partisan allegiances, as well as the dominance of slaveholders, was very similar to that disclosed in Table 4, with the exception of stronger support for Bell and Douglas from the older town middle class. In the western Tennessee Valley, Douglas had a decided advantage over Breckinridge in attracting the Northern and foreign-born. A much larger amount of unimproved acreage and a less intensive agriculture which put more stress on corn production once again characterized the Bell farmers as opposed to the Breckinridge. This held true in Butler, the one county where the two parties could be directly compared. The largest cotton producers in the Tennessee Valley favored Breckinridge over Douglas.[35]

Mobile, the cotton emporium of southern and central Alabama, was the only large metropolitan area in the Deep South aside from New Orleans. Its urban parties were factionalized along a number of lines. In terms of age and wealth, the Breckinridge and Douglas groups were very similar, but the Bell party revealed the greatest strength among those fifty and over worth under $25,000, and the weakest among the younger, wealthier politicians. Slaveowning lawyers and farm-

[34] This supports the finding of J. C. Oldshue, "The Secession Movement in Tuscaloosa County, Alabama," unpublished master's essay (University of Alabama, 1961), 97–98, that the Whigs' rural vote in Tuscaloosa was concentrated in hilly areas devoted to small-scale farming, not the plantation regions.

[35] The disparity between the two rival Democratic organizations in Autauga County was more muted than in other areas, a testimony to the success of the respected Douglas planter, Bolling Hall, in attracting dissident Democrats.

ers easily favored Breckinridge. The servicing agents of the cotton crop, factors, brokers, and buyers, virtually ignored Breckinridge; eleven of the thirteen who were politically active favored Bell or Douglas. For the rest of the business community, nativity and slaveholding status were the key variables affecting party allegiances. Nonslaveholding merchants, businessmen, and clerical help comprised 7% of the Breckinridge sample, about 20% of the other two. The slaveholders of this class, except those who were Northern born and backed Bell by a wide margin, were not as sharply divided in their allegiances. About 30% of the Breckinridge politicians belonged to this class, as compared to 40% of the other two parties. As a whole, the Bell and Douglas nonslaveholders were more likely to be members of the town middle class, the Breckinridge nonholders to be lawyers.[36]

Few party samples were found in the low slaveholder concentration counties, a reflection of the dearth of newspapers in these areas. Jackson, a strong Breckinridge county, was the only one where a direct comparison between two parties was possible. There, the Breckinridge party was considerably younger and wealthier than their Douglas opponents. The wealthier activists favored the former at all age levels, though most strongly by those in their twenties and thirties. The Douglasites had a much higher percentage of nonslaveholders, 54% to 19%. Most of this differential was based on their appeal to older yeomen farmers.[37] Among slaveholders only farmers age forty and over owning fewer than ten slaves favored Douglas. The Douglasites of Marshall, a county lost by Breckinridge, were poorer and lacked support from young wealth when compared to the Breckinridge politicians in the neighboring counties of Jackson and Calhoun. The Douglas men were favored by more nonslaveholders, businessmen,

[36] Even in these decidedly urban parties, nonslaveholders were in a minority. Their influence ranged from 36% in the Bell sample to 23% in the Breckinridge.

[37] These yeomen farmers owned less land and of poorer quality than the slaveholders in either party. None of them grew cotton, whereas a majority of the slaveholding farmers did.

Northern born, and all those in their fifties worth under $25,-000. To the extent that twelve Bell supporters in Calhoun were representative of their party, they arrayed nonslaveholders and town interests against the county's dominant Breckinridge party, controlled by slaveholding farmers and lawyers.

The preceding data permits some firm conclusions about active party membership. The Breckinridge politicians, independent of wealth, were consistently younger than the Bell supporters. In the counties carried by Breckinridge the effect of greater wealth within each age bracket was to increase the preference for Breckinridge. The opposite held true in those counties lost by him, revealing that the traditional assignment of wealth to the Whigs was valid only in those areas where they were the majority party or close to it. Regardless of an area's politics, younger wealth was more prone to back Breckinridge, the older wealth Bell. The Breckinridge farmers and planters were not only younger than their Bell counterparts, but were also engaged in a more commercially exploitive agriculture as shown by their greater cotton production, lower ratios of corn to cotton outputs, and smaller amounts of unimproved acreage. Lawyers clearly favored the Democrats; businessmen and artisans either split their allegiances or backed Bell.

The contrasts between the Douglas and States' Rights Opposition organizations also help explain their divergent ideologies. The former, more closely akin to the Bell politicians in age, wealth, and occupations, likewise adhered to a conservative position. The States' Rights groups most often paralleled the Breckinridge politicians in their attraction for young slaveholding farmers and planters committed to cotton production and hence had a similar ideological thrust.

III

As in Alabama, Mississippi politics in the 1850's evolved toward a one-party system. In the face of external threats to slavery, all Whig efforts at combating the Democrats' vote-getting appeals to Southern unity proved abortive. By 1859 the Whig organization failed to run even a full slate of candidates for state offices. Significantly, Mississippi Whiggism developed nothing analogous to the States' Rights Opposition movement in Alabama. While many Whigs in the latter state backed the gubernatorial bid of William Samford in 1859, a candidacy demanding a more aggressive defense of Southern rights, Mississippi Whigs ran H. W. Walter on the negative platform of opposition to the re-opening of the African slave trade, to Congressional protection of slavery in the territories, and to secession in the event of a Republican triumph in 1860.[38]

That the Whigs of Mississippi were more willing to accept political stagnation than run the risk of embracing a radical ideology which threatened social and economic stability was a reflection both of their great wealth and proximity to prime, undeveloped cotton lands. The strength of the party was in the Delta.[39] This triangular area north of Vicksburg formed by the basins of the Mississippi and Yazoo Rivers contained alluvial soils more conducive to a heavily capitalized agriculture than even Alabama's Black Belt. The soil in the Delta, more fertile and less susceptible to erosion, supported agricultural units with an average cash value more than twice that of those in the Black Belt. In the 1850's these incomparable cotton lands absorbed an influx of planters wealthy enough

---

[38] Donald M. Rawson, "Party Politics in Mississippi, 1850–1860," unpublished Ph.D. thesis (Vanderbilt University, 1964), *passim*; Reuben Davis, *Recollections of Mississippi and Mississippians* (Boston, 1891), 378; *Mississippi Democrat*, July 16, 1859; Percy Lee Rainwater, *Mississippi: Storm Center of Secession, 1856–1861* (Baton Rouge, 1938), 100.

[39] Seven out of the eight counties that Bell carried with an outright majority were in the Delta. Sunflower was the only county lying entirely within the Delta that he lost. Four river counties below Vicksburg which had very narrow bands of alluvial soil along the Mississippi are not considered as Delta counties since their predominant soil was brown loam and loess.

to exploit the land. In comparison, Alabama Whiggism did not have as much wealth to protect nor as much available land for the expansion of plantation agriculture. Consequently some Alabama Whigs, and particularly the younger adherents, rejected their party's conservatism for a more belligerent stance which held out the hope of more slave territory.

The geographic distribution of membership in the Bell and Breckinridge central executive committees in Mississippi epitomizes the Whigs' limited state-wide appeal.[40] Whereas the latter represented all the major areas of the state, the Bell committee was heavily weighted in favor of Hinds and Warren, two older, plantation-dominated counties. Greater wealth and age distinguished the Bell leadership. Only two members of the eight-man committee were under the age of forty and half had property holdings in excess of $100,000. A majority of the Breckinridge committee was in their thirties; measured by median holdings, they were half as wealthy as their opponents, $38,500 to $77,500. Lawyer-planters at the top of their profession, such as William Sharkey and William Yerger of Hinds and C. C. Shackleford of Madison, controlled the Bell committee. Farmers and planters, followed by lawyers, were characteristic of the Breckinridge. Wm. W. W. Woods, Breckinridge editor of the *Mississippi Free Trader* was the only nonslaveholder in either group.

County leaders performed the same functions as in Alabama. With speed and efficiency the regular Democratic county organizations answered the state chairman's call for county conventions to sustain the action of the bolting delegates at Charleston and to select county delegations of the same persuasion for the state convention scheduled for Jackson in June. Little opposition to this course materialized in southern and central Mississippi. Pro-Douglas resolutions, such as one by Elisha Dismukes of Noxubee to "re-affirm the old Democratic doctrine, that we will support the nominees whoever they may be," were quickly voted down. Franklin

[40] For the Breckinridge committee see the *Mississippi Democrat,* Dec. 24, 1859; the Bell is in the *Weekly Vicksburg Whig,* May 2, 1860.

County Democrats even resolved not to support Douglas under any circumstances and requested the Mississippi delegation at Baltimore to withdraw and nominate another candidate if faced with a Douglas nomination. The county chairmen had done their jobs well. The official party organ, the Jackson *Mississippian*, could rightfully boast of the state convention's "firm resolve not to abate one job or title of the demands heretofore made in behalf of Mississippi by her representatives in the Charleston Convention, nor to erase a single motto which they have written upon her banner."[41]

There were signs of recalcitrance in parts of northern Mississippi. Meetings in Calhoun and Chickasaw, though not condemning the Charleston bolters, stressed the need for harmony and unity in the Democratic party as the surest way to preserve Southern rights. Serious battles over the resolutions which would bind the county delegates erupted in at least four northern counties. The Pontotoc convention was the most severely split. Efforts by R. W. Flournoy, a future Douglas elector, to denounce formally any attempts that had been or might be taken to split the Democratic party raised a storm. Party regulars, led by C. D. Fontaine, a young lawyer, gained control of the meeting and voted down the Flournoy resolution. Those voting in the minority walked out.[42]

By comparison the Whig county conventions were placid affairs. Meetings were held in late March and early April in response to the call of William Sharkey, chairman of the central committee, for a state convention of the Opposition Party in Jackson on April 23. The convention, which appointed an electoral ticket and delegates to the Constitutional Union Convention at Baltimore, was poorly attended. Only about one-fourth of the counties, some by proxy, were represented in the roll call of the delegates present; most of these were river counties or older, interior areas such as Madison and Holmes.[43] After this state conclave, the Whigs limited them-

[41] *Semi-Weekly Mississippian*, May 25, 29, June 1, 1860.
[42] *Ibid.*, May 22, 29, June 4.
[43] *Weekly Vicksburg Whig*, May 2, 1860.

selves to ratification meetings and fund-raising clubs on the local level.

By age and wealth the Breckinridge and Bell county leaders broke down as shown in Table 5.

TABLE 5

Mississippi County Leaders

| Age | Party | Party Membership by Age & Wealth | | | Total | |
		Under $25,000	$25,000– $49,999	$50,000 & Over	N	%
Under 40	Breck.	18	6	7	21	31
	Bell	10.5	3	10.5	9	24
40–49	Breck.	13	3	18	23	34
	Bell	3	10.5	21	13	34
50 & Over	Breck.	10	6	19	24	35
	Bell	16	5	21	16	42

Summary of Wealth & Slaveholdings by Party

	Breck.	Bell
Median Wealth	$42,000	$50,017
% Slaveholders	91	89
Median Holding	21	33

SOURCES: Various 1860 newspaper accounts. See Appendix B.

The county leaders did split along age lines but not as sharply as in Alabama.[44] The Whigs' ability to attract more young, wealthy politicians here than in Alabama undoubtedly reflected their party's greater state-wide appeal in Mississippi. Bell's most consistent followers derived from planters over the age of fifty (18% to 10%) and Breckinridge's from lawyers under forty (16% to 5%). Natives of the Upper South were about three times as likely to be in the Bell camp.

[44] The preponderance of age for Bell was even heavier than the table would indicate. Those age sixty and over comprised 16% of the Bell sample, only 6% of the Breckinridge.

Only six local Douglas leaders were found. Included were two merchants and just one planter, James Bryson, a fifty-two-year-old Irishman from Noxubee County. The paucity of the sample mirrored the weakness of the Douglas movement in Mississippi. Douglas leaders were often dismissed as office-hungry Democrats and members of the opposition. Breckinridge editors pointed out disdainfully that the delegates at the Douglas state convention in Holly Springs represented a mere eleven counties. The convention's president, James H. R. Taylor, was a chronic loser in politics who had dallied with the Whigs. He had run against the regular Democratic nominee in his congressional district in 1855 and lost; voted for Fillmore in 1856; had made futile bids for state offices as an independent in 1857 and as an opposition candidate in 1859. The chairman, B. Sugg, a wealthy old planter, had unsuccessfully run for the legislature in 1851 against the Democrats. The delegates could hardly claim to speak for the Democracy; R. D. Shropshire and L. J. Galloway were Whig editors from eastern Mississippi; B. N. Kinyon, a lawyer who had not been an active Democrat since 1853; Elisha Dismukes and J. D. Brooks of Noxubee were Whigs; and R. W. Flournoy and Daniel B. Wright, Democrats of just local importance according to the Mississippian.[45]

The Mississippi party activists encompassed the same range of delegates and party workers that was encountered in Alabama. The editors, those molders and purveyors of public opinion, were again considerably younger and poorer than their fellow politicians. The typical editor from either party was a nonslaveholder in his twenties or thirties. The Bell group had a higher percentage of those born in the North or Upper South. The importance placed on a good press can be

[45] This assessment of the Douglas leadership was taken from the *Semi-Weekly Mississippian*, Aug. 7, and the *Mississippi Democrat*, Aug. 11. Both were Breckinridge organs and decidedly not impartial observers. Yet their main argument—that Douglas leaders were political outsiders who had never exercised much power within Democratic ranks and were unrepresentative of any significant segment of the Mississippi Democracy—remains valid.

seen in Governor Pettus' dispatching of his private secretary, James Campbell, to edit the Brandon *Herald* during the campaign. The Democrats also made sure that they did not lose control of the leading paper in eastern Mississippi, the Paulding *Eastern Clarion*, with the death of its editor, Simeon Roe Adams, in April of 1860. A local party leader purchased the paper for $6,000.[46]

During its colorful and at times violent history, the Mississippi press had served as a steppingstone for young politicians. Editing a paper, together with taking up law, were the two most common entries to political power for those lacking sizeable land and slave holdings. Many combined both avocations. Jehu A. Orr, a South Carolinian, settled in Houston, Chickasaw County as a young man. He read law under W. S. Featherston and in 1846 commenced practice with Featherston as his partner. In 1849 he and J. M. Thompson, another young lawyer, bought out the Houston *Southern Patriot*, renamed it the *Southern Argus*, and used it as a Democratic campaign sheet. From this point on Orr's advancement was rapid. In 1850 he was elected secretary of the Mississippi Senate, served in the lower house in 1852–53, was appointed district attorney for the Northern District, and was a Buchanan elector in 1856. In 1860, still young at 32 and with property holdings in excess of $100,000, Orr was honored as one of his county's two delegates to the Secession Convention.[47]

High slaveholder concentration counties that Breckinridge carried yielded samples of the two major parties, as shown in Table 6.

[46] *Weekly Vicksburg Whig*, April 25, 1860; J. J. Shannon to Mrs. Isabella A. Adams, May 15, 1860, Simeon Roe Adams and Family Papers, MDAH.

[47] In his essay on the Mississippi press in *DBR*, xxix (1860), I. M. Patridge, a co-editor of the Vicksburg *Whig*, stressed, 509: "The press has furnished to Mississippi nearly all of her leading politicians." "Reminiscences of J. A. Orr," J. A. Orr Papers, MDAH; T. N. Martin Manuscript, "Historical Sketch of Chickasaw County, And Also of the Towns of Houston and Okolona," MDAH.

TABLE 6

Politicians in Breckinridge,
High Slaveholder Density Mississippi Counties

Party Membership by Age & Wealth

Age	Party	Under $25,000	$25,000–$49,999	$50,000 & Over	Total N	%
Under 40	Breck.	30%	8%	11%	159	49
	Bell	23	9	9	82	40
40–49	Breck.	9	6	13	89	28
	Bell	10	10	13	67	33
50 & Over	Breck.	4	7	12	75	23
	Bell	10	5	13	55	27

Party Membership of Slaveholders by Age & Occupation

Occupation	Party	Under 40	40–49	50 & Over	Total N	%
Planters	Breck.	8%	10%	9%	85	26
	Bell	6	10	10	53	26
Farmers	Breck.	13	9	9	101	31
	Bell	9	12	11	67	33
Lawyers	Breck.	8	3	1	38	12
	Bell	2	2	1	10	5
T. M. C.	Breck.	2	1	1	10	3
	Bell	5	1	2	18	9

Summary of Wealth & Slaveholdings by Party

	Breck.	Bell
Median Wealth	$29,600	$33,250
% Slaveholders	85	84
Median Holding	21	21

SOURCES: Breck.—38 from Rankin, 35-Noxubee, 31-Madison, 30-Oktibbeha, 27-Franklin, 26-Kemper, 23-Yalobusha, 21-Pike, 19-Holmes, 19-Jefferson, 18-Copiah, 12-Monroe, 10-Carroll, 8-Wilkinson, 6-Claiborne; Bell—53 from Holmes, 42-Madison, 25-Kemper, 24-Copiah, 16-Noxubee, 15-Oktibbeha, 12-Claiborne, 6-Carroll, 6-Wilkinson, 5-Rankin.

Young wealth was more prone to back Bell here than in Alabama, but, in the main, these party profiles paralleled those in Alabama. Natives of the Upper South and the North more frequently backed Bell (22% to 13%). No clear-cut differences in agricultural practices emerged.

A Douglas organization in Noxubee County was one of the few uncovered within the state. These party delegates were considerably older and less wealthy than the Breckinridge regulars in Noxubee. The young politicians worth over $25,000 favored Breckinridge 37% to 8%. Breckinridge's slaveholding support rested more on farmers and planters under the age of 40 and professionals; Douglas' on merchants and the older farmers and planters. A greater attraction for those born outside the Deep South and the nonslaveholding town middle class further distinguished the Douglas group.[48]

Columbus, the county seat of Lowndes County, was the commercial center of eastern Mississippi. Located on the Tombigbee, it exchanged the region's cotton for supplies from the Mobile market. The Democrats were usually the minority party within the town limits, but their great strength in the countryside enabled them to control county politics. This town-country dichotomy was reflected in the political organizations. Rural interests played twice as great a role in the Democratic group; town elements, including artisans, favored the Whigs by two to one.

Samples from the high slaveholder density counties lost by Breckinridge have been divided into three groups—those from the urban counties, the Delta areas of exceptionally great wealth, and the other rural counties.

In the Delta the Breckinridge sample was younger due to its strong attraction for the young politicians with more than $50,000 in property. Those worth less than $50,000 over the age of forty were Bell's most consistent followers. Planters

[48] As a group, nonslaveholders comprised 23% of the Douglas sample and 14% of the Breckinridge. More than 90% of the Breckinridge politicians were born in the Deep South; only 60% of the Douglas.

solidly backed Breckinridge unless age fifty and over. The smaller slaveholding farmers, especially those who produced fewer than fifty bales of cotton and had large amounts of unimproved acreage, backed Bell at all age levels.[49] The other occupational categories revealed no marked pattern of allegiances.

Panola and Tallahatchie were two northern counties without the Delta's great concentration of wealth. The sharpest contrasts between the parties in Panola occurred with the adherence of the young very wealthy politicians to Breckinridge and of those over the age of fifty worth under $50,000 to Bell. Bell's slaveholding support from physicians, businessmen, and older farmers was higher than Breckinridge's. The latter had a large edge among the younger planters. The five nonslaveholders and three skilled workmen in the small Douglas sample of twelve from Panola suggest that the Douglasite leadership relied more heavily on those not directly benefiting from slavery. The fourteen-man Breckinridge contingent from Tallahatchie, a very young group with a median age of thirty-five, was dominated by small slaveholding farmers in their thirties and forties.

Breckinridge lost the four relatively urban counties (that is, those containing a town in excess of 1,000 population) with high slaveholder densities. Three of these—Adams, Hinds, and Warren—were staunch Whig areas. The fourth, Marshall, had a normal Democratic majority of 55% that was denied Breckinridge by the 10% Douglas vote.

The support of slaveholders by age and occupation, as shown in Table 7, was fairly uniform except for the two to one preference for Bell expressed by farmers over the age of fifty. Among nonslaveholders, professionals were more likely to favor Breckinridge, businessmen to back Bell. Northerners made up equal percentages of both parties but natives of the Upper South went strongly for Bell, 29% to 13%, and the foreign-born for Breckinridge, by 7% to 1%.

[49] This was the case in Yazoo, the one Delta County where samples of both parties were found.

TABLE 7

Politicians in Anti-Breckinridge, High Slaveholder Density Mississippi Urban Counties

Age	Party	*Party Membership by Age & Wealth*				
		Under $25,000	*$25,000– $49,999*	*$50,000 & Over*	*Total* N	*Total* %
Under 40	Breck.	20%	8%	11%	69	39
	Bell	17	6.5	9	61	33
40–49	Breck.	12	8.5	16	65	37
	Bell	6	12	16	63	34
50 & Over	Breck.	5	6	14	43	24
	Bell	9	9	16	61	33

Summary of Wealth & Slaveholdings by Party

	Breck.	*Bell*
Median Wealth	$37,000	$40,000
% Slaveholders	87	85
Median Holding	20	19

SOURCES: Breck.—84 from Hinds, 31-Adams, 31-Warren, 31-Marshall; Bell—74 from Hinds, 65-Warren, 25-Adams, 21-Marshall.

Breckinridge carried all the Mississippi counties where slaveholders did not constitute a majority of the family units. There were few extant 1860 newspapers from these areas, but the excellent state-wide political coverage of the *Mississippian* still made it possible to locate sizeable numbers of Breckinridge Democrats. Unfortunately, no Bell or Douglas paper performed the same function, and only scattered samples of these two parties were found.

In these counties of rapid growth and medium size farms (where 25 to 49% of the families owned slaves), the Breckinridge Democrats were in the aggregate about the same age but poorer than their counterparts in the plantation dominated counties. Most were slaveholders, but their median holding of ten, half that found in the high slaveholder density counties, put them on a much lower tier of the slaveholding hierarchy. Farmers owning fewer than thirty slaves comprised nearly half the sample. As a group, these farmers were the cutting edge of the expanding cotton frontier. These smaller producers, lacking the capital to compete in the Delta, had fanned out into the prairie and shortleaf pine soils of eastern and central Mississippi opened up by railroad transportation in the 1850's. Ambitious, even more destructive of the soil in their agricultural practices than the planters, the small farmers devoted most of their resources to cotton and slaves. They were proud of owning slaves and their demand for more was a major factor in pushing up slave prices.[50]

Support from slaveholding professionals and businessmen, 13% and 5% respectively, was comparable to that of other Breckinridge samples. The bulk of the 20% nonslaveholding minority were farmers and lawyers. The scattered and small group of thirty Bell activists revealed more backing among businessmen and nonslaveholders and less among farmers.

The Douglas movement in northern Mississippi was represented by a party sample found in Pontotoc. Compared to the Breckinridge men in the bordering counties of Tippah and Lafayette, these Douglasites with their median property holdings of $8,000 were less than half as wealthy. The Douglas set was especially weak among the young, wealthy politicians, planters, and professionals, but attracted more businessmen and nonslaveholders.

In the low-slaveholder-concentration counties, a party sample was found in just one, a Bell group in Tishomingo, a county barely carried by Breckinridge. Small slaveholders domi-

---

[50] Paul W. Gates, *The Farmer's Age: Agriculture, 1815–1860* (New York, 1968), 138. Of the slaveholding yeomanry, Daniel Robinson Hundley, *Social Relations in Our Southern States* (New York, 1860), 197–198, wrote: "[he] is very proud of being a slaveholder; and when he is not such, his greatest ambition is to make money enough to buy a negro." James C. Bonner, "Profile of a Late Ante-Bellum Community," *AHR*, XLIX (July, 1944), 673–674, observed: "Large planters in the 1850's were putting more money into land and less into slaves. In contrast, smaller planters were apparently demanding more slaves."

nated the organization. Farmers made up the greatest single bloc of slaveholders, followed by businessmen, and then professionals. Businessmen made up the largest contribution to the 31% nonslaveholder minority. About one in three of these Bell politicians were members of the town middle class, one of the highest percentages found for any of the Mississippi county organizations.

The same basic pattern of active party membership that emerged in Alabama repeated itself in Mississippi. The major exception was the greater success of the Mississippi Whigs, more united than their party in Alabama, in competing with the Breckinridge party for the allegiance of young wealth. The one region where young wealth decidedly favored Breckinridge was in the Delta. Lawyers and the younger planters and farmers tended to work for Breckinridge; businessmen and the older farmers and planters, especially native Virginians, were Whiggish. Wherever contrasts appeared in agricultural practices, the Breckinridge planters produced more cotton than their Bell counterparts.[51]

IV

The party profiles from Alabama and Mississippi permit the formulation of an interpretive framework for politics in the newer cotton states on the eve of the Civil War, both in general terms and in the specific characteristics of the various parties. A wealthy elite dominated the parties. Politically, the slaveholders held as disproportionately large a share of power as their monopolization of the South's wealth and social status would indicate. In those counties where slaveholders comprised at least 25% of the family units, about 80% of all those politically active owned slaves.[52] Most of these men

[51] These cotton differences appeared in Yazoo, Hinds, and Noxubee, three of the five counties for which direct comparisons were feasible. In Madison cotton production was comparable and in Panola the Bell planters had a slight edge.

[52] Both the number of slaveowners and the size of their holdings

were farmers or planters, born in the older slave states, having migrated to the Southwest either as children with their parents or as young men on their own. Mobility and an incessant drive for land and slaves had marked their early careers. They accepted the efficacy and morality of slavery as a social norm, as the underlying condition in the competition for wealth and status. This competition was their forte and they had excelled in it by staking out personal fortunes on the raw Southwestern frontier of the 1840's and 1850's. By 1860 they were the leaders of an agricultural aristocracy which supervised the wealth and garnered the prestige of the communities in which they lived. They were accustomed to command; indeed, their very success was a testimony to this trait. In recalling the planters whom he had known, H. S. Fulkerson noted that "they were slow to regard any as their equals except those of their own class."[53] These men, the natural spokesmen for the slave South, all agreed that the preservation of slavery was absolutely essential for the maintenance of social order and their own elite position.

Slaveholding farmers and planters accounted for half of the politically active. The bulk of the remainder, also slaveholders, were professionals, about 20%, and the town middle class, 10-15%. Professionals, who comprised less than 2% of those employed in either Alabama or Mississippi, had the highest rate of political participation for any group. The advantages that politics gave lawyers have already been seen. The keen competition among lawyers for state offices was reflected in the volatility of the Alabama lower house's membership in the 1850's. The three elections held during the decade produced a turnover ranging from 76% to 88%. Many lawyers were content to use politics as an aid to their careers, but others made a profession of it. This accounts for

---

have been understated since holdings were checked only for the county in which the various politicians resided. Some of them held slaves in more than one county.

[53] H. S. Fulkerson, *Random Recollections of Early Days in Mississippi* (Baton Rouge, 1937), 16.

an increasingly greater influence of lawyers from the lower to the higher echelons of the party structure. At the very top, the central executive committees, lawyers were in command. Physicians were not quite as prone to enter politics, nor to exercise as much state-wide power. While a political career could expedite their planter ambitions, it also could be dispensed with more easily. Medicine was not as competitive as the law, and the young physician could make his fortune faster than a lawyer. He had a ready market in attending plantation slaves. "On some estates a physician permanently resides, whose time may be supposed sufficiently taken up in attending to the health of from one to two hundred persons. Often, several plantations, if the 'force' on each is small, unite and employ one physician for the whole."[54]

The small number of businessmen and clerks in politics was in keeping with the town's subordinate role in Southern life. Most of those who were active were slaveowners whose political ambitions extended beyond that of the average storekeeper's desire for a postmastership or seat on the city council.[55] They were the more successful of the business community, putting their profits aside to finance their own advancement into planter status. While few could hope to emulate a Edmund Harrison, commission merchant and member of the States' Rights party in Lowndes County, Alabama, whose 1,500 acre plantation produced 379 bales of cotton in 1859, all could find politics useful. Land speculations, legislative action on banks and insurance companies, the routing of railroads—these were matters that directly affected the businessman. A railroad depot in town meant more farmers and cotton for the countryside and more profits for the merchant who purchased this cotton and sent it to market.

The 20% minority of nonslaveholders were young men, usually in their twenties or thirties. The older nonslaveholders had little to protect or to gain from political activity. Noteworthy was the very small role played by the yeomen farmers

---

[54] Ingraham, *South-West*, 121.
[55] Atherton, *Southern Country Store*, 192.

who, in most areas, comprised a majority of the nonslave-holding populace. They were easily overshadowed in political participation by professionals and businessmen. This casts doubt on Owsley's assertion that the nonslaveholder who owned land must have been important politically since he voted and was courted by both parties and hence, "whatever influence the planters exercised over the political action of the common people was of a personal and local nature."[56] The vote cannot automatically be equated with political power, particularly when the voter represents a class with next to no influence in the decision-making process. When the elite that controls a society's wealth also dominates its politics, sets its options, and defines its goals, then the question of who votes, or how fervently he is courted, is largely immaterial. The Southern politician could indulge in any amount of egalitarian rhetoric as long as he held slavery sacrosanct, and it was precisely slavery that rendered the nonslaveholder economically extraneous and socially inferior. When the yeoman farmer voted, and most did, there was little for him to decide. Both candidates were more likely than not to represent slavehold-ing interests. Potential class tensions would have been drained by playing upon the common man's antiplanter resentments and Negrophobia and by defining the chief threat to his well-being and way of life as external in nature in the form of Northern abolitionism. The slave system was never questioned, only its standard-bearers at any given moment.

Insistence on the need for protection of slavery in the territories was the crucial issue for the Breckinridge Democrats since their prime goal was the maintenance of slavery as a vigorous, growing institution capable of satisfying the aspirations of the ambitious, young politicians who characterized their supporters. The preponderance of youth and lawyers in the Breckinridge camp was also an extension of the support which had made the Democrats, whose label, membership, and party machinery were inherited by the Breckinridge

[56] Frank L. Owsley, *Plain Folk of the Old South* (Chicago, 1965), 139.

forces, the majority party in Alabama and Mississippi. As the Whig press correctly noted, the Democrats ran well because they attracted the young. The Democrats had always run strongly in frontier areas and in the 1850's their hold on the young was enhanced by their stress on Southernism. The young politician coming to maturity in the 1850's was conditioned to viewing the North as a threatening and hostile force. His formative years had coincided with the escalation of sectional rancor—the controversy in the late 1830's over the presentation of antislavery petitions on the floor of Congress, the rise of abolitionism, the struggle to annex Texas, Northern efforts to blame the Mexican War on Southern avarice for more slave territory, the Wilmot Proviso, the wrangling over the Compromise of 1850 and its near rejection in the Deep South, and, in the 1850's, a whole series of hate-provoking confrontations capped by "Bleeding Kansas" and John Brown's raid. Foreign to his experience, as it was not to older Southerners, was the lingering image of the Union as a workable coalition between co-equals, providing essential services, such as surveyors to lay out the wilderness or troops to put down the Indian menace. The party that preached that the South must look to herself for her salvation and reject an overly hostile North would win his allegiance.[57]

Unless he had inherited wealth, the young politician would have begun to amass his land and slaves in the 1850's, a time of rising prices and decreasing profits. Land, slaves, provisions—everything needed to stock a plantation—were increasing. Had the prices of cotton, most planters' chief source of income aside from an occasional sale of slaves, risen commensurately, then no pinch would have been felt. As it was, prices stabilized between 9¢ and 10¢ a pound, and this put the small planter and newcomers to cotton agriculture at a disadvantage. The former was unable to maximize his profits

---

[57] These same considerations also influenced the leaders in the agitation to reopen the African slave trade. These men were significantly younger than their opponents. See Ronald T. Takaki, *A Pro-Slavery Crusade* (New York, 1971), 9–22.

by capitalizing on the greater efficiency of a large-scale operation, nor would he find it easy to add to his supply of land and labor. The latter was faced with a much heavier initial cost than had prevailed a decade earlier. He needed plentiful credit, available from 6% to 10%, to get started, and then had to expand production as rapidly as possible to pay back his debts and achieve solvency—a process, if successful, likely to take several years.[58]

The emergence on a mass scale of antislavery sentiment in the North was a real threat to such a young slaveholder. It imperiled his newly won and not yet solidified status, and by demanding that a cordon be drawn against any future expansion of slave territory denied him the opportunity to acquire more land at cheap prices or to start anew in a virgin area. If he wanted immediate relief from high slave prices by importing fresh supplies from Africa, he knew the North would never allow it. These young slaveholders were improving their position but the conditions for breaking into the slave system in the 1850's made them susceptible to the appeals of any party which promised economic relief. The Democrats offered just such a program. In Mississippi it was a four-pronged affair consisting of: (1) adding land through expansion into Mexico, the Caribbean, and Central America; (2) decreasing labor costs by reopening the African slave trade; (3) lowering the marketing costs of cotton by eliminating the Northern middlemen through the establishment of direct free trade with Europe; (4) cutting transportation fees by extending internal improvements, especially railroads.[59] This program, which easily lent itself to demands for economic independence based on secession, was popular with the rising young slaveholders since it was framed in response to their needs.

[58] Charles S. Davis, *The Cotton Kingdom in Alabama* (Montgomery, 1939), 155, 163, 183, emphasized that even an established plantation was run on credit. The planters rarely had cash on hand to pay for local purchases.

[59] Rainwater, *Mississippi*, 68.

A third factor accounting for the Democrats' hold on the younger politicians was their advantage in patronage distribution. As the majority party, they had more jobs and favors at their disposal. The posts of marshal, judge, district attorney, collector, postmaster, and land agent were the real plums, but favors of any sort were eagerly sought by those seeking a competitive edge. Robert S. Tharin, a young lawyer dissatisfied with his practice in Wetumpka, Alabama, felt that he could not secure enough business to support himself and his family. As a solution, he wrote Congressman William P. Miles of South Carolina asking him to use his influence on Representative James Stallworth of Alabama to induce the latter to take in Tharin as a law partner. Tharin wanted to practice in Stallworth's home county of Conecuh in the town of Sparta, "a place of rising importance" offering many openings to a young lawyer. A well-placed political friend could take care of a relative in need of work. William Acklen, a Democratic leader from Huntsville, tried to secure from Senator Clay the post of Land Office Registrar in Huntsville for his son Theodore. Luckless Theodore, however, had just gotten married, was poor, had no taste for the law, no qualifications for farming, and lost out on the appointment.[60] The Democrats were the source of most of these favors on the state and federal level and hence had more to offer the young.

Lawyers favored the Democrats because the party promised the most rapid advancement. Law was an open competitive field demanding ambition and a keen sense of political reality from its practitioners. The young lawyer who joined the dominant party in local politics greatly increased his chances for success. He was close to, and in time would become part of, the decision-making group for his community; the option of local and state offices was open to him. In addition to the majority position of their party in most areas, the Democrats had one other great advantage in at-

[60] Robert S. Tharin to Wm. P. Miles, June 13, 1860, Miles Papers, SHC; William Acklen to Clement C. Clay, Dec. 17, 1856, Clay Papers, DU; Theodore Acklen to Clay, Dec. 30, 1856, *ibid.*

tracting lawyer support.[61] The party's aggressive assertion and defense of Southern rights struck a responsive chord in those social elements such as lawyers who were striving for the material benefits and social pre-eminence which the enjoyment of these rights would bring. In short, the Democrats were arguing for the protection and extension of the very status that lawyers were hoping to attain.

The conservatism of the Bell forces rested not on any greater wealth or higher percentage of large slaveholders, but rather on their age and social composition.[62] The elements that distinguished the Whigs—older politicians born before 1810, the town middle class, natives of the North and upper South—had a social ethic that could accept and even demand a compromise with the North on the expansion of slavery. The older small slaveholding farmers, the agrarian group that supported Bell the strongest, had a secure and settled niche in life. With the drive and ambition of youth behind them, they had little use for an ideology that stressed growth and a widening of opportunities for slaveholders.

The Bell planters were concentrated in the planting districts opened up and settled no later than the 1830's.[63] These were prime cotton areas, the Alabama Black Belt and the Mississippi Delta below Vicksburg, and they attracted a heavy migration from the upper South. Abandoning their badly worn fields, members of the landed aristocracy of Virginia were in the forefront of this migration and reaped the most benefit from it. Their new plantations in the Southwest provided them with a life of wealth and a base and rationale for participation in local Whig politics. Combining with the Whig planters already entrenched in these areas, they con-

[61] In both Alabama and Mississippi the Whigs received the bulk of their lawyer support in areas where they competed with the Democrats on equal terms.

[62] Once again the exception was the extremely wealthy and Whiggish upper Delta counties in Mississippi. Even here, however, the Whigs' support among the politically active planters was confined chiefly to those individuals age fifty and over.

[63] See Chapter 3.

stituted the rural leadership of the party. Men of this class in the 1850's were in the best position of any to withstand the economic pressures of higher prices for land and slaves. Since their plantations were stocked, the main concern was in maintaining their productive capacity. Higher slave prices actually worked to their advantage by increasing the value of the slaves they held. The need for fresh land necessitated by the exhaustion of the old was a more compelling problem, but here foresight and capital resources still gave established wealth room to maneuver. Farsighted planters, like Benjamin Grubb Humphreys, had invested in the fresh lands of the upper Delta. After his plantation in Claiborne County started to fail in the 1840's, he moved his planting interests up river to land he had purchased in Sunflower. When B. L. C. Wailes needed land in 1856, he had the time to shop around. Finding most of what was offered in Adams and Wilkinson counties badly eroded, he sent his son Levin out to check on sites near Grant Lake, Arkansas, and along the Yazoo River. He finally purchased 1,280 acres of uncleared land across the river in Louisiana for $6,400 and considered himself fortunate; most of the planters there valued adjacent lands from $10 to $30 an acre.[64]

Humphreys, Wailes, and fellow Whigs of their class were part of an older elite. For them the Union provided the laws and institutions which protected their wealth. The good life was here and now, and they saw no reason to risk it in uncertain expansionist schemes. For a generation their political action had been a rear-guard movement to maintain what they enjoyed both from fanatic Northerners and, at least as much, from overzealous Southerners who would risk all to extend the benefits of slavery to younger social elements.

The rural Whigs' chief allies came from the urban factors and the merchants and businessmen of the towns. These groups were essential to the financing and marketing of the

[64] Percy L. Rainwater, ed., "The Autobiography of Benjamin Grubb Humphreys," *MVHR*, XXI (Sept., 1934), 231–255; Sydnor, *B.L.C. Wailes*, 89.

cotton crop but they were not at the core of the Southern reality or dream—that distinction must be given to the master who directed the black labor that produced the South's wealth. On the periphery of Southern expectations, commercial interests could not shape the policy or direction of the party. Their major accomplishment was in reinforcing the national framework in which the old Whig planters felt most comfortable. Representing Northern capital and servicing a Southern market, business favored the party that sought to unite the capital interests of both sections. Not only the seaport factor with accounts running into the hundreds of thousands but also the storekeeper in the small interior towns had good reason to be doubtful of Southern chauvinism. Without credit and goods provided by Northern capitalists and wholesalers, they could not operate. In turn they passed this credit along to the farmers. As explained by Lewis Atherton, "in other words, when all middle transactions are eliminated, the eastern wholesaler actually furnished the southern farmer with credit on which to operate and accepted as security a lien on the farmer's crop."[65] A shrinking base of good cheap land or higher labor costs did not directly affect these groups. Except in so far as they themselves were planters, businessmen were not involved in rural competition. As long as the volume of cotton from the countryside remained high, the merchants' profits were assured. Their main problem was to prevent their access to the Northern money market being blocked by sectional tensions.

Another factor which affected Whiggism among the town middle class was their birthplaces. As a group, they had the highest ratio of any politicians born in the upper South and the North. In the commercial center of Mobile, less than one-quarter of the Bell merchants and factors were natives of the Deep South; close to one-half were Northerners. Whether a New Yorker or a Virginian, such men were not as culturally predisposed to focus all their energies on land and slaves. They had personal friends and business associates outside of

[65] Atherton, *Southern Country Store*, 129.

the Deep South and had come from a background which either did not encompass slavery or had accepted it for generations as the prerogative of a mature, polished aristocracy long past its period of greatest growth. Their concept of the good society included the planter, a status to which many of them aspired, but was also flexible enough to place a premium on other forms of wealth and capital dependent on a working relationship with the North.

The Douglasites agreed with the Bell forces that the Breckinridge party was forcing extreme, unacceptable demands upon the North. Ideologically bound in their opposition to Breckinridge and the desire for sectional compromise, both parties shared a similar social base. The Douglas Democrats were older and more likely to be businessmen, Northerners, or foreign-born than the Breckinridge men; the party held little attraction for lawyers and young slaveholding farmers. The Douglas candidacy, combined with the clarity of the issues and the critical importance attached to them by their party, had forced a hard decision on many Democrats. The dissidents were those party elements who, being most removed from the needs of the cotton frontier, stood to gain the least from the expansion of slavery. This was particularly true of the nonslaveholders who backed Douglas in greater numbers than the other two parties.

Breckinridge warnings of a nonslaveholders' rush to Douglas were overstated but not completely incorrect. The only two county organizations found in either state which contained a majority of nonslaveholders were for Douglas.[66] The first of these in Jackson County, Alabama, a region of small farms in a northeastern mountainous corner of the state, was dominated by the older yeomanry. In sharp contrast to their 39% contribution to the Douglas organization, the yeomanry comprised only 5% of the Breckinridge party. Although confirmation from other equally poor northern counties is lacking, the Douglas sample in Jackson was probably an accurate

[66] Inclusion of two smaller Bell samples in Madison (19 men) and Calhoun (12 men), Alabama, would bring the number to four.

index of his appeal to yeomen in the state's Appalachian area. His strongest showing came in these mountains, and it was the one area where his rural vote did not trail his town support.

The other nonslaveholder controlled Douglas organization was in the western Black Belt county of Greene. In common with most of the politically active nonslaveholding Douglasites in southern Alabama, these men were drawn predominantly from town businessmen and artisans and had a high percentage of Northerners and the foreign-born.[67] This pattern repeated itself in Mobile and Montgomery. With the lowest incidence of land ownership of any of the politicians, this group was too young, too poor, and in many cases, too recently arrived in the South to be actively thinking of a career in planting. They reacted negatively to the Breckinridge campaign since its demands had little relation to their own needs. Their support enabled Douglas to outpoll Breckinridge in Mobile and Selma.

Bell was also popular with these nonslaveholding town elements. The main difference in his backing was the absence of the foreign-born. Fearful both that immigrants were an unassimilable proletariat and a corruptible lot ready to do the bidding of the Democrats in return for small favors, the Whigs in the mid-1850's had lashed out against the foreign-born. Pitched battles broke out in many Southern cities, and the Know-Nothing Whigs succeeded only in cementing the immigrants' Democratic loyalties. Bell could not shake this stigma and the foreign-born shunned him for Douglas.[68]

The traditional juxtaposition which assigns wealth and large slaveholders, merchants, and planters to the Whigs and

[67] Of the Douglas sample in Greene 25% were nonslaveholding business and artisan groups; the same town elements contributed only 6% to the Breckinridge party. Moreover, 21% of the Douglasites were nonslaveholders born in the North and abroad.

[68] W. Darrell Overdyke, *The Know-Nothing Party in the South* (Baton Rouge, 1950), *passim*. During the campaign *The Mississippi Free Trader*, Oct. 8, 1860, taunted the Whigs for having "abused the foreign-born population in language of the coarsest kind."

the yeomanry and slaveholding farmers to the Democrats oversimplifies and distorts the structure of politics in Alabama and Mississippi. Economic status or occupation did not influence party affiliations so much as did age and social position within the context of cotton agriculture. By representing and speaking for those who gave the South her dynamism— young slaveholders, lawyers, men on their way up driving for planter status—the Breckinridge Democrats encapsulated the ambition and energy of a society which saw itself fighting for its very existence. The party's fervid defense of slavery also promised the poor whites that the blacks would never become their social or economic competitors. The Whigs were in the minority because they had lost their vitality a generation earlier. Older slaveholders, commercial interests, and town groups were the repository of its conservative values. By default the party had yielded the yeomanry to the Democrats since the 1820's when Andrew Jackson first won their allegiance. The Whigs and the Douglas Democrats relied on those with something to save, be it an accepted aristocratic way of life or commercial ties with the North, and those with little to gain from slavery expansion, such as older small slaveholding farmers. This appeal was too limited, too cramped for a politician with his whole career in front of him. Insistence that slavery could be protected within the Union could not satisfy those who feared that the Union was a brake on their own slaveholding ambitions. As a result, the Breckinridge Democrats swept to power while the Whigs stagnated and the Douglasites were checkmated.

THREE

THE VOTERS RESPOND

I

THE social energy represented by the Breckinridge leadership had to be translated into an ideology which would galvanize Southern anxieties and hopes as well as answer the needs of those who were politically active. In successfully appealing to specific groups within the limits drawn by the South's political economy and social ideals, the Breckinridge Democrats summed up and amplified the thrust of slave society on the eve of the Civil War. Their more conservative opponents failed to offer Southerners a competing vision which could blunt their racial fears or satisfy their ambitions.

The keynote of the Breckinridge ideology was its sense of crisis. The Republicans were described as the implacable enemy of slavery who would unceasingly attack the institution. Like a disease, slavery was to be quarantined, denied room to expand, and forced to atrophy. After abolishing slavery in the District of Columbia and other areas of federal jurisdiction, the Republicans would prohibit slavery in the territories and then the slave trade between the states. They had to be stopped now, the true Southerner had to work for a Breckinridge victory, or else the result would be "to yield up our claim to carry slaves into the territories—to say, that slavery shall remain where it is—to grow denser—to become less profitable, and finally *unprofitable*—to ferment—and at the last to reach the Seward culmination and be abolished."[1]

From the perspective of the Breckinridge forces who insisted that the expansion of slavery through congressional guarantees of the rights of slaveholders was the only real

[1] *Mississippi Free Trader*, July 30, 1860; *Montgomery Weekly Mail*, quoted in the *Mobile Daily Advertiser*, May 29, 1860.

issue, and that upon its resolution hinged the survival of the slave South, the stances of both Bell and Douglas were anathema. The Whigs vaguely and rather pompously stood on the Constitution and proclaimed Bell as the only truly national and conservative candidate. If problems over slavery in the territories arose, let the courts, and ultimately the Supreme Court, decide the matter.[2] But such advice could scarcely comfort a slaveholder outraged at the Republicans' denunciation of the Dred Scott decision. The Douglas Democrats had their formula of popular sovereignty. No matter how many slave codes Congress might pass, the settlers of a territory would still control the question of slavery: "slave property will never go to a territory where the people do not want it, and if they do want it, then no protection from Congress is needed." Mere cant and hypocrisy was the rebuttal of the Breckinridge supporters. "If slave property be not adequately and sufficiently protected in the Territories, by statutory law, it will not go to them; and if it does not go, the States now growing, and hereafter to grow out of them will all ask and receive admission as free States." The Douglas doctrine "of excluding slavery by non-action and unfriendly legislation" would be just as fatal as Lincoln's, only slower.[3]

Rather than denying the importance of the territorial issue, the Bell and Douglas forces claimed that the Breckinridge men had transformed it into a "humbug, and a cheat," a cheap device of demagogues to court votes. They were quick to point out that the resolutions of A. G. Brown of Mississippi,

[2] Many conservative Democrats agreed. "Whenever the Supreme Court becomes abolitionized then will be time enough for Revolution." F. L. Claiborne to W. N. Whitehurst, May 12, 1860, William N. Whitehurst Papers, MDAH. The Whigs also hoped that the courts could defuse popular sovereignty, an issue which they regarded as theoretically national in form but unsettling in its practical operation.

[3] *Letters of Hon. John Forsyth, of Alabama, Late Minister to Mexico, to Wm. F. Samford, Esq., in Defence of Stephen A. Douglas* (Washington, 1859), 2; *Speech of Hon. Albert G. Brown, delivered at Crystal Springs, Copiah Co., Miss., September 6th, 1860* (Jackson, 1860), 5, 6.

introduced in the Senate back in January, 1860, and demanding just such a Congressional slave code for any territory
where slavery was inadequately protected, received all of
five votes. Clearly, they reasoned, most Southerners realized
that agitation of the issue could have no practical benefit.
The present Union contained no territories particularly well
suited to slavery and, even if it did, the South had no slave
surpluses to send into the territories.[4]

Although the moderates were certain that no immediate
necessity required additional Congressional protection of
slavery and although few had the missionary zeal of
A. G. Brown who "would spread the blessings of slavery like
the religion of our devine master," they did agree that eventually the South would have to expand. Since they felt this
expansion was inevitable and would not become imperative
for at least another generation, the Bell and Douglas parties
alike counseled patience. They asserted that the Pacific Coast
could still be reclaimed for slavery and noted that the anarchy
in northern Mexico made these states an easy prey for Southern
expansionists. The Douglas press seized upon the passage of
proslavery legislation by the territory of New Mexico as solid
evidence of the victories being won for the South by popular
sovereignty. If it could accomplish this in an area not especially attractive for slavery, "cannot the South afford to trust
the same principle when we acquire more Territory from
Mexico *still further South*, and with slavery already established in the North and East so that fugitives cannot escape
to free territory?"[5]

The Breckinridge editors replied that New Mexico was
hardly a fair test of the Douglas doctrine. The territory was
very thinly settled and many of the slaveholders were tran-
sient army personnel who happened to own a few slaves.
Moreover, if Douglas did not believe there was something

[4] Huntsville *Southern Advocate*, May 9; *Natchez Daily Courier*,
May 29, 1860.

[5] *The Mississippi Democrat*, Oct. 2, 1858; *DBR*, xxvii (1859), 219;
Mobile Daily Register, March 29, 1860.

immoral about slavery, he would never have admitted the right of any territorial legislature to discriminate against it in the first place.[6] But, above all, the dangers of restriction were too grave to permit the South to place her faith in vague hopes for the future. The South needed immediate guarantees of equal access to the present *and* future territories before the Republican menace became too powerful to resist.

In comparison the reopening of the African slave trade was a muted issue. The position taken by the delegates at the Vicksburg Southern Convention in May of 1859 placed the future Breckinridge Democrats in the forefront of the movement, with the Whigs furnishing the opposition.[7] The topic was a factor in the Mississippi elections of 1859. Whig candidates labeled the introduction of African slaves "a social and moral evil" and accused Democrats of advocating repeal so as ultimately "to bring about a dissolution of the Union." The Democrats, aware of the question's political divisiveness, tried to avoid it. "Its agitation at this particular time may do much mischief—it may distract and divide the South, when we ought to be united as one man, but it can eventuate in no good." H. J. Harris explained to Jefferson Davis that he had voted with the Whigs on the issue at the Vicksburg Convention because "I honestly thought the democratic party would be destroyed by the agitation of the question, *at this time.* ..."[8] When the Democrats did discuss the slave trade, they invariably linked it with the acquisition of more territory in a program which would restore to the South her former glory

[6] Paulding *Eastern Clarion*, Aug. 29; Port Gibson *Tri-Weekly Southern Reveille*, Aug. 16, 1860.

[7] *DBR*, XXVII (1859), 94–103, 205–220, 360–365, 470–471, covers the convention and includes many of the key debates and resolutions on the slave trade.

[8] Walker Wade Plantation Diary, Sept. 14, 1859, MDAH; *The Mississippi Democrat*, June, 18, 1859; Harris to Davis, June 7, 1859, *Jefferson Davis, Constitutionalist: His Letters, Papers and Speeches*, ed. Dunbar Rowland (Jackson, 1923), Vol. IV, 56.

within the Union and eventually enable her to eclipse the North in power and prestige.

The territorial and slave trade demands inevitably led to an assessment of the existing Union. So closely identified was the Breckinridge party with these issues and so impractical, if not impossible, was their attainment within the Union, that the Bell and Douglas parties argued that forcing them on the public was merely a pretext for disunion. Back in March of 1860 conservative Democrats were warning of "a Disunion Party in Alabama." Secession was allegedly the real aim of this group and they hoped to accomplish it by completely sectionalizing the Democratic party. Party fidelity would be equated with support for the expansion of slavery and the African slave trade, and "extreme ground on the question of slavery in the territories." The subsequent Democratic split at Charleston and Breckinridge campaign confirmed these earlier fears of the conservatives. In July the *Hayneville Watchman* neatly summarized the Whig indictment when it announced for Bell. The goals of the Whigs were:

> . . . to show the conservative elements of the North, that there is a Southern party with whom they can cooperate, which is aiming neither to steal land from nations with whom we are at peace by fillibusterism, nor to re-open the African slave trade in disregard of law; nor—most heinous of all—"to precipitate the cotton states into revolution;" and finally, to save the Constitution, to preserve the Union, and to enforce the laws.

Mississippi Whigs charged that the whole territorial question and Breckinridge candidacy were part of the same plan which "originated in the mad scheme of certain ambitious, disaffected, would-be leaders, who hope to bring about a dissolution of the Union."[9]

[9] *Alabama Beacon*, March 30; quoted in the *Mobile Daily Advertiser*, July 17; *Natchez Daily Courier*, Aug. 16, 1860.

Another favorite accusation of the conservatives was that their opponents actually wanted Lincoln elected if Breckinridge lost since this would furnish them with an excuse for secession. The Democrats enjoyed a national majority, but the actions of Southern extremists resulted in two sectional candidates who would split the party vote. The odds on Lincoln, which were already good, then became almost insurmountable. Late in the campaign the Breckinridge forces rejected an appeal made by the Whigs and Douglasites in some localities to forget party lines and unite behind any conservative candidate with a chance of defeating Lincoln. This was the last straw for the conservatives, who interpreted the rejection as proof positive of their opponents' evil designs.[10]

The sequence of events in 1860 lends support to the conservatives' charge of a plot to break up the Union. The radicals entered the Charleston Convention in April determined to rule or ruin. Nothing would satisfy them short of an unequivocal party declaration that slavery was entitled to the same rights in the territories as any other form of property, backed by Congressional legislation protecting its status where it was threatened. Using L.Q.C. Lamar as an intermediary, Jefferson Davis urged the Mississippi delegation to remain in the convention and combine with the other Southern states to deprive Douglas of the two-thirds majority required for the nomination. Lamar "insisted that if they could get a living, practical representative of our principle it would be better than to go out upon a mere verbal symbol." But Davis' efforts were to no avail. The Douglas forces were irrevocably committed to their candidate and to popular sovereignty. Driven on by the shrill Charleston press Mississippi stood firm, forced Alabama to do likewise, and led the bolt. Neither side would compromise at the reconvening of the splintered convention a month later and each put up their own candidate. The Democracy was irrevocably split

[10] *Weekly Panola Star*, Sept. 13; Huntsville *Southern Advocate*, Sept. 26; *Alabama Reporter*, Oct. 25, 1860.

and the chances apparently enhanced for a Republican victory which the Breckinridge party (and some of its opponents) claimed would be sufficient cause for secession.[11]

Further evidence can be found in the writings of the extremists. Robert Barnwell Rhett, an unabashed secessionist from South Carolina and a theoretician of the movement, laid out a virtual ground plan for secession in January of 1860. He began by castigating Southern rights Democrats as hypocrites for attempting to work with Northern Democrats in Congress. The national Democracy, he asserted, was nothing more than a spoils party with no principles and a portion of it, the Douglas wing, differed from the Republicans only in its mode of attacking the South. The needs of the national organization explained why Southern rights were always sacrificed for party gain and why the Southern people, at least in the cotton states, were more ready to sustain "a bold and decided course" than their representatives in Washington. The solution was obvious. Southern politicians "must cut loose from party ties and yield old party aspirations." Since Southern rights men could have no hope of controlling the Charleston Convention, the faithful, led by Alabama and Mississippi, should walk out on the issue of popular sovereignty and the interpretation of the Dred Scott decision. The bolt would secure two major objectives. It would lead to the creation of

a southern state-rights Democratic party organized on principles and with state-rights candidates upon whom to rally. This will ensure the defeat of the double-faced "na-

[11] Lamar to Christopher H. Mott, May 29, 1860, quoted in Edward Mayes, *Lucius Q. C. Lamar: His Life, Times, and Speeches, 1825–1893* (Nashville, 1896), 83; Roy Nichols, *The Disruption of American Democracy* (New York, 1967), 288–304; Steven Channing, *Crisis of Fear, Secession in South Carolina* (New York, 1970), 203–208. Austin L. Venable, "The Conflict between the Douglas and the Yancey Forces in the Charleston Convention," *JSH*, VIII (1942), 226–241. The Breckinridge press nearly unanimously recommended secession in the event of Lincoln's election.

tional"—Democracy so called—and make up the issue between the sections, with a resistance party already formed to meet the event of a Black Republican President elected by the North.[12]

However convincing the conspiracy theory of secession might appear when applied to a few individuals, such as Rhett, there is simply not enough documentary evidence with which to prove that a significant range of the Breckinridge leadership plotted disunion.[13] They were certainly willing to accept secession and after Lincoln's election exerted incredible pressure toward that end. But whether secession was always their goal before Lincoln's election, and whether they undertook concerted action to insure his election by splitting the Democracy, is a moot point. What is incontestable is the fact that the Breckinridge Democrats posited terms for the security and perpetuation of slave society which were impossible to achieve within the Union. Having made these demands, they had quite consciously narrowed the alternatives to revolution, humiliation, or the defeat of Lincoln by their own Southern rights candidate. Some Breckinridge men were undoubtedly "plotters" who welcomed secession; others, and probably the majority, embraced secession only after the failure of their combined effort to defeat Lincoln and gain acceptance of Southern demands.

Unless the South forced the issue of her territorial rights in 1860, the Breckinridge leaders feared that slavery would

[12] R. B. Rhett, Jr., to Wm. P. Miles, Jan. 29, 1860, Miles Papers, SHC.

[13] Ollinger Crenshaw, *The Slave States in the Presidential Election of 1860* (Baltimore, 1945), noted, 300, that the papers of the radicals dealing with the key events of 1860 and the secession crisis are "relatively scarce." Channing, *Crisis of Fear*, 152–166, applies the conspiracy theory to South Carolina, but most of his evidence rests on the role of Rhett. Quitman of Mississippi, who died in 1858, undoubtedly can also be considered as an outright disunionist. In 1857 Reuben Davis, *Recollections of Mississippi and Mississippians* (Boston, 1891), 370, quoted Quitman as claiming that he and his friends had a set policy whose "aim and end is disunion."

108

be irretrievably and fatally weakened. Unable to compete with free labor in the territories and growing ever weaker relative to the antislavery North, the South had to defend her right to expand or accept the slow death of her slave civilization. The victory of another Northern Democrat would be meaningless since the South had gained nothing from Democratic administrations throughout the 1850's, and the defeat of a Democrat pledged to popular sovereignty would not present an issue which would prepare Southerners for further resistance. Secession was one response, and it was always touted as the most likely solution; but another alternative was a South united behind her own candidate and in a strong bargaining position if the presidential election were thrown into the House of Representatives. Many Southerners predicted just such a contested election when they first heard of the Charleston split.[14] Although by September Breckinridge politicians were conceding Lincoln's victory, they initially had overestimated Douglas' strength in the North, and ironically it was the inability of Douglas to seriously challenge Lincoln in the free states which ensured his election. The Breckinridge party then immediately fell back on secession.[15]

Conservatives rarely distinguished between conspiracy and intransigence.. In fact, if any party was guilty of a conspiracy to destroy the Union, it was the Breckinridge Democrats, but intransigence characterized three of the parties in 1860. The portrayal of the Breckinridge men as uncompromising doctrinaires prepared to fight for their values if they could not get their own way can be applied with as much truth to

[14] For example, see J. H. Hammond to Prof. Harry Hammond, April 27, 1860, James H. Hammond Papers, LC. By the fall only conservatives still clung to this hope. See B. Fitzpatrick to Leonidas Howard, Oct. 22, 1860, Benjamin Fitzpatrick Papers, SHC; J. Henly Smith to A. Stephens, Oct. 8, 1860, Alexander H. Stephens Papers, LC.

[15] Of course this result had been foreseen and even anticipated. See the letter from "States' Right Man," Richmond *Enquirer*, June 15, 1860.

the Republicans and the Douglas Democrats. The Douglas followers refused to negotiate at either the Charleston or Baltimore Conventions and were just as unwilling to accept Southern demands as the South was to take no for an answer. Meanwhile the Republicans remained unyielding on the crucial issue of slavery's expansion. Although the Bell party appealed for sectional reconciliation, their position had little value since it avoided the problem which had created the crisis. Thus, rather than viewing the events of 1860 as the unfolding of a conspiracy, it is more helpful to recognize that the politicians were true to the values and interests of their respective sections and that at best these values precluded compromise.

In response to being labeled disunionists the Breckinridge party mounted a counteroffensive. The slogan—"Disunion, which follows a perverted Union, is the work of the perverters"—epitomized this tactic. Southerners were told they would have to choose between slavery or the Union. Occasionally the Spirit of '76 was invoked:

> Were the Whigs of the Revolution, the men of 1776, who withdrew their allegiance from George III and sat [sic] up for themselves and posterity the mighty Republic of ours Secessionists? and were not those who opposed them Tories? when *might* attempted to deprive them of their just *rights*, and they dared to act as freemen, were they Secessionists?[16]

A few Breckinridge editors wore their disunionism like a badge and openly proclaimed that a division of the present Union into at least two distinct governments was the best solution to sectional hostilities. More common was a denial of favoring secession per se. Rather, claimed the Breckinridge press, they were simply being honest and true to the South by admitting that the very fact of Lincoln's election

[16] *Montgomery Weekly Mail*, June 8, *Mississippi Free Trader*, Aug. 6, 1860.

110

would be cause enough for secession, the highest form of Southern patriotism. Why waste a vote on Bell or Douglas? The election of either would close the territories to slavery as effectively as Lincoln's. To argue that slavery could be protected within the present Union was pure chicanery, for if slavery could not expand, it was doomed. Breckinridge alone stood unequivocally for Southern rights, and his election offered the slave South its only chance for survival.[17]

In the middle of the campaign the *Weekly Vicksburg Whig* attacked T. J. Wharton, Mississippi's attorney general and a leading Breckinridge supporter, for describing himself at a political barbecue in Terry the year before as " '*a disunionist, a filibuster and a Congo pirate.*' " Wharton's reaction was a testimony to his political sagacity. He readily admitted that "in a note of levity" he had once spoken of himself as a " 'Cuba filibuster and Congo pirate.' " Such an admission could only enhance, not hurt, his party's voter appeal. He did deny ever having declared himself a " 'disunionist.' " By his denial Wharton paid homage to what was perhaps the single most effective campaign tactic of the opposition— branding the Breckinridge party as disunionists who would lead the South into a bloody civil war. Warnings to the voters that unless a conservative was elected—"you will have to leaves your homes and take up the line of march for the battle field"—hurt the Breckinridge campaign. H. S. Van Eaton reported from Wilkinson County that the election would be close. "The Bell men are getting up a *big scare* on Disunion & all that & I should not be surprised if Bell carried the County." "We will do all we can but *paeans* to the Union sound musically to the masses and I fear the worst. . . ." Similar assessments were made in Alabama. Septimus D. Cabiness correctly foresaw that Breckinridge would lose the entire Tennessee Valley with the exception of Jackson. The Bell and Douglas forces were hammering away at the theme

---

[17] *Camden Register*, quoted in the *Mobile Daily Advertiser*, July 18; *Mississippi Democrat*, April 7; *Clayton Banner*, Sept. 6, 1860.

"that it is the settled purpose of the Breckinridge party to *precipitate* a revolution, with a view to the destruction of the Federal union."[18]

The other issues in the 1860 campaign derived logically from the position taken by the parties on the viability of slavery within the Union. The first of these was the question of militarism. The Breckinridge Democrats, asserting that slavery was not safe from the diabolical machinations of Northerners of John Brown's ilk and aided immeasurably by the popular uproar and revulsion over Brown's raid at Harper's Ferry, applauded the legislation passed by the Alabama and Mississippi legislatures which had financed and enlarged the volunteer military companies.[19] The governors of both states were appropriated large sums, $200,000 in Alabama and $150,000 in Mississippi, with which to purchase arms for the volunteer militia. Inducements were offered to make volunteer service more attractive. In Mississippi all members of the volunteer companies performing their required nine days of duty were exempted from jury, road, and street duty for one year; every company received $9 for each of its members who fulfilled the nine-day requirement. Volunteer officers took precedence over militia officers of the same grade. Under this legislation the volunteer companies mushroomed. Requests for arms poured into Governor Pettus' office and the martial spirit was blended with the defense of Southern rights.

> Our citizens to a man should use every effort to get up a military spirit in our state—if we will maintain our rights

[18] *Weekly Vicksburg Whig*, Sept. 19; *Semi-Weekly Mississippian*, Sept. 21; *Selma Morning Reporter*, June 1, 1860; Van Eaton to W. N. Whitehurst, Sept. 11, 1860, Whitehurst Papers, MDAH; Cabiness to Gov. Moore, Oct. 29, 1860, "A. B. Moore Correspondence Relating to Secession," ed. Miles B. Howard Jr., *AHQ*, 23 (Spring, 1961), 6.

[19] *Mississippi Free Trader*, May 28; *Clayton Banner*, Aug. 9, 1860; *Acts of the Seventh Biennial Session of the General Assembly of Alabama* (Montgomery, 1860), 36, 37 and *Laws of the State of Mississippi passed at a Regular Session of the Mississippi Legislature* (Jackson, 1860), 128, 129 and 247–254.

in or out of the Union, we must fight. Abolition has got the entire control of the free States & it means to control the Southern States. We must fight or give our consent to be plundered now of our Slaves & our rights in the Territories, and it will not be long till we will have to submit to being plundered in our homes.

New companies sprung up at such a rapid rate that in some areas there was a call for retrenchment and concentration of resources on the older, better established companies. "Seriously, we cannot for the life of us see the use of so many military organizations in Noxubee county. We have four or five companies in our county, and altogether there are not more active members than enough to keep up two efficient companies."[20]

In addition to feeding Southern chauvinism, the volunteer companies performed useful social functions in this isolated, rural society. Military encampments and competition in drilling and target shooting were frequently public affairs, with the citizen soldiery performing their skills in front of an admiring audience. Flavellus G. Nicholson, a lieutenant in the Quitman Light Infantry near Shuqualak, Mississippi, treated his militia duty as a social occasion of the first rank. On July 4 the company, accompanied by "several ladies," took a train to Lauderdale Springs where they marched, had a picnic, toasts, and danced at night. In the middle of September an encampment was held near Shuqualak. The twenty-first was the company's "big day. A great many persons were present—gentlemen & ladies—we gave them a fine dinner—we had target firing & Hamilton got the first prize—we done some fine drilling, and when the crowd left I believe they were all highly pleased." More parades and balls kept the company busy during October.[21]

[20] A. C. McEwen to Gov. Pettus, Feb. 29, 1860, Governors' Records, MDAH; *Macon Beacon*, Jan. 9, 1861.

[21] John Hope Franklin, *The Militant South 1800–1861* (Boston, 1966), 173–186; Flavellus G. Nicholson Diary-Journal, July through October, 1860, MDAH.

113

The capstone to these sociomilitary functions of the volunteer companies was provided by the State Agricultural Fair held at Holly Springs in mid-October. John J. Williams, secretary of the Mississippi Agricultural Bureau, had induced the state to sponsor bounties of $300 and $150 to be paid to the best-drilled militia units, all of whom were invited to encamp as part of the fair. Dour old Whigs grumbled over all the political posturing at the fair, but the Democrats were well pleased. The Agricultural Bureau, under the presidency of Thomas J. Hudson, a Breckinridge legislator from Marshall County, had been controlled by the secessionist wing of the Mississippi Democrats since its inception in 1857. These agricultural politicians encouraged the county agricultural societies to become both forums for secessionist ideas and fulcrums for aiding local militia companies.[22]

Leadership in the volunteer companies came primarily from young Breckinridge politicians. At a convention of the State Military Board in Jackson on May 29, 1860, twenty delegates were enrolled.[23] Out of this group of volunteer captains and lieutenants, at least fourteen were active in the politics of their counties. Twelve were Breckinridge men. Youth and small slaveholdings characterized these Breckinridge supporters. Of the eleven found in the census returns, nine were under the age of forty and only three owned more than thirty slaves. Farming, followed by the professions, comprised the bulk of their occupations.

Rank and file support for the volunteers was drawn from a wider social base. The Westville Guards, a company that must have appeared positively resplendent in their uniforms of "dark blue with yellow buff trimmings, cap with red-toped [sic] pompoon [sic]," was one of the newer companies formed in the fall of 1860. On September 18 the Breckin-

[22] *Semi-Weekly Mississippian*, May 1, 1860; B.L.C. Wailes Diary, Oct. 15, 1860, DU; John Hebron Moore, *Agriculture in Ante-Bellum Mississippi* (New York, 1958), 197–205.

[23] *Semi-Weekly Mississippian*, June 4, 1860.

ridge county chairman, L. B. Walker, wrote to Pettus asking for arms and his permission to hold an election for officers. He included a list of the volunteers.[24] Over half of the members owned no slaves and among the slaveowners, holdings under ten were most common. A majority was under the age of thirty and about 40% of them reported no property holdings. Occupationally the group was very diversified with farmers and sons of slaveholding farmers making up the largest single contingent. Here in Simpson County the call to defend the South was answered in the main by the young men on the fringes of the slaveholding oligarchy.

The reaction of the Bell and Douglas forces to their opponents' sponsoring of military measures was one of dismay. They interpreted the military appropriation acts as part of "a mad scheme of disunion and treason." "We charge directly, on the proofs, that the fire-eaters of our own and of other States, have formed a plan to break up the government; that the military preparations made by our late Legislature are part of that plan and that the plan is now advancing to completion." Short of coming down hard on the disunion theme, the best tactic of the conservatives in attacking the military acts was to stress the higher state taxes imposed to pay for the appropriations. The *Vicksburg Whig* denounced the commutation tax of $1 per head plus 5% of one's state tax as unconstitutional taxation designed to support a standing army. It was a waste of the people's money and would be used only to fatten the pockets of a few glory-seeking Democratic leaders.[25] The antimilitary feeling in Alabama was more intense and better directed. The state's $200,000 Military Appropriations Act was closely contested in the legislature, passing in the Senate by only one vote. The voting on the bill was along

[24] Walker to Gov. Pettus, Sept. 18, 1860, Governors' Records, MDAH.

[25] *Semi-Weekly Mississippian*, Sept. 21, quoting the opposition; Greenville *Southern Messenger*, Sept. 5; *Weekly Vicksburg Whig*, Sept. 19, 1860.

North-South sectional lines which coincided with the major non- and -slaveholding areas of the state.[26] This initial opposition to the measure in northern Alabama, coupled with the imposition of a 5% state surtax for a military fund, gave opponents of the bill a ready-made weapon to use against Breckinridge in the presidential campaign.

Opposition centered in the Whig areas of western Alabama and the Douglas strongholds in the Tennessee Valley. The tax collectors of Greene and Sumter Counties resigned in protest over the surtax. Thomas J. Clark, the Whig county chairman in Pickens, urged the citizens not to pay the additional tax of "that most iniquitous bill." The Huntsville *Southern Advocate* pointed out that the army law "was voted for by nearly all the Seceders and voted against by nearly all of the National Democracy." Meetings to devise legal means of resisting the military tax were held throughout the Valley in the early fall. One such meeting in Waterloo, Lauderdale County, railed against "the military disunion tax."[27]

Although the issue was costing them votes in the northern portions of both states, the Breckinridge supporters refused to soften their stand on the need for military preparedness. The *Clayton Banner* listed slave revolts, the election of a Black Republican, and John Brown type invasions as some of the possible contingencies that the Military Act was designed to prevent. In the face of such dangers $200,000 would not even be adequate for military defense. The efforts of Bell men such as Joseph W. Taylor of Greene, an elector for the state at large, in linking the military appropriations with a disunion plot were attacked with savage sarcasm. Taylor was so true to the South, it was suggested, that he just might advance money for the passage home of any murderous Yankee aboli-

[26] For the Senate vote, see *Senate and House Journal, 1859–'60* (Montgomery, 1860), 210, and the House vote, 430; in Mississippi the military appropriations act passed with little opposition, *Semi-Weekly Mississippian*, Sept. 21, 1860.

[27] *Pickens Republican*, Aug. 3; Huntsville *Southern Advocate*, Aug. 15, Nov. 7, 1860.

tionists captured in the South.[28] As the campaign progressed, the South was portrayed as increasingly insecure by the Breckinridge editors. By October they were painting lurid pictures of the degradations which would befall the South when Lincoln unleashed his army of from 200,000 to 500,000 Wide Awakes upon the South.[29] To make matters unspeakably worse, the ranks of this army were swelled with free blacks.

> In many parts of the North, the Wide Awakes are composed mainly of *Negroes*. Lincoln's strength is in no inconsiderable degree swelled by buck Negroes; and these are the people that Yankee emissaries ask the South to submit to. But it is not possible that Southern white men can be guilty of such baseness—Southern *women* will not permit it!

Having conjured up such a threat, a paper like the *Montgomery Mail* quite consistently could thunder: "Let the boys arm. Everyone that can point a shot gun or revolver should have one."[30]

Another issue which characterized the participants in the campaign was the philosophical defense of slavery promulgated by certain Breckinridge editors. This defense, which adhered to the main tenets of George Fitzhugh's critique, was more of an aggressive assertion of the unique historical role of the slave South than a passive rebuttal of abolitionists' charges. Far from being a moral blot on the American conscience, slavery was providing freedom-loving whites with

[28] Cabiness to Moore, Oct. 29, 1860, "A. B. Moore Correspondence," *ADAH*, 6, 7; W. C. Falkner to Gov. Pettus, Dec. 28, 1860, Governors' Records, MDAH; *Clayton Banner*, Aug. 9, 1860.

[29] The various estimates on the size of the Wide Awakes (a rather harmless campaign auxiliary of the Republicans) will be found in the *Mississippi Free Trader*, Oct. 1; *Semi-Weekly Mississippian*, Sept. 28; and the Pratteville *Southern Statesman*, Sept. 29, 1860.

[30] *Mississippi Free Trader*, Nov. 12; *Montgomery Weekly Mail*, quoted in the Canton *American Citizen*, Nov. 3, 1860.

their only opportunity of erecting stable republican institutions. The French, English, and Yankees had all the liberty and equality they could ever want, but as long as they remained isolated individuals in a capitalist society which made labor beholden to capital for its bread and daily wants, their freedom availed them nothing. The position of free labor was steadily worsening, class antagonisms were on the rise, and a virulent reform mania was undermining the safety of all property. In blissful contrast to this inherent instability stood the slave South. "The social *status* of the South at the present time affords the nearest approximation to a sound and stable Democracy, which the modern world has ever witnessed." Combining labor and capital in the person of the slave, the South avoided the mutually exclusive economic hostilities of a free society. The slave, under the paternalistic care of his owner, performed the menial tasks and back-breaking labor. As a result, the status of all whites was elevated and an aristocracy of race held sway, rather than a vulgar and socially injurious aristocracy of wealth.[31]

The editors who most consistently followed the above line of reasoning clearly saw, however crudely, that abolitionism was related to the growing industrialization of the North. Rooted in the very fabric of Northern society, it was not a passing threat or one that could be compromised away. J. H. Smith, the young Georgian editor of *The Southern Era* in Opelika, Alabama, argued:

> No modern 'free labour' society has yet wrought out a sound social theory. Revolution after revolution must be consummated ere the social *status* in France, be restored. The continual drainage by emigration has preserved England from the influence of social deterioration. And the same difficult problem is now presented to the 'free labour' States of North America; and thus far there is no promise of a speedy nor safe solution. The 'free labour' North looks to Abolition as her principle safety-valve. And if she can

[31] Opelika *Southern Era*, Feb. 14, 1860.

but gain an indefinite respite by destroying the institution of slavery, 'let the South perish!,' will be the decree of her utilitarian wisdom.

The South had such a well-balanced social system that it could withstand even this menace were it not for its shrinking supply of indispensable slave labor. Instead of prospering, the South found itself "in the condition of a besieged fortress." She could not place any trust in national platforms or parties. "The Union is no longer a refuge, but an absolute *prison*." The remedy was obvious. "She must arise in the majesty of her strength, shake off the shackles and resolve, that in the form of an INDEPENDENT CONFEDERACY, *she will conquer or perish!*"[32]

Starting from a class analysis based on the contradictory labor systems of the North and South, Smith insisted that the very definition of what constituted human justice and personal and property rights differed in the two sections. "That which is right to the Southron, is a mortal sin in the eyes of the cold-blooded Northerner. That which is the highest and most sacred kind of property to the Southern citizen, is, in the estimation of his 'free labour' friend, nothing but stolen goods, tyranny, robery [sic] and crime." Such a basic incompatibility made talk of compromise at best hypocritical and at worst dangerously deceptive.[33]

The tracts in Jefferson Buford's *Clayton Banner* were quite similar to those of Smith, only more extensive. This lawyer-editor was speaking from firsthand experience when he discussed sectional enmities. As the leader of a 350-man expedition to Kansas in 1856, he had contributed far more than most Southerners in the effort to stake out new slave frontiers. The expedition was financed by donations and Buford's sale of forty slaves. Beginning their journey with high hopes and Bibles given them by the citizens of Montgomery, and carrying a banner which read "The Supremacy of the White Race" and on the reverse side "Kansas, The Outpost," the expedi-

[32] *Ibid.*, Feb. 14.   [33] *Ibid.*, Feb. 14.

tion nevertheless wound up an abject failure. Buford absorbed a personal loss of about $15,000. He had gambled on a clever piece of land speculation and lost. Each colonist in the group had pledged to give Buford his preemption claim of 160 acres and receive back only 40 acres. Buford would have profited handsomely if the expedition had succeeded. As for the crew of Southerners that accompanied Buford, James, his younger brother, described them best: ". . . men of no prominence in the communities where they lived, mostly without a local habitation or name, and what was worse, as they showed up in the end, without integrity of character."[34]

The Kansas episode may well have imparted to Buford's political thinking an incisiveness and inflexibility not found in many of his contemporaries. There can be no doubt that his 1860 essays combine a sophisticated defense of slavery with an unyielding attack on free society in a manner that often rivals Fitzhugh. Buford's main premise, reiterated throughout the campaign, was that universal suffrage and republican institutions could survive only in a slave society. "What are the antagonisms now really at war among us? Nothing—absolutely nothing but anti-Slavery, with consequent Anarchy and depressing Despotism on the one side, and African Slavery with attendant Universal Suffrage and Republican Institutions, peace, order and human progress on the other." Slavery, by excluding the poor and propertyless from citizenship, provided a built-in social stabilizer. A free society lacked any comparable institution performing such a necessary conservative function. Northern poor were already supporting radical schemes which would topple the social order. Given enough time, the poor would take advantage of their universal suf-

---

[34] Elmer LeRoy Craik, "Southern Interest in territorial Kansas, 1854–1858," *Collections of the Kansas State Historical Society 1919–1922*, xv (1923), 399; quoted in Walter L. Fleming, "The Buford Expedition to Kansas," *TAHS*, iv (1904), 191. Barbour County produced the leader of another Kansas expedition, Henry D. Clayton. For his wife's recollections of the trip, see Victoria V. Clayton, *White and Black Under the Old Regime* (New York, 1899), 62–81.

frage to divide up all property; this, in turn, would lead to anarchy which could be quelled only by a despotism. The South could not afford to sit by smugly and watch these frightening events come to pass. Abolitionism, the worst of all reform "isms," was on the verge of a great victory. The election of Lincoln would doom slavery. "The most besotted Union-saver a[s] the South knows full well that Lincoln's platform is 'no protection to slavery, but universal freedom, fraternity and equality;' necessarily leading to negro conservators of the peace, with no pigs, poultry or potatoes for the white man." Bell and Douglas, by ignoring the right of slavery to expand, would only delay the inevitable destruction of slavery.[35]

Secession was the only way out of this impasse. On this score Buford chided his fellow politicians for not better preparing the people. The average politician made the mistake of treating sectional differences as a mere property question, not as an institutional problem. This failure, plus the lingering nostalgia over the glories of the Union, blinded him to the fact that the present confederacy had already accomplished its historical mission of creating two distinct and antagonistic civilizations. The South, once it ensured the survival of slavery by tearing itself loose from the North, alone was capable of maintaining the free institutions so beloved by the common man.[36]

The Bell and Douglas parties addressed themselves to the points raised by a Smith or Buford only in an oblique fashion. That there were no irreconcilable, inevitable antagonisms between a free and a slave society was implicitly assumed. Many of their party leaders were representatives of northern capital; here was proof that conservatives of both sections could work together amicably based on common interests. Surely the Boston textile manufacturer and New York cotton exporter were vitally interested in the preservation of slavery. Besides,

[35] *Clayton Banner*, July 19, Aug. 16, 1860.
[36] *Ibid.*, Oct. 18.

121

not all of the Republicans were guilty of antislavery prejudices. Many of them, especially in the Northwest, were party
members out of a disgust at the type of Democratic corruption recently exposed by the Covode Committee.[37]

Conservatives conceded that Northern society was unstable
and plagued by a moral decay which had spawned a reform
mania, but common sense should tell the Southerner that
within the Union lay the best hope for the protection of slavery. Since the days of the Founding Fathers, the Union had
been an effective shield, protecting equally all forms of property. Secession, which meant revolution and certain war, was
slavery's greatest threat. Admittedly both sections had their
agitators, but it was a moot point as to who was more to
blame for the current crisis, the abolitionists or the fire-eaters.
"The ultra abolitionists North are in favor of Disunion, to get
clear of slavery, as some of the ultras in the South are for disunion to get rid of abolitionists!" The safest policy for the
South was to trust its conservative friends in the North and
repudiate the radicals in their own midst, that "set of reckless
political quacks who set themselves up as the peculiar guard-
ians of Southern honor and the judges of Southern fealty."[38]

The campaign of 1860 also made explicit many of the attitudes held by the parties toward the nonslaveholder. The
Breckinridge men continued the usual Democratic practice of
posing as his special friend. Indeed, the praise heaped upon
the nonslaveholder was at times quite fulsome. "As a class,
there are no men [in] the South truer to her institutions, more
zealous in defence of her rights, or more jealous of any en-
croachments upon her interests than the non-slaveholding
population." Nevertheless, such laudations were often juxta-

[37] *Speech of William C. Smedes Esq.* . . . (Vicksburg, 1860), 36–37.
David E. Meerse, "Buchanan, Corruption, and the Election of 1860,"
CWH, xii (June, 1966), 116–131, discusses how skillfully the Republicans developed the issue of corruption. The Buchanan Administration was particularly embarrassed by the findings of the Covode Committee, a Republican dominated House committee.
[38] Huntsville *Southern Advocate*, April 4; *Weekly Vicksburg Whig*,
Oct. 31, 1860.

posed, without the slightest hint of irony, with the dogma that the South must entrust its leadership to the slaveholders. For this reason Douglas was branded a dangerous candidate. To win in the South, cautioned the Breckinridge press, he must attract the nonslaveholders' vote. "At all events it will raise up throughout the South—what has never been there before —a political party composed mainly of nonslaveholders, and arrayed in opposition to that supreme control over the politics of Southern States, which the slaveholding interest has always enjoyed." Not only would such a faction be opposed to secession, but, should a Republican be elected president, its rank and file might very well be converted into a Southern Republican party.[39]

Further proof that the slaveholder had to be vigilant was the alleged existence of a mysterious poor man's abolitionist society, known as the Friends Z. Society. Centered in southwestern Alabama and across the state line in Mississippi, the society was reported to have more than a hundred members. They were branded abolitionists for taking an oath against fighting to protect the property of the rich. The Breckinridge editor Isaac Grant was aghast at a letter which originally appeared in the *Mobile Daily Tribune*. Identifying himself only as a National Democrat, the letter writer was a nonslaveholder. He bitterly complained about having to hire slaves at double prices and warned the large slaveholders and their "dupes" that men such as himself valued the Union over slavery. The planter should be chary of his property, for if secession ever occurred it could result in class warfare. Grant labeled the letter "about as first-rate a specimen of abolition sentiment and incendiarism as could be found in the wigwam of Chicago or the Tabernacle in New York."[40]

[39] *Democratic Watchman*, July 11, 1860; *Montgomery Advertiser*, quoted in *ibid.,* July 11. This was a common fear of many Democrats. "The truth is, I fear, a union party at the South now means an abolition party—not at first, it may be—but through quick transitions." Lawrence Keitt to Miles, Oct. 3, 1860, Miles Papers, SHC.

[40] Claiborne *Southern Champion*, June 29, Aug. 10; quoted in the *Clarke County Democrat*, July 5, 1860.

Of course, if the opposition charged that the nonslave-holder had no business in a party which would break up the Union if its own definition of the slaveholder's rights was not made the law of the land, the Breckinridge press paraded all the arguments on how slavery benefited the poor and how very loyal to the South were these poor. Pierre Soulé, the most influential Douglas supporter in Louisiana, argued that nonslaveholders had no direct, tangible interest in the pres-ervation of slavery; therefore, they should vote for Douglas, the candidate who spoke for all Southerners, not just the slaveholders. After first accusing Soulé of inciting envy and class dissension, Breckinridge editors then referred to the let-ter published by A. G. Brown in rebuttal. Slavery elevated all whites by placing them above the blacks. The nonslaveholder had the greatest material and social interest in its preserva-tion, and if slavery were destroyed, the resultant chaos would fall heaviest on the poor. Breckinridge was really waging the poor man's contest, for only his platform would protect slavery.[41]

When the Whig planter Stephen Duncan, one of the wealth-iest men in the South, publicly stated that he would sell out and leave the South rather than face the heavy direct taxes which secession would necessitate, he was called a traitor and just the kind of rich snob the Breckinridge party was fighting against. In contrast the poor man was hailed as the truest friend of the South. Even if he could afford to leave, he would remain and fight for Southern rights. This was shrewd politics. The river planters of Duncan's class were very unpopular. Wiley P. Harris spoke of how their "insufferable arrogance and ostentation at home and abroad drew upon them actual antipathy everywhere. . . ." The same political astuteness could be seen in the Democrats' reaction to the opposition's charge that Breckinridge was not a proper candidate for the South since he did not own slaves. "It is as much to say that

[41] *Mississippi Free Trader*, Oct. 22; *Semi-Weekly Mississippian*, Oct. 5, 12, 1860.

a man's fealty to the Constitution, and to the rights of his native South depends upon the number of negroes he gives in to the tax assessor." It was dangerous incendiarism. "Produce this impression upon the public mind, and how long suppose you, before the less informed, of Southern non-slaveholders would become, in reality, hostile to the institution."[42]

The Whigs viewed the nonslaveholder with an air of aristocratic detachment. Their position was akin to feeling that any problems posed by the nonslaveholder would go away if ignored. What particularly irritated them about the Breckinridge crusade on behalf of the nonslaveholder was its claim that the poor had a greater stake in the preservation of slavery than the wealthy. Such sermonizing was "miserable demagoguery." "It is criminal and wicked—aye, it is anti-Southern and free-soilish—thus to encourage persons not to purchase slaves. It is the most direct and certain method of limiting the number of slave-owners, and thereby lessening the interest in the perpetuity of the institution which only the master can feel." Nonslaveholders spouted such nonsense, rallied public opinion against the slaveholder, and called him an abolitionist if he professed his property to be safe within the Union. The real abolitionists were those who so slandered their fellow citizens. True statesmanship required an emphasis on the virtues of slaveownership as the proper reward for diligence and ambition. The slaveholder had already revealed his capacity and ability to lead and should be the natural spokesman for Southern rights. But, wherever possible, and on their own conservative terms of working for the Union, the Whigs welcomed support from the yeomanry and praised their moderation and patriotism.[43]

The Douglas approach varied according to the section of

[42] Percy Lee Rainwater, *Mississippi: Storm Center of Secession 1856–1861* (Baton Rouge, 1938), 141–142; quoted in *ibid.*, 143; Paulding *Eastern Clarion*, Sept. 12, 1860.

[43] *Weekly Vicksburg Whig*, Oct. 31; *Eutaw Whig*, cited in the *Mobile Daily Advertiser*, April 18, 1860.

the state. In the Alabama Black Belt the conservatism of wealth was stressed over the party loyalty of the nonslaveholder. Dallas County, with the largest slave population in the state, was applauded for holding the state's first Douglas ratification meeting. It was emphasized that the meeting was fully controlled by large slaveowners and was attended almost exclusively by slaveowners. In northern Alabama where the yeomanry was a major political force the Douglas appeal was directed at the true followers of Andrew Jackson's principles, the "honest yeomanry" and "Democratic masses."[44]

Throughout the 1860 campaign, the parties had staked out clear ideological positions. An aggressive, militant defense of Southern rights characterized the Breckinridge Democrats. They shunned any moderation, boldly proclaimed the need of the South to expand, demanded federal protection of slave property within the territories, and emphasized irreconcilable differences between the sections. In pushing military preparedness and in posing as the champion of the nonslaveholders, they sought to widen their appeal by exploiting the fears and ambitions of the Southern masses. The Whigs and Douglas Democrats were ideologically aligned by their common desire to find a safe middle ground. They admitted the South's right to expand but denied that such expansion was of immediate concern; they viewed a congressional slave code as fine in theory but unnecessary, and certainly not worth pursuing at the cost of destroying the Union; they recognized that self-defense required military precautions but decried loud saber rattling which only intensified sectional tensions; they asked for the support of nonslaveholders but denounced demagogic appeals. For the Breckinridge Democrats a crisis confronted the South; for their opponents any such crisis was the product more of the machinations of greedy Breckinridge politicians than of any conflicts which could not be resolved within the Union.

[44] *Selma Sentinel,* cited in the Gainesville *Independent,* July 21; Huntsville *Southern Advocate,* July 11, 1860.

II

The voter response to these competing ideologies paralleled the social composition of the parties' leadership. Although Breckinridge carried by an absolute majority well over half of Alabama's counties and over three-fourths of those in Mississippi, he did quite poorly in towns and cities with a total white population of 1,000 and over, and is shown in Table 8.[45]

Significantly, the two large Alabama towns which Breckinridge did carry by an absolute majority, Montgomery and Tuscaloosa, were the only ones in which the slaves outnumbered the whites. The higher concentration of slaves with the resulting greater concern for security precautions by the whites might account for the voting behavior of the two towns. Voting statistics on the county seats, the most common, and in many areas the only centers of town life in the Deep South, are scattered and at times incomplete. Where extant, the returns further reflect the strong rural appeal of the Breckinridge campaign. Whenever the largest town in a county differed sharply from its surrounding countryside in voting behavior (defined by a variation of 10% or better in the Breckinridge and anti-Breckinridge vote), the balance usually favored Bell or Douglas. Ten out of fifteen towns followed this pattern.[46]

[45] W. Dean Burnham, *Presidential Ballots 1836–1892* (Baltimore, 1955), 260–274, for the Ala. county returns; 552–570, for Miss. A typographical error by Prof. Burnham credits Douglas with 411 votes in Hinds County, Miss., instead of the correct total of 41; see Presidential Election Returns, Series F, Vol. 85, MDAH. Ollinger Crenshaw, "Urban and Rural Voting in the Election of 1860," *Historiography and Urbanization: Essays in American History in Honor of W. Stull Holt*, ed. Eric Goldman (Baltimore, 1941), noted that both Lincoln in the North and Breckinridge in the South ran strongest in rural areas.

[46] Except for Oxford, found in the *Mobile Daily Advertiser*, Nov. 9, all the Miss. returns are from the official returns, MDAH. The Ala. towns, with the exceptions of Grove Hill, *The Clarke County Democrat*, Nov. 15, and Guntersville, Peggy Jane Duckworth, "The

TABLE 8

Urban Vote in Alabama and Mississippi, 1860

City	Total Pop.	% Slaves	Breck. %	Bell %	Doug. %
Alabama					
Mobile	28,441	27	29	33	38
Montgomery	8,741	50+	54	38	8
Huntsville	3,549	44	25	31	44
Selma	3,124	42	27	40	33
Tuscaloosa	3,920	61	51	48	1
Kingston	1,960	37	32	24	44
Mississippi					
Natchez	6,404	33	38	44	18
Vicksburg	4,560	31	45	47	8
Jackson	3,178	34	49.5	47	3
Holly Springs	2,986	36	None Found		
Columbus	3,304	48	47	49	4

SOURCES: *The Eighth Census: Population of the United States in 1860*, comp. Joseph C. G. Kennedy (Washington 1864), 9, for the Ala. cities; 271 for Miss. Election returns for Montgomery were found in the Secretary of State Files, Presidential Election, 1860, ADAH; for Mobile, the *Mobile Daily Advertiser*, Nov. 11; for Huntsville, *The Southern Advocate*, Nov. 14; for Selma & Kingston, the *Alabama State Sentinel*, Nov. 14; and for Tuscaloosa, the *Independent Monitor*, Nov. 9. The returns for Jackson and Columbus are in Presidential Election Returns, Series F; for Natchez, *The Mississippi Free Trader*, Nov. 12; and for Vicksburg, the *Daily Vicksburg Whig*, Nov. 9.

The Breckinridge managers were well aware of the party's weakness in nonrural areas. "The town vote is against us— always has been" admitted the Democrats of Columbus, Mississippi. Occasionally they imported their rural adherents to vote at city boxes in an attempt to embarrass the Whig opposition. Their problem in 1860 was particularly tacky. Many

---

Role of Alabama Black Belt Whigs in the Election of Delegates to the Secession Convention," unpublished master's essay (University of Alabama, 1961), 45–47, were from the ADAH.

of their Irish supporters, nearly all of whom were nonslave-holders clustered in seaport cities such as Mobile and New Orleans or the larger interior towns, found the more temperate stand of Douglas more agreeable than the strident, pro-slavery emphasis of the Breckinridge campaign.[47] Efforts at stemming this defection were largely unsuccessful because to many Breckinridge leaders such apostasy simply confirmed their suspicions that lower class naturalized citizens were abolitionists at heart. John T. Morgan of Alabama, a Breckinridge elector at large, publicly accused the Irish and Germans of inclining toward Republicanism and being *"opposed to slavery on account of the negroes coming in opposition to them in blacking boots and doing other such services."* The head of the Breckinridge party in Louisiana, John Slidell, denounced the foreign vote in New Orleans to President Buchanan. "In the city seven eighths at least of the votes for Douglas were cast by the Irish & Germans, who are at heart abolitionists."[48]

The towns, with their ties to Northern capital and business groups and a work ethic that was not directly related to the use of the land and slave labor, shied away from the agitation of issues which stressed the rights of the slaveholders and the acquisition of more slave territory. The Whiggism of the factors, merchants, and storekeepers, and the Douglas leanings of the foreign-born shopkeepers and artisans were thus a reflection of both the town's middleman function in the Southern economy and its uneasiness over demands from which the countryside stood most to gain. Whatever their uneasiness, however, cities and towns simply did not command enough

[47] *Mississippi Democrat*, Oct. 1, 1859; *Weekly Vicksburg Whig*, Nov. 14, 1860; Roger W. Shugg, *Origins of Class Struggle in Louisiana* (Baton Rouge, 1968), 145. Foreign-born immigrants comprised 40% of the total population of New Orleans; 25% of Natchez's; and 24% of Mobile's. Ella Lonn, *Foreigners in the Confederacy* (Baton Rouge, 1940), 4.

[48] *Mobile Daily Advertiser*, Sept. 18, 1860; quoted in Shugg, *Origins of Class Struggle*, 145–146.

votes to alter the ideology of a party which, by speaking for and dominating the countryside, could control state politics.

The rural vote for Breckinridge was impressive. Fortunately, Bell and Douglas combined had sufficient pockets of support to allow for a contrast by which to highlight the characteristics of this vote. As an aid in analyzing the voting pattern, the following organizational technique has been employed. Alabama's fifty-two counties and Mississippi's sixty counties were divided into three political groupings: (1) strong Breckinridge counties defined by a Breckinridge vote of 60% and greater; (2) moderate defined by a Breckinridge vote of 50% to 59%; (3) anti-Breckinridge defined by a Breckinridge vote of less than 50% (see maps on pages 132–133). Each group was in turn subdivided into: (a) counties where slaveholders were in an absolute majority as measured by the ratio of slaveholders to families; (b) counties where this ratio ranged from 25% to 50%; (c) counties where the ratio was less than 25% (see maps on pages 134–135). After blocs of counties were identified by their politics and extent of slaveholdings, demographic and economic variables were then used to formulate in Tables 9 and 10 a rough political ecology of the vote.

The most striking feature revealed by these maps and tables is the relationship between growth rates and the size of the Breckinridge vote in medium and high slaveholder concentration counties. In Alabama Breckinridge carried seven of the fifteen counties where the slaveholders were in a majority.[49] His strength was in those areas where plantation agriculture was expanding most rapidly; conversely, he ran weakest where the plantation had already reached its peak. Wilcox, Lowndes, and Montgomery in the Black Belt, and Perry, on its northern border, were the only plantation-domi-

[49] The figure would be eight if Dallas, a county lost by Breckinridge because of the city vote of Selma, is included. Dallas planters did well enough in the 1850's to maintain their county's ranking as the leading cotton producer in the state.

130

nated counties which experienced a net gain of whites during the 1850's.[50] They were also the counties registering the heaviest gains in slave population. These four counties not only all went for Breckinridge but also were precisely those Black Belt areas that showed the greatest drop in Whig support from the last presidential election.[51] Millard Fillmore, the American Party candidate in 1856, had run stronger than Bell in all four counties, his margin ranging from 14% in Lowndes to 8% in Perry. The three other Breckinridge counties in this category were Marengo and Sumter in the western Black Belt, and Pickens, whose southern border included the northwestern tip of the Black Belt. Marengo and Sumter were in the process of consolidating their plantation systems. Both exhibited a net loss of free population and total farm units in the 1850's, as the small farmers left looking for cheap land. The large increases in slaves, improved and unimproved farm acreage, and doubling of cotton production bespoke the rising prosperity of the planters. The same process was occurring in Pickens with the smaller producers. Here the small slaveholder, owning less than twenty slaves and farming under one hundred acres, was the dominant factor in agriculture. His commitment to cotton was so strong that the cotton crop more than doubled during the 1850's, while corn production registered a scant 2% increase.

The planting counties lost by Breckinridge had reached their apogee of plantation development no later than 1850.

[50] The term plantation-dominated refers to counties in which a majority of the farm units were in excess of 100 acres. The Black Belt, named after the color of its soil, was a belt of black, sticky, and very fertile prairie soil, extending in a crescent shape east-northeast in south central Alabama from the Mississippi line to a point just east of Montgomery. Invaluable for the following discussion were the superb soil maps in *Tenth Census of the United States: Report on Cotton Production in the United States* (Washington, 1884), Eugene W. Hilgard, special agent in charge, Part I for Mississippi and Part II for Alabama.

[51] Dallas showed a 10% drop in Whig support but some of this Whig vote went to Douglas, who polled 19% of the county's vote.

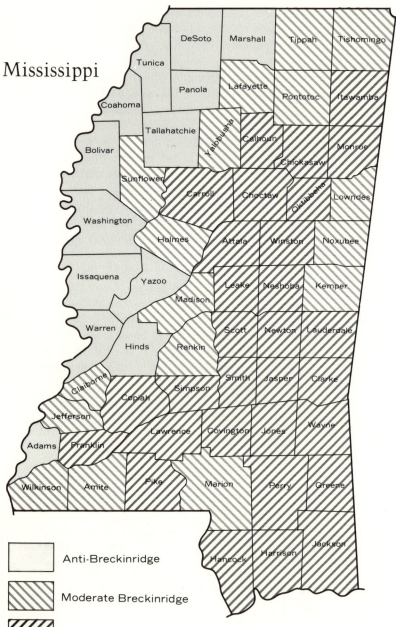

Presidential Vote in Mississippi and Alabama, 1860

Mississippi

DeSoto
Marshall
Tippah
Tishomingo
Tunica
Panola
Lafayette
Pontotoc
Itawamba
Coahoma
Tallahatchie
Calhoun
Monroe
Bolivar
Chickasaw
Sunflower
Carroll
Choctaw
Oktibbeha
Lowndes
Washington
Holmes
Attala
Winston
Noxubee
Issaquena
Yazoo
Leake
Neshoba
Kemper
Madison
Warren
Scott
Newton
Lauderdale
Hinds
Rankin
Smith
Jasper
Clarke
Claiborne
Simpson
Copiah
Jefferson
Lawrence
Covington
Jones
Wayne
Adams
Franklin
Wilkinson
Amite
Pike
Marion
Perry
Greene
Hancock
Harrison
Jackson

Anti-Breckinridge

Moderate Breckinridge

Strong Breckinridge

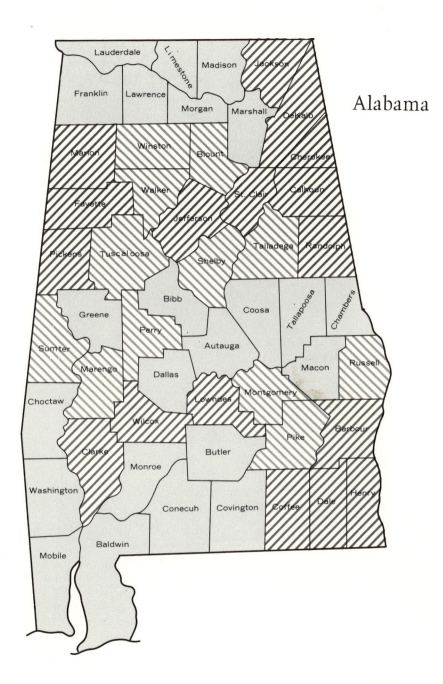

Alabama

Slaveholdings and Slave Growth Rates in Mississippi and Alabama

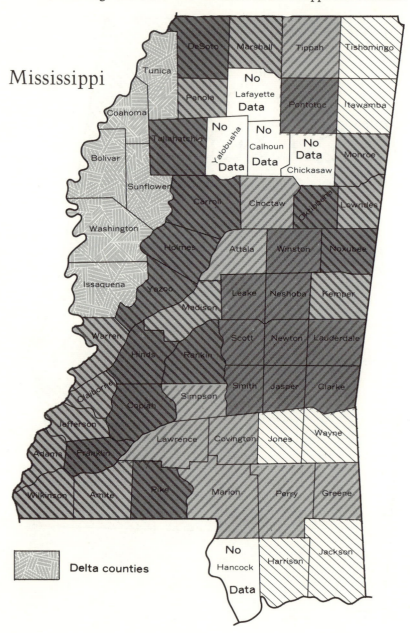

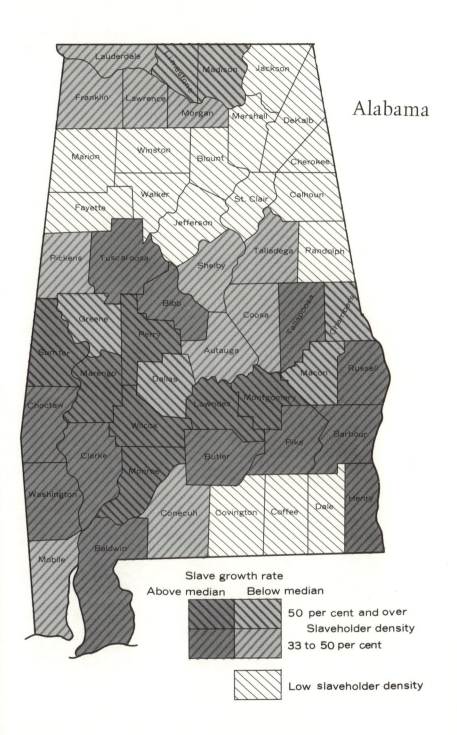

Alabama

Slave growth rate

Above median   Below median

50 per cent and over
Slaveholder density
33 to 50 per cent

Low slaveholder density

TABLE 9

Voting, Slaveholdings, and Growth Factors,
1850–1860, in Alabama Counties

Rel. Breck. Strength	No. of Counties	% Median White Pop. Change	% Median Slave Pop. Change	% Change Farms	% Change Improved Acreage	% Change Unimproved Acreage	% Change Cotton Production	Median % Change Breck. Vote Against 1856 Dem. Vote
High Slaveholder Concentration Counties								
Strong	3	+15.0	+32.0	+ 2	+43	+26	+141	+ 5
Moderate	4	+ 4.5	+22.0	−13	+28	+15	+115	+ 2
Anti-Breck.	8	− 6.5	+11.5	−10	+28	+ 3	+ 68	−11
Medium Slaveholder Concentration Counties								
Strong	3	+54.0	+54.0	+37	+66	+117	+133	+ 9
Moderate	5	+26.0	+40.0	+41	+56	+ 91	+109ᶜ	− 2
Anti-Breck.	13ᵃ	+22.0	+19.5	+21	+45	+ 68	+ 58	−12
Low Slaveholder Concentration Counties								
Strong	11	+35.0	+49.0	+48	+73	+166	+156ᵈ	− 2
Moderate	3	+47.0	+95.0	+25	+52ᵇ	+298	+384	−42
Anti-Breck.	2	+52.0	+90.0	+82	+131	+413	+192	−32

SOURCES: W. Dean Burnham, *Presidential Ballots 1836–1892* (Baltimore, 1955), for county voting statistics; population rates based on *Compendium of the Seventh Census,* comp. J.D.B. DeBow (Washington, 1854) and *The Eighth Census: Population*; farm, acreage, and crop statistics from *Compendium of the Seventh Census* and *The Eighth Census of the United States, 1860: Agriculture* (Washington, 1864); family figures for both 1850 and 1860 from *Statistics of the United States (Including Mortality, Property, & C...)* in 1860 (Washington, 1866) 340 for Alabama and 345 for Mississippi.

ᵃ Mobile County is not included. The urban nature of the county with more than two out of every three whites living in the city of Mobile sets it off from the predominantly rural

ᵇ Acreage statistics are based on only two counties. Winston was omitted due to the probability of error in the 1850 figures which credit the county with more improved acreage than unimproved.

ᶜ Tuscaloosa County was omitted from cotton statistics since published figures are inconsistent (show a drop in cotton production from 73,561 bales in 1850 to 26,035 in 1860). The 1850 figure is probably out of line.

ᵈ The cotton percentages for the low slaveholder concentration counties are quite deceiving since such small and relatively insignificant cotton totals are being used. Of more relevance is the fact that of the six counties in this group producing at least 5,000 bales in 1860, all were found in the strong Breckin-

Voting, Slaveholdings, and Growth Factors,
1850–1860, in Mississippi Counties[a]

Rel. Breck. Strength	No. of Counties	% Median White Pop. Change	% Median Slave Pop. Change	% Change Farms	% Change Improved Acreage	% Change Unimproved Acreage	% Change Cotton Production	Median % Change Breck. Vote Against 1856 Dem. Vote
			High Slaveholder Concentration Counties					
Strong	6	+22.0	+ 43.5	+ 6	+ 45	+ 88	+160	+ 6
Moderate	12[b]	+ 5.5	+ 30.0	+ 9	+ 39	+ 25	+153	+ 1
Anti-Breck.	13[c]							
Rich Delta	5[d]	+92.0	+273.0	+81	+236	+244	+518	+ 4
Others	8[e]	+ 9.5	+ 33.5	−14	+ 40	+ 44	+117	− 7
			Medium Slaveholder Concentration Counties					
Strong	18[f]	+43.0	+ 59.5	+24	+ 79	+ 93	+258	+ 2
Moderate	4[g]	+13.0	+ 28.0	+17	+ 56	+ 51	+108	+ 1
Anti-Breck.	0	–	–	–	–	–	–	–
			Low Slaveholder Concentration Counties					
Strong	6[h]	+24.0	+ 40.0	− 7	+ 48	+ 48	+124[i]	+ 8
Moderate	1	+42.0	+154.0	+19	+112	+ 23	+191	−15
Anti-Breck.	–	–						

SOURCES: See note on same for Table 9.

[a] The following counties have been omitted from the correlation table: Sunflower, Washington, and Hancock because the 1860 census returns on them have been lost; Calhoun, Lafayette, Chickasaw, and Yalobusha since portions of the latter three were taken in 1852 to form Calhoun. For the sake of consistency they have been included in the numerical listing of the counties.

[b] Returns missing for Sunflower County; Yalobusha omitted.

[c] These thirteen counties have been subdivided as shown because of the singular nature of the capitalized agriculture practiced in the five Delta counties of Bolivar, Coahoma, Issaquena, Tunica, and Washington. A discussion of the inordinately high concentration of agricultural wealth found in these five counties will be presented in the text.

[d] Returns missing for Washington County.

[e] There is some unavoidable distortion in this part of the table since Yazoo, one of the counties lost by Breckinridge, was carried by him in the countryside. If Yazoo is considered as a Breckinridge county in terms of the dynamics of its plantation agriculture and if the population data is viewed from a different perspective, then the following pattern appears. Whereas four-sixths of the strong Breckinridge counties and seven-elevenths of the moderate ones increased by a minimum of 5% in white and 15% in slave population, only one-seventh of the "other" anti-Breckinridge counties did so.

[f] Calhoun and Chickasaw omitted.

[g] Lafayette omitted.

[h] Returns missing for Hancock County.

[i] No cotton returns were given for Harrison and Jackson Counties in 1850, and they have been omitted from the cotton statistics.

Chambers in the eastern piedmont, Macon on the eastern fringes of the Black Belt, and Greene in the western Black Belt all had a heavy outflow of whites during the decade. The slave economy of these three counties was generally growing at a pace far below that set by their Breckinridge counterparts. A fundamental reason for this sluggishness was the shrinking base of good farm land. Total farm acreage in Macon actually decreased from 1850 to 1860 and the additions in Chambers and Greene were among the lowest in the entire state.[52] Unimproved acreage decreased in all three counties as planters were forced to cut drastically into the supply of uncleared land which had been their best hedge against soil exhaustion.

Madison and Limestone in the Tennessee River Valley of northern Alabama were the centers of a once flourishing plantation agriculture. With the advantages of good cotton land in its fertile limestone valleys and a transportation outlet in the Tennessee River, the region attracted Georgia planters as early as 1809. Once established, the plantation regime showed little growth after 1850. Soil exhaustion and the opening of better cotton lands in new regions gradually weakened the agricultural preeminence of the Valley planters and their position as spokesmen for their class on a state-wide basis. Both counties barely increased their cotton output in the 1850's and whites and slaves alike were leaving. Clement C. Clay has left us with a vivid picture of this process.

> Our small planters, after taking the cream off their lands, unable to restore them by rest, manures, or otherwise, are going further west and south, in search of other virgin lands, which they may and will despoil in like manner. Our wealthier planters, with greater means and no more skill, are buying out their poorer neighbors, extending their plantations, and adding to their slave force. The wealthy few, who are able to live on small profits and to

[52] Dallas was the only other county with a net drop in farm acreage. Franklin was the one county which registered a smaller increase than Chambers or Greene.

give their blasted fields some rest, are thus pushing off the many, who are merely independent.

Heavy Democratic majorities continued to be registered but they rested upon an ideological base which looked upon the privilege-hating, Union-loving yeomanry of Andy Jackson's day as the custodians of political virtue and was openly leery of the motives of the Union-hating cotton nabobs of southern Alabama. With "the bond of union *seeming* to be a common dread," Bell and Douglas forces were sympathetic to each other's motives and combined, denied Breckinridge a majority in Madison and Limestone.[53]

Breckinridge lost only two counties in this high slaveholder concentration group which experienced vigorous growth in the 1850's—Choctaw and Monroe in southwestern Alabama. The 14% Douglas vote in Choctaw and 19% in Monroe were enough to cost Breckinridge a majority and reflected an erosion of his support among the small, nonslaveholding farmers. Precinct returns for Monroe reveal that the Douglas defectors were centered in Claiborne, an old river town on the Alabama that earlier had been a distribution point for immigrants on their trek northward from Mobile, and in the more subsistence-oriented eastern half of the county in such beats as Burnt Corn and East's Store.[54]

The correlation of high growth rates with a preference for Breckinridge was also characteristic of the range of Alabama counties in which slaveholders made up a large minority of at least 25% of the total families. Commercial agriculture was prevalent in most of these counties but on a smaller scale than prevailed in the Black Belt. The smaller planters and farmers with limited capital resources or shorter lines of credit had an opportunity to acquire land and expand pro-

[53] Thomas P. Abernathy, *The Formative Period in Alabama, 1815–1828* (Montgomery, 1922), 11; *DBR*, xviii (1855), 727; Cabiness to Moore, Oct. 29, 1860, "A. B. Moore Correspondence," ADAH, 6.

[54] W. Brewer, *Alabama: Her History, Resources, War Record, and Public Men. From 1540 to 1872* (Montgomery, 1872), 435; Claiborne *Southern Champion*, Nov. 9, 1860.

duction in these counties which was frequently denied them in more settled areas. This secondary expansion of the cotton belt can be seen most readily in those counties carried by Breckinridge. They formed a rough crescent which flanked the Black Belt on the north, east, and south and were peripheral centers of cotton production. His strongest showing came in Henry and Barbour, two counties in the red hills of southeastern Alabama, and Clarke in the southwest. All the indices pointed to an upsurge in economic activity. Whites were pouring in and bringing their slaves with them, land was being cleared or earmarked for future use, and cotton production increased close to two-and-a-half fold in the 1850's. Enjoying the same growth but at a more leisurely rate were the moderate Breckinridge counties of Russell and Pike, to the north and west respectively of Barbour, and Tuscaloosa, Shelby, and Talladega, three hill counties in central Alabama. Navigable rivers provided market outlets for their cotton, and the two that were isolated, Shelby and Talladega in the non-navigable Coosa River Valley, worked energetically for railroad transportation. By the late 1850's the Alabama and Tennessee Rivers Railroad, which both counties had supported since 1848, was completed from its origin in Selma through southeastern Shelby and across the Coosa River into Talladega.[55]

Within this slaveholding category of counties Breckinridge ran weakest in those areas least suitable to the large-scale production of cotton. Whereas five of the eight counties he carried ranked in the top twenty of the state in cotton output, only two of the twelve counties he lost did so. Lacking extensive stretches of available, quality land and, in many cases, good transportation facilities, the anti-Breckinridge counties were more popular with a yeomanry interested in grain and livestock farming than with commercially minded small planters and farmers specializing in cotton. The different agricultural emphasis in each set of counties was reflected in

[55] John Hardy, *Selma: Her Institutions and Her Men* (Selma, 1879), 107–109.

the Breckinridge counties producing only 29.1 bushels of corn for every bale of cotton, as opposed to 43.5 bushels of corn per bale in the anti-Breckinridge counties.

Lauderdale, Franklin, and Lawrence in the western Tennessee Valley all dropped out of the top twenty counties in cotton production during the 1850's. Suffering from the same problems as their wealthier neighbors to the east, Limestone and Madison, these anti-Breckinridge counties faced a serious decline in their slave-based economy. Corn production fell, the cotton output and slave labor supply stagnated, and whites left. Morgan, another Valley county, showed a little more growth but this was attributable to nonslaveholders moving in. Three hill counties in central Alabama, Bibb, Coosa, and Tallapoosa, were lost by Breckinridge. They had poorer market outlets and land less adaptable for cotton than the three Breckinridge hill counties. As a result, their farms were valued on the average about 50% less, there was a higher percentage of small farms, and land ownership was more widely distributed. Autauga in the heart of the state was slipping as a center of cotton production and failing to attract sizeable numbers of whites or slaves.

The other four counties in this group were in southern Alabama. Only one of them, Butler, lying just south of the Black Belt, had a growth rate based on the use of slave labor which was comparable to that of the Breckinridge counties. The Whig stronghold was among the farmers and planters occupying the prairie soil of the Chunnenuggee Ridge in the northwestern corner of the county. Using this as their base, and with no competing centers of large-scale cotton production emerging in the oak uplands and pine forests of central and southern Butler, the Whigs were just able to hold the county for Bell in 1860.[56] Conecuh to the southwest of Butler, and Washington and Baldwin in the basins of the lower Tombigbee and Mobile Rivers respectively, were among the oldest counties in the state. Light, sandy soil covered with

[56] From 58% in 1852, the Whig vote declined to 51% in 1856 and 1860.

141

vast stretches of pine was a predominant feature of all three. Lumber and distilled turpentine, not just cotton, were major producers of wealth. The white influx in the 1850's, consisting of small farmers and squatters, exceeded the slave increase in all three counties.

Breckinridge nearly swept the Alabama counties in which slavery was weakest. His strength was based on the fantastic party loyalty of the yeomanry who, from the inception of their counties as political units, returned heavy Democratic majorities election after election. This loyalty had been shaped by the charisma of Andrew Jackson, folk hero par excellence, enshrined in party mythology as part Indian fighter, part leveler of special privileges, and always as the friend of the common man. The small farmers who moved into Alabama after successive Indian cessions opened up land in the 1820's and 1830's were the staunchest of Jackson men. Democratic leaders from the Black Belt, cleverly playing upon the yeomanry's resentment of the status and wealth of the planter and directing it against the Whig party as a whole, found the Jackson men of the north to be more than willing allies in their efforts to neutralize Whig power. The passage of the White Basis system in 1843 and the gerrymanders of 1843 and 1853 crippled Whig strength throughout the state.[57]

Concentrated primarily in the hilly and mountainous region of northern Alabama these Breckinridge counties were locked into poverty and isolation. The prospects for a cash income by many of the farmers who occupied even the best lands were bleak. As the Appalachian Mountains sloped to the southwest from DeKalb toward Tuscaloosa, fertile land was to be found in the valleys and coves interspersed between the parallel ridges. The farmer's cash crop had to be cotton, for that was the only crop that could bear the expense of

[57] Abernathy, *Formative Period*, 105. The White Basis system eliminated slaves as an element in apportionment for state offices. Carlton Jackson, "The White Basis System and the Decline of Alabama Whiggery," *AHQ*, 25 (Fall and Winter, 1963), 246–253.

marketing. At that he had to pay about $6 to place one bale on the seaboard, and since neither the soil nor climate was particularly suited for cotton, he had to devote about five acres to produce that bale. Grain and livestock farming which would not have been as destructive of the soil were neglected. Unprofitable as this agriculture was, land was cheap, and as soon as some gave up and left for Arkansas or Texas, others moved in.[58]

Eleven out of the twelve Breckinridge counties in this group from northern Alabama subsequently voted against immediate secession. Party loyalty was the main reason why more of these voters did not initially favor the softer stand on slavery taken by Bell or Douglas, but this allegiance was reinforced by two other factors. In the first place, these counties had an utter dearth of towns which could attract and nourish a Whig movement. Second, isolated and insular as they were, with poor means of communication, few newspapers, and a high rate of illiteracy, the counties were the least receptive of any in the state to new ideas. The Douglas supporter in the Tennessee Valley had vastly superior means of promoting his man, of hammering away at the regular Democratic constituency. Nothing short of the fear of secession and war could shake the party allegiance of the Breckinridge Democrat in the mountains.[59]

Breckinridge ran as well in Mississippi as his opponents had feared. By the middle of September, Bell forces were beginning to admit privately that their best hopes lay in running a strong second so as to deter the Breckinridge leaders in Mississippi and other Southern states from embarking on secession. This hope proved to be ephemeral; Bell carried just eleven counties, including three by a plurality. A partisan description of the difficulties Douglas would encounter in securing an electoral ticket in Mississippi—

[58] See A. Battle, "Alabama Railroad Projections," *DBR*, xxvii (1859), 196–205.

[59] Even so, in half of these counties Douglas attracted at least 20% of the normal Democratic vote.

"There isn't [sic] 7 leading men in the State that would serve. They would feel themselves personally degraded to do so"— was off the mark more in style than in substance. A Douglas State Convention at Holly Springs on July 30 attracted delegates from a mere eleven counties. DeSoto, on the Tennessee line, was the only county to give Douglas as much as 20% of its vote. In Alabama Douglas received at least that much of the vote in fifteen counties.[60]

The wider distribution of slave ownership in Mississippi accounts for much of Breckinridge's greater popularity there than in Alabama. Based on the county unit, the median percentage of slave ownership in the former state was 51%; in the latter it dropped to 33%. Except for the pine barrens of southeastern Mississippi and the northeast highlands region of Tishomingo and Itawamba, the rest of the state had soil well suited for slaves and cotton. Most of the northern half of Alabama was too mountainous or hilly for slavery to flourish, and in the north where it had prospered, in the Tennessee Valley, slavery was a stagnant institution by the 1850's. As a result, slavery was concentrated in the southern half of the state. This neat geographic polarity of slavery created sectional antagonisms which were effectively exploited by the Douglas forces in their attacks on Breckinridge. The Douglas movement in Mississippi never got off the ground because it did not have a comparable, well-defined area of antiplanter resentment to serve as a springboard for its campaign. The region with the greatest potential in this context was the piney woods section. But here, especially in the coastal counties of Hancock, Harrison, and Jackson, the majority of the population consisted of grazers, hunters, charcoal burners, and squatters and not a yeomanry owning its own land and practicing subsistence agriculture as in northern Alabama. These voters were the most apathetic

[60] Mississippi Citizens to Crittenden, Sept. 14, [1860], Crittenden Papers, LC; M. D. Haynes to Davis, March 31, 1860, *Jefferson Davis, Constitutionalist*, IV, 229; *Mississippi Democrat*, Aug. 11, 1860.

in the state.[61] Without even a semblance of a Whig organization bidding for their vote, they habitually supported Democrats who catered to their Negrophobia. Bell actually ran stronger in a wider range of Mississippi counties than he did in Alabama but, unaided by any serious Douglas defections in the Democratic ranks, posed only a weak challenge to Breckinridge.[62]

The Mississippi counties with a high concentration of slaveholders included the only ones lost by Breckinridge in the state. As in Alabama, there was a correlation between Breckinridge strength and the speed at which slavery and a slave-based agriculture were spreading. Small to medium slaveholding farmers, not planters, made up a majority of the landholders in the six strong Breckinridge counties. On the average no more than 5% of the farms were larger than 500 acres and more than half were under 100 acres. The rapid extension of slavery, acreage, and cotton production revealed that these areas offered excellent opportunities for the ambitious lower and middle tiers of the slaveholding hierarchy. The moderate Breckinridge counties were distinguished from the above group by their slower rates of growth and the greater prevalence of the plantation. Half of the ten had more than 20% of their farm units in excess of 500 acres and in all but two, farms greater than 100 acres were the rule. The planters in these brown loam and prairie counties were expanding their cotton output at a tremendous rate. Since 1850 four of them had jumped into the state's top ten in cotton production.

The anti-Breckinridge counties were divided into two groups. The first group consisted of the very wealthy Delta counties north of Vicksburg—Issaquena, Washington, Bolivar, Coahoma, and Tunica. Occupying an alluvial plain de-

[61] Only Adams County had a lower vote turn-out in 1860 than the piney woods counties of Harrison, Jackson, and Jones.

[62] Bell drew at least 40% of the vote in 25 Mississippi counties; in Alabama the number drops to 15.

145

scribed by L. Harper, the state geologist, as "of inexhaustible fertility, every acre of which is able to produce from sixty to eighty bushels of corn, and from one and a half to two bales of cotton," these counties possessed unparalleled cotton lands. A lush, nearly impenetrable wilderness, subject to frequent floodings, the Mississippi-Yazoo Delta was not developed until the 1850's. By then some 310 miles of continuous levees, built and supervised by a state Levee Board, allowed drainage systems to be completed. Planters from worn-out lands down river moved in with their slaves and a boom was on.[63] A labor equivalency of $100 per acre was necessary to prepare the land for cultivation, and many planters required private levees, but the results could be a bonanza. From 1853 to 1857 land assessments for taxation in the five submerged counties on the Mississippi more than tripled to $23.5 million. In 1860 the average value of a farm in each of the five was in excess of $30,000. The extremely high capitalization of agricultural operations in the Delta prohibited all but the wealthy from a chance to compete for the alluvial lands.[64] Its political corollary was the understandable conservatism of a planter class which supervised one of the greatest concentrations of wealth in the South.

The other group of counties lost by Breckinridge included the old Whig heartland of Warren and Adams along the lower Mississippi, Hinds to the east of Warren, and a cluster of four northwestern counties. Natchez and Vicksburg were the

[63] *DBR*, XXIII (1857), 644; John K. Bettersworth, *Confederate Mississippi: The People and Policies of a Cotton State in Wartime* (Baton Rouge, 1943), 132; Frank A. Montgomery, *Reminiscences of a Mississippian in Peace and War* (Cincinnati, 1901), 32–33; Percy L. Rainwater, ed., "Autobiography of Benjamin Grubb Humphreys," *MVHR*, XXI (Sept. 1934), 231–255.

[64] *DBR*, XXV (1858), 389, 440. Yazoo and Claiborne were the only other counties with an average farm value in excess of $15,000; in Alabama the farms of Dallas at $13,097 had the highest average value. In 1860 only 4 out 40 holders of land in Issaquena were non-slaveholders; in Bolivar only 32 out of 252. Herbert Weaver *Mississippi Farmers, 1850–1860* (Nashville, 1945), 76–77.

146

cultural and political nexus of the polished, urbane aristocracies of Adams and Warren. Shorn of their former political dominance by the coming to power of the staunchly Democratic counties of central and northern Mississippi carved out of the vast Choctaw and Chickasaw land cessions of 1830 and 1832, these proud old-line Whigs had settled into a sulking lethargy.[65] They could still control local politics given the static nature of the area. There was some growth in Natchez and Vicksburg during the 1850's, but few farmers were moving into the countryside since the best lands had long since been engrossed and much of the rest were badly eroded. Hinds was another settled plantation area receiving few whites. Its rural economy though was more robust than that of Adams and Warren. Farm units dropped by a third and cotton output nearly tripled in the 1850's as its planters were enlarging their productive capacity. From a peak of 60% in 1856, the Whig vote dipped to a bare majority in 1860. With the exception of Panola the northwestern counties were normally Democratic. Douglas splinter factions in DeSoto, Marshall, and Tallahatchie were just large enough to prevent a Breckinridge majority. The corn and cotton of the region were shipped north to Memphis. These close economic ties to Tennessee, a more balanced agriculture than further south that did not place so much emphasis on cotton, and a matured economy that was no longer assimilating whites all contributed to blunting the Breckinridge rhetoric keyed to expansion and the rights of the slaveholders.[66]

---

[65] "By the 1850's many men of the Natchez region, especially those who were older and wealthier, had eschewed politics and turned their thoughts in other directions." Charles S. Sydnor, *A Gentleman of the Old Natchez Region, Benjamin L. C. Wailes* (Durham, 1938), 76.

[66] *The Weekly Panola Star*, Aug. 30, 1860; Sam Bowers Hilliard, "Hog Meat and Hoecake: A Geographical View of Food Supply in the Heart of the Old South, 1840–1860," unpublished Ph.D. thesis (University of Wisconsin, 1966), 316; Joseph Karl Mann, "The Large Slaveholders of the Deep South, 1860," unpublished Ph.D. thesis (University of Texas, 1964), 147.

A large bloc of eighteen counties with medium concentrations of slaveholders gave Breckinridge overwhelming support. Forming an inverted "V" in eastern Mississippi with its apex in the north central plateau and black prairie lands of Calhoun and Chickasaw, extensions south into the central prairie, and its base in the long leaf pine belt, this cluster of counties was the fastest growing region of the state for yeomen farmers and small slaveholders. Less than one in ten of the slaveholders owned twenty or more slaves, and about 75% of the farm units were under 100 acres. Not wealthy enough to compete in the Delta and stymied in other areas by the consolidation of landholdings, the smaller producers had migrated into these counties in search of land and a cash crop. The recently completed Vicksburg and Meridian Railroad, bisecting the region from west to east, triggered much of this expansion. Forest, a station depot in Scott County, typified the area's rapid growth. "Twelve months ago it had not a single house, now it presents a commanding appearance, and is a place of considerable business, and will ship six or seven thousand bales of cotton next crop, with the prospect at no distant day of being the county seat of Scott County, in the place of Hillsboro. The other depots farther east, are bran[d] new places." The railroad opened up new lands for commercial agriculture, and the slave frontier was booming.[67]

The Mississippi counties with the lowest concentration of slaveholders were a traditional Democratic bastion that Douglas failed to dent. Of the five counties in the southeastern pine belt, Jones was the only one in which the ratio of farms to families was greater than 50%. As previously stressed, a landholding yeomanry was not in the majority here. With poor soil and a pastoral economy, augmented by the sale of some farm surpluses in the Mobile market, the region turned to its pine forests as its main source of wealth. Susan Dabney Smedes, daughter of the patrician Dabneys of Hinds County, noted that "The people in the 'piney woods' counties . . . were

[67] Paulding *Eastern Clarion*, Dec. 26, 1860.

almost totally uneducated. They had but little use for money, subsisting on the products of their little patches, and cows, pigs and fowls. They were frequently 'squatters,' living on government lands." Untouched by the outside world, the mass of the voters habitually backed the Democratic label.[68]

The beat, or election precinct, was the smallest voting unit and correlation of beat voting with the socioeconomic profile of individual beats would provide the best foundation for an analysis of political behavior. Unfortunately, little of the necessary groundwork has been laid. What has been done reveals that in mixed soil areas Breckinridge ran strongest in the plantation districts and weakest among the hill farmers. The same was true in Dallas. Here the anti-Breckinridge rural vote was centered in the shortleaf pine belt of the northeastern portion of the county.[69] A study by Joseph Allen Hazel on the geography of slavery in the Deep South pinpointed by post offices the distribution of slaves in five Alabama counties. For one of these counties, Franklin in the western Tennessee Valley, the coincidence of extant beat returns and well-defined areas of slave concentrations made possible a rough analysis of beat voting. The good cotton lands and best transportation facilities in Franklin were in the northern half of the county; the high tableland of the southern portion was best suited to small-scale farming. Breckinridge carried six of Franklin's twenty beats. Five out of the six beats were located. The three in the northern half included Tuscumbia, which lay on the Memphis and Charleston Railroad and had the highest number of slaves in the

[68] J.F.H. Claiborne, "Trip Through the Piney Woods," *PMHS*, IX (1906), 487–538; Nollie W. Hickman, "Logging and Rafting Timber in South Mississippi, 1840–1910," *JMH*, XIX (July, 1957), 154–164; Susan Dabney Smedes, *Memorials of a Southern Planter*, ed. Fletcher M. Green (New York, 1953), 99.

[69] J. C. Oldshue, "The Secession Movement in Tuscaloosa County, Alabama," unpublished master's essay (University of Alabama, 1961); Kit C. Carter, "A Critical Analysis of the Basis of Party Alignment in Lowndes County, Alabama, 1836–1860," unpublished master's essay (University of Alabama, 1961); election returns, Secretary of State Files, ADAH.

county; Barton, which ranked second in number of slaves among the towns along the railroad; and Alsoborough, south of the railroad. The Breckinridge beats of New Berg and Mountain Springs were the leading slave centers for the southeastern part of the county. In the four beats where slavery was weakest, Breckinridge attracted only 29% of the vote.[70]

An examination by the author of beat returns in Butler County, a region of small farms and one of the few Alabama counties where the census was taken by beats, found the more successful slaveholding farmers who had not yet advanced into the planter class to be for Breckinridge. Butler's fifteen beats were ranked according to their wealth.[71] The farmers and planters along the Chunnenuggee Ridge in the northwest made up the wealthiest beats and, as their neighbors in Lowndes, were the centers of Whig strength. In the middle range of beats, Breckinridge areas were distinguished from those of Bell by a greater prevalence of small to medium slaveholders and an economy that was producing more farmers of moderate wealth. Within the five poorer beats Bell was a solid favorite in Owen's, Breckinridge in Smut Eye, and both ran closely in the other three. The farmers in Smut Eye owned more slaves, better land, and had larger farms than those in Owen's.

III

The voting coalitions dictated much of the strategy of the party chieftains. Each party shaped, and in turn was shaped

[70] Joseph Allen Hazel, "The Geography of Negro Agricultural Slavery in Alabama, Florida, and Mississippi, circa 1860," unpublished Ph.D. thesis (Columbia University, 1963), 184–202. Slaves numbered under 100 at six post offices. The conclusion on the Breckinridge vote is based on the four that definitely could be associated with beats.

[71] The median of the total property holdings of all the adult white males residing within each beat was determined. The wealthier beats had median holdings of $2,000 and above; the middle group between $1,000 and $1,999; and the five poorer beats under $1,000.

by, the needs and aspirations of their respective constituencies. The insistence of the Breckinridge Democrats on the right of slavery to expand and on the need for Congressional protection wherever the slaveholders' rights were being infringed spoke directly to the rising planters and slaveholding farmers of the newer cotton areas. Planters whose status was not secure, parvenus eagerly acquiring land and slaves, the more mobile small- and non-slaveholders, gave the cotton frontier its vitality. By articulating the demands of this frontier, by promising every white on his way up that competition would remain open, that the South would always have land and slaves for the ambitious, and by demanding of the Yankee that the territories be kept accessible to slavery, the Breckinridge men harnessed the energy and reaped the votes of the most dynamic regions in the countryside. Simultaneously, they used blunt racist appeals to hold the regular Democratic vote of the poor whites and to reinforce the white fear that room would have to be found for the growing black population before it became a social menace.

The Bell Whigs were more placid about the rights of slaveholders. Drawing for their support upon factors and merchants in cities, planters and farmers in the mature plantation areas, and hill farmers outside of the black belts, the Whigs lacked a constituency with a sense of urgency on the slavery question. Although all of this group would gladly have accepted more land and slaves, the acquisition of them was not of immediate concern. The economic activity of the businessman was dominated by his dependence on outside sources of capital, much of which originated in the North, of the established or very wealthy planter by the maintenance of what he already had, and of the hill farmer by his concern with getting in a crop sufficient to his family's needs with perhaps a small surplus for market. In essence, the Whig constituency either financed and serviced plantation agriculture, had grown accustomed to the status it provided and accepted its prestige and rewards as a way of life, or had given up active pursuit of it.

151

Moreover, many of the Whiggish areas had been weakened economically by the rapid expansion of the cotton frontier. Economic diversification, soil restoration, and the accumulation of capital in the older plantation belts were all made more difficult by the outflow of population, skills, and labor resources to new regions. In the generation before the Civil War Whig Congressmen constantly decried the burden placed on their home districts by the availability of fresh lands elsewhere. They attacked the cruelty and greed of the aggressive cotton entrepreneurs and denounced filibusters as young "elegant men, having nothing to live upon and doing nothing, and nothing to do anything upon."[72] The Whigs were both the South's economic old guard and her paternalistic conscience, but neither could save them from political decay.

Douglas supporters tended to be peeled away from those layers of the normal Democratic coalition whose function and place in the slave economy overlapped that of the Whigs. Urban and town Democrats found Douglas very attractive and he outpolled Breckinridge in three out of the four largest cities in Alabama. The foreign-born small tradesmen and artisans had an alternative in Douglas. Their loyalty to slavery had been questioned first by the Whigs during their Know-Nothing phase in the mid-1850's and then by the Breckinridge Democrats in 1860. Voting for Douglas enabled them to keep their party credentials without going over to the hated Whigs with their air of social snobbery. Planters in the agriculturally static Tennessee Valley and the yeomanry in the uplands of the Valley also backed Douglas. For them the expansion of the plantation was either behind them or had never been the focal point of their activities.

[72] *Congressional Globe*, 35th Congress, 2d Session, 1059. For Whig arguments against expansion on moral, economic, and political grounds, see *ibid.*, 1058–1063 and 1344–1361. Whigs from the upper South were particularly concerned since their states had suffered the longest and most severely from the effects of migration, but the same factors were at work by the 1850's in scattered Whig sections of the lower South, such as the old plantation district of central Georgia and parts of the Alabama Black Belt.

FOUR

EXPLOITING THE FEARS

As LONG as Breckinridge held the bulk of the normal Democratic vote, he was virtually assured of victory in the South. But to maximize this vote and to prepare the South for secession, if Lincoln were elected, the Breckinridge party exploited the siege mentality and near panic which had gripped wide areas of the lower South. Uneasiness over severe food shortage, a fear of alleged abolitionist plots to burn down towns or entice slaves to revolt, and the crisis psychology whipped up by vigilance committees and squads of Minute Men alarmed Southerners and resulted in a pervasive sense of insecurity and personal danger. As trumpeted in the Breckinridge press, the Union began to appear less as a place of refuge than as an external menace which threatened the safety and well-being of those citizens who lived in a slave society.

I

The summer of 1860 was the hottest and driest that most Southerners could remember. "The heavens are as brass and the streets are as a sea of molten lead" was one paper's description of the intense heat. Some called it the hottest spell since the summer of 1828, others referred to the unprecedented drought, and all agreed that complaints about the hot weather and failing crops had never been so widespread. The drought, which was general throughout the South, was particularly devastating in the central and southern regions of Alabama and Mississippi. Corn, the slave's handout and the common man's staple, was the crop hardest hit.[1]

[1] Canton *American Citizen*, Aug. 4; Diary of Ann L. Hardeman, July 28, in Oscar J. E. Stuart and Family Papers, MDAH. On August

153

Reports during the summer coming in to J. J. Williams, Secretary of the Mississippi Agricultural Bureau, all stressed the drought and the poor corn prospects. By August 1 he was expressing the consensus of most Mississippians. "In a few favored section[s] of the State corn enough and to spare, will be made, but in the main the crop is an entire failure." He pinpointed a few north central counties in the watersheds of the Yazoo and Big Black Rivers as areas where the drought was least severe.[2]

The drought ruined the harvest in the southern two-thirds of Mississippi. A letter writer to the Mississippian summarized the plight of those in the eastern section.

> Our early corn is not more than one-fourth crop, and late corn is entirely ruined. We will not make to last till Christmas. Cotton is unually light; it cannot now be brought enough to make a half crop.
>
> Failing in corn would not be so bad if we were making cotton enough to buy provisions. But we are neither making bread nor anything to buy it with. This is the case mostly in Scott, Newton, Neshoba and Leake.

A correspondent from Marion, Lauderdale County, noted that spirits were depressed. The crops were a failure and garden plots had long since burned up. The *Southern Star* of Noxubee County feared that the area would not produce half of the normal cotton crop; "add to this the almost entire failure of

---

16, the *Jacksonville* (Ala.) *Republican* noted that "The drought appears to have been general throughout the South and the Southwestern states, including Missouri and a portion of Kansas." Corn, because of its high moisture requirement during the tasseling stage, was especially vulnerable to droughts; Sam Bowers Hilliard, "Hog Meat and Hoecake: A Geographical View of Food Supply in the Heart of the Old South, 1840–1860," unpublished Ph.D. thesis (University of Wisconsin, 1966), 43–44. For the importance of corn, see Donald L. Kemmerer, "The Pre-Civil War South's Leading Crop, Corn," *AgH*, XXIII (Oct., 1949), 236–239.

[2] *Semi-Weekly Mississippian*, July 10, 17, Aug. 1.

the cotton crop for several counties below this, and the failure of at least one-half of the planters to make corn enough to do them, and the prospect looks indeed gloomy." Most of the blame was put on the drought, but the worm, mayfly, and late, untimely rains had compounded the problem.[3]

Wretched and distressing were adjectives commonly used to describe the crops in the southwestern counties of Amite and Wilkinson. The *Amite Democrat* of July 25 reported corn production only one-fifth of normal and a cotton output down by two-thirds. Just to the north in Claiborne and Copiah only the river planters and those who planted along the Big Black had good crops. Benjamin Wailes, a very careful planter committed to soil conservation and crop diversification, considered himself fortunate for breaking even on his Fonsylvania plantation "when so many others have done much worse." Northern Mississippi escaped the worst of the drought. The Grenada *Rural Gentleman* estimated crops in the North to be off by about one-third, a welcome contrast from central Mississippi where they were "*almost* a total failure."[4]

The drought-induced crop destruction was just as severe in Alabama. On July 27 the *Montgomery Weekly Mail* labeled the corn crop of Alabama and Georgia "an absolute failure. Excepting only an occasional fair crop, on some stream, or in some other specially favored locality, the yield cannot be equal to local needs." In the same issue under a column headed The Weather and Crops, excerpts from newspapers across the state corroborated the *Mail's* pessimism. By August the Eufaula *Spirit of the South* had written of corn and cotton and warned that if the drought continued, peas and potatoes would also "be cut grievously short." A distraught citizen from Coffee County wrote the *Mail* saying

[3] *Ibid.*, July 27; *Mobile Daily Advertiser*, Aug. 18; quoted in the *Weekly Panola Star*, Sept. 20.

[4] *Weekly Vicksburg Whig*, July 25; *Natchez Daily Courier*, July 26; *Port Gibson Reveille*, Aug. 23, quoted in *ibid.*, Aug. 28; B.L.C. Wailes Diary, Oct. 20, DU; quoted in the *Weekly Vicksburg Whig*, Sept. 12.

that crops there were so bad that many were talking of petitioning the legislature for debtor stay laws which would prevent the levy and sale of property for the payment of debts until another harvest.[5]

The Black Belt planters were not as fortunate as their counterparts in the Mississippi Delta. They suffered more from the drought and did not have as much alluvial or overflow lands to fall back on. Wilcox, Lowndes, Greene, Montgomery, and Dallas were all Black Belt counties that reported short, poor crops. William P. Gould, a planter in Boligee, Greene County, undoubtedly spoke for many of his neighbors when he jotted in his diary for August 7: "I have had no heart to witness the destruction in the field and have not been further than the Gin-House today." A few favored areas in the Tennessee Valley survived the drought in the best shape. A pro-Douglas paper in Tuscumbia felt the crops in northern Alabama were the best in the state. This good fortune probably did not extend much south of the Valley, however, for the mountainous counties of Cherokee, Calhoun, and Blount reported short crops.[6]

The immediate effect of the crop shortages was a sharp increase in grain imports from the Northwest and a subsequent price rise in foodstuffs. In late May the Mobile press noted that in the last three or four weeks receipts of corn from the West had been the highest ever known. Corn was the principal freight item on the New Orleans steamers and schooners coming into Mobile, with the bulk consigned for transshipment to the interior. Western corn was available in the Mobile market at 90¢ a bushel but freight cost inflated prices in the interior to well over a dollar. In Montgomery, an important trading center in central Alabama, the seasonal drop in corn prices never occurred. Corn had rarely ever risen above 50¢ a

[5] *Montgomery Weekly Mail*, July 27; quoted in the Huntsville *Southern Advocate*, Aug. 15; *Montgomery Weekly Mail*, Aug. 17.

[6] William P. Gould Diary, Aug. 7, ADAH; *States' Rights Democrat*, Aug. 3.

bushel in previous summers but in late July it was selling from $1.25 to $1.30 and was still rising.[7]

This pattern was a common one. The *Mail* expected prices to reach $2.00 by Christmas in eastern Alabama and western Georgia. Pressure against hoarding and profiteering was strong. "We would advise those who have it to sell to be satisfied with good profits, and let *better* alone. A word to the wise is sufficient." But such warnings were largely futile. In December Mobile merchants were filling grain orders only if accompanied by cash. Many Southerners had no recourse but to pay the high prices or starve. Asked the *Blountsville Pioneer*, speaking for an isolated, rocky county where corn sold as high as $2.30 per bushel and wheat sold for $2.00: "What will become of us poor devils who have neither corn, or money to buy it with?"[8]

These poor devils were indeed in bad straits. Their ruined crops had left them in need of foodstuffs while simultaneously they were unable to find the cash or credit necessary to meet exorbitant market prices. Their hardships were compounded by a short wheat crop which had been severely damaged by a late winter frost in northern Alabama and Mississippi.[9] As a result, famine was a distinct possibility as early as the spring of 1860. In May reports came out of Randolph County, Alabama, of persons "actually starving." The problem worsened and spread in the ensuing months. "We do not see how a scarcity, approaching famine, is to be avoided in the middle eastern counties, next year," warned the *Montgomery Weekly Mail*. From Choctaw County came a December prediction

[7] *Mobile Daily Advertiser*, May 27; Paulding *Eastern Clarion*, Aug. 8; *Weekly Montgomery Confederation*, July 27.

[8] *Montgomery Weekly Mail*, July 20; *Macon Beacon*, July 18; *Mobile Register*, quoted in the *Southern Advocate*, Dec. 19; quoted in the *Montgomery Weekly Mail*, June 1.

[9] *Weekly Vicksburg Whig*, April 18, May 23; *Weekly Panola Star*, May 10; *Southern Advocate*, Sept. 26; *Autauga Citizen*, July 26. In the early fall western wheat was bringing up to $10 a bushel in northern Alabama, *Southern Advocate*, Sept. 26.

that within two months, eight out of ten families would be both out of corn and without money to purchase supplies.[10]

Accounts out of Mississippi were equally gloomy. "In many localities they report starvation staring the people in the face unless something is done to supply the deficiency of breadstuffs." By September conditions in the southeastern counties had so deteriorated that one paper captioned its article on the region, "A Famine in Mississippi." Most alarming in either state were the ominous threats of armed rebellion heard in Barbour County, Alabama. The county had experienced food shortages since March and the subsequent drought placed the poor in an untenable position.

> We have been informed from reliable authority that in the lower part of this county the people are reduced to the most straightened [sic] circumstances in consequence of the scarcity of provisions. The suffering is confined chiefly to the poorer classes who have not the means of providing themselves with the wants of life; and we understand that if provision is not made immediately to secure those wants unto them, they will take them by force of arms from those who happen to have them.[11]

To head off such potentially dangerous confrontations between the haves and have-nots, as well as for humanitarian considerations, planters in some areas organized Relief Clubs. The purpose of these clubs, as explained by General William B. Trotter of Quitman, Mississippi, whose plan received the most publicity, was to provide corn for the indigent free of cost. Every member of the clubs was called on to contribute $100 for the purchase of western corn to be distributed by local officials. Only those with the ability to pay would be

[10] *Wedowee Mercury*, quoted in the *Southern Advocate*, May 23; *Montgomery Weekly Mail*, July 20; *Mobile Register*, quoted in the *Southern Advocate*, Dec. 19.

[11] *Grenada Rural Gentleman*, quoted in the *Weekly Vicksburg Whig*, Sept. 12; *Weekly Panola Star*, Sept. 13, *Clayton Banner*, July 26.

charged for the supplies. Public relief meetings were held in Mississippi's Wilkinson County, her central regions, and in Pickens County, Alabama. At best these measures afforded only temporary and stopgap relief. More substantial assistance was delayed until March of 1861. Then at the behest of Governor Pettus the Mississippi Secession Convention empowered the boards of police in the central counties to issue bonds on borrowed state funds to meet the corn famine.[12]

The severity of the drought made a food crisis inevitable, but some were quick to stress that the planters' overemphasis on cotton had made a bad situation worse. Foreseeing bad times ahead, the Eufaula *Spirit of the South* entreated planters back in March to plant more corn, less cotton. Another Eufaula paper, commenting in June on the area's heavy importations of foodstuffs at high prices from the Midwest, put much of the blame on the planters. Concerned only with cotton and slaves, they went into debt to buy corn. The same theme was harped on by the *Alabama Reporter* which felt it was shameful that Talladega should be dependent on the North for its hay and on Indiana and Illinois for its corn. If high prices continued, added the paper, perhaps the planters would be taught a lesson. In July the *Mail* singled out the small planters in the uplands for censure. They "cannot be induced to believe that their first duty is to secure an abundance of the necessaries of life; so they plant all their best lands in cotton."[13]

Despite all the homilies and criticisms directed against the cotton mania, Southern agriculture was less diversified in 1860 than it was a decade earlier.[14] The social prestige and

[12] *Missouri Advertiser*, quoted in the *Pickens Republican*, Aug. 2; *Weekly Vicksburg Whig*, Dec. 5, *Macon Beacon*, July 18; *Pickens Republican*, Oct. 18; John K. Bettersworth, *Confederate Mississippi: The People and Politics of a Cotton State in Wartime* (Baton Rouge, 1943), 21.

[13] Quoted in the *Clarke County Democrat*, March 8; Eufaula *Express*, quoted in the *Southern Advocate*, June 6; *Alabama Reporter*, April 19; *Montgomery Weekly Mail*, July 27.

[14] Robert R. Russel, *Economic Aspects of Sectionalism, 1840–1861*

economic power which cotton growing alone could provide were too enticing a goal to permit advocates of reform to make much headway. Cotton, the cash crop, and the one that promised fastest relief from debts, was planted on the best soil and received the most care. Many planters believed it was cheaper to import corn and pork than to divert land and slaves for their production. In addition, poorly developed home markets offered little incentives to produce foodstuffs for local consumption. These economic factors, plus the eventual absorption of the agricultural reform movement into the greater enthusiasm for Southern nationalism, precluded any significant changes in the countryside. As James Bonner has pointed out, agricultural reform began in the 1840's with an intense devotion to the soil and a critical attitude toward the plantation system. It then moved toward crop diversification and economic nationalism. By the late 1850's it was stressing cotton and an aggressive stance on slavery.[15] Thus, with the reform impulse having been channeled off into political directions, the ravages of the 1860 drought were exacerbated by an agriculture which stressed cotton over food production.

All segments of Southern society suffered from the drought. As usual the hardships fell heaviest upon the poor. By the late summer they were running out of food with no means of purchasing any. While most small planters had credit connections to draw on for food supplies, they were nonetheless in a sharp economic bind. A bad cotton crop meant insufficient revenue to pay off last year's debts, and the need to purchase essential foodstuffs forced them to go into greater debt to tide them over the winter. The inability of the country-

(New York, 1960), 203; for lack of crop diversification in Alabama, see Charles Davis, *The Cotton Kingdom in Alabama* (Montgomery, 1939), 187; for Mississippi, Bettersworth, *Confederate Mississippi*, 136.

[15] *DBR*, xxv (1858), 390; Hilliard, "Hog Meat," 135; James C. Bonner, "Advancing Trends in Southern Agriculture, 1840–1860," *AgH*, xxii (Oct., 1948), 248–259.

side to pay for goods and services hurt the merchant. By July many were "complaining that they can make no collections because all the money of their customers is necessarily expended in buying provisions." Nearly everyone felt the pinch of tight money. From Greensboro, Alabama, Sereno Watson wrote his brother Henry in October that many planters were experiencing hard times because a short crop of poor cotton and carry-over debts from last year had made money tight. "Montgomery papers report money scarcer than it has been since '37. Some of the reports may be exaggerated for political effect."[16]

As a result of the bad crops, lack of credit, and deepened debts, the economy was strained to muster enough capital to meet the cost of importing and distributing food supplies. The wealthy in town and country were obviously in the best shape to withstand the dislocations imposed by the drought. Large planters, with their holdings in the Delta and on bottom lands, had the highest percentages of fertile, well-watered lands. Many owned plantations in more than one county and hence had insurance against a ruined crop in one locality. In general, the northern sections of Alabama and Mississippi were less affected than areas farther south. They had the double advantage of a bit more rain during the summer and an agriculture with more emphasis on grain production.

In an election year the response to the drought was bound to become enmeshed in politics. No one could argue that the deep South had any choice but to draw heavily on the Northwest for food supplies and animal feed. Even rabid Breckinridge newspapers took solace in the fat granaries of the free states. They assured their readers "there is no necessity for the alarm which seems to pervade some sections as to the scarcity of provisions next year. The immense grain crop of the northwest will certainly keep the price of provisions down to a lower figure than it has been during the past year." After noting that the price of supplies had skyrocketed, the opposi-

---

[16] *Montgomery Weekly Mail*, July 27; Sereno Watson to Henry Watson, Oct. 8, Henry Watson, Jr. Papers, DU.

tion press reasoned that only a fool would deny that the cotton states' very dependence on the North for indispensable food supplies was a most powerful argument for the preservation of the Union. In the words of the *Alabama Reporter*, a Bell paper:

> An exchange suggests that a worse time for precipitating the cotton States into a revolution than the present, could not have been selected. The grain crop of the cotton States is almost a complete failure, Alabama, it is believed, will not make corn enough to bread the people for six months. Georgia, Florida, Mississippi[,] Louisiana and Texas make similar reports. The very States that are expec[ted] to lead in the precipitating movement, will be compelled to draw on the free States of the North West for corn to supply them during the coming year.

The implication was no less clear to the *Southern Advocate*, the leading Douglas paper in the Tennessee Valley. With pride it reminded the voters that the Northwest was Douglas territory, the home of good, staunch Democrats who would defend the rights of the South at the same time they were feeding her in her hour of need. Pointing to the food shortages in Barbour County, a Breckinridge stronghold, the paper asked: "Would a revolution of the Cotton States help the people there?"[17]

Logic may have been on the side of the Bell and Douglas forces, but the Breckinridge press employed sarcasm, appeals to Southern chauvinism, and outright denials of any economic crisis to counteract their opponents' argument. This became especially clear during the campaign for delegates to the secession conventions. In Pickens County, Alabama, the co-operationist nominee, Henry Stith, expressed concern over the plight of the indigent should immediate secession close off the Northwest as a source of food. This problem could

[17] *Clayton Banner*, Aug. 30; *Alabama Reporter*, Aug. 16; *Southern Advocate*, July 25, June 6.

.not be wished away, he added, since the South now had less food per capita than at any time in recent memory. All this elicited from the secessionist *West Alabamian* was the following *non sequitur*. "Would it not have made Lord North laugh? if our revolutionary fathers had said with solemn earnestness, 'wait till we make a little more corn and raise a few more hogs and then we will resist British oppression!' " Almost every December issue of the Vicksburg *Daily Evening Citizen* was filled with accounts of utterly destitute Northern workmen being thrown out of work by pitiless employers. In antithesis, all Southerners, both white and black, were portrayed as happy and contented. Few journals ignored the famine conditions in Mississippi more explicitly than the *Brookhaven Advertiser*. In reply to a Whig paper's question as to what the people would have to eat next year should Mississippi immediately secede, the *Advertiser* answered: "Why, neighbor, corn cake and bacon on week days, and hog and hominy on Sundays."[18]

II

Only the incessant reports of ubiquitous abolitionists plotting slave revolts, setting fires, and poisoning wells upset the South's equilibrium more severely than the drought. Concern over internal security, always a powerful impulse in a slave society, reached pathological proportions during 1860. In a public essay J. A. Turner, a planter-industrialist from Georgia, heatedly warned: "What we are called on to guard against now—this very day, this very hour—is the host of abolition emissaries who are scattered abroad throughout the length and breadth of our land, who permeate the whole of Southern society, who occupy our places of trust and emolument."[19]

[18] *Pickens Republican*, Dec. 13, *West Alabamian*, Dec. 19; quoted in the Vicksburg *Daily Evening Citizen*, Dec. 18.
[19] *DBR*, xxix (1860), 70.

In one respect the hysteria that swept the slave states in 1860 was an intensification of traditional Southern fears.[20] Travelers in the late 1850's were taken aback by the hostility and suspicion they encountered. W. H. Venable and Alexis E. Holcombe, two students from Ohio, toured the lower South in the winter and spring of 1858 and soon discovered it was ill advised to be seen talking with slaves or to be identified as Northerners. They met a Yankee schoolmaster in a small Mississippi town who had been given thirty days to leave or face a lynching. The Englishman Robert Russell was told by a Northern peddler that he always tried to pass himself off as a Southerner while in the South. If his customers knew he was from the North, they would assume he was an abolitionist and conduct no business with him. James Stirling, a crusty Scotch Presbyterian, was disgusted with the hostility he found. "I had to endure more espionage on the Mississippi than in Austrian Italy. There you have to do only with paid professional spies: here your fellow-traveller is your spy." Olmsted observed that Southerners rarely felt secure. A planter with whom he spent the night near Natchez insisted on barricading their door, even though it made the room too warm. "You don't know," he said, "there may be runaways around."[21]

Olmsted quickly perceived the source of the South's insecurity. It was not outside agitation; that was only a scapegoat. Rather, it was the overwhelming need for control de-

[20] Ollinger Crenshaw, "The Psychological Background of the Election of 1860 in the South," *NCHR*, xix (July, 1942), 260–279, and Donald Brooks Killey, "Harper's Ferry: Prelude to Crisis in Mississippi," *JMH*, xxvii (Nov., 1965), 351–373. Steven Channing, *Crisis of Fear, Secession in South Carolina* (New York, 1970), 17–57, examines this phenomenon in South Carolina.

[21] W. H. Venable, "Down South Before the War," *Ohio Archaeological and Historical Publications* (Columbus, 1893) Vol. ii, 488–513; Robert Russell, *Economic Aspects of Sectionalism, 1840–1861* (New York, 1960), 301; James R. Stirling, *Letters from the Slave States* (London, 1857), 58; Frederick Law Olmsted, *A Journey in the Back Country* (London, 1860), 30.

manded by the system itself. This could be seen in the fearsome police machinery prevalent in Southern towns with their citadels, sentries, passports, grapeshot cannons, and daily public whippings. Slaveholders were apprehensive of the unsettling examples that free labor could have not only on their slaves but on poor whites who received no direct benefit from slavery. Unable to acknowledge their most deeply held fears, they blamed outsiders for their feelings of insecurity and told the nonslaveholders that all danger was from outside the system. Any real or imagined threat to slavery immediately invoked alarms of a slave revolt. "Any great event having the slightest bearing upon the question of emancipation is known to produce an 'unwholesome excitement,' even in parts of the country where the slave population is, and has least reason not to be, peculiarly contented with its condition."[22]

The presidential election of 1856 had been one such great event. The election marked the emergence of the Republicans as a national party. Their candidate John C. Frémont was a rank abolitionist in the eyes of the South. The mere posing of this new threat of abolitionist control of the national government's executive branch was sufficient to touch off rumors of slave revolts and mob action throughout the South. In the early fall of 1856, a wave of panic swept Kentucky and Tennessee, where it was most intensive, spread into Missouri and Arkansas, then the Gulf States, and, completing the cycle, hit Virginia and Maryland by December.[23]

The events of that year were a prelude to the excessive anxieties of 1860. The intervening years had witnessed John Brown's raid in the fall of 1859 with its incalculable damage to the South's sense of security. The shock waves set off by

[22] Olmsted, *Journey*, 451, 474–475.

[23] Harvey Wish, "The Slave Insurrection Panic of 1856," *JSH*, v (May, 1939), 206–222. Wish felt there must have been some actual slave plots but added (p. 222), "much can be explained away by a counter-thesis of a panic contagion originating in the unusual political setting of the year."

the raid left Southerners psychically unbalanced as rumors of impending abolitionist invasions became rampant and never ceased.

In December, 1859, Governor Pettus of Mississippi ordered the militia to muster at Jackson to defend the state arsenal from a rumored invasion. Even Vicksburg's "oldest and most quiet citizens" were alarmed at a report that their city was to be attacked on Christmas night. These pillars of the community met at the office of Brooke and Smedes on December 5, 1859, and decided to enlarge the military forces, have the swamps north of the city searched for guns and suspicious persons, and impose a special tax on slaves of up to $1 a head to finance these measures. A committee of ten was formed and they rushed off to Jackson that night to secure approval for their plan from the county's three representatives in the state legislature. The strong opposition of Representative William C. Smedes, who "smelt disunion and fire eating," was the deciding factor in the plan's veto by the Whig representatives. The committee itself had second thoughts and only three members argued in behalf of their military preparations.[24] The conservatism of the Whigs and their sure knowledge that talk of slave uprisings would most benefit the Democrats had defused a dangerous situation that might have thrown Vicksburg into panic.

The South went into 1860 with its nerves taut and the excitement of the campaign heightened the tensions. Benjamin F. Riley recalled that his county of Conecuh, Alabama,

> was convulsed by the canvass. Little else was done this year, than discuss politics. Vast crowds would daily assemble at the places of popular resort, to canvass the questions at issue. Stump speaking was a daily occurrence. Men were swayed more by passion than by calm judgment.

Out of Texas in early July came reports of a widespread and fiendish abolitionist conspiracy to burn down towns and to

[24] James Roach Diary, Dec. 5, 1859, SHC; Warren County's three members in the legislature were Whigs.

166

supply slaves with strychnine for use in their masters' wells. Highlighted by the press and political orators, the news reached into every corner of the South. Deep in the interior of Alabama Sarah R. Espy recorded in her diary the dreadful state of affairs. "The country is getting in a deplorable state owing to the depredations committed by the Abolitionist especially in Texas; and the safety of the country depend[s] on who is elected to the presidency." Closer to home, the menace could appear anywhere. The *Sumter Democrat* noted in September that their region's good fortune in being spared insurrectionary plots was at an end for "now they have been discovered almost immediately upon us." The paper mentioned the discovery of hidden arms in Greene County, the arrest of an itinerant abolitionist in Wilcox, and the rumor of an abolitionist soap dealer in Sumter. The threat was so pervasive, the South so overrun with abolitionist agents, that eternal vigilance was demanded of all. Warned the *Montgomery Advertiser*: "Let us not slumber whilst the enemy is now prowling about our very doors, and the torch of the incendiary lights up the whole Northern horizon in the onward march of the enemy."[25]

Just who was the enemy and what were his actual crimes? In their zeal to identify the culprits and pass the word along, Southern newspapers usually included some specifics; wherever possible they gave a full description of the guilty party, much like that of a wanted poster. The following individuals were listed by the Alabama and Mississippi press in 1860—a journeyman harness maker; an Irish ditcher; a shoemaker and daguerrean artist, born in England and a former resident of New York; two Methodist preachers; someone passing himself off as a Virginia schoolteacher but probably a New England Yankee; a minister-doctor (believed to be a leader of the abolitionist Friends Z. Society); a doorkeeper

[25] Benjamin F. Riley, *History of Conecuh County, Alabama* (Blue Hill, Maine, 1964: reprint of the 1881 Columbus, Ga., ed.), 153; Sarah R. Espy Diary, Aug. 11, 1860, ADAH; quoted in the *Montgomery Weekly Advertiser*, Sept. 19, *ibid.*, Oct. 10.

of a canvas show on the Fair Grounds; a soap dealer; a Southern hired hand; a clock mender disguising himself as a Baptist or Methodist preacher depending upon the locality; a German traveler; the keeper of a whisky shop; a traveling corn doctor; an Ohioan; a Canadian painter; an itinerant for the Middle Deer Creek Colored Mission; a New Yorker; an Englishman; a traveling Northern ambrotypist; the seven-member Clark family who were forced to flee Texas; a Philadelphia drummer; a German; two Northern mechanics; some gypsies; and railroad hands.

Most of these men were strangers, itinerants just passing through. Sometimes their presence alone was sufficient to touch off a near panic. Poor William Blucher had a harrowing experience. "This German was travelling the road leading from Claiborne, Miss., to Shubuta, Miss., and walked into the yard of Edward P. McCarty, in an impudent manner, which alarmed his lady, who ran to a school near by and alarmed the scholars, who ran home and reported an insurrection among the negroes, which was all false." Blucher was questioned by a hastily arranged committee which ascertained that all he wanted in the first place was a drink of water. He was not punished, only ordered to leave the county as soon as possible.[26]

Few of the accused held a trusted position in Southern society. Not only were they outsiders, but they were usually engaged in lowly occupations. They catalyzed a region's fears and frustrations in part because they were different, surrogates for the hostile outside world which harshly condemned the South as immoral and threatened, so it seemed, to plunge the section into a race war. With little property, they had neither roots nor standing in the community. With few friends to defend their good name and possessing little to which the average Southerner aspired, they made tempting scapegoats.

Undoubtedly there were some native abolitionists and sympathizers in the deep South but they were rarely men-

[26] Paulding *Eastern Clarion*, Oct. 10.

tioned in newspaper accounts. Olmsted met a slaveholding abolitionist in Mississippi and asked if it was safe for him to be vocal about his beliefs. "I've been told a hundred times I should be killed if I were not more prudent in expressing my opinions, but, when it comes to killing, I'm as good as the next man, and they know it. . . ." Hundley felt that most Southern abolitionists came from among poor whites. He was most likely, Hundley reasoned, to be the son of a hard working yeoman family with one of the parents, usually the mother, of poor white origins. The future abolitionist was bright and ambitious and fiercely resented his lack of status and the contempt shown him by those of a higher social class. Eventually he would raise his status but the old resentment would continue to smolder until it vented itself in abolitionism. Hundley had no sympathy with such a type. "We know he may delude himself into the belief, that the social position of his father as well as that of his mother's family connection is due mainly to the institution of slavery; but is this an excuse for treason?"[27] Support for Hundley's contention comes from the stress placed on the poverty of those belonging to the alleged Friends Z. Abolition Society. While there are serious doubts as to whether such a society ever existed, its format of pitting poor against rich apparently conformed to the Southerner's conception of how such a society would be organized. Moreover, many also believed that the poor urban immigrants were potential abolitionists.

The actual deeds of the accused abolitionist emissaries fell far short of the imagined heinous crimes for which the newspapers publicly condemned them. Loose talk and unauthorized contact with slaves, frequently combined in the charge of "negro tampering," were the indiscretions which led most of the suspected abolitionists into trouble. The journeyman harness maker was found "holding improper conversation with slaves" on two consecutive nights and was stripped and

[27] Olmsted, *Journey*, 179–180; Daniel Robinson Hundley, *Social Relations in Our Southern States* (New York, 1860), 275–276.

169

whipped as punishment. The Montgomery *Mail* was indignant over such leniency. "We protest against the whipping of these people. They should be hanged, or not touched." Patrick Kelly, an Irish ditcher, was arrested near Alenton, Alabama, on suspicion of plotting a revolt. Kelly had foolishly gotten drunk the night before in the slave quarters and was cared for by a slave who had also been drunk. His behavior nearly resulted in a mob hanging some blacks. A letter writer to the pro-Douglas newspaper in Montgomery emphasized that the Kelly incident was "no jest[,] it did actually occur right in a Breckinridge community, and many more will, no doubt, be heard of before the election."[28]

In this atmosphere strangers had to be very careful of what they said. Individuals were detained, tried by vigilance committees, sometimes whipped or tarred and feathered, and ordered to leave an area immediately for such crimes as paying compliments to John Brown, supposedly telling the slaves they would be freed once Lincoln was elected, or simply declaring oneself a Republican.[29] A New Yorker, by the name of Bundy, was arrested while traveling on a railroad in Florida because his fellow passengers had overheard him say he was a Republican. Bundy "swore on his knees" that he had no idea what Black Republican meant. His impassioned plea saved him temporarily but the *Mail*, whose inflammatory invective was consistently in a class by itself, felt that the committee should reconsider the case and "vote him 'a halter gratis.' " Thought control reached its logical conclusion when a committee in Carroll County, Mississippi, conducted a meeting "to try the purport of language" used by one Edward Mortimer, an Englishman. He was deemed an abolitionist and a "nuisance" and ordered to leave the county.[30]

[28] *Clarke County Democrat*, Aug. 16; quoted in *ibid.*, Aug. 16; *Weekly Montgomery Confederation*, Sept. 21.

[29] *Semi-Weekly Mississippian*, April 27; *Montgomery Weekly Advertiser*, Nov. 7; *Weekly Vicksburg Whig*, Aug. 29.

[30] Montgomery *Mail*, quoted in the *Semi-Weekly Mississippian*, Sept. 25; *ibid.*, Sept. 25; *Semi-Weekly Mississippian*, Sept. 28.

At least the abolitionists who exposed themselves through careless language could be identified and expelled, but what of those who were silent and devious, lurking everywhere, scheming, setting fires, and hiding arms for the eventual uprising? These fiends, the South convinced itself, were truly the gravest threat of all. Suspicious fires were reported in many localities and the entire towns of Crystal Springs, Mississippi, and Port Hudson and Minden, Louisiana, were said to have burned down. Towns organized vigilance committees to examine all transients and rid themselves of all incendiaries. One committee bought a small cannon, fired it every night at nine o'clock, and automatically arrested anyone found on the streets after that hour "as dangerous and suspicious characters." So inhuman was the enemy supposed to be that he was even charged with using cemeteries to further his ends. One popular story concerned the burial of a coffin filled with arms and ammunition. The culprits, a roving band of gypsies in one version and a stranger with a deceased brother in another, had received permission from the local authorities for the burials and would have succeeded were it not for the excessive weight of the coffins. In both cases they made good their escape before their treachery was unearthed.[31]

By the summer and fall of 1860 whites in Alabama and Mississippi seemed incapable of retaining their self-control. Fears of slave revolts were so intensely felt that they tended to feed self-fulfilling expectations. Typical were the details of an attempted "Negro insurrection" near Plattsburg, Mississippi, in a heavily Democratic and drought stricken east central region of the state. On September 20, C. D. Kelly was chastising his cook-woman. Probably in an effort to lessen her punishment, she blurted out the particulars of a slave plot in which, after the cooks had poisoned the white families' food, the field hands were to rise up with the assistance of

---

[31] *Mississippi Free Trader*, Sept. 24, Oct. 29; *Weekly Vicksburg Whig*, May 9; *Natchez Daily Courier*, Sept. 4; *Memphis Argus*, quoted in *Weekly Montgomery Confederation*, Nov. 30.

friendly whites and strike for their freedom. Kelly promptly gathered up five or six men and went around the plantations indiscriminately whipping slaves. His neighbors then formed a vigilance committee of twenty-five with an executive council of twelve to meet weekly and pass judgment on the suspected culprits. The council was specifically authorized to punish or acquit as it saw fit since it was believed that "the law is too tardy in its course, even if it could be effectual in its process, to obviate the dangers and punish the offenders in troubles of this character." A week later, after many slaves were rounded up and interrogated, the cook-woman's story was substantiated by "those that were induced to make confessions. . . ." As a result thirty slaves and a white man were arrested. The latter was G. Harrington, a traveling ambrotypist, born and educated in the North. He had been under suspicion since his arrival in the county back in May because of his frequent conversations with slaves. At least one slave and a white, identified only as "an abolition artist," probably Harrington, were hung.[32]

Another documented slave plot occurred in late August near Talladega, Alabama. Two local citizens were arrested on charges of inciting the slaves to burn down the town and murder its inhabitants. A day after his arrest one of the accused, Lem Payne, was hauled out of jail and lynched at three in the morning. The slaves were said to be restless because of their belief that a Black Republican was a Negro.[33] Supposedly, if one were elected president, he would set them free. Despite many arrests only one slave was convicted and sentenced to be hung. The excitement lasted about three weeks and was widely mentioned in the press of Alabama and Mississippi. At its height the uproar was described by a Whig planter, James Mallory: "Vigilance committees have been formed in every neighborhood, great prejudice against

[32] This account was taken from a letter dated Oct 1 printed in the *Semi-Weekly Mississippian*, Oct. 9.

[33] As a note of derision, Southerners invariably referred to the Republicans as Black Republicans.

northern people, political discussions have been no doubt the cause of the present disturbances." The events at Talladega sparked insurrection scares in other Alabama towns. In Greensboro,

> there were all sorts of reports brought in yesterday, respecting plots among the Railroad hands & neighboring negroes for a "rising" tonight,—with very little foundation as it seems, perhaps none at all,—& this with numerous accounts, no two alike, of recent [uprisings] at Selma & Talladega—where they have hung a white man on negro evidence,—set the town all in a stir.

The regular and volunteer patrols canvassed the countryside around Greensboro for slaves; of those who were jailed one was guilty of leaving his plantation and "having been caught in bed with his wife without a pass."[34]

The Plattsburg and Talladega incidents were the best documented slave revolts in Mississippi and Alabama. Since there is no reason to believe that they were atypical of other revolts, they can serve to illustrate the basic nature of this threat and the white reaction to it. Immediately apparent was the absence of any actual armed uprising. For all the talk of murder and pillage, none occurred; the plot was always nipped in the bud. Nonetheless the reaction of the white community to the slightest hint of trouble among the slaves was a spontaneous consensus that there existed an imminent danger which at all costs had to be combatted. Such a consensus and the fear that underlay it were institutionalized in the formation of vigilance committees which, by their very presence, prolonged the sense of crisis. By ferreting out additional plotters, these committees reinforced the community's belief that a real and pervasive threat to their safety existed. The fear of abolitionists was so intense that it led to a readiness, almost a need, to believe in their presence. This belief mani-

[34] *Alabama Reporter*, Aug. 30; James Mallory Diary, Aug. 28, SHC; Sereno Watson to Henry Watson, Sept. 4, Henry Watson, Jr. Papers, DU.

fested itself first in rumors, then in the discovery of suspected plotters, regardless of the fact that no act of violence had been committed, and finally sustained itself by creating extralegal vigilance committees which gave final credence to the omnipresent fears.

These committees had a sweeping mandate from the people. One formed at Laurel Hill, Mississippi, on September 11 for Neshoba and Leake Counties saw its functions as twofold: "to insure protection against the secret Emissaries of the Abolitionists of the North, and to prevent the promulgation [sic] of sentiments prejudicial to the Institution of slavery, as it exists among us." At its organizational meeting the committee pointed to abolitionist outrages in Kansas, Virginia, and Texas "where the Bowie-Knife, the Torch and Poison seemed to be the favorite means of general extermination. . . ." Since they had reason to believe the enemy was in their midst, they resolved "to bring such offenders under the laws of our country, and where its arm may prove too short, or imbecile, to dispense the punishment due to such crime, we will fall back upon the common law of our nature, self-preservation, that ours, like other lands, may not have to mourn in sack-cloth and ashes." It was also resolved to tighten up and rigidly enforce the slave patrol laws. Small slaveholding farmers dominated the committee, which was chaired by William A. Slaughter, a Breckinridge politician. They must have taken their task seriously for a month later the Vicksburg *Whig* reported that five whites and forty slaves had been arrested in Leake.[35]

Vigilance committees appeared throughout the deep South. From the few whose membership can be determined, it seems that the Whigs avoided them. The committee from Collirene Beat in Lowndes County, Alabama, was led by planters active in the Breckinridge campaign. Out of a special slave patrol of twenty-five men, which was formed in early September to help police the town of Greenville, Alabama, ten were active

[35] *Semi-Weekly Mississippian*, Sept. 25; *Weekly Vicksburg Whig*, Oct. 10.

174

politically—seven for Breckinridge and three for Bell.[36] More-over, charges that these committees were guilty of political intimidation came only from the Bell and Douglas press. John Hardy of the *Selma Sentinel* accused a mob of whipping a local resident, James G. Bagley, solely because he was a Bell man. The Breckinridge Selma *Issue* retorted with the account of a meeting which resolved public thanks to those individuals responsible for the act. They charged that Bagley fully deserved his whipping since he had publicly stated that if secession and war ever came, he would go back North and fight against the South. The Vicksburg *Whig* claimed that the vigilance committee of St. Martinsville, Louisiana, had ordered Judge Lewis, a Bell elector, out of town after he had given a Bell speech.[37]

These excesses were not uncommon, though usually they were directed against slaves and strangers. An irate citizen informed Samuel M. Meek, district attorney for Mississippi's sixth district, of an outrage committed near Buckhorn on July 24 and 25. A group of men calling themselves a vigilance committee went down to the home of a Mr. Hastings and in his absence arrested and carried off John, one of his slaves. The following day, with neither the jurors nor the witnesses duly sworn, John was hung. Other slaveholders were concerned over the safety of their property. J. E. Taliaferro wrote Governor Pettus complaining of the brutal murder of one of his slaves while he was absent. He believed that the culprit was in the vicinity of Huntsville and asked Pettus to issue a requisition to the Alabama governor for the proper writ to extradite the man back to Mississippi. "The shooting of negroes by overseers, and other irresponsible men of the country, is becoming too common a thing among us, and I deem it nothing more than right that an example shall be made of this man Mooney."[38] Hilery J. Lanier was tried

---

[36] Hayneville *Chronicle*, Sept. 20; *Greenville Southern Messenger*, Sept. 19.

[37] Selma *Issue*, Oct. 17; *Weekly Vicksburg Whig*, Aug. 29.

[38] A. S. Kirk to Samuel M. Meek, Sept. 29, Samuel M. Meek and

at a public meeting in Georgetown, Mississippi, and found guilty of slave tampering. The committee readily admitted "the evidence is not such as to convict him in a court of justice" but still felt there was no reasonable doubt of his guilt. They ordered Lanier to leave the county within thirty days and, if he failed to comply, his punishment was decreed as one hundred lashes on the bare back for every additional day that he remained.[39]

Even when their actions degenerated into mob rule, the vigilance committee had the full support of the Breckinridge press. Frequently these editors whipped their readers into a frenzy and then demanded ever stronger actions to suppress the abolitionist threat. The Montgomery *Mail* argued that the South was infested with abolitionist agents because she had been too slow to hang the fiends as soon as they were caught. "The whole South needs a *thorough expurgation*. . . . Now the time has come for wiping these creatures out. Let a strict search *everywhere* reveal them—it *will* bring them to light—and let THE ROPE do the rest." The *Clayton Banner* was equally emphatic in its demand for the lynching of all suspected abolitionist emissaries.

> We are utterly opposed to the nonsense of rail-riding, taring [sic] and feathering, &c., or any other mere indignity; it only makes the Devil in them more fierce. If strangers come among us and by their voluntary conduct render themselves liable to a *just suspicion*, it is their own fault or misfortune, and our *safety demands* that *all such be rendered incapable of prowling about and putting into execution their apparent designs.*[40]

Family Papers, MDAH; J. E. Taliaferro to Gov. Pettus, Aug. 21, Governors' Records, MDAH. The extent to which violence directed against slaves was a reflection of class divisions among the whites has yet to be investigated. Such murders of slaves might well have been one means by which the poor whites could vent the frustrations of their stunted role in Southern life.

[39] *Semi-Weekly Mississippian*, Nov. 2.

[40] *Montgomery Weekly Mail*, Aug. 31; *Clayton Banner*, Sept. 27.

Too many segments of Southern society responded affirmatively to these calls for acts of violence. In so doing they were continuing a pattern of mob rule that Clement Eaton has traced back to the beginnings of the abolitionist movement in the 1830's. He noted that after 1831 Southern mobs and vigilance committees were a major factor in governing and shaping local public opinion. The continued existence of frontier conditions, the custom of dueling, illiteracy, and, above all, the antislavery controversy were cited as reasons for the persistence of mob rule. Another dimension of this phenomenon was given by Charles Sydnor who pointed out that certain features of Southern society—the exclusion of black testimony in the courts, the rural isolation, the planter's authority, and an unwritten social code which governed personal relations—sharply curtailed those areas of life directly governed by the written law. In the West geographic distances restricted the scope of the law; in the South the same was accomplished by the social order.[41] These arguments help explain the Southerner's flouting of law in 1860. Conditioned to view the law more in terms of custom and the felt needs of the community and less in terms of a written statute that had to be obeyed, the Southerner in time of crisis was quite prepared to resort to extralegal devices which his community demanded as necessary for its own self-preservation.

The Whigs were disturbed by the growing reign of terror and correctly ascribed much of the blame to the Breckinridge forces. Wherever possible they tried to exert a moderating influence. The Vicksburg *Whig* explained that unfounded stories of slave revolts were commonplace in every presidential election year and "gotten up for party purposes." When investigated, nine out of ten reports turned out to be unfounded. During the furor in Talladega over the slave revolt the Bell paper, the *Alabama Reporter*, stressed: "We hope that prudent councils will prevail and that those who are

[41] Clement Eaton, "Mob Violence in the Old South," *MVHR*, xxix (Dec., 1942), 351–370; Charles S. Sydnor, "The Southerner and the Laws," *JSH*, vi (Feb., 1940), 3–23.

177

officiating will keep the excitement within proper bounds."
A few days later it reported that calm was being restored
but warned that many exaggerated accounts had been circulated. The Whigs were very skeptical of most of the tales
recounting abolitionist intrigue. The Montgomery *Post* said
it would report all the facts relating to the Texas insurrection,
but meanwhile it had only "loathing and contempt" for those
who would use these troubles for political gain. This skepti-
cism was shared by the Douglas press.

> The horrid accounts of Abolition plots and incendiary
> and murderous designs of the Abolitionists, as at first dis-
> closed in the Breckinridge papers, have been so frequently
> modified, and sometimes altogether contradicted, that we
> have felt a reluctance to copy them in our columns, as they
> have been the means of causing a great deal of unnecessary
> and painful anxiety and alarm to our wives and children,
> especially.[42]

The sensationalism of the Breckinridge press was one both
of rhetoric and content. The Texas troubles, according to the
Mississippian, were unparalleled for "diabolism of intent—
revolting cruelty—and savage ferocity. . . . The details present a fertility of wicked invention and an exuberance of de-
pravity sickening to all but the most hardened in vice, villainy,
cruelty and corruption." No disturbance was too trivial to be
overlooked. In Occaquan, Virginia, some Republicans openly waved a Lincoln banner and attempted to raise it on a
Liberty Pole. To the *Mississippian* this was nothing less than a
renewal of the irrepressible conflict. A week later the paper
admitted that nothing much had come of the affair since the
Republicans had refused to fight, but the impression of a
narrowly avoided battle remained.[43]

In extensive press coverage the plot in Texas, which was

[42] *Weekly Vicksburg Whig*, Oct. 24; *Alabama Reporter*, Aug. 30;
Montgomery Weekly Post, Aug. 1, Sept. 26; *Weekly Montgomery
Confederation*, Nov. 2.
[43] *Semi-Weekly Mississippian*, Aug. 3, 1, 7.

characterized by the Breckinridge editor Jefferson Buford as an example of "practical Lincoln-ism," received the most play. The Talladega revolt ran a close second. The Breckinridge treatment of this affair angered J. J. Seibels of the Montgomery *Confederation*. He quoted from an item in the *Blountsville Pioneer* to show how accounts of the insurrection were grossly exaggerated by claims that eight slaves were hung and thirty more were incarcerated and how it was used for political effect; voters were urged to rally behind Breckinridge or face more abolitionist emissaries. Seibels asked "in what way a dissolution of the Union is to prevent the evils complained of?" Scare tactics were also employed by the *Clayton Banner*. "If an organized band of Abolitionists are bold enough to fire Southern towns before Lincoln's election, what may we expect from them afterwards? Think of this, men of the South, before you consent to divide the votes of the Southern States in November."[44]

The lurid exploitation of the abolitionist menace by the Breckinridge press was difficult to counteract because the vast majority of Southerners hated and feared the antislavery movement. To be soft on abolitionism or to downplay it as a real danger was promptly equated with being untrue to the South by condoning murder and racial warfare. Thus, the most politically expedient tactic of the Whigs and Douglasites was to accuse the Breckinridge party of, in effect, being the abolitionists' best friend by its constant emphasis on, and exaggeration of, the abolitionist menace. The Vicksburg *Whig* ridiculed the Democrats for raising a storm over a few book peddlers who were accused of selling what the Democrats called incendiary books. "Well, it appears that every Democratic member of Congress from this State is engaged in circulating the late speech of Senator Seward. . . . If a speech of Wm. H. Seward is not an incendiary document, what is?" The Brandon *Herald* replied for the Breckinridge forces. In its coverage of the Bell state convention it charged the prin-

[44] *Clayton Banner*, Aug. 9; *Weekly Montgomery Confederation*, Sept. 28; *Clayton Banner*, Aug. 9.

cipal speakers—W. L. Sharkey, A. R. Johnston, and General Henry—with a willingness to submit to a Republican victory and with denouncing the fire-eaters in harsher terms than the abolitionists. "It does not require the ken of a prophet to tell to which side they will len [sic] when the contest comes. *It would be well for slaveholders to watch these men, lest managers of an underground railroad may be found in their midst at some future day.*"[45]

And so the recriminations reverberated throughout the campaign. The Whigs were labeled quasi-abolitionists for making light of the abolitionist outrages and not declaring in advance that Lincoln's election would be cause enough for secession. They answered in kind by likewise stigmatizing the Democrats for leading the slaves to believe that hordes of abolitionists were fighting for their freedom, that they had an invincible political friend in the North who would set them free, and that even native Southerners harbored abolitionist sentiments. "There is a law in this State against inciting slaves to rebellion. Every man who charges a portion of his fellow-citizens with being abolitionists, violates it, and deserves to be arrested and trotted off to jail.[46]

III

The taproot of the near panic in 1860 lay deep in the Southern consciousness. It is clear that the whites' sense of insecurity and numbing fear that they might lose control over the slave population were major factors in the paranoia with which so many reacted to the mere rumor of abolitionist emissaries. But this savage and intense response was also part of a community effort to promote internal unity and to maintain self-respect by exposing and then punishing those alleged agents of the outside world which had morally condemned the

[45] *Weekly Vicksburg Whig*, April 4. Ever since Seward's "Irrepressible Conflict" speech in 1858, he had been denounced in the South as the archetypical abolitionist Republican. Quoted in *ibid.*, May 9.

[46] *Ibid.*, Oct. 31.

South and threatened to unleash the slaves upon Southern whites.[47]

If the South were to protect herself against her enemies, white unity was essential, and any doubts over the morality or social utility of slavery had to be expunged. Incoming literature was rigidly censured, laws against manumission were tightened, and native antislavery groups, such as the Quakers of North Carolina, were forced to leave or cease spreading their beliefs.[48] Consequently, although the author of a pro-slavery polemic once wrote Governor Pettus of Mississippi that some Southern Christians were "greatly troubled in conscience by the continued reiteration that 'slavery is a sin'— and free their slaves," there is very little evidence that many Southerners harbored guilt feelings over slavery. Excessive brutality was condemned, but harsh discipline as an integral control mechanism was accepted by all. Thus, when an overseer stripped naked and publicly whipped a slave on the streets of Mobile, he was adjudged guilty in court not for any cruelty but for the social indiscretion of performing the act in the view of a lady.[49]

Nonetheless attitudes over the institution were beset with contradictions and tensions. Slave traders and overseers, those most intimately connected with the dehumanizing and strictly economic side of slavery, had low status. As Thomas B. Carroll put it: "Money made in buying and selling human beings, though slaves, was not quite so good as money made other-

[47] For this insight into the Southern response I am indebted to an article by David Brion Davis which dealt with similar social phenomena, "Some Themes of Counter-Subversion: An Analysis of Anti-Masonic, Anti-Catholic, and Anti-Mormon Literature," *MVHR*, XLVII (Dec., 1960), 205–224.

[48] Clement Eaton, *The Freedom-of-Thought Struggle in the Old South* (New York, 1964), *passim*.

[49] Thomas McGill to Gov. Pettus, Nov. 18, 1860, Governors' Records, MDAH; *Mobile Daily Advertiser*, June 17, 1860. The most subtle and carefully delineated case for Southern guilt is presented by Charles G. Sellers, Jr., "The Travail of Slavery" in Sellers, ed., *The Southerner as American* (Chapel Hill, 1961).

wise."[50] Moreover, Southerners had a curious aversion to referring to slaves as slaves; most commonly they were just "negroes." Up to the Civil War newspapers still found it necessary to publish tracts defending the morality of slavery.

These tracts typically began with an affirmation of the writer's Christianity. "I have no idea of being unprincipled—I have no idea of being delinquent in my moral duties—I have no idea of deliberately violating the moral government of God," assured William Grayson, a Yazoo planter. In reconciling his Christianity with his role as a slaveholder, Grayson elaborated on the stock themes of the Southern defense of slavery. On the one hand, he was simply a passive agent of God's will. "The curse of the involuntary servitude of the African race arose in the legislation of God in consequence of the filial irreverence of one of the sons of Noah" (Ham, whose progeny subsequently became black). However, Grayson was also careful to distinguish between a moral and an immoral evil. The former was ordained by God in consequence of man's fall from grace and in this sense slavery was morally evil, just as were all social relations, "*all conditions of life.*" Northern Methodists who sought the extirpation of slavery as an evil were as wrongheaded as they would be if they attempted to reform the evils of childbirth, a social necessity which involved pain and danger but which was still moral since it was God's will. These antislavery critics had made two basic errors. Although the true Christian knew that man could not alter God's will, the abolitionists held to the infidel belief that social evil was wrong (not imposed by God), and this resulted in the false notion that civil legislation could eliminate evil. Since the abolitionists lacked faith in the efficiency of the Gospel, they naturally were guilty of an unchristian impatience with the moral evils of life. According to Grayson, man should wait on the Gospel "until these evils can be ameliorated by *Christ's method, by moderation,* which

[50] Thomas B. Carroll, *Historical Sketches of Oktibbeha County* (Gulfport, Miss., 1931), 84.

looks to the voluntary or free abandonment of what is wrong upon the part of rebellious men and women."[51]

The moral justification of slavery became part of white folklore since the masses had been indoctrinated for a generation by their ministers to view slavery as a divinely ordained institution which was a blessing to the blacks. Of course, as Cassius Marcellus Clay once noted with biting sarcasm, "If it [slavery] be proved damnable, the church South stands in the same category. What, therefore, is to be done? They must defend themselves, lest a white cravat become disreputable, and the boys in the street hoot at a black gown!" In its extreme form this defense assumed a religious fervor. Brown of Mississippi "would spread the blessings of slavery like the religion of our divine master" and newspapers argued that it would be far better for the African taken off an illegal slaver to remain in this country under a master than to be returned to his own land and a life of "the most abject servitude without the benefits of civilization and Christianity."[52]

The result of these ideological defenses was not so much an acceptance of slavery as a positive good so much as it was a fatalistic resignation that slavery could not be abandoned or greatly modified without far greater social, racial, and economic evils. An Alabama farmer undoubtedly spoke for many of his class when he told Olmsted that "I don't think it's right to hev 'em slaves so; that's the fac—taant right to keep 'em as they is." But he had prefaced his criticism with the standard racial refrain that emancipation would mean the

[51] *Semi-Weekly Mississippian*, June 19, July 3, Nov. 13, 1860. A stimulating reinterpretation of the proslavery advocates as men alienated from their society has been offered by David Donald, "The Proslavery Argument Revisited," *JSH*, xxxvii (Feb., 1971), 3–18.

[52] James W. Silver, *Confederate Morale and Church Propaganda* (New York, 1967), 13–24; Cassius Marcellus Clay, *The Writings of Cassius Marcellus Clay: Including Speeches and Address* (New York, 1848), 434; A. G. Brown speech, *Mississippi Democrat*, Oct. 2, 1858; *Semi-Weekly Mississippian*, June 12, 1860.

destruction of white values and civilization inundated by thieving black masses too lazy to work and eager only for the chance to marry white women. That was why he "wouldn't like to hev 'em freed, if they was givine to hang 'round."[53]

However much the South may have been at peace with herself, the abolitionists would not leave her alone. They played upon the latent class antagonisms between slaveholders and nonslaveholders, impugned the morality of Southerners, and posed a physical threat to safety. At a time of crisis such as a national political campaign when slavery was daily discussed in the press and by the parties, the abolitionist menace was magnified since Southern values were constantly being debated and the future of slavery called into question. Southern doubts over their ability to maintain slavery intensified, and the need for white unity grew ever more urgent. By telling themselves they were infiltrated by abolitionist agents, Southerners were at least able to give a tangible expression to their fears and find an outlet for their concerns over security as the increased number of exposed emissaries became a perverse testimony to the effectiveness of internal vigilance. Any qualms over slavery were crushed as social conformity became a fetish. Planters and dirt farmers, town and rural dwellers banded together in what was not just a negative act of self-defense but a positive assertion of Southern values which physically and directly freed their communities of all who would disturb the social order or moral consensus.

By 1860 the Southern need for respect from others was overpowering. The Protestant South was a land of religious orthodoxy deeply resentful of any imputations that she was less moral than others. In responding to attacks on her peculiar institution by arguing back that slavery was good, she was not necessarily cloaking inner feelings that slavery was really wrong. More logically, this was a reaffirmation, both to themselves and to the outside world, of the essential goodness of their institutions which, being moral, fully deserved the re-

[53] Olmsted, *Journey*, 217–219.

spect of others. This demand for approval colored much of the opposition to the federal laws which treated as pirates those who participated in the African slave trade.

> The people of the South, through representatives in the federal Legislature, must assert their rights, without hesitation or equivocation. It will be difficult for the northern people to regard slaveholders and slavetraders (half the southern people trade in slaves directly or indirectly) as their moral and religious equals or to treat them as such, so long as the southern people tamely permit their own government to brand them as pirates, or no better than pirates, or something worse.[54]

The dignity of the Southerner might be affronted anywhere. In Congress slavery was constantly on trial and denounced as barbarous and unchristian. Although they generally shared the Southerner's racism, Northern critics combined their prejudice with their own vision of Christian progress to ridicule the paternalistic and humane image of slavery. In a classic expression of sectional antagonisms during the spring of 1860, Owen Lovejoy, a Republican congressman from Illinois, reminded the slaveholders that "the principle of enslaving human beings because they are inferior is this: if a man is a cripple, trip him up; if he is old and weak, and bowed with the weight of years, strike him, for he cannot strike back; if idiotic, take advantage of him, and if a child, deceive him." In his most cutting remark, he condemned slavery as an institution which "drags slaveholding communities further below the plane of the Christian civilization of the age, then the civilization which the slave receives elevates him above the plane of heathenism by being in these Christian communities." Barksdale of Mississippi and Martin of Virginia retorted that the "meanest slave" was Lovejoy's superior and that he would be hung "as high as Haman" if he ventured into the South. But the damage had been done. Once again the South

[54] *Semi-Weekly Mississippian*, April 10, 1860.

185

had seen her ideals and moral self-esteem defamed as she was told that her alleged virtues were her very real shame.[55]

Not even attendance at a statistical conference in England could insure the Southerner freedom from gross insults. Mississippi's two delegates walked out of such a meeting in protest after their attention had been called to the presence of a black delegate who, to their disgust, was praised by many in attendance.[56] There was no escaping the scorn and abuse. The South was becoming western civilization's moral pariah and no one would let her forget it. Her reply was an increasingly vigorous defense of slavery as a positive good and a concomitant statement of its right and need to expand. There is no reason to read guilt into either reaction. Any society under attack magnifies its virtues, and the South had very sound reasons to believe that she had to expand for her survival. In clear conscience she turned the tables on the abolitionists and accused them of being the moral transgressors by conspiring "to teach their progeny to regard us as barbarians and semi-savages, themselves, assuming to be responsible to other nations and to Deity, for our conformation to their standard of morality which places us upon a social equality with slaves, and gives to negroes equal authority with ourselves in affairs of government. . . ."[57]

Although this moral counterattack buttressed the Southerner's sense of his own worth, he was still prone to panicky revulsion over the abolitionists since the latter posed such a direct threat to his status. As previously noted, it was the Breckinridge press which exaggerated and exploited the abolitionist menace. Political considerations were foremost since

[55] *Congressional Globe*, 36 Congress, 1 Session, Appendix, 203–207. Such attacks were one of the prime grievances listed by Southern political meetings. See the *Daily Mississippian*, Dec. 1, 1860.

[56] *Semi-Weekly Mississippian*, Aug. 21, 1860. Southern hypersensitivity on the issue of white supremacy was revealed by the extensive press coverage given to the incident.

[57] From resolutions passed at a secessionist meeting in Newton County, Mississippi, on December 8; Paulding *Eastern Clarion*, Dec. 19.

the creation of an omnipresent external threat could be used as a justification for the South's uniting behind the party which exposed the enemy and promised to eliminate him. Who would dare suggest compromise with a foe who was plotting insurrection in one's very midst? But these political motives were predicated on the interests of those who formulated party policy, the politicians, and those who responded to this policy, the constituency. The Breckinridge party, with a higher percentage of young slaveholding politicians than either the Whigs or Douglasites, and a voting coalition more heavily centered in the newer, rapidly growing cotton areas, spoke for those who were most sensitive to the abolitionist threat and most prone to hyperbolize it. Their self-respect as slaveholders, a recently acquired status, was denigrated by the abolitionists and, lacking the buffer of self-assurance secured through time by the older planters, this status was more vulnerable to attack. With their hopes for advancement not yet abandoned, still in the process of accumulating rather than protecting property, these younger social elements were prepared to believe the worst of those pledged to destroy the basis of their future wealth and position. The older Whig planters and farmers either already enjoyed an accepted pre-eminent prestige or were more rooted in their social station. They feared the abolitionists, but this fear was more detached, less hysterical than in younger slaveholders since the abolitionist was not a deterrent to a goal they were still actively seeking.

The masses of Southerners, uneducated and isolated, joined the abolitionist witch hunt because the mere suggestion of his presence brought closer to home the spectre of emancipation. For they were the Southerners who would be thrown into bitter economic, and perhaps even social, competition with the freed blacks. No longer would their self-respect automatically be reinforced by a color line separating free from slave. To be deprived of their legally defined superiority over the blacks was equated with unthinkable degradation. "How would you like to see one of your children on an equality with an african.

187

(jest think of it, when I do it raises all my spunk, and I would fite my self before I would submit to it)."[58]

The drought and the abolitionist panic heightened tensions throughout the South and were major contributors to a state of mind which was prepared to accept any change as one for the better. In looking back over the year, James Mallory, who had witnessed the destruction of his crops and the slave insurrection scare in Talladega, remarked that "altogether it has been one of the most remarkable ones in the history of this country. . . ."[59] The year was climaxed by secession.

[58] Frank A. Thert to his brother, Dec. 29, 1860, Crutchfield—Fearn —Steele Family Papers, MDAH.
[59] James Mallory Diary, Dec. 31, 1860, SHC.

FIVE

MOBILIZING FOR SECESSION

LINCOLN'S election, the dreaded eventuality, occurred on November 6, and the reaction in the South was all that the conservatives had feared. In little more than two months, Alabama and Mississippi seceded along with the other cotton states. Secession stands as the only political revolution in the history of the American republic. Its roots may be traced back about as far as one wishes, but the immediate justification and impetus for the movement were a direct outgrowth of the 1860 presidential campaign.

I

The electioneering provided a forum for a politics of intensity which led to an inevitable climax in the election itself. All parties agreed that the election was the most important ever to be held. Whigs and Douglasites viewed it as the last chance to preserve the Union and protect slavery. The election transcended mere politics, argued the Montgomery *Post*.

> The issue now before the people of Alabama is not simply whether the State shall be carried by Bell, or Breckinridge, or Douglas; but that other and greater question is before them—Union or disunion; for as the State may go in the present election, so it will be most likely to go when the question of secession shall be presented directly to them, as it will be in the case Lincoln should be elected.[1]

According to this logic, a vote for Breckinridge was a vote for disunion. Had not Southern extremists, out of political greed and personal ambition, deliberately split the Democratic

[1] *Montgomery Weekly Post*, Oct. 31.

189

party at Charleston so as to ensure the election of a Republican as a minority president, thus forcing the issue of secession upon the South? "I know they say this was not their object," wrote Alexander Stephens, a leading Georgia Whig. "But it seems to me this will be the result." The Breckinridge press portrayed the election as a national referendum which would decide the safety of the South and the future of her institutions.[2] The stickler was that either could be guaranteed only by a Breckinridge victory, and his defeat would leave the South with no recourse but to secede.

The party faithful responded in record numbers to the campaign appeals. Newspapers, pamphlets, speeches at political barbecues, village crossroads, and from the pulpit flooded the voters with the issues and increased political awareness. Benjamin F. Riley, the historian of Conecuh County, Alabama, reported an unusually great demand for political literature during the campaign and a keen interest in the issues. "This, acting in concert with the frequent discussion of these principles on the stump, in the social circle, and in the homes, awakened inquiry and stimulated the mental energy of the youth of the country."[3]

The voters were reminded up to the very last moment of what was at stake. On election day at Herbert's precinct, Neshoba County, Mississippi, a banner was held in front of the polls by two little brothers of the Walsh sisters. These young women of the county had prepared a banner emblazoned with the number of stars and stripes corresponding to the slave states. Its motto read: "Death rather than submission to a Black Republican government."[4]

[2] *Natchez Daily Courier*, May 29; Alexander H. Stephens to Henry H. Armstrong, Aug. 25, Henry Halcomb Armstrong Correspondence, ADAH. "In two weeks the most important political battle ever fought in the Republic will take place—a battle upon the issue of which depends the institutions of the South and the safety of our homes and firesides"; *Mississippi Free Trader*, Oct. 29.

[3] Benjamin F. Riley, *History of Conecuh County, Alabama* (Blue Hill, Maine, 1964: reprint of the 1881 Columbus, Ga., ed.) 146.

[4] Paulding *Eastern Clarion*, Nov. 14.

The voter participation reflected the campaign's intensity. In Alabama 79% of all the eligible voters turned out at the polls. By comparison, 70% had voted in 1856, the first time that a Republican was in the running, and only 47% in the uninspired Pierce-Scott election of 1852.[5] The same story unfolded in Mississippi—a rising interest in national elections during the decade culminating in a participation rate greater than 80% in 1860. The cities and the poorer isolated regions in the mountains and pine belts had the most lethargic voters and prevented the turnout in both states from approaching 85%.

News of Lincoln's election was instantly met throughout the deep South with the resigned feeling that the final crisis was at hand. All the fears and frustrations brought to the surface by the campaign now had a focus. "The die is cast—No more vain regrets—Sad forebodings are useless. The stake is life or death—," exclaimed Mrs. Chesnut of South Carolina on hearing the news. Others set down in their diaries their belief in the inevitability of secession and the impending confrontation with the North. "It is now certain that Lincoln is elected, and the Southern States are making ready to withdraw from the Union. There are fearful times in store for us, I greatly fear, for war will be the final result of such withdrawal." A minister's wife recorded that her family was expecting the call to arms any day. But she was ready. "In anticipation of the coming storm, I['ve] been practicing shooting, assiduously."[6] This spontaneous reaction was the secessionists' first great advantage. Given Lincoln's election, everyone expected that something had to be done.

The party press reacted in predictable fashion. True to their word, the Breckinridge editors immediately called for

---

[5] Clanton W. Williams, ed., "Presidential Election Returns and Related Data for Ante-Bellum Alabama," *AR*, II (Jan., 1949), 68–73.

[6] Mrs. Mary B. Chesnut, *A Diary from Dixie*, quoted in J. G. Randall and David Donald, *The Civil War and Reconstruction* (Boston, 1961), 136; Sarah R. Espy Diary, Nov. 25, ADAH; Margaret J. Gillis Diary, Nov. 15, ADAH.

secession. "Mississippi knows her duty and will discharge it to the letter," reported the *Mississippian*. To the editor's "great joy," sentiment for secession was said to be nearly unanimous throughout the state. At once this paper, the most influential Democratic voice in Mississippi, insisted that secession should be immediate and carried out "independently of all others." Other Democratic papers repeated refrains on the same theme. The time for talk was over, "there is no alternative left the South but to strike bravely for liberty, property, honor and life, or basely submit to the domination of the trained hands of hungry fanatics who will be precipitated upon her to eat out her substance and sap the pillars of her prosperity." The racist appeal was brought front and center. Property in slaves would be destroyed and the freed blacks, placed on political and social equality with whites, would barbarize Southern civilization. Southerners could "not consent to bow down to abolition rule, and quietly see the south free-negroised, and themselves[,] their wives, and their children degraded to the level of the free negro."[7]

The conservatives had a herculean task simply to be heard. They decried the Republican victory as loudly as any, though taking some satisfaction in blaming the outcome on the Breckinridge forces. Charging that the disunionists did not want Breckinridge elected, the Tuscaloosa *Independent Monitor* insisted that his role was "to carry a large number of slave States, and thereby afford them a pretext for attaching all the Southern States to the coattail of South Carolina, and let her drag them out of the Union." The disunionists might yet be foiled, hoped the conservatives, if only the South were patient enough to avoid rash action. Secession meant revolution and war and the South owed it to herself to be dead certain she was right before embarking on such a dangerous course.[8]

[7] *Semi-Weekly Mississippian*, Nov. 9; Hayneville *Chronicle*, Nov. 8; Pratteville *Southern Statesman*, Nov. 10.
[8] Tuscaloosa *Independent Monitor*, Nov. 16.

The Vicksburg *Whig*, one of the more outspoken papers, dared to argue that, unacceptable as the Republicans undoubtedly were, they at least deserved to be judged by their performance. Lincoln's party had not committed any overt aggressive acts against the South. If they were to do so while in office, the South would still have the courts and the Constitution as a means of defense. Failing in that, the South would then be justified in claiming secession as the last resort. At stake were Southern rights in the federal territories, and secession now would be *"a total abandonment of all our interest in these Territories forever."* Equally bold was the stand of the Canton *American Citizen*. Its editor, John F. Bosworth, deplored the Republican triumph but felt that secession would be a calamity "a thousand times more to be deplored." He counseled acquiescence to the new order and added that there was no need to panic. Lincoln could do little without Congress, which was in the hands of conservatives. The South could afford to wait four years and then unite behind a conservative national man, like Douglas or Alexander H. Stephens of Georgia. Secession would not bring any further security to slave property nor gain the South another foot of slave territory.[9]

Most of the other conservative papers were less sanguine in their suggestions. They admitted that Lincoln's election was too grave a threat to let pass without resistance. Since in their view immediate and separate state secession entailed too many risks, they recommended that the South either wait until a bloc of states could go out in a cooperative movement or give the North one last chance by presenting her with a list of Southern grievances drawn up by a convention of all the slave states.[10]

The initial party reactions foreshadowed the lines of debate in the upcoming elections for delegates to the secession con-

[9] *Weekly Vicksburg Whig*, Nov. 14; *American Citizen*, Nov. 10.
[10] *Alabama Reporter*, Nov. 15; Tuscaloosa *Independent Monitor*, Nov. 23.

ventions. These conventions provided the mechanism for secession. Called by the respective Southern governors, they were empowered to decide the mode of resistance for their states, including the ultimate power of deciding for or against secession. South Carolina, Alabama, and Mississippi were in a perfect position to lead this movement. Their governors— William H. Gist, A. B. Moore, and John J. Pettus—were personally and politically committed to secession in the event of Lincoln's election. On October 5 Gist confidentially had written his fellow chief executives informing them that he would ask the legislature to call a special convention to take his state out of the Union if faced with Republican rule. Accordingly on November 5, when the legislature met to choose presidential electors, Gist made his request; it was compiled with on the thirteenth.[11] Moore and Pettus had already been authorized by their legislatures as early as February to take such action. Moore had an express mandate to call a special convention and Pettus could point to legislative resolutions deeming an abolitionist victory so serious a menace "as to justify the slaveholding States in taking counsel together for their separate protection and safety." On November 14, a day after South Carolina's action, Moore and Pettus issued calls for conventions.[12]

The first organized pressure for secession in Alabama had come on November 10 out of a meeting in Montgomery.

[11] James G. Randall and David Donald, *The Civil War and Reconstruction*, 2d ed. (Boston, 1961) 135; Charles E. Cauthen, "South Carolina's Decision to Lead the Secession Movement," *NCHR*, xviii (Oct., 1941), *passim*.

[12] Joint Resolution of the Alabama Legislature, Alabama, *Acts, of the Seventh Biennial Session of the General Assembly of Alabama* (Montgomery, 1860), 685–687; letter of Feb. 10, 1860, submitting the resolutions of the Mississippi Legislature, Governors' Records, MDAH. Technically, Moore waited until Lincoln was officially elected by the presidential electors on December 5. On November 14, however, he made known the dates he would set for the election and the meeting of the convention. Ralph A. Wooster, *The Secession Conventions of the South* (Princeton, 1962), 51.

Young slaveholding Breckinridge lawyers from southern Alabama controlled the meeting which publicly asked Moore to state his intentions in regard to the legislative resolution which called for a state convention. Moore replied on November 12 that Alabama and the rest of the slave South must secede to ensure their future security. In Mississippi Pettus' only doubt was over the means of secession. On November 22, four days before the special legislative session was to convene, he arranged for a private meeting in Jackson with the state's Congressional delegation. L.Q.C. Lamar and both senators, Davis and Brown, argued for joint secession not to take effect until March 4. The other representatives, Singleton, Barksdale, and Reuben Davis, held out for separate state secession to take effect immediately. Pettus cast the deciding vote in favor of the latter position.[13]

Jefferson Davis' defeat at this meeting was significant for it marked the second time during the year that the advice of the recognized national leader of the Mississippi Democracy was disregarded on a crucial issue. Davis had failed to stem the Mississippi delegation's defection at Charleston and now once again was in the backwater of state politics. Just how far out of touch he had become can be seen in his November 10 letter to R. B. Rhett, Jr. Isolated on his plantation, Davis made it clear that he had not discussed Lincoln's election with others and was offering his personal opinion on what should be done. He then proceeded to misread totally the political climate in Mississippi. He doubted that the legislature would either call for a state convention or appoint delegates to a Southern convention. Given a convention of the slave states, the proposition to secede without support from neighboring

[13] Carrollton *West Alabamian*, Nov. 28; Edward Mayes, *Lucius Q. C. Lamar: His Life, Times, and Speeches, 1825–1861* (Nashville, 1896), 86–87; Reuben Davis, *Recollections of Mississippi and Mississippians*, (Boston, 1891), 391–392; O. R. Singleton to W. T. Walthall, July 14, 1877, Dunbar Rowland, ed., *Jefferson Davis, Constitutionalist: His Letters, Papers, and Speeches* (Jackson, 1923), Vol. VII, 560–562. Representative John J. McRae did not attend.

states "would probably fail." Should South Carolina secede first and not be followed, then Mississippi probably still would not secede because she lacked a good ocean port and had no geographic connection with South Carolina. The only way that solitary action by South Carolina could trigger secession throughout the South would be as the result of Northern overreaction in the form of an invasion or naval blockade of the state. If the North simply used her navy to collect duties from ships before they entered Charleston, there was little the rest of the South could do. *"My opinion is, therefore, as it has been, in favor of seeking to bring those States into co-operation before asking for a popular decision upon a new policy and relation to the nations of the earth."*[14]

Party leaders at the local level, in contrast to Davis, had a firm grasp of where Mississippi politics were heading. From Pontotoc County Charles D. Fontaine reported "Mississippi will secede. Our people are ripe for it." During the canvass in this county the Breckinridge Democrats had been frank and said they were for secession should Lincoln be elected. "I at least took the ground we would secede first and cooperate afterwards." Fontaine insisted that the people were far in advance of their leaders. All they demanded was some known figure to step in and lead. "Who will show the way[?] Where is Jeff Davis? Will he let this auspicious moment pass by?" In reference to the key Jackson meeting of November 22 Pettus was urged by G. Harrison of Columbus to accept nothing less than immediate secession. "If we have any remedy, either in, or out of the Union it can only be made available in my opinion, by prompt secession." Cooperation would not work and besides, "without the consent of Congress, how can the States South make treaties, or union with each other, unless each one for it self first withdraws from the Federal Union? & resumes its individual sovereignty—."[15]

---

[14] Davis to R. B. Rhett, Jr., Nov. 10, Rowland, ed., *Jefferson Davis*, IV, 541–543.

[15] Fontaine to Pettus, Nov. 12, and Harrison to Pettus, Nov. 18, Governors' Records, MDAH.

The keynote of this early response, as foreseen by Fontaine, was the decision against cooperative action. As explained to Pettus by State Rights Gist, William's brother, "do not ask for a Southern Council, as the Border and non-acting States would out vote us & thereby defeat action. Let your State immediately assemble in Convention." What the governors wanted was an informal assurance that they would not be acting alone. "If your Legislature gives us the least appearance that you will go with us," Governor Gist wrote Pettus, "there will not be the *slightest difficulty* and I think we will go out at any rate."[16]

Having absorbed the lessons of the past, the secessionists were worried that action formally dependent on the prior agreement of other states would lead to delay and stalemate. Southern resistance to the Compromise of 1850 had collapsed once Georgia declared for acceptance. The gathering of slave state delegates at Nashville in June of 1850 turned out to be harmless, and its most radical act was a resolution asking for the extension of the 36°30′ Missouri line westward to the Pacific. Delay and the cooperative approach had proved fatal to the secessionists in South Carolina and Mississippi, the originators of the Nashville movement. The nine months between the call for the convention and its actual meeting had given the conservatives time to mount a counterattack and the formula of united action had enabled the moderates to restrain those who opposed any compromise.[17]

More recently, futility had marked South Carolina's proposal for a Southern convention to protest John Brown's raid and the growing strength of Republicanism. Only Mississippi responded affirmatively. She appointed delegates, but the convention, scheduled for Atlanta in June of 1860, never took place. Hiram Cassedy, one of the delegates, was dis-

---

[16] S. R. Gist to Gov. Pettus, Nov. 8, Governors' Records, MDAH; Wm. H. Gist to Gov. Pettus, Nov. 6, *ibid.*

[17] Holman Hamilton, *Prologue to Conflict, The Crisis and Compromise of 1850* (Lexington, 1964), *passim*; Avery Craven, *The Coming of the Civil War* (Chicago, 1966), 264.

gusted by such a show of weakness. Furious over the farce which the Atlanta Conference had become, he concluded that it meant either that Mississippi's sister states did not realize the dangerous position they were in or, if they did, were dangerously apathetic. He declined to go under these circumstances. "I almost despair for the South and think that our fate is fixed for a want of unanimity in action among ourselves." For a confirmed secessionist the Nashville and Atlanta affairs could only reinforce the advice of John A. Quitman, given in 1858 shortly before his death. If secession were to succeed, the initiative must come from the cotton states and be accomplished by state conventions which would declare the right and need of secession. The actual act should be deferred only until each state had conferred with others as to the best time and manner of withdrawal.[18]

By the middle of November the campaigns for the secession conventions were under way. The elections revolved around the counties. Each Alabama and Mississippi county was entitled to as many delegates in their conventions as they had representatives in the lower house of their state legislatures.[19] The opposing candidates most commonly referred to themselves as secessionists or cooperationists. The former were the immediate and separate state secessionists with a platform which demanded no delay and no prior binding agreements with other states. The latter insisted that the slave states, faced with a common threat, should react in a united manner. Safety demanded that secession should be by blocs of states, not individually. At the very least, if the state conventions decided on separate state secession, then the issue should be referred back to the people for their approval or rejection. This group also encompassed the conditional

[18] Avery O. Craven, *The Coming of the Civil War*, 1st ed. (Chicago: Phoenix, 1960), 413; Cassedy to Gov. Pettus, May 24, 1860, Governors' Records, MDAH; Quitman to John Marshall, Feb. 1, 1858, J.F.H. Claiborne, *Life and Correspondence of John A. Quitman* (New York, 1860), Vol. II, 253.

[19] Alabama, *Acts*, 686; *Journal of the Senate of Mississippi. Called Session* (Jackson, 1860), 19.

unionists who argued that one last effort should be made to save the Union. They wanted all the Southern states to meet in convention and draw up a list of grievances to be presented to the North as an ultimatum. In practice, contemporaries usually did not draw a distinction between the two terms. Walker Brooke, a Mississippi delegate from Warren County, explained: "I was elected by a large majority, as what is known as a co-operationist—which means, as I understand it, one who was in favor of united Southern action for the pur· pose of demanding further guarantees from the North, or, failing in that, the formation of a Southern Confederacy."[20]

Under these circumstances secession would appear to have been a foregone conclusion. The right or desirability of secession was rarely called into question during the campaign debates, only the best means of bringing it about. However, it is very misleading to lump together all Southerners as secessionists since this overlooks the paucity of alternatives left open to the conservatives. Jeremiah Clemens, a key organizer of the cooperationist movement in northern Alabama, explained in his correspondence during the crisis the problems faced by the conservatives and the only tactics by which they might stem secession. Since "our friends outside of the State may sometimes misunderstand our tactics," he outlined his plans to Senator Crittenden of Kentucky on November 24. His initial hope that the combined Bell-Douglas vote would carry Alabama had been proved wrong. This setback was compounded by some important Bell politicians, such as Thomas H. Watts of Montgomery and William S. Phillips of Dallas, announcing for immediate secession: "their defection will do ten times the mischief it would have done if they had supported Mr. Breckinridge." The reaction against Lincoln had been so intense, Clemens continued, that if the election for delegates were held tomorrow, two-thirds would vote for separate state secession. The conservatives had but one

[20] *Proceedings of the Mississippi State Convention, Held January 7th to 26th, A.D. 1861 . . .* , by J. L. Power, Convention Reporter (Jackson, 1861), 13–14.

chance. "*Time* is everything to us, & if we fail to gain that we are lost." Delay would enable passions to subside and give the South, gathered in a convention of the slave states, an opportunity to present her real grievances to the North. These injustices, headed by Lincoln's election on an antislavery platform, the North's personal liberty laws, and her refusal to obey the fugitive slave law, had to be redressed. Where possible, additional guarantees must be granted to protect Southern rights in the future. Cooperationists could not afford the luxury of debating the right or wrong of secession. "There are some prejudices which can not be removed—some opinions which, however irroneous [sic], can not be changed. To these we must withdraw opposition in the present crisis, or we shall lose all." Such an admission of secession's legality might also convince the North of the severity of the crisis.[21]

Two days later, in elaborating on these views to William B. Wood of Florence, Clemens pinpointed the difficulty. "We have before us the double duty of preserving the Union, & of obtaining redress for grievances, which undeniably exist, & security against other aggressions which we can not fail to see are impending." The mood in both sections had put Southern moderates in a bind. Active secessionists assumed that war would not result and that, even if it did, one Southerner could whip three Yankees. Northerners and those who voted for Lincoln—characterized by Clemens as the antislavery men, unmerciful fanatics, and those envious of what they believed to be a South filled with large slaveholders living in luxury and idleness—still refused to take the South's grievances seriously and thought secession was but an empty boast. Southerners had cried wolf too often in the past and now, for

---

[21] Clemens to Crittenden, Nov. 24, Crittenden Papers, LC. Appended to the letter was the Huntsville circular of November 19 calling for no opposition on the "abstract question of secession" but "a conference of all the Southern States before any act of secession is consummated." It was drawn up and distributed by Clemens and was affixed with 100 signatures.

the sake of safety alone, they must convince the North that they had the power to force them to obey the Constitution. Unless firm guarantees were now won, the South would be faced with the gradual weakening of slave interests until general emancipation was forced upon her. Clemens was pessimistic but saw his plan as the best hope for avoiding civil war and anarchy. Otherwise, the North would try to coerce a divided South. "They will not *call it coercion*, but that is what it will be. They will call it, the enforcement of the laws, & the alternative will be presented to us, of submitting to the collection of Federal revenue in our seaport towns, or assuming an attitude of armed rebellion."[22] Clemens had desperately groped for a policy which would protect both slavery and the Union, but, given the refusal of the Republicans and Douglasites to accept Southern demands, even his position would make secession virtually inevitable.

II

The secessionists had nearly all the advantages in what passed for a debate of the issues in the period between Lincoln's election and the convening of the state conventions. Dr. Moody, speaking at a precinct meeting in Tippah County, Mississippi, summed them up in his remark that the secessionists were "do somethings" and the Unionists were "do nothings." What the secessionists could do was considerable. Pressure exerted by the governors was of incalculable value in furthering the cause. As commanders in chief of their states' military forces, they could take decisive action which would force the issue and cut away all middle ground. On January 3, 1861, Governor Moore ordered the Alabama First Volunteer Regiment to occupy Forts Morgan and Gaines, and the United States Mt. Vernon arsenal in Mobile Bay. He had planned this move carefully. Two weeks earlier he had in-

[22] Clemens to Wm. B. Wood, Nov. 26, Samuel Alexander Martin Wood Papers, ADAH.

structed that the facilities be scouted and any troop or arms movements be noted. In a letter accompanying his seizure order, which he justified as an act of self-defense, he stressed: "You will of course perceive the necessity, as Alabama has not yet seceded, aside from any other considerations, of avoiding, if it be possible, the sacrifice of life." To the extent that it was feasible, all federal property was to be preserved and protected. The seizures went off without a hitch since the fortifications had been grossly neglected and were an easy prey.[23]

The conservatives, helpless to prevent a decision which was beyond their control, could only sit by and fume. "This act of the Governor of Alabama exceeds in usurpation of power any thing that has yet been done even in South Carolina," Thomas McClellan wrote his wife from the convention; "they passed their ordinance of Secession before they took the forts in that State, but here it is done two days before the assembling of the convention."[24]

Correspondence coming in to Moore and Pettus during November and December was filled with requests for arms from volunteer companies, free military advice, reports of revolutionary new military inventions, and offerings of service for the defense of the South. C. Williams of St. Louis waxed eloquent over the business possibilities inherent in the impending war. "Having, as I believe, made some important improvements in projectiles and fire-arms, it would seem that there could not be a more fitting opportunity for their introduction than the present time,—in the defense of right and justice against might and wrong." From the Mobile & Ohio

[23] Samuel Andrew Agnew Diary, Typed Volume III, Dec. 12, p. 193, SHC; Gov. Moore to Colonel J. B. Todd, General Order No. 1, Jan. 3, 1861; Moore to Todd, Jan. 3; and Todd to Moore, Jan. 4, John B. Todd Papers, ADAH, Thos. J. Butler to Moore, Dec. 24, 25, 1860; H. Maissey to Moore, Dec. 26, Governor A. B. Moore Correspondence, ADAH.

[24] T. J. McClellan to his wife, Jan. 6, 1861, Thomas Joyce McClellan Letters, ADAH.

Railroad came an offer to transport free of charge all munitions needed in the defense of Mississippi.[25]

The governors fanned the secession ardor by contracting through agents and personal friends for the purchase of all available arms. Secretary of War Floyd was besieged by Southern agents seeking arms. Particularly diligent was J. R. Powell, appointed by Moore as the munitions purchasing agent for the state of Alabama. In the space of a month, before he was hastily called back to Montgomery by Moore for apparently overextending himself, Powell had procured $46,452 worth of arms, including cannons, gun carriages, and caissons. By early January the Washington market was about picked clean. A cavalry company in Adams County sent a man to Washington to acquire arms but he was too late and found that Jefferson Davis, under Pettus' orders, had bought up all the Maynard Rifles, 800 in all. He asked Pettus to reserve 75 of them for the use of the cavalry. They were really needed, "the more particularly as we live where the plantations are large and the white population is comparatively small." The arms mania knew no bounds. A Clinton, Mississippi, merchant requested arms for a company of 14- to 18-year-old boys. A committee of cadets from an Alabama military institute tendered their services for the defense of the homeland, observing that "even a sling and two pebbles in the hands of a brave youth, may be instrumental in doing good service in a good cause."[26]

[25] C. Williams to Pettus, Nov. 26, and L. J. Fleming to Pettus, Dec. 1, Governors' Records, MDAH. The railroad was not about to bite the hand that fed it. Davis, *The Cotton Kingdom in Alabama* (Montgomery, 1939), 132, noted that the road's major source of earnings came from freighting cotton.

[26] Memorandum, dated 1861, in the J. R. Powell Folder, 1860, Moore Correspondence, ADAH; Wm. T. [?] Martin to Pettus, Jan. 8, 1861, and J. W. Welborn to Pettus, Jan. 22, Governors' Records, MDAH; Committee of the Cadets of the Glennville Collegiate and Military Institute to Moore, Nov. 30, 1860, Moore Correspondence, ADAH.

By the appointment of seccesion commissioners to each of the state conventions the governors neutralized the conservatives' demand for cooperation between the states. These commissioners were liaison men sounding out opinion at the various conventions and relaying back the information. The official instructions of W. S. Featherston, Mississippi's commissioner to Kentucky, were to inform the people of that state through their executive that Mississippi was preparing to hold a convention to consider her relations with the North, and "to express the earnest hope of Mississippi that Kentucky will co-operate with her in the adoption of efficient measures for the common defense and safety of the South." This was as far as the radicals would go toward "co-operation." One secessionist paper described the role of Stephen F. Hale, Alabama's commissioner to Kentucky: "Though he has no power to bind the States to a positive conclusion, yet he can ascertain sentiment and report to our convention. Another course would be illegal and treasonable. What more can 'co-operation' ask for? Let the people be undeceived. Cooperation as it is used, means *submission*, and nothing else." No commitments were to be made, no state's action was to be dependent on another's. Instead the commissioners acted as ambassadors of secession. They gave speeches backing immediate secession and their reports were used at propitious moments to influence the delegates. On December 19 the Vicksburg *Citizen* hailed the actions of the commissioners as "beginning to tell most powerfully in favor of immediate and separate secession." The governors had handled the situation perfectly for they had made sure that the men they appointed were top ranking politicians in their own right who were loyal to the cause of immediate secession. Of Alabama's sixteen commissioners only Robert H. Smith of Mobile was a cooperationist. All owned slaves and fourteen were or had been lawyers.[27]

[27] W. S. Featherston Paper, MDAH; *Alabama Beacon*, Dec. 21; Ralph A. Wooster, *The People in Power: Courthouse and Statehouse in the Lower South, 1850–1860* (Knoxville, 1969), 57, 89, 90; Vicks-

The radicals were able to ride the crest of prosecession sentiment generated by the presidential campaign. The pressure had been building for a long time. In Mississippi local meetings called in 1859 to nominate delegates to the Democratic State Convention provided a forum for secession arguments. Typical of the resolutions passed were those of a precinct meeting in West Point declaring that "in addition to the many wrongs, heretofore inflicted upon the South, the election of a Black Republican to the presidency, upon strictly sectional ground will be sufficient cause for the slave states to withdraw from the Union." The *Mississippi Democrat* in November, 1859, announced that the people through various county meetings had left no doubt that secession must be the South's response to a Republican triumph.[28]

By the summer and fall of 1860, the momentum was snowballing. Participants in a Breckinridge ratification meeting at Camden, Alabama, agreed with their state representative T. K. Beck that, should Lincoln and Hamlin be elected, "WE WILL RESIST THEIR INAUGURATION BY FORCE if necessary." Mississippi meetings in October were more specific in their means of resistance. A bipartisan group in Carroll County urged Pettus to call the legislature into special session on Lincoln's election and advised a conference of all the Southern states to determine what should be done.[29] No one could top the solution proposed by Jefferson Buford on the editorial page of the *Clayton Banner*. He argued that the South should wait no longer than three weeks after Lincoln's victory before the first states seceded. He hoped that such an ominous threat as an abolitionist president would suffice to

---

burg *Daily Evening Citizen*, Dec. 19; Durward Long, "Alabama's Secession Commissioners," *CWH*, IX (March, 1963), 57.

[28] *Mississippi Democrat*, May 28, Nov. 5, 1859.

[29] Quoted in Greenville *Southern Messenger*, July 18; *Semi-Weekly Mississippian*, Oct. 26, J. F. Terrell and D. C. Glenn, speaking at a meeting in Harrison County on October 15, made a similar demand but mentioned no conference of the slave states. *Ibid.*, Oct. 29.

invoke secession, but he had his doubts. Firm and ruthless action would be necessary.

> It must be by *coup d'etat*, or it will fall through and fail. South Carolina, with her abstractions and nonsense, will be calling for a convention and discussing, in field and fire-side, the question of disunion. This folly will end only in servile insurrections. Already the mere Presidential canvass is provoking them everywhere. The direct question of Union or Disunion, of slavery *vel non*, will inevitably give them birth. The Legislatures have sovereign power. . . . Let the Governor convene the ordinary Legislature; let it the next day declare the Union dissolved, and pass an act, de-nouncing as traitors, and putting out of legal protection, whoever may gainsay the measure. This done, and univer-sal suffrage, with its indispensable slavery basis, is perpet-ual. With any other course schism and bickerings ensue, and an enemy's party is organized among us, which, backed by the federal power, will effectually cripple and destroy us.[30]

As the governors well knew, the convention plan of secession was preferable to Buford's more drastic scheme. The result would be the same, but the calling of a convention elected by the people clothed the process with the aura of legality. A simple legislative declaration of secession had a much greater chance of creating a dangerous counterattack from the con-servatives.

The spontaneous sense of crisis invoked by Lincoln's elec-tion gave the secessionists tremendous leverage which they never allowed to wane. It was his failure to take into account this crisis psychology that made Davis' assessment to Rhett so woefully inadequate. The secessionists made no such mistake and through exhortations in favor of vigilance committees, companies of Minute Men, and volunteer companies main-tained the excitement at a fever pitch.

[30] *Clayton Banner*, Sept. 20.

On the eve of the presidential election the Montgomery *Confederation* accused the Breckinridge Democrats of openly flaunting their secessionist aims. The Breckinridge men were going around Montgomery wearing blue cockades "as an emblem of revolution and disunion"; their papers were urging the formation of Minute Men into clubs or associations, with the motto "Resistance to Lincoln is obedience to God." Conservatives had no doubts that these clubs were to be used as pressure groups for secession. "Clubs of Minute Men are being formed daily all through the south, whose duty it will be to aid any state to secede," wrote John Hall to his father Bolling, a cooperationist leader. The Vicksburg *Whig* denounced such organizations as unnecessary and incapable of accomplishing anything worthwhile. "Its purposes, if its objects are understood, are to do what the laws of the State have ample power to do. Whatsoever is proposed to be done beyond that, is unlawful."[31]

The Minute Men were organized to defend the South and to promote secession. Since there was no real enemy for them to fight until war broke out, they concentrated on the latter function during the secession crisis. The constitution and by-laws of the charter group in Edgefield, South Carolina, provided a model generally used throughout the South. Members resolved to "solemnly pledge 'our lives, our fortunes and our sacred honor' to sustain Southern constitutional equality in the Union, or, failing in that, to establish our independence out of it." To this resolve the *Mississippian* added the specific duty "not to permit a corrupt and mercenary band of office-holders to be installed in their midst by a Black Republican President." Under no circumstances was such a party to be allowed to gain a foothold. These potential traitors who would divide the South had to be stopped at once. "Strong remedies may be required, but the issue involves consequences of vast magnitude, and the remedy must be proportionate to the

[31] *Weekly Montgomery Confederation*, Nov. 2; John E. Hall to his father, Nov. 6, Bolling Hall Letters, ADAH; *Weekly Vicksburg Whig*, Nov. 14.

disease." The Minute Men of Copiah County, Mississippi, went further than most. They pledged to assist any Southern state to secede, even if Mississippi herself chose to remain in the Union.[32]

In addition to suppressing dissent, the Minute Men also played a direct political role. In Selma they constituted the nucleus for the immediate secessionist party. Formed on November 7, the organization soon decided to meet every Wednesday evening and to wear the blue cockade. The club was structured along party lines, complete with committees for finance and correspondence. Although lip service was given to cooperation and concerted action, it was thought "impolitic and impracticable to make such cooperation and concert a condition precedent to the secession of Alabama." On November 14 they became the first group in the county to announce a candidate for the secession convention. Their choice was William S. Phillips, a prestigious Whig planter who had served as president of the Bell state convention in May. Phillips, along with a young Breckinridge lawyer, John T. Morgan, was nominated on the separate secessionist ticket at Cahaba five days later. The Selma Minute Men were a bipartisan group led by experienced politicians. The typical member was in his twenties or thirties and drawn from the professional and business community. Two-thirds owned slaves.[33]

The Jackson Minute Men were organized on November 13 after a general resistance meeting had adjourned. Although the initial meeting was chaired by a Whig, W. P. Anderson, the club was dominated by Breckinridge politicians. Only four of the sixteen members whose politics could be ascertained were Bell supporters.[34] The participation of Governor Pettus

[32] *Mississippi Free Trader*, Nov. 19; *Semi-Weekly Mississippian*, Nov. 9, 20.

[33] *Alabama State Sentinel*, Nov. 21. The membership will be found in the same issue.

[34] Members were found in the *Semi-Weekly Mississippian*, Nov. 16, and the *Daily Mississippian*, Dec. 1. The politics of ten others was un-

and the two Breckinridge editors in the city, E. Barksdale and R. H. Purdom, revealed the importance placed on the organization by the Breckinridge party. Characteristic of the membership was its youth and heavy support from professionals. All but two were slaveholders, and the majority had holdings of less than twenty slaves. The club exerted strong pressure in favor of the secessionist position. They resolved that every member should consider himself a delegate to the county nominating convention in Raymond on December 10 and feel "duty bound to attend." At the convention Minute Men controlled the committee on resolutions and two of their members, Wiley P. Harris and W. P. Anderson, were chosen for the three-man separate secessionist ticket. They had also made certain that the dangers to the South were publicized. The Vicksburg *Whig* charged them with ordering "for distribution" 10,000 copies of an abolitionist article which had appeared in the Chicago *Democrat*. The paper weakly added that the circulators of this incendiary material should be "arraigned before the grand jury, as such proceedings are in direct and palpable violation of our excellent State Law.[35]

Consistent with its behavior during the presidential campaign, the Breckinridge press led the call for the formation of vigilance committees in every Southern community to protect lives and property. The abolitionists were pictured as more menacing than ever. "According to late accounts there has been a renewal of Abolition outrages in Kansas which are preliminary to contemplated invasions of Missouri, Arkansas and Texas to avenge the recent punishment of antislavery emisaries [sic] in the last named State. The triumph of Lincoln is bringing forth its fruits already." Any enemy of Southern institutions, no matter how cautious or harmless he ap-

---

known. Of 16 Minute Men identified in Vicksburg, 9 had been for Breckinridge, 3 for Bell, and 4 were unknown. They were primarily a young group of businessmen; half owned slaves. See *Semi-Weekly Mississippian*, Nov. 20.

[35] *Daily Mississippian*, Dec. 1; Weekly Vicksburg Whig, Nov. 28.

peared, had to be expelled. "Let us watch out and *hang every non-resident white who becomes liable to suspicion.*—We must get rid of the dangerous, even at the expense of some innocent strangers." Reports of slave uprisings were cited to vindicate these draconian measures. In vain, conservatives repeated their charge that such reports and abolitionist news in general were blown out of proportion by the Breckinridge forces to futher disunion. "The real purpose is to exasperate the South, and thus to *widen the breach* between it and the North."[36]

Fears over internal security peaked during the Christmas holidays when rumors of slave revolts were rampant. The revolts conformed to the earlier pattern in sharing more of the characteristics of self-fulfilling expectations than of a real, distinct threat. In Sardis, Mississippi, a black mechanic was whipped and made to confess to an insurrectionary plot planned for the night of December 26. The citizenry immediately formed a vigilance committee and "examined" the slaves. As usual, nothing came of the affair. The local paper ventured that the slaves of Panola County were never under better subjection than they were on that Christmas Day. John C. Brahan, a Bell planter, publicly labeled the slave's confession a complete fabrication.[37] The vicinity of Pratteville and Autaugaville in central Alabama was another area that convinced itself a disaster had narrowly been averted. The press admitted that the details of the revolt were hazy. "The plot at this place [Pratteville] had not been well understood among the negroes, and their ideas were much confused, some telling one thing and some another. However, the most of them had heard that Lincoln was elected, and took it for granted that they were to be free."[38] Some were ready to join "Lincoln's

[36] *Semi-Weekly Mississippian*, Nov. 23; *Montgomery Weekly Mail*, Nov. 30; *Clayton Banner*, Dec. 20; *Weekly Vicksburg Whig*, Nov. 14.

[37] *Weekly Panola Star*, Dec. 20, 27.

[38] *Autauga Citizen*, Jan. 3, 1861. This was a common complaint. The *Weekly Panola Star* suggested on December 13 that the masters tell their slaves "that the election of Lincoln had nothing in the

army" when it marched South. No slave rebellion broke out in Autaugaville, but this did not prevent the hanging of one white and three blacks.[39]

Grounded more in anxiety than reality, news of slave revolts nonetheless convinced most Southerners that they were faced with a genuine threat. "We are anticipating great trouble this Christmas, and indeed I think we may, I'm afraid to close my eyes at night," confided one woman in her diary. A worried Mississippian asked of Senator Crittenden: "Our negro population are now contented and cheerful, but how long will they continue to remain so, when every effort is being made by so many persons of the non-slaveholding States to turn [them] down loose upon us as so many infuriated wild animals?"[40]

The vigilance committees gave secession an incalculable boost. On one level, their members were direct participants. The Collirene Beat Committee from Lowndes County, Alabama, after quickly coming out for separate state secession and the convening of the state convention as soon as possible, represented their beat on the county convention's nominating committee. Furthermore, the committees enabled the average Southerner, the nonpolitician, to involve himself personally in the defense of his own community. For example, of the forty-five men who joined three beat committees in Panola County, Mississippi, only ten had been active in the presidential campaign.[41] By so collectivizing the sense of crisis, the vigilance groups transferred the threat of Lincoln's election from the realm of political rhetoric to that of personal experience. Joining such a group was both a commitment to the homeland

---

world to do with them or their freedom, but has reference to the question of making new slave States."

[39] *Autauga Citizen*, Jan. 3, 1861.

[40] Margaret J. Gillis Diary, Dec. 29, ADAH; F. M. Aldridge to Crittenden, Dec. 31, Crittenden Papers, LC.

[41] Hayneville *Watchman*, Nov. 23; *Weekly Panola Star*, Dec. 27, 1860, and Jan. 10, 1861. Since large samples of both major political parties were found in Panola, I feel that this ratio is fairly accurate.

and tacit admission that the secessionists were right all along, that the abolitionists would fire their homes and free their slaves. The police functions that these committees abrogated to themselves—especially the power to seize anyone suspected of tampering with slaves and to deal with such in any way they saw fit—were an exercise in effective home rule that rendered useless talk of preserving the Union.[42] Of what use was a government that could not protect one's family and property and forced him to band with others for self-defense?

The enthusiasm with which the committees performed their police duties was frightening. Even when they were long established in their communities, some Northern businessmen were summoned before local committees to answer vague charges. On hearing of one such incident befalling a business associate, an Iowa cattleman wrote an angry letter to Jefferson Davis and A. G. Brown. Arguing that this conduct injured innocent parties and hurt the Southern cause among its friends in the North, he suggested that Davis use his influence with leading Southerners to prevent any future actions of this kind. The wife of a patrician planter echoed the feelings of many conservatives when she wrote: "Christmas will soon be here & I suppose vigilant committees will be active and no doubt but in many instances will be too active, for both white & black."[43]

Most importantly, the vigilantes in ruthlessly enforcing conformity contributed to the atmosphere of violence and hysteria that made attempts at rational debate futile at best and personally dangerous at worst. Conservatives sensed this from the very beginning but were powerless to check it. On the eve of the campaign for the secession convention the

---

[42] The Springport committee in Panola even resolved to "take notice of, and punish all and every persons who may be guilty of any misdemeanor, or prove themselves untrue to the South, or Southern Rights, in any way whatever." *Weekly Panola Star*, Jan. 10, 1861.

[43] W. F. Magraw to Davis and Brown, Jan. 3, 1861, Rowland, ed., *Jefferson Davis*, IV, 562–563; Mrs. Clara Young to Robert Tweed, Dec. 15, Robert Tweed Papers, SHC.

Tuscaloosa *Independent Monitor* reported that in some areas of the state "it is considered heretical and unsafe to utter a sentiment in favor of reconciling our differences with the North, even were such a thing possible." The *Monitor's* charge was borne out in the subsequent campaign. Dissenters were open game for past or present transgressions; they were viciously ferreted out and free expression was suppressed. The Handsboro *Democrat*, in commenting upon the lynching of one Allen McIntosh by a vigilance committee, spoke of the matter as if the community had rid itself of a nuisance. "McIntosh kept a little whiskey shop on one of the roads leading into Hansboro [sic], and has long been considered a man of very suspicious and dangerous character. Whether he was dealt with for any recent outrage, or simply on account of his general bad character, is not stated." John H. Aughey, a Northern born Unionist preacher riding circuit in Attala and Choctaw, was exposed to the terror prevalent in north central Mississippi. He quoted a secessionist candidate boasting over the "glorious news from Tallahatchie. Seven tory-submissionists were hanged there in one day, and the so-called Union candidates, having the wholesome dread of hemp before their eyes, are not canvassing the county; therefore the heretical dogma of submission, under any circumstances, disgraces not their county."[44]

Another Northerner, Sereno Watson, was shocked at the frenzy he witnessed in the Alabama Black Belt town of Greensboro. Writing back home to his brother Henry, whose plantation he was tending, Sereno noted:

> This people is apparently gone crazy. I do not know how to account for it & have no idea what might be the end of it. Union men, Douglas men, Breckinridge men are alike in their loud denunciation of submission to Lincoln's administration. There are of course those who think differ-

[44] *Independent Monitor*, Nov. 16; quoted in the Paulding *Eastern Clarion*, Dec. 26; John H. Aughey, *Tupelo* (Lincoln, Nebraska, 1888), 30–31.

ently but they scarcely dare or are suffered to open their mouths.

John Harvey, editor of the Whiggish *Alabama Beacon*, had called for a Union meeting and the secessionists immediately "stopped the paper." Most of the handbills announcing the meeting were torn down and the Unionist cause looked hopeless since the secessionists would not permit any opposition to form. "It seems to be their endeavor here as elsewhere to browbeat & bully into silence those whom they cannot persuade to go with them & so to make it appear that there is but one opinion throughout the South." Sereno was sickened by the spectacle. "I would like to breathe free air once more, —have the privilege of speaking as I think, & feel that I am a freeman."[45]

Southern Whigs reacted in a similar vein. Their elitism had always precluded them from ever fully trusting the people, but now they were astounded by the popular mania for secession. James Mallory attended a political discussion in Sylacauga, Alabama, and came away with the impression that "the people are mad, they seem to be determined to sell their liberties to satisfy their passions." Through the press and at county nominating conventions Whigs tried to restore order. At a meeting in Canton, Mississippi, Wesley Drane offered a resolution condemning the curtailment of personal liberties by mob rule. Illegal and cowardly assaults upon individuals were becoming all too frequent, he claimed, and were a disgrace to the South. The Montgomery *Post* warned against too much sensationalism. These were certainly troubled times, conceded the editor, and valid causes for apprehension existed, but undue popular excitement had gotten out of hand. "A general alienation of feeling, a disregard of law, and the cultivation of revolutionary passions, all tending to anarchy and misrule, is being most fearfully developed amongst our people—reason is ridiculed, judgment is overridden by excited feeling, and pas-

[45] Sereno to Henry Watson, Nov. 17, Henry Watson, Jr., Papers, DU.

sion reigns supreme." Even a secessionist paper suggested restraint. The *Southern Watchman* urged the citizenry to be careful of what they said and not to go around saying they would hang every man who disagreed with them.[46]

Conservatives outside of the South were also amazed by the mass enthusiasm for secession. Supreme Court Associate Justice John A. Campbell asked ex-President Franklin Pierce, a Northerner still respected in the South, to use his influence in behalf of Southen moderates. They need all the help they can get, he wrote. "There is a wild & somewhat hysterical excitement in all the Southern States and especially in the tier of States from South Carolina west, to the Mississippi." He feared that the leading politicians in these states had already succumbed to "the apparently popular feeling" for secession.[47]

One stimulus after another agitated the masses. William Gould was in Eutaw a few days after Lincoln's election and observed the furor instigated by the wild rumors coming in on the telegraph dispatches. The reports announced a revolution in New York City with Black Republicans burning down the Astor House, fusionists destroying the *Tribune* office, and Wide Awakes storming the Custom House, only to find that Secretary of the Treasury Cobb had removed the public funds to Charleston ten days earlier. "With patriotic zeal some proposed to start immediately and help our friends, the Fusionists[,] to annihilate the Black Republicans. Others, and by far the greater number, thought we would soon have fighting enough at home, and talked loudly of guns and trumpets— minute men and militia." On the following day Gould noted that he had read nothing in the papers about the supposed New York uprisings, but it is to be doubted how many of the Eutaw crowd took the trouble to do the same. The excitement in Eutaw was commonplace. The street corners of Montgom-

---

[46] *James Mallory Diary*, Dec. 20, SHC; Canton *American Citizen*, Dec. 1; *Montgomery Weekly Post*, Dec. 24; quoted in *Alabama Reporter*, Dec. 5.

[47] Campbell to Pierce, Dec. 19, Campbell-Colston Papers, SHC.

ery, in the words of the *Confederation*, were "crowded with persons, agitated, perplexed and maddened by the alarming news that has reached our city within the last week."[48] The rumor mill kept churning. Other telegraph reports told of the assassination of the ex-governor of Virginia, Henry Wise; Cobb was taken prisoner for removing the public funds; 7,000 abolitionists were marching on Washington. A rumor that was especially prevalent in December and was carried in many newspapers had Andrew Johnson of Tennessee killing Jefferson Davis in a Washington street fight.[49]

City and countryside alike experienced the epidemic of violence. The mayor and city council of Savannah offered a $100 reward for information leading to the arrest and conviction of the city's lynch mob leaders. Mobile's mayor, J. M. Withers, issued a proclamation calling upon the citizens to disband "all secret and unlawful associations" which had been dispensing their own justice. Beginning on November 21 a card, signed by the Vigilance Committee, appeared daily in the advertising columns of the Mobile *Advertiser* and ordered all free blacks to leave the state within ten days. If they remained, "they will be waited upon by a Vigilance Committee and dealt with to the extreme of the law." It was this atmosphere which led the cooperationist *Advertiser* to decry threats of intimidation voiced against supporters of their ticket. The paper was forced to plead that cooperationists were as loyal to the South and slavery as any group.[50]

In rural areas the outbreaks of violence took on a quasi-ritualistic aspect. A Northerner, identified only as a Philadelphia drummer (i.e., traveling salesman), appeared in the vil-

[48] William P. Gould Diary, Nov. 12, 13, ADAH; *Weekly Montgomery Confederation*, Nov. 16. Mary Eleanor Thompson to her son Elias, Jan. 14, 1861, Benson-Thompson Family Letters, DU, described a similar scene in Marion, Alabama, of excited street crowds avidly awaiting day after day the latest news.

[49] John E. Hall to Bolling Hall, Nov. 11, Hall Letters, ADAH. Most noteworthy of the Davis-Johnson rumor was the wide publicity that it received.

[50] *Mobile Daily Advertiser*, Dec. 9, 20, 23.

lage of Ripley, Mississippi, on December 8. Within a few hours news circulated that he was a Lincoln supporter. At nine o'clock in the evening the citizens were awoken by the clanging of bells and the firing of cannon. Armed to the teeth, they formed a procession and marched around town accompanied by the blare of band music and the glare of torches. They stopped at the hotel and questioned the drummer. Some of the mob wanted to lynch him at once; others said wait, see if he really was a Lincoln man, and then lynch him. For the time being he was able to convince them that he was not for Lincoln, in fact had not even voted in the election. This satisfied the mob but they agreed to hold another trial in the morning. "They then dispersed with the hope [of] having some more fun in the morning; but early, ere the sun was up, he was off for parts unknown." Tom West, apparently a mentally retarded individual, provided the sport in the nearby town of Batesville. West was caught meddling with slaves and selling them liquor. As punishment, the words "Negro Tamperer" were stamped in large letters on the back of his coat and half of his head and beard were shaved. He was shipped from Panola to Memphis; an Adams Express Company messenger was entrusted with $16 to be used to send him further north.[51]

Sudden murder struck both master and slave under these conditions. Robert Williams, the wealthiest man in Yalobusha County, was murdered by "one of his negro men" on November 16. The slave had been frightened by Williams' promise to whip him for failing to split rails correctly. The common folk were encouraged not to forget such tragedies. By coincidence, several thousand people were in Holly Springs the following day to witness the hanging of Dick, who had killed his overseer in the spring. In late December near Houston, Mississippi, a slave, saying he wanted to be free, refused to obey his master. "His master walked into the house, got his gun, and

[51] *Semi-Weekly Mississippian*, Dec. 21; *Memphis Appeal*, quoted in *ibid.*, Dec. 21. West was referred to as "a person of somewhat imbecile mind." A slightly different version appeared in the *Weekly Panola Star*, Dec. 20.

shot the negro dead, then called up the balance of his servants, and asked them if they wanted to be free."[52]

The volunteer companies completed the triumvirate of paramilitary organizations pushing for secession. Recruitment accelerated once the Republican triumph was a fact. "Volunteer Companies are forming in every little town and village and not a day passes but finds some of the Companies in the County drilling and getting ready for the conflict. . . . Whenever we are ordered I am going though I may never get back home again, but it is a risk we will have to run." By early January the war spirit was everywhere. "There seems to be great excitement throughout the entire County—Companies are organizing & wearing badges—& besides many other demonstrations of Antagonism—War! War!! War!! is the cry throughout North & South!" The companies vied with one another in requesting arms from the governors and offering their services to the states. Typical of their resolutions were those of the Enterprise Guards, proclaiming "that our organization being Military, we are the more bound to defend our State when assailed by Foreign or domestic foes; and believing that the aspect of political matters now portends such contingency, we do *unanimously* offer our Services to Gov. Pettus[,] Such Service to be rendered at a moment's notice." The companies pressured the governors to convene the state conventions and supported immediate secessionist candidates. To bolster his arms request for the Salem Minute Guards, T. F. Murphy informed Governor Moore that he was a fervent secessionist, had been for a number of years, and that he and his friends would work "to elect Secessionists Straight."[53]

[52] *Macon Beacon*, Nov. 21; *Coffeeville Intelligencer*, Dec. 22, quoted in the Vicksburg *Daily Evening Citizen*, Dec. 28.

[53] Alonzo B. Cohen to his sister Irene, Jan. 12, 1861, Alonzo Boyet Cohen Letters, ADAH; Diary of Ann L. Hardeman, Jan. 5, 1861, in Oscar J. E. Stuart Papers, MDAH; Resolutions of the Enterprise Guards to Pettus, Nov. 21, Governors' Records, MDAH; T. F. Murphy to Moore, Nov. 24, Moore Correspondence, ADAH. See also, T. Lomax to Moore, Nov. 22, *ibid*.

With their pomp and pageantry, the volunteer companies lent a martial air to secession. Their parades, band music, and banners made for a colorful spectacle which drew the people together and enabled all to share in the sense of excitement. Resistance to the Republicans became a community celebration. These ceremonial functions of the companies, as well as their more prosaic task of cowing dissenters with the strength of their numbers, were fully appreciated by the secessionist leaders. In Barbour County, a call went out for the eight companies which comprised the Third Regiment of the Alabama Volunteer Corps to muster in Clayton on the day of a mass resistance meeting. Some 3,000 to 4,000 people were in attendance; the meeting was preceded by a grand military demonstration, a flood of oratory, and the presentation of a flag to the regiment by President Holmes of the local Female College. The volunteer captains played a prominent role in the meeting which followed. Joseph Jones chaired the committee on nominations and Alpheus Baker and J.W.L. Daniel were chosen as secessionist candidates.[54]

III

The tensions of the secession crisis were also heightened by economic dislocations. Crops, and particularly foodstuffs, had been damaged by the drought.[55] Many planters were hard pressed to meet their debts from the previous year and everyone suffered from the high food prices. Then, as money was already becoming tight, the reaction to Lincoln's election provoked a major economic crisis. In the wake of the suspension of payments in the South by the New York banks, North-

[54] *Clayton Banner*, Nov. 19, 22. The estimate on the crowd was taken from Lewy Dorman, "Barbour County History," MS, 507, UA.

[55] Contemporary accounts agreed that cotton was less damaged than the food crops. The actual drop in cotton production, the only crop on which we have firm statistics for both 1859 and 1860, was 15%; from 4,508,000 bales in 1859 to 3,841,000 bales in 1860. See *The Statistical History of the United States from Colonial Times to the Present* (Stamford, Conn., 1965), Series K, p. 302.

South trade came to a virtual halt. Credit dried up as entrepreneurs refused to commit their capital in the unsettling
political circumstances.

In the commercial centers of the Lower South—Memphis,
Mobile, and New Orleans—cotton piled up and business
stagnated. Many New Orleans merchants suspended payments on December 1 and 4. The city's gloom deepened in
the ensuing weeks. E. W. Dorr reported: "Very little doing
in our business & there is no telling what losses business men
will meet with before these times settle down—Never saw so
much distress in money affairs before." He felt that matters
were worse there than in Mobile but supposed prospects
would improve once Louisiana seceded. Frank Valliant, a
Breckinridge central committee member from Mississippi,
visited New Orleans in the middle of December. After noting
that "business is almost at a standstill," he pinpointed the effect such distress would have on secession. "I find that the
secession movement is if anything stronger here than in Mississippi, everyone appearing to think that they can not possibly be in a worse situation than they now are."[56]

In the interior the hard times were just as bad. Complaints
over the scarcity of provisions and lack of money were heard
everywhere. "I never knew any thing equal to it—No money,
and no confidence in any one's ability to pay—," lamented
a Montgomery planter. A Byhalia, Mississippi, dry goods
merchant fretted in his diary over his pressing financial troubles and the difficulty of getting up drafts to pay off old debts.
Mary E. Thompson, in describing conditions back home in
Marion, Alabama, to her son Elias who was attending the
University of Alabama, summarized the problems faced even
by the well-to-do.

The people no longer talk of peacible [sic] secession, war
must follow, we have no money, nor provisions, it is almost

[56] Dorr to W. T. Walthall, Dec. 20, 24, William T. Walthall Papers,
MDAH; Valliant to Marian Rucks, Dec. 14, Rucks-Valliant Family
Papers, MDAH.

impossible for the best men to raise one hundred Dol, with all the notes I hold, I cannot raise money enough to pay my tax, I have not succeeded in hiring all the servants yet & I fear I cannot, they are going low, all business has stopped, except that that is really necessary.[57]

Most of the nonslaveholders earned only a scant cash income and under normal circumstances were not drawn into the market economy. If their crops or those of neighbors failed, they lacked the financial resources to make up the deficit and supply their own needs. Even with greatly increased food shipments from the Midwest, foodstuffs were scarce and prices exorbitant. After quoting the market prices on a variety of staples, the Huntsville *Southern Advocate* added: "everything else at the same famine prices, and money scarcer than ever known!" Relief meetings for the indigent were called and reports of starvation continued to come in as they had during the summer and fall.[58] Probably best off among the poor were the hunters and fishermen of the piney woods who lived off the forests and streams.

Pressure was exerted on the governors to provide some economic relief. A meeting in Greenville, Alabama, representing "the Commercial and Agricultural interests of Butler County," asked the governor to call a special session of the legislature before the state convention met. They wanted the legislature to remove the penalties which the banks otherwise would incur for suspending specie payments. Such action was warranted, the resolutions argued, because the present financial troubles were politically inspired and neighboring states had already done the same. The Greenville meeting expressed

[57] Wm. H. Ogbourne to his sister, Dec. 14, James B. Bailey Papers, SHC; Thomas B. Webber Diary, Jan. 6, 1861, DU; Mary E. Thompson to Elias, Jan. 2, 1861, Benson-Thompson Family Letters, DU.

[58] *Southern Advocate*, Nov. 28; *Weekly Vicksburg Whig*, Dec. 5; *Southern Advocate*, Nov. 14. As estimated by the *Mobile Daily Advertiser* on Dec. 22, the increases in food imports from the Midwest were: 500% for wheat, 171% for corn, 39% for flour, 22% for bacon, and 5½% for pork.

widely felt demands and consequently on December 17 Moore issued an executive proclamation explaining his position. He decided not to call the legislature into special session for two reasons, both based on his assumption that Alabama would soon secede. Secession would necessitate a special session to act on certain legislative adjustments; to call yet another session he felt would be a wasteful expense at a time when economy was of the utmost importance. In addition, the call for such a session would trigger a run on the banks. This could not be risked since Alabama would need all her resources and all her specie after she had seceded. However, Moore fully concurred that specie suspension was an economic necessity. He pointed out that his December 4 letter to the banks had authorized suspension and that all but two banks had done so.[59]

Demands for debtor relief in the form of stay laws were also voiced. As William Garrett of Coosa County argued, with money so scarce and the prospect of higher taxes to support the expanded military apparatus, there should be a temporary suspension of the law "which allows a party to take judgment at the *first court*." The financial community was against such action, and, following their advice, Moore did nothing on the subject. Northern creditors, a group exceedingly vulnerable to reprisals, did not fare so well. Various county bar associations met and resolved to stop collecting or receiving for collection any debts held by Northerners against citizens of their state. The Lowndes County bar of Alabama even added that they would use their influence "to prevent such collections by others, as far as we properly can."[60]

The economic crisis and its resultant hardships intensified the sense of desperation experienced by most Southerners

[59] John K. Henry to A. B. Moore, Dec. 18, and Governor's Moore's Proclamation of Dec. 17, Moore Correspondence, ADAH.

[60] Garrett to L. Parsons, Jan. 12, 1861, Lewis Parsons Letters, ADAH; L. C. Tutt to A. B. Moore, Dec. 5, Moore Correspondence, ADAH; Hayneville *Chronicle*, Nov. 15, see also the *Clayton Banner*, Dec. 6.

after Lincoln's election. The secessionists played upon this desperation and used it brilliantly to further their revolutionary aims. In a fascinating letter written to William Samford back in October, Henry Wise had foreseen perfectly the relationship between economic conditions and the prospects for secession. "Whilst cotton is up and times flush of cash you can't wake men up to revolution at 6 o'clock in the morning. The *Domineerers* may lose Submissionists by making hard times. If that be the effect, let the cause come."[61] The secessionists did not create the hard times (except insofar as they contributed to Lincoln's victory), but they capitalized on the fact that economic distress left Southerners open to the argument that secession alone offered a way out of their distress. Bold and prompt action would leave the South with a clean slate and enable her to control her own economy free of Yankee dominance. After all, as Frank Valliant had noted, with times so bad how could they possibly get worse?

IV

Southern church opinion solidly supported disunion. In an age when religion was still at the core of one's values, this was a considerable advantage to the secessionists. The church could not be neutral. The Republican threat was too pervasive, and the church itself was too closely identified with slavery for this powerful institution to stand aside. Its ministers would have made a mockery of their own beliefs had they argued that the South could accept a national administration that branded as immoral the central feature of Southern life. Religious leaders were as quick as any to see in the abolitionists an all-powerful enemy. "CAN THE UNION BE SAVED?" asked the *Baptist Correspondent*. "Not if the North proposes to force upon the South a President and Vice-President, elected by Northern fanatics, to carry out their fell purposes of *injustice, despotism* and *wholesale murder* upon

[61] Wise to Samford, Oct. 21, 1860, William F. Samford Papers, SHC.

the unoffending people of the South." Ministers added to the hysteria by sermonizing on the murderous designs of the abolitionists and local congregations backed resistance efforts. On the first Sunday in December, the Baptist Church of Christ in Bethesda, Mississippi, passed resolutions approving Pettus' call for an extra session of the legislature preparatory to secession. They stressed that the church did not meddle in politics or party questions, but that the present crisis was one which involved "the vital interests of our *homes* and *firesides*." Therefore, they interpreted the governor's call not as mere politics but as "a warning voice to the people that we may put our house in order—for our enemies are marshalling their forces for our destruction."[62]

The church needed no prodding to favor secession. Whigs had long complained that ministers were bringing politics into the pulpit, especially disunion politics.[63] The secessionist press, however, took no chances and assumed the role of reminding the church of its duty.

> The Southern church would be palpably untrue to its mission if it remained quiescent while the North demands an "anti-slavery Bible and an anti-slavery God." It cannot serve God and Mammon at the same time, and hence it must stand with the South in this crusade of the North against all that is sacred and right, and beneficent in Southern civilization.

Secessionists were delighted by the Thanksgiving Day sermons delivered in New Orleans by the Reverends Dr. Palmer (Presbyterian) and Dr. Leacock (Episcopalian). All the religious defenses of slavery were given, and particular stress was placed on the South's God-given obligation to protect slavery from atheistic Northern fanatics. The sermons were

[62] *Baptist Correspondent*, Dec. 5; *Clayton Banner*, Nov. 1; Resolutions of the Baptist Church of Christ at Bethesda, Oktibbeha Co., to Gov. Pettus, Governors' Records, MDAH.

[63] See the condemnation of the Rev. Dr. P. P. Neely in the *Alabama Reporter*, April 26, 1860.

widely publicized. The press carried front-page columns, headed "The Duty of Resistance to Northern Oppression taught in the Pulpit"; frequently both sermons were reprinted in full. The sermons had tremendous propagandistic value to the secessionists. The *Mississippi Free Trader* compared Palmer and Leacock to "the prophets of old" for telling the South her duty and reminding her that " '*if the South bows before the throne of Black Republicanism, she accepts the decree of restriction and ultimate extinction, which is made the condition of her homage.*' " E. Barksdale drew a frightful moral from Palmer's sermon.

> The triumph of Abolitionism, will be the triumph of discontent, riot, blood-shed, atheism, and every manner of foul thing to pervert the understanding and corrupt the hearts of men. It runs riot over the Northern States. Shall we not protect from its leprous embrace this fair land of our inheritance? If you are a patriot—if you are a *christian* —listen to the voice of the man of God.[64]

While some ministers such as T. W. Caskey of Jackson took a direct role in secession by helping organize Minute Men, chairing resistance meetings, and serving as delegates, the church had proved itself a valuable ally by simply lending her moral support to the movement.

Appeals to racism constituted the secessionists' single most effective tactic. The issue cut across class lines and laid bare the Southerner's most basic fear, equality with blacks. Whether expressed in the poor white's vicious hatred of the black or the planter's ego-fulfilling paternalism, a racism which demanded that the black be enslaved was the bedrock of Southern values.[65] The Republicans, by proclaiming emancipation

[64] *Montgomery Weekly Advertiser*, Dec. 5; *Semi-Weekly Mississippian*, Dec. 7; *Mississippi Free Trader*, Dec. 10; *Semi-Weekly Mississippian*, Dec. 11.

[65] "The 'white trash' of the South . . . have a personal dislike of the negroes which the planters do not all share." James R. Stirling, *op. cit.*, 86. James H. Hammond to Lewis Tappan, Sept. 6, 1850, Ham-

as their ultimate goal, forced every Southerner to face the consequences of huge numbers of freed blacks within his midst. This prospect was unthinkable since everyone believed that free blacks were a worthless, corrupt, and vice-ridden lot. The whites were professedly doing them a favor by keeping them enslaved and attending to their needs. Free them and everyone would suffer. A poor white told Olmsted: "I don't know anybody, hardly, in favor of that. Make 'em free and leave 'em here and they'd steal everything we made. Nobody couldn't live here then."[66] The planter was spared the non-slaveholder's fear of social and economic competition with ex-slaves, but emancipation, aside from the question of monetary compensation, would destroy both the greatest prop to his self-esteem, his authority as master, and the basis of his enshrined class position.

The Ashville *St. Clair Diamond* rhetorically asked, why did Southerners want to secede? Its crude answer—"because they don't wish to be ruled by a 'nigger' "—epitomized the secessionists' racist appeal. On one level, the answer referred to the belief that Lincoln's running mate, Hannibal Hamlin of Maine, was a mulatto. More basically, it touched upon the

---

mond Papers, LC, makes the same point. Ulrich B. Phillips, "The Central Theme of Southern History," *AHR*, xxxiv (Oct., 1928), puts this racism in historical perspective.

[66] Frederick Law Olmsted, *A Journey in the Back Country* (London, 1860), 203. These prejudices were also all too common in the North. Joseph B. Howell, the uncle of Jefferson Davis' wife and a conservative Philadelphian who described himself as "a northern man with Southern feelings," wrote his brother William, a resident of the South: "Had the slaves never been interfered with by Northern Emissaries, they would now be in a happy and contented state. There is no comparison in their position to that of the free negro of the north. They are clothed and supported in health, sickness and old age. The labor extracted from them is in no wise equal to that performed by the white Laborer here. And the free negroes in our cities and country taken as a body, are a mass of vice and idleness compared to them." Joseph to William Burr Howell, Dec. 10, 1860, William Burr Howell and Family Papers, MDAH.

racial consequences which Southerners predicted would result from accepting Republican rule. In unison the newspapers, and especially the Breckinridge press, announced that Lincoln's election was the prelude to racial amalgamation in the South. The great contest for control of the national government between those who held that men of every color were equal and those who believed that the black and the Indian were naturally inferior to the white man had been lost.[67] Now, no eventuality was too remote nor any degradation too lurid to be undeserving of mention in the secessionists' propaganda.

Early in the convention campaign the *Mississippian* claimed that the real aim of the Lincoln party was, "unmistakably and unquestionably," first to overthrow slavery and then to tear down the barriers between the races by placing blacks on a complete equality with whites. As the election approached, it reminded the voters that the only choice was between a free Southern Confederacy and "a Northern free negro despotism." To the young men of Mississippi, the paper framed a special argument. It asked if they realized that under the Black Republicans those born in a slaveholding state would be stigmatized and all federal places of distinction, such as the army and navy, would be closed to them. "The free negroes of the North will occupy a higher position than the noblest and worthiest son of the South." Clearly no self-respecting young Southerner could accept such a government, that is, "unless you are false to every instinct of your chivalric natures, false to your mother, and false to God and the land that bred you."[68]

No segment of Southern society would be immune to the sickening consequences of racial equality. Treating the freed blacks as equals would result in "marrying and giving in

[67] *St. Clair (Ala.) Diamond*, Dec. 5; *Semi-Weekly Mississippian*, Nov. 2. The resolutions passed at a public meeting in Buena Vista, Mississippi, on July 21, 1860, and reprinted in the *Mississippian* on Aug. 14, are a good example of the Southern formulation of the different racial policies in the two sections.

[68] *Semi-Weekly Mississippian*, Nov. 13, Dec. 11, 18.

marriage with them." What about schooling? In October the Montgomery *Mail* had asked: "Do you believe in sending your sons and your daughters—aye, your *daughters!*—to school with negroes and in asserting that the negro is their intellectual equal?" Submission to the Republicans and their doctrine meant an endless series of horrors. Andrew Henry, the young Irish editor of the *West Alabamian*, drew a most terrifying picture.

> Submit to be governed by a sectional party whose grand aim is not to raise the negro in the scale of being, but to sink the Southern white men to an equality with the negro! Submit to have our wives and daughters chose [sic] between death and gratifying the hellish lust of the negro!! Submit to have our children murdered, our dwellings burnt and our country desolated!! Far better ten thousand deaths than submission to Black Republicanism.[69]

The secessionists placed special emphasis on the dangers which emancipation held for the nonslaveholders. On November 16 the Montgomery *Mail* published John D. Phelan's letter which spelled out why they should support immediate secession. He reasoned that the essence of the antislavery movement was its belief that the races were inherently equal. Hence, blacks were entitled to the same status as whites in all civil and religious matters, including "the great and sacred *institution of marriage*." "A few generations will see a *mulatto race* possess this country, as they now do Mexico and Central America." The wealthy had the means to hold themselves above this degrading spectacle or to leave the country, but the poor had no such defense. They must awake to the danger now and strike for secession.[70]

In elaborating on this theme in a speech at a mass meeting in Columbiana, Alabama, on November 30, in the state's hilly central area, Phelan addressed himself to the region's non-

[69] *Clarke County Democrat*, Nov. 29; *Montgomery Weekly Mail*, Oct. 5; *West Alabamian*, Dec. 12.
[70] *Montgomery Weekly Mail*, Nov. 16.

slaveholding majority. He told them that the South must secede since slavery was doomed within the Union. If slavery were destroyed, the effects would be disastrous for "the poor and middling classes." As of now, these classes enjoyed slavery's greatest benefits. Not only were they freed from degrading menial labor, but, "where negro slavery exists, a white man's face, without further guarantee of any sort, is the sure and undisputed badge of a certain degree of superiority and respectability." Furthermore, nonslaveholders controlled the government here in Alabama, slavery produced the wealth, and the slaveowners paid more in taxes on their slaves than all Alabamians did on their land. But the doctrine of Negro equality, if accepted for a moment, would change all this. It would lead to emancipation. After the rich had fled, "the poor and the improvident will be left, unavoidably, to the unhappy fate of free *negro society and dominion* for themselves and free *negro amalgamation* for their posterity." For the same purposes of internal solidarity, newspapers reprinted portions of DeBow's essay, "The Interest in Slavery of the Southern Non-Slaveholder." Stressed were his arguments that out of the nonslaveholding class were derived the planters and the South's leaders in industry and politics, that if not himself then the nonslaveholder's children would advance, and that the fruits of slavery were indispensable and distributed among all classes.[71]

The importance of the racial issue cannot be overemphasized. Secessionists employed it in the press and on the stump; nearly every resistance meeting cited the threat of racial equality as a leading justification for secession. Volunteer companies swore to defend white supremacy with their lives. The Calhoun Guards of Pickens County declared that the Black Republican doctrine could lead only to Negro equality and thus was "a doctrine we claim no fellowship with, and will forever fight against even to the spilling of blood."[72] Rac-

[71] *Montgomery Weekly Advertiser*, Dec. 19; *Montgomery Weekly Mail*, Dec. 14.
[72] *West Alabamian*, Nov. 28.

ism was the secessionists' greatest weapon. They knew precisely what Southerners dreaded the most and by constantly exacerbating this fear and identifying it with the Republicans succeeded in building up tensions and hatreds which looked to secession as an outlet.

The atmosphere of anxiety and violence in which the secession campaign took place was itself an immense advantage to the secessionists. Every facet of Southern life was touched by the crisis, every fear was exposed. Since slavery and its concomitant racial accommodations were so central to Southern existence, indeed comprised the only reality which the South cared to accept, any threat to slavery could have had no lesser effect. The secessionists recognized this crucial fact and acted upon it by seizing the moment of crisis and channeling into political action the general discontent with the status quo and forebodings over the future. Above all, they acted as if conforming to the dictum laid down by Henry Wise. If Lincoln is elected, and he will be, Wise had written William Samford, the South must secede then or never. "What can we do? Appoint 'committees of safety' and organize 'minute men' as in Revolutionary times. If masses and conventions won't—let the few who will meet and arm—and, if they can do no more, alarm."[73]

The successful revolutionary must create effective organizations and arouse the masses. The secessionists did both. They elicited mass support for secession by playing on the common man's two greatest fears. As Stirling had predicted in 1857: "Hatred of 'Abolitionism' (which with them is identical with 'the North'), on the one hand, and jealousy of the nigger on the other, will ever make this miserable mob a ready tool in the hands of a fanatical party."[74] Aided by the leadership which the governors provided and their control of the Breckinridge press, the secessionists formed paramilitary groups and participated in resistance meetings. In so doing they created the machinery which would force secession.

[73] Wise to Samford, Oct. 21, 1860, Samford Papers, SHC.
[74] Stirling, *Letters*, 95.

SIX

RHETORIC FOR REVOLUTION

THE ideological battle over withdrawal from the Union not only mirrored the strengths and weaknesses of the secessionists and cooperationists, but it also foreshadowed the paralyzing indecision which was to hamstring the efforts of the conservatives. The debate hinged on two points: the desirability of immediate, separate state secession as opposed to a slower, cooperative movement with the action of any one state dependent upon the behavior of others, and the question of whether or not the decisions of the state conventions should be final or referred back to the people in a referendum.

I

The secessionists were confident and aggressive. At the start of the campaign, they contemptuously brushed off conservative charges that the Breckinridge party was responsible for Lincoln's election; such attacks at this time, they suggested, better became the open enemies of the South than her supposed friends. From the beginning they pressed the offensive. On November 8 the Hayneville *Chronicle* announced: "Two parties will take the field, one for action, prompt and efficient; the other to eulogise the glories of the Union, and preach submission to the sway of Black Republicanism."[1] Secessionist ideology assented a quick, direct, and positive solution to the terrible threat that everyone agreed faced the South. It warned that delay could lead only to greater dangers and outlined the advantages of immediate action.

[1] *Woodville Republican*, quoted in the *Mississippi Free Trader*, Nov. 26; Hayneville *Chronicle*, Nov. 8.

231

Economically, the sooner that the South seceded, the sooner would she have full control over the marketing of her staples. In addition, she would minimize the unsettling effects of the crisis on her commercial and financial interests. Appeals were made to Southern honor and pride. Immediate secession would gain the South the moral advantage by proclaiming to the world the righteousness of her cause, but procrastination would be taken as a sign of doubt, of weakness, and of internal division. Had not the South in the past already exposed herself to ridicule by assuming a lofty stand only to back down at the moment of crisis? In political terms the South was warned not to forget that until March 4 a president friendly to her interests, James Buchanan, would be in power. "He knows that we are wronged and endangered by Black Republican ascendancy, and he will not, we have a right to suppose, lend himself to carry out their bloody policy."[2]

Delay increased the chances that Lincoln would be inaugurated and be in a position to use force or blandishments to keep the South within the Union. With their keen grasp of political loyalties and party workings, the secessionists warned that soon all federal patronage would be in the hands of the Republicans. Henceforth, the South would have no voice in the formulation of domestic and foreign policy. Local appointive officials, such as postmasters and customs agents, might well be abolitionists, and the South would be powerless to stop their appointment. They would be loyal to their party employers, and "if Lincoln's election is submitted to for a moment, Southern men will take office under him—then become his partisans. Then an abolition party is formed among us; the South demoralized and all is lost." Republican foreign policy would aim to strengthen the North and "to circumscribe, weaken, and finally, to crush the South." Slavery must expand to survive, and not only would the Republicans never allow this, but they ultimately would try to

[2] Charleston *Mercury*, quoted in the *Semi-Weekly Mississippian*, Nov. 9.

govern the South's slaves. "What will be the result? Look at
St. Domingo."[3] The South's best defense, it was insisted, was
immediate secession which would give her time to form a
united and strong confederacy to combat the Republicans
on equal terms when they took office.

Another secessionist argument had an air of finality about
it that was difficult to refute. It pointed out that the heart of
the problem was the belief held by a majority of Northerners
that slavery was sinful and that those who lived under a government which recognized the institution were partly responsible for its continuance and hence shared in the moral
guilt. Despicable as the abolitionists were, the South should
at least grant them their sincerity. "If a dog dies in your own
yard and becomes a stench in your nostrils, and you have
the power to remove it, will you not do it? Do you ask the
Abolitionists to do less with your slaves? Would *you* do less,
believing as they do?" No amount of talk, no wasting of
valuable time could convince the abolitionists otherwise. How
could you change the conscience of a whole people? J. B.
Hancock, a Breckinridge leader reporting to Governor Pettus
on secession sentiment in Lauderdale County, put it best.
There would be many

> who believe if the South will present a bold front it will
> roll back the tide of public opinion in the North & North
> West. Many of us think differently and believe that the
> people of North & North West, having sucked in abolition
> feeling and sentiment from the breasts of their mothers, had
> it taught them in lullaby songs at the sides of their cradles,
> been taught it in school rooms, from the pulpit and stump
> until the[y] have become so imbued with feelings hostile
> to slavery, that nothing that the South [could do] could

[3] *Clayton Banner*, Dec. 20; *Montgomery Weekly Advertiser*, Nov.
14; Troy (Ala.) *Southern Advertiser*, Dec. 7 and Nov. 14. Toussaint
L'Ouverture led a successful and bloody revolt on this West Indies
island in the 1790's against the French. The memory of this uprising
was a constant nightmare to Southerners.

change their deep rooted hatred of our institution, and that secession is the only remedy.[4]

In attacking cooperationism, the secessionists stigmatized it as a mere subterfuge for submission. It was all the more dangerous because of its deceit; "they [cooperationists] will not *at first* advocate passive submission, but will try to delude the people by pretending to be for resistance in co-operation with other states." No intelligent person really doubted that the Southern states would band together after secession and no state need dread having to stand alone, said the Paulding *Eastern Clarion*, but to make such cooperation a precondition before secession was unnecessary. At worst it was a delaying tactic which tried to gain time during which the South would lose patience and quietly give in to Republican rule. It was this concern which compelled Representative David Clopton of Alabama to denounce L.Q.C. Lamar's proposal for making secession in Mississippi contingent on secession in eight other states; it "would defeat the whole movement." Consultation was acceptable. By this the secessionists meant that every state was free to consult with others as to the timing of secession in the hope that all would go out at about the same time. This was precisely the function of the secession commissioners. If any more unity was required, say for self-defense, then the individual states instinctively would come to each other's aid. Republican attempts to push a force bill through Congress would expose their treachery to the Upper South and rally these states behind those who had already committed themselves.[5]

For the most part, though, secessionists downplayed the possibility of war. The *Mississippian* noted that the U.S. Army consisted of no more than 20,000 men, one-half of

[4] Auburn *Sketch Book*, Nov. 16; J. B. Hancock to Gov. Pettus, Nov. 14, Governors' Records, MDAH.

[5] *Hayneville Chronicle*, Nov. 15; *Eastern Clarion*, Dec. 12; Clopton to C. C. Clay, Dec. 13, Clay Papers, DU; Auburn *Sketch Book*, Dec. 7; Charleston *Mercury*, cited in the *Semi-Weekly Mississippian*, Nov. 9.

whom were Southerners, scattered along the western frontier. The present Congress would not arm Lincoln with the authority and appropriations to atack the South and it would be two years before the Republicans could hope to dominate Congress as the result of new elections. By then an impregnable Confederacy would protect the South. Have no fears of war, counseled the *Clayton Banner*. Since the Northern and British economies were based on cotton, neither the Yankee exporter nor the Manchester textile manufacturer would permit war to disrupt the flow of white gold. However, in their private correspondence the secessionists were much more pessimistic and talk of peaceable secession nearly vanished. "If Lincoln makes fight as I doubt not he will I think you had better be getting ready to meet Genl. Scott at the head of 200,000 wide awakes," Pettus informed Jefferson Davis on December 31. Writing from the secession convention in Jackson, Charles D. Fontaine told his wife that "Coercion of the South[,] a War of Conquest and Subjugation is the apparent Sentiment & gaining ground in the North. We are preparing to 'welcome them with bloody hands & hospitable graves.' "[6]

Secessionists bristled at their opponents' charges that they were revolutionaries and anarchists. In rebuttal they portrayed secession as "this great conservative movement for self-preservation." By insisting that cooperation was illegal since it violated Article 1, Section 10 of the Constitution which forbade any state from forming an alliance with another state or raising an army, the secessionists proclaimed themselves as true constitutionalists. Admittedly they were revolutionaries but only in the same sense that the term was applied to the illustrious Founding Fathers. These men, too, had been victims of oppression who fought for their inde-

[6] *Semi-Weekly Mississippian*, Nov. 13; *Clayton Banner*, Nov. 15; Pettus was quoted in Donald M. Rawson, "Party Politics in Mississippi, 1850–1860," unpublished Ph.D. thesis (Vanderbilt University, 1964), 300; Fontaine to his wife, Sally Ann, Jan. 13, 1861, Charles D. Fontaine and Family Papers, MDAH.

pendence. They did not tear down society but by building upon the old created a new and stronger compact which guaranteed freedom and stability. Their great accomplishment had been defiled and violated by Northern fanatics and now the patriots of the South must strike anew for their liberties.[7]

The weakest link in the secessionists' case was their opposition to a referral back to the people of the secession conventions' action. Wherever possible they tried to avoid the issue lest they appear as plotters seeking to subvert the popular will. In dealing with it, they argued that there was no precedent for the popular ratification of the actions of a convention. In the instance of the present conventions, the members, as duly elected representatives of the people, were said to be fully empowered to speak for the people. The election itself was a referendum on the state's future course. Both parties had an equal opportunity to present their sides and no one could cry foul. The cooperationists were simply trying to delay secession as long as possible. The time spent in another election would be wasted and would be better spent in readying defenses and forming a new government with sister states.[8]

These were the main contours of the secessionist position. Variations were normally a function of the particular needs or politics of a local area. For example, in the cooperationist stronghold in the Tennessee Valley the *Florence Gazette* found it expedient to balance its attacks on cooperationism with support for the concept of referring back any decision on immediate and separate secession. Other secessionist papers in the northern sections of Alabama and Mississippi struck a similar compromise. The yeomanry in these hills and mountains were lukewarm secessionists, so why not gain the major prize, their support for secession, by conceding a minor point which the convention could always reject. Spe-

[7] *Semi-Weekly Mississippian*, Nov. 9; Hayneville *Chronicle*, Nov. 15; *Montgomery Weekly Advertiser*, Nov. 28.

[8] *Mississippi Free Trader*, Dec. 24; *Semi-Weekly Mississippian*, Dec. 25.

cialized arguments appealing to local pride were employed, such as the one in Mobile directed toward the business community. Interior dealers who formerly had traveled to the North for their goods would now turn to Mobile "as they ought always to have done." These profits, plus those accruing from the establishment of direct trade with foreign nations, would enrich the city and fulfill her destiny as "the commercial metropolis of all the Gulf coast east of New Orleans."[9]

In contrast to their adversaries, the cooperationists were confused and hesitant. Their one great advantage, the inertia of existing institutions, was constantly eroded away by the popular fears and suspicions which led many to reject the legitimacy of the status quo. The obstacles that they had to overcome were stupendous since Lincoln's election had given the initiative to the secessionists, and there was nothing the cooperationists could do to regain it. The flow of events which would shape the popular decision was beyond their control. It was up to the Republicans to offer a meaningful compromise or to persuade the secessionists to agree to a delay. In the meantime Southern conservatives were caught in the middle. The cooperationist editor of the *Weekly Panola Star*, M. S. Ward, knew the feeling. "Some few weeks since we were of the opinion that something might be done to save the Union, by cooperation conventions of the Southern States, but the hope is entirely disapated [sic] by the current of events. The Republicans of the North are as unyielding as the fire-eaters of the South."[10]

The conservatives' basic premise was that secession most probably would lead to war, higher taxes, and economic chaos. To avert this calamity, every means of redress should be exhausted. Some diehards maintained that the South could still protect herself within the Union. Conservative men controlled both the House and the Senate and could block all

[9] *Florence Gazette*, Nov. 28; *Mobile Daily Advertiser*, Nov. 18.
[10] *Weekly Panola Star*, Dec. 27.

executive appointments and appropriations for at least two years after Lincoln's inauguration. In the time thus gained, the North might repent, and the South could afford to wait as long as the Republicans committed no overt, aggressive acts.[11] Once the viability of this minority position was dissolved by the popular demand for immediate action, conservatives fell back on an argument for a united front. The Southern states were bound together by slavery, so they should react as one to outside threats. In unity there was strength. If all the slave states came together and presented their demands, then perhaps the North would listen.[12] But this position smacked too much of submission; it was attacked as putting the South in the role of a supplicant rather than of a gallant defender of her rights.

Most conservatives opted for cooperationism. How many of these men were sincere secessionists and how many were frustrated Unionists who grasped at cooperation as a delaying tactic is difficult to determine. Fortunately, the question is largely irrelevant. Any Unionist, if he wanted to be heard at all, had to be for cooperation. Those cooperationists who did favor secession as an end in itself were going against the whole grain of the movement. Without the benefit of hindsight no one, of course, knew how the crisis would resolve itself. To counsel delay and unified action was correctly interpreted by the immediate secessionists as a course which still left room open for maneuver and reconciliation. The longer that secession was put off the greater the chance, however small to begin with, that the Republicans would give in and offer just enough to the South of defuse secession.[13]

---

[11] This argument left the conservatives wide open to the following type of counterattack. "We want no more 'overt acts.' We have had them at *Harper's Ferry*, in *Kansas*, in the *conflagrations* in Texas, in the wide spread *incendiarism* throughout the Southern States." Auburn *Sketch Book*, Nov. 9.

[12] Tuscaloosa *Independent Monitor*, Nov. 23.

[13] Though not conclusive, the weight of evidence indicates that most cooperationists were in the frustrated Unionist category and at

The cooperationists' problems were reflected in the negative tone of their ideology. Most significant were those points which they had to concede. As Jeremiah Clemens so well understood, discussion of the right of secession had to be waived. Debating the issue would only discredit the cooperationists. The South did have legitimate grievances, granted the cooperationists, which must be redressed as the price for continuing the Union. A Huntsville meeting on December 8 listed these grievances in the form of demands. The North must faithfully adhere to the Fugitive Slave Act and repeal her obnoxious personal liberty laws; guarantees must be given that in the District of Columbia and wherever Congress had jurisdiction slavery would not be abolished and that there would be no interference with the interstate slave trade; and it must be stipulated that the territories were free to decide on slavery as they saw fit. In addition, the meeting recommended a constitutional amendment requiring the President to be chosen alternately from free and slave states. Nor could conservatives deny that Southerners were personally endangered by the abolitionists. The Whiggish Montgomery *Post* explained: "It is not that we love the Constitution and the Union less (that is of themselves) but because we love our firesides and homes, our families and friends, our rights and interests, our liberties and institutions more, and feel that he who would not sacrifice all else on behalf of these domestic relations, is unworthy the name of American freeman."[14]

Cooperationists likewise had to agree that the root of the present crisis was the Northern belief that slavery was morally wrong. Recognizing this fact, many conservatives lost heart

---

best reluctant secessionists. Benjamin G. Humphreys recalled that while many Whigs went over to the Democrats after Lincoln's election, "others resorted to the miserable dodge of 'wait till all the States can cooperate and all go out together.'" Percy Lee Rainwater, ed., "Autobiography of Benjamin Grubb Humphreys," *MVHR*, XXI (Sept., 1934), 243.

[14] Huntsville *Southern Advocate*, Dec. 12; *Montgomery Weekly Post*, Dec. 19.

and concluded that reconciliation was impossible. "The only remedy is a *change* of *public* opinion north, that of the people as a people. Such a change *cannot* be *hoped for*," wrote Henry Watson to a Northern friend. The Montgomery *Post* admitted that the South could never expect peace within the Union unless Northern sentiments and prejudices were transformed, or at least accommodated to respect slavery as an institution. Grasping at straws the Mobile *Advertiser* hoped that, since the North felt so strongly against slavery, perhaps she would be relieved to see the South secede and allow her to go in peace. Finally, in their most damaging admission, conservatives acknowledged that given a choice the South could dispense with the Union, but not with slavery.[15] By permitting the debate to be polarized in this manner, the cooperationists weakened their entire argument. In effect they were saying that in the last analysis the Southerner must decide between a mere political arrangement and a way of life. The secessionists could not have been more pleased, for reducing the crisis to the same options was a cardinal theme of their campaign. However, one ought not be too harsh on the cooperationists. They were trapped in an insoluble paradox. They wanted both the Union and Northern guarantees on slavery, and by 1860 these two goals were mutually exclusive. The stronger they pushed for the one, the weaker were their chances of obtaining the other.

Having conceded so much, what positive arguments were left to the cooperationists? In enumerating the inherent advantages which they believed cooperation offered the South, the conservatives came closest to mounting an offensive. They, too, made appeals to Southern honor. Her nine million citizens were strong enough to act cautiously without fear of "being crushed, should they not rush precipitately and rashly into revolution." By combining their resources, the states would impress the North with their strength and mini-

[15] Henry Watson to H. Barnard, Dec. 23, Watson Papers, DU; *Montgomery Weekly Post*, Nov. 28; *Mobile Daily Advertiser*, Dec. 7; letter of D. C. Anderson in *ibid.*, Nov. 27.

mize the chances of war. They would be able to share the costs of defense and restore financial confidence. A united South would be recognized as a nation sooner by foreign powers. While working together to build a strong edifice for protection and future prosperity, the states should not fear taking a reasonable amount of time. Southern congressmen should remain in Washington until Lincoln's inauguration and thus prevent the passage of legislation injurious to the South. Delay would enable the wishes of sister states in the upper South to be taken into consideration. Most importantly, the states must not move so quickly that the wishes of the people were ignored. Since such a short time was allowed for convention campaigns to debate such momentous issues, any action taken by the conventions should be referred back to the people.[16]

As the prospects for compromise grew dimmer, the co-operationists increasingly emphasized that their program gave conservatives a safety valve. The conservatives' greatest worry, and the fear which underlay their insistence that if secession must come it should be as smooth a transition of power as possible with minimal disruptions of property and institutions, was that the radicals would plunge the South into anarchy. Thus, conservatives soon realized that they had to exercise some control over secession in order to protect their own interests. The Mobile *Register*, a Douglas paper, argued this point effectively. There were only two courses left open to the South. "One, a mere hurrah movement, in which all the evils of revolution will be let loose, and the demons of anarchy will riot at will; in which frenzied appeals will take the place of reason, demagogues usurp the seats of statesmanship, and secret leagues supercede [sic] constituted authority." Politically, this would result in the Balkanization of the South; splintered and weak, she would be as pitiful as the South American republics. The effect on public and pri-

[16] Resolutions of Vicksburg Union Meeting of Nov. 29, quoted in *Daily Mississippian*, Dec. 1; *Autauga Citizen*, Dec. 6; speech of Daniel Chandler, *Mobile Daily Advertiser*, Dec. 18.

vate property would be disastrous. On the other hand the South could emulate the wisdom and patience of the revolutionary forefathers,

> so that we have at least a firm foundation laid for a new edifice ere the old one is razed to the ground. By such a course the worse evils attending so important a change will be essentially lessened, perhaps wholly removed, and the transition effected without vital injury to any of our important interests. Whether it shall be the one or the other depends on the conservative men of the country. Other choice, we repeat, they have none.

Mobile's Whig paper, the *Advertiser*, used the same logic in justifying its support of the cooperationist slate. Both tickets, it was admitted, would probably act the same at the convention, but they felt their men were better equipped for the task of building a new government.[17]

Cooperationism appealed to conservatives on three different levels, all of which were interdependent. It provided the last hope of saving the Union; failing in that, it could function as a stabilizing device minimizing the dangers to the South and maintaining order; lastly, it was a mechanism which promised conservatives a voice in the new order. Individuals interpreted the movement according to their own needs. For Jeremiah Clemens, it was a political tool, an effort to buy time. "No good may come of it, but no evil *can*." William Gould, a Whig planter in the Alabama Black Belt, reluctantly embraced cooperationism as the lesser of two evils. He analyzed his dilemma in his diary and left a rare, introspective account of a conservative planter's reaction to the secession crisis.[18]

[17] Quoted in the *Weekly Montgomery Confederation*, Nov. 23; *Mobile Daily Advertiser*, Dec. 23.

[18] Clemens to Crittenden, Dec. 25, Crittenden Papers, LC. The following account on Gould is taken from his diary. The quotations will be found in the entries for Oct. 16, Nov. 24, and Dec. 23, ADAH.

Gould was a sixty-year-old, Massachusetts-born planter who had grown wealthy in the South. In 1860 he owned a 1,500-acre plantation and 53 slaves, with a total value in excess of $100,000. Members of his class had the greatest economic stake in preserving the Union. Though active in politics, Gould was not a very astute politician. As late as the middle of September he expected Bell, or "the Union ticket," to carry every Southern state except South Carolina. Within a month news that Pennsylvania had gone Republican and pessimistic reports on the fusion movement in New York forced Gould to consider the effects of a Lincoln victory. He was amazed by the spread of Republicanism, "the greatest wonder of this wonderful age." "I cannot bring my mind to the belief that it will end in dissolution of the Union but it cannot be denied that there are troubles ahead and the wisest cannot foretell the result."

When Lincoln's election was a fact, a calamity which Gould blamed on the "Yanceyite," he assumed a wait-and-see attitude. The instant and contagious demands for secession soon made a mockery of Gould's hopes for a calm, dignified reaction to Republican rule. He took small solace in articles urging conciliation and moderation that he found in the press of both sections. "They ought to be read and re-read —but I fear will only be sneered at by the leading Demogogues [sic] who have set their hearts upon disunion, and nothing but disunion." After refusing to attend a separate secessionist meeting in Eutaw, he participated in the cooperationist movement. He was honest in rationalizing his actions. Since October 26 (the first time he acknowledged the inevitability of Lincoln's election), "my views have been modified to some extent. Circumstances change—and I must either change with them or stand alone." He found himself retreating from one position to another. Initially he favored giving Lincoln a chance and waiting for some unconstitutional act. When that hope proved illusory, he held out for a national convention, composed of two delegates from each state, which

243

just might be able to hammer out a compromise. Finally he settled for a Southern Convention. He would accept their decision. "Whatever it may be I shall feel bound to submit, as the best that can be expected under existing circumstances. In changing my opinion, I do not, by any means admit that my first position was not the right one. . . ."

Henry Watson was another transplanted Yankee who had found wealth in the Black Belt. Returning to his plantation near Greensboro in the middle of December from a trip North, he found conditions as bad as his brother Sereno had written him. He quickly realized that the only hope of even staunch Unionists was "to advise delay till a sufficiency of the states may agree to secede together to make the new government a repectable [sic] one. I have ceased to expect that Reason will resume her sway." Delay would cool off the excitement and increase the chances of sound conservative men being elected to the state convention; they could be trusted, he felt, to secure a good Constitution.[19]

James L. Alcorn was too ambitious a politician to let the main chance pass him by. When he immigrated to Mississippi in 1844, he was a struggling young lawyer from the Kentucky frontier. Rising rapidly in the economic and political circles of Coahoma County, he was by 1860 a wealthy planter and a power in Whig politics. He was a perfect representative of the younger Delta Whiggery; proud and cultured, possessing a sense of duty and the ability to lead, and with a progressive conception of the state as a promoter of social and economic welfare. He championed the cooperationist cause on the stump and in the convention. His plan was rejected but Alcorn was not overly discouraged. Writing his wife on the day the ordinance of secession was passed, he was quite proud to report that his speeches had been received splendidly and that his fellow delegates placed the utmost confidence in him. Since he had no doubt that he would be elected a brigadier general, the military post he desired, he had turned down a

[19] Watson to Messrs. Thayer and Peck, Dec. 14, and Watson to H. Barnard, Dec. 23, Watson Papers, DU.

seat in the Provisional Congress to meet at Montgomery.[20] Alcorn had supported cooperationism as long as it could be defended as legitimate dissent. When faced with secession, he had made certain that he would be close to the center of power and in a position to exert his customary leadership.

As a movement to block immediate secession by separate state action, cooperationism failed. In this regard the conservatives labored under insurmountable odds. The governors were against them, the victorious Breckinridge party machinery was controlled by their opponents, and the common people were too fearful and angry to heed moderation. Too many were resigned to secession. A Methodist minister wrote: "Secession seems to be the order of the day. It is, perhaps, the only remedy left, and much as I deplore it, I greatly prefer it to such strife and injustice as we have suffered for years past."[21] Furthermore, cooperationists were caught on the horns of a cruel dilemma. They were committed to the Union but the price they demanded for its continuance was clearly unacceptable to Northern opinion. Indeed, these very demands were the crux of the whole crisis. However, for those who feared anarchy more than secession, cooperationism was a partial success. The states did secede in relative proximity to one another and rapidly formed a Confederacy. Disruptions to institutions and property were kept at a minimum. If only the Yankees had agreed to let the South leave in peace, conservatives were prepared to live with the revolution they so dreaded.

II

The counterpart of the ideological contrasts between the parties was the manner in which each waged its campaign for convention delegates. The secessionists' tactics were de-

[20] Lillian A. Pereyra, *James Lusk Alcorn, Persistent Whig* (Baton Rouge, 1966), 3–4; Alcorn to his wife, Jan. 15, 1861, James Lusk Alcorn Papers, MDAH.

[21] Eugene V. Levert to Francis J. Levert, Dec. 1, Levert Papers, SHC.

signed to sustain the resistance spirit ignited by Lincoln's election and to neutralize any opposition. They immediately called for resistance meetings which demanded secession. At the same time these calls were couched in nonpartisan rhetoric which identified secession with Southernism and opposition with petty partisanship. Care was taken to include a prominent Whig on the secessionist ticket; this solidified the claim that their cause was above politics and further divided the conservatives. Wherever necessary they agreed on compromises in the wording of resolutions in order to achieve unanimity behind one secessionist slate. Thus, the main objective of electing secessionists was assured and the politically divisive debates on the merits of immediate action versus delay and cooperation were avoided. Compromise resolutions sacrificed nothing since they generally were so vaguely worded as to permit secessionists to interpret them to their own advantage before the voters.

The conservatives were as weak and divided in campaigning as they were hesitant and defensive in their ideology. In many counties they put up no organized opposition to the secessionists or allowed themselves to be satisfied with resolutions that did not specifically exclude cooperative action. In other areas the conservatives had trouble agreeing on candidates and organized too late. These belated efforts could do little to stem the secessionist tide. A suggestion of the Selma *Sentinel* that Alabama conservatives meet in a state convention at Selma on December 5 came to naught. Mississippi conservatives did succeed in holding such a convention at Vicksburg on November 29 but only four counties were represented.[22]

In the Alabama Black Belt, the initial resistance meetings were controlled by the secessionists and the conservatives never did mount an effective counterattack. On November 12 a meeting in Selma voted down the cooperationist resolution of John W. Lapsley, a Douglas lawyer. N.H.R. Daw-

[22] *Alabama State Sentiniel*, Nov. 21; *Daily Mississippian*, Dec. 1.

son's resolution—"that we, the citizens of Selma, are opposed to living under a government with a Black Republican President"—passed. Dawson was a Breckinridge lawyer and chairman of the local Minute Men. A week later the secessionists nominated their convention slate, a ticket neatly balanced between an elderly Whig planter and a young Breckinridge lawyer. They ran on an ambiguous platform which the pro-Douglas Selma *Sentinel* criticized as "a two-faced concern." The paper, warning conservatives not to be deceived, argued that the nominating convention knew full well that both candidates were immediate secessionists and that Judge Pettus, chairman of the committee on resolutions, favored such a course. Furthermore, the meeting had voted down any referral back to the people. There was a week's delay before the cooperationists held their nominating convention. Their bipartisan slate was late in the field, conceded that the state must secede, and made a poor showing, obtaining only 26% of the vote. Though the secessionists were in complete charge, they apparently took no chances. If we are to believe John Hardy, editor of the cooperationist *Sentinel*, rural postmasters interfered with deliveries of his paper.[23]

The secessionists were as successful in the rest of the Black Belt. In Lowndes County they nominated candidates as early as November 17. The only show of opposition at the nominating meeting came from a Douglas planter, John P. Cook, who resolved that the governor should ask the legislature to pass a law requiring an election to decide whether or not Alabama should even hold a state convention. Breckinridge had carried 61% of the county's vote and the radicals saw little need to appease the opposition. Both their candidates were Breckinridge men who stated unequivocally they were for immediate and separate secession. Indeed, the cooperationists never surfaced. The Whigs were disorganized with many voters having followed their county leaders into the States' Rights Opposition movement in the latter half of the

[23] *Alabama State Sentinel*, Nov. 21, Dec. 5, 19.

decade. Conservative papers did suggest that Dr. F. C. Webb, a Whig physician, and Benjamin Harrison, a Douglas planter, be chosen as cooperationists, but a scheduled nominating meeting in Hayneville on December 2 was called off. On election day the Whigs boycotted the polls rather than vote secessionist.[24]

Secessionists also ran virtually unopposed in Marengo, Montgomery, and Perry. The 40% Whig minority in each county was left adrift by the inaction of its leadership. In contrast the Breckinridge men moved surely and swiftly. Montgomery's first resistance meeting was held on November 10 and declared for immediate secession. Another meeting four days later enrolled the names of those favoring separate state action and formed a Central Safety Committee, thus linking secession with self-defense. The committee justified its existence by claiming that the *"public conscience"* of the now dominant North was implacably hostile to Southern institutions. Its members were a very effective pressure group which raised funds, corresponded with the secessionist leaders, and prepared rabid, prosecessionist addresses. The secessionist nominees, Thomas Hill Watts and William Lowndes Yancey, were chosen on November 17 and deftly balanced the county's two main political groups. Watts, a young lawyer-planter and Bell elector, was one of the most influential Whigs in southern Alabama. He had run unsuccessfully for Congress in 1855 and then moved into the States' Rights Opposition party. Ever since his widely publicized Tuskegee speech of September 13 in which he announced that Lincoln's election would be sufficient cause for secession, he had been a perfect candidate for the secessionists. Yancey had long been

[24] Hayneville *Watchman*, Nov. 23; Kit C. Carter, "A Critical Analysis of the Basis of Party Alignment in Lowndes County, Alabama, 1836–1860," unpublished master's essay (University of Alabama, 1961), 67; Benton *Weekly Herald*, Nov. 15, Dec. 6; Peggy Jane Duckworth, "The Role of Alabama Black Belt Whigs in the Election of Delegates to the Secession Convention," unpublished master's essay (University of Alabama, 1961), 123.

identified in the public mind as the leader of disunion. As fitting as his inclusion on the ticket was, his presence was bound to rankle many conservatives who viewed him as the personification of the enemy. Running Watts with Yancey mollified much of this discontent and enabled the ticket to present a united front. Montgomery conservatives did not offer an opposing slate. They had lost two key leaders, J. J. Seibels, editor of the Douglas *Confederation*, and Daniel Sayre, editor of the Whig *Post*. After Lincoln's election Seibels sold out his interest in the paper and Sayre resigned. Both papers deplored the haste and sensationalism of the secessionists but their efforts at rallying the conservatives educed such a weak response that they did little more than hold a cooperationist meeting on December 5 with some like-minded citizens of Pike County.[25]

In the western Black Belt counties of Sumter and Pickens the cooperationists fared little better. In the former county they did not agree on a candidate until December 10, just two weeks before the election. In touting their choice, Willis V. Hare, the cooperationists attempted to avoid the usual campaign rhetoric. Their clever, but futile, strategy was to stress that Hare, a large slaveholding farmer, offered the voters a welcome relief from having to select their representatives from among only lawyers. If the farmers were flattered, they hid their feelings well. The secessionist candidate, a young Breckinridge lawyer, received over 95% of the vote. In Pickens the cooperationists were better organized and polled about a quarter of the vote. Their strength was among the county's yeomen hill farmers. It was the presence of this group in much larger numbers than the rest of the Black Belt

[25] *Weekly Montgomery Confederation*, Dec. 7, Nov. 23; *Montgomery Weekly Post*, Nov. 14; *Montgomery Weekly Advertiser*, Dec. 5. Although there are no accounts of the campaign in Marengo and Perry, we do know that in Perry the secessionists pulled off a masterful stroke by choosing as one of their candidates James J. Bailey, one of the most popular Whigs in the county who repeatedly had been re-elected as probate judge.

that enabled these cooperationist candidates to employ a conditional unionist ideology usually found only in northern Alabama.[26]

Greene, Breckinridge's weakest planting county, was the only Black Belt county where the cooperationists made a respectable showing. They were led by John G. Harvey, the veteran editor of the *Alabama Beacon* and a conditional unionist who argued his position forcefully. On November 16 he issued a call for a Union meeting in Greensboro on the following day. The secessionists, in danger of losing the initiative, first tore down the handbills announcing the Union meeting and then met on November 19 and decided to establish a "Southern Rights Press." A committee of three was formed to write William H. Fowler of Tuscaloosa inviting him to edit a secessionist paper. Harvey, who back in July had been pressured by his subscribers to cease his editorial endorsement of Douglas, was now forced to sell his paper to Fowler. He explained that after seventeen years as the *Beacon*'s editor he was most reluctant to sell out but had no choice because of "the strong antagonism of opinion and views between himself and many of his subscribers. . . ." With Harvey removed, the secessionists sought to consolidate their victory by placating conservatives with mild and confusing resolutions. A Greensboro meeting declared on the twenty-fourth that Alabama should secede "without any further delay than may be necessary to obtain in the speediest manner a consultation with other slaveholding States, in the hope of securing their co-operation in a movement which we deem essential to our safety." These resolutions were seconded in Eutaw two days later.[27]

The conservatives did not take the bait. They knew that the resolutions meant anything anyone wanted them to mean and feared that the secessionists would use them as a guise

[26] Gainesville *Independent*, Dec. 15, Duckworth, "Role of Alabama Black Belt Whigs," 112.

[27] Sereno Watson to Henry Watson, Nov. 17, Watson Papers, DU; *Alabama Beacon*, Nov. 30.

to slip two of their own into the convention unopposed. In early December both factions held nominating conventions. The secessionists chose two lawyers, one from each major party; the cooperationists put up two Whigs, a planter and a lawyer. There was no longer any need for the pretense of harmonizing different opinions, so the secessionists flayed cooperationism as illegal and treasonable submission. The secessionists won with 61% of the vote, but they had been forced to extend themselves.

Autauga, on the Black Belt's north central border, was the one southern county with substantial planting interests which the cooperationists came close to carrying. Their movement was based on Bolling Hall's Douglas organization, a cohesive group which had won for Douglas his largest vote in southern Alabama with the exception of Mobile. A bipartisan resistance meeting, chaired by the Whig industrialist, Daniel Pratt, called for a county convention in Kingston on November 24. The Kingston convention was a raucous affair. The pro-Douglas *Citizen* blamed it on "that old partyism"; the Bell and Douglas supporters, as well as conservative Breckinridge men, sought harmony, but "*the Separate State Action Yanceymen* were determined to have things their own way, or not at all." The trouble began when the chairman, Dr. W. C. Penick, a Breckinridge planter-physician, appointed the committee on resolutions. Passing over such leading conservatives as the Hall brothers, Senator Fitzpatrick, and Daniel Pratt, he stacked the ten-man committee with seven Breckinridge supporters. According to the *Citizen*, these seven were "young and inexperienced men" whose only qualification was that they "happened to have voted with the Yancey party heretofore." Party lines held in the committee. The majority report demanded separate secession and the minority report of the three Douglas members held out for cooperative action with a majority of the Southern states. In voting on a motion to take the majority report from the table and vote on its adoption, a division was called. Since such a large crowd (some 500 to 600) was in attendance

251

and control was difficult in the meeting hall, the convention retired to the street, formed two lines, and had the tellers take the vote. At this point confusion broke out. The cooperationists felt they were being shortchanged, refused to go back in, and proceeded to hold their own meeting. Within a few hours each party had chosen their candidate.[28]

In the county canvassing, the secessionists played up racist appeals, and the fact that their nominee, Dr. George Rives of Coosada, had been selected from "not among the politicians, but the sturdy yeomanry"; he was "the man on whom all might unite without feeling any sting of old party prejudice." On their part cooperationists defended their program as one which would avert civil war. The election was very close; the secessionists won with 51% of the vote. Hall carried seven of the county's ten beats but, by being crushed in the two largest beats, Autaugaville and Pratteville, both of which represented the cotton regions in the Alabama River Valley, lost the election.[29]

South of the Black Belt the cooperationists carried only one county, Conecuh. Indecision and lack of organization once again plagued their efforts. However, conservative setbacks in southern Alabama were expected since most of the region had gone heavily for Breckinridge. It was in counties such as Mobile and Butler where the Whigs traditionally were very strong that cooperationists' failures to stop immediate secession hurt their cause the most.

[28] *Autauga Citizen*, Nov. 22, 29.

[29] Pratteville *Southern Statesman*, Dec. 8; *Autauga Citizen*, Dec. 6. Hindsight suggests that the cooperationists made a serious tactical blunder in not nominating Daniel Pratt. By coincidence a special legislature election was held at the same time to fill a vacancy in the Alabama House. Pratt ran as a Whig and on a cooperationist platform. He won with 57% of the vote. His showing closely paralleled that of Bolling Hall the cooperationist nominee, in all the beats except Pratt's home district of Pratteville. Pratt lost the precinct, but only by 5 votes; Hall lost it by 160. In addition, Pratt ran nearly as well as did Hall in his home district of Chestnut Creek.

The city of Mobile, though giving Breckinridge only 29% of its vote, favored the secessionists' candidates by two to one. The cooperationists lost all seven wards. This was a crucial defeat for the conservatives, for Mobile had been the center of the Douglas movement in the southern part of the state and, with its extensive trade relations with the North, offered the cooperationists unique advantages. The conservatives' first mistake was in misreading public opinion. The Whiggish Mobile *Advertiser* wanted the people's role in the crisis minimized. The paper suggested that each county select its "best men" and send them uncommitted to the convention. Deferring to the judgment of their leaders, the people should trust them to devise the proper means of resistance. Meanwhile the secessionists began enlisting supporters; they utilized popular discontent as a political tool rather than attempting to ignore it.[30]

The secessionists' campaign began on November 15 when a bipartisan meeting endorsed immediate secessionist resolutions. Though forced to react, conservatives still vacillated. Their appeals to Unionism rang hollow when the dwindling Unionist ranks had no leaders or organization with which to combat the secessionists and their campaign sputtered from the start. On the twenty-third the *Advertiser* announced a slate of four convention candidates. None of them had been publicly nominated and two subsequently declined to run.[31] The secessionists held their nominating meeting on December 1. Their four-man ticket offset two Breckinridge men with a Douglas and a Bell supporter.

The conservatives, bewildered and leaderless, waited two weeks before they entered their own convention slate. No Breckinridge men would consent to run so the ticket was

[30] Clemens to Crittenden, Dec. 25, Crittenden Papers, LC; *Mobile Daily Advertiser*, Nov. 15.

[31] *Mobile Daily Advertiser*, Nov. 16, 20. John Forsyth, editor of the Douglas *Mobile Register*, and D. C. Anderson, a Breckinridge lawyer, declined in public letters printed in the *Advertiser* on Dec. 14.

divided between Whigs and Douglasites. The defiance of late November by now had been drained. "This election is *no cause* for a dissolution of the Union, but it is *the occasion* that demonstrates the true sources of our danger," explained Daniel Chandler in the keynote speech of the cooperationist meeting. Another speaker admitted that the overthrow of the government was necessitated by the need to protect slavery. Some secessionists led by Colin J. McRae tried to disrupt the meeting, but they need not have bothered. The cooperationists accepted watered down resolutions which agreed to separate state secession to take effect as soon as four coterminous states joined Alabama. Only if these four states hung back should secession be referred back to the people. Nothing better revealed the conservatives' difficulties than the absence from their nominating meeting of C. C. Langdon, a Connecticut born editor who had championed Mobile's Whigs for twenty years. In a public letter Langdon criticized the cooperationists' feeble efforts and pointedly disassociated himself from their resolutions.[32]

The cooperationists had little more than a week in which to campaign. Much of this time was spent in efforts to convince the voters of their Southernism. They granted the inevitability of secession and insisted that they too were "for resistance, prompt, vigorous and effective." They were not proposing any unreasonable delay but were only working to ensure that secession would proceed smoothly and Alabama would not be left alone. In an appeal to business support, the cooperationists were portrayed as men "who have large interests to be affected by the measures they will be called upon to consider, and thus afford strong personal guarantees of their fidelity, if elected, to the grave and important trust confided to them." These last minute endeavors failed and the cooperationists lost badly. While threats of intimidation directed against cooperationists should not be overlooked,

[32] *Ibid.*, Dec. 18, 20. Florida, Mississippi, Georgia, and South Carolina were the four coterminous states.

their defeat can be traced to their indecision and slow re-action to political realities.[33]

Butler County registered no active opposition to secession. Its two convention delegates were nominated together on an immediate and separate state secessionist platform and swept all but five of the 696 votes cast in the delegate election. With only one ticket in the field, this election elicited such little voter response that two out of every three who voted in the presidential election stayed away from the polls. Breckinridge and Bell supporters alike stayed home, as there was no cor-relation in the beat returns between the decline in the seces-sion vote and the strength of any one party.[34]

A public call for a meeting of all citizens, regardless of party, at the Greenville courthouse on December 1 provided the organizational initiative for secession. Thomas Hill Watts, John W. A. Sanford, and the famous Yancey were scheduled to speak. "Let everybody come. On the same day, those who are opposed to submission to Lincoln will nominate candi-dates for the Convention." The tone had been set for the up-coming selection of delegates. A nonpartisan common front would be stressed, leading secessionist orators were to be brought in, and the issue reduced to secession or submission.[35]

The Greenville meeting was orderly and well-controlled. Yancey and Thomas Watts spoke and resolutions in favor of *"Separate State Action"* passed unanimously. Samuel J. Bolling, an old line Whig and probate court judge, and John McPherson, a Breckinridge yeoman farmer, were chosen as the county's candidates. The convention's leaders were a bipartisan group of wealthy Greenville slaveholders. On the twenty-four-man nominating committee, the Breckinridge

---

[33] *Ibid.*, Dec. 19, 23.

[34] Duckworth, "Role of Alabama Black Belt Whigs," 70.

[35] Greenville *South Alabamian*, Nov. 24. On December 12 the Greenville *Southern Messenger* carried the only account of a precinct meeting. This was held in Monterrey on November 30. The older Whigs boycotted the meeting which passed secessionist resolutions calling for cooperation only after secession had been accomplished.

party was represented by six members and the Whigs by only one. The committee was dominated by small-to-medium size slaveholding farmers, men in their thirties or forties who were wealthier than most of their neighbors but who had not yet advanced into the planter class of great wealth and large slaveholdings.[36]

The meeting had performed its task so well, and Bolling and McPherson played their nonpartisan roles so skillfully, that no serious opposition emerged against the secessionist slate. In justifying the Whigs' inaction, their paper, the Greenville *Southern Messenger*, claimed that both candidates stood for "the *fullest* and *most unlimited*, consultation and co-operation of the Southern States, before the act of secession. . . ." Hence, the editors were pleased that a tentative call for a second nominating meeting had been dropped. Such action they felt, would "create division or dissension among the people." They concluded by stating that they had always believed McPherson to be "a secessionist, *per se*," and were reluctant to support him and Bolling, but now felt more confident in doing so.[37]

Why the Whigs professed such confidence in the secessionist ticket is a mystery. The resolutions passed at the December 1 meeting clearly and unmistakably demanded immediate and separate state secession. Neither McPherson nor Bolling was on public record as construing them any differently and their subsequent action at the state convention was of a straight-out character. Furthermore, the Greenville meeting had even ignored the earlier request of the *Southern Messenger* that it be stipulated that any separate secession by Alabama should be subject to the voters' approval. Perhaps the Whig editors were simply being realistic. After all, Judge Bolling, a leading Whig and one of the largest landholders in the county, was on the ticket; he certainly met the paper's criterion of sending only the "wisest and best men" to the

[36] *Southern Messenger*, Dec. 5.
[37] *Southern Messenger*, Dec. 12, 19.

Convention and his judgment was to be trusted. No opposing group had stepped forward and why risk being branded a submissionist in a hopeless cause? By taking the position they did, however disingenuous, the editors at least formally maintained a conservative posture.[38]

In a striking example of the state's sectionalism, northern Alabama overwhelmingly backed the cooperationists. Only one county, Calhoun, went secessionist. Here the cooperationists had the advantages implicit in belonging to a popular majority. With mass support and extensive newspaper encouragement, they were assured of receiving a fair hearing. Unionist editors were not forced out of business and public opinion, though shocked and upset by Lincoln's election, had not reached the paranoic levels of southern Alabama. Strangers were suspect but there were no calls for the immediate outlawry of all Northerners.[39] Rational debate was still possible.

Operating from a favorable base which they lacked south of the mountains, the conservatives here were organized and disciplined. Their candidates were nominated as soon as, if not earlier than, those of the secessionists. In most areas they seized the initiative. Jeremiah Clemens of Huntsville drew up and distributed by November 19 a cooperationist circular signed by 100 citizens. He rallied the conservatives, made certain their case was presented to the people, and put the secessionists on the defensive. Resolutions passed at a meeting in Ashville on December 1 exemplified the more positive tone of the northern cooperationists. They would ever defend Southern rights but stated that "these Rights can be better

[38] *Southern Messenger*, Nov. 21, 28, Dec. 5.

[39] Down in Barbour County the *Clayton Banner* argued on December 13 that "The immediate outlawry of all who after this date may come among us from the land where they educate and send forth emissaries to incite insurrections, secret poisonings, murders and house burnings at the South, is necessary and justifiable on the ground that *most of those who come have more or less connection* with the criminal objects mentioned."

preserved and secured in the Union than by Secession and Dissolution." The "mere election" of a president and vice-president, whatever their opinions, was not a sufficient cause for disunion. They were strongly opposed to separate state secession and demanded that no state secede without the previous consent of the upper South.[40]

To shore up their minority position the secessionists resorted to two stratagems. They usually yielded the point of referring any secession ordinance back to the people and they sought noncontroversial nominees who were not identified by the public with radical planter demands. For example, in St. Clair County they nominated a sixty-two-year-old merchant, Alemeth Byers. He was billed as a long resident of the county and "one who is not nor never has been an aspirant for any office." In Franklin County they ran a Whig physician and a public school teacher.[41]

In some cases all the secessionists wanted from such candidates was the use of their names. Their original nominees in Tuscaloosa County were Basil Manly, the area's best known Baptist minister, and D. Garland, President of the University of Alabama. Charles Manly, Basil's son, informed his father that the committee on nominations did not expect him or Garland to actively canvass the county. If they felt a canvass was necessary, they would attend to it. A few days later Charles reported that Judge Moody, the secessionists' leader, did not want Basil to feel compelled to accept publicly the nomination. If he did, fine, but it was not obligatory. "They did not wish you to suppose that they considered you a *candidate* in the ordinary sense of that term." The secessionists lost the county, but their tactics did assure them of support from the clergy and professors. Robert Jemison, one of the cooperationist candidates, acknowledged this opposition and resented it.[42] The secessionists won only one northern county,

---

[40] *St. Clair Diamond*, Dec. 5.

[41] *Ibid.*, Dec. 5; Tuscumbia *States' Rights Democrat*, Dec. 7.

[42] Garland declined because of his duties at the University and was replaced by A. S. Nicholson, a Breckinridge lawyer. Charles

but they were more competitive there, carrying on the average 40% of the vote, than were the cooperationists in the south, who averaged only 15% of the vote.

III

Mississippi conservatives held a state convention at Vicksburg on November 29, but only four counties sent representatives—Adams, Warren, Rankin, and Hinds. The Breckinridge press jumped on this poor showing and ridiculed the conservatives for their futility. Of course, claimed the *Mississippian*, no Breckinridge men were present and "but an infinitesimal part of the Bell party." Weak as the Vicksburg convention was, it was nonetheless crucial for defining the issues on which the election for delegates would be contested. By coming out for cooperation, a Southern convention, and referral back, the convention offered the voters a choice and claimed to provide "the only prevention of ruin to our commercial, our agricultural, and our mechanical interests, of oppressive taxation, and of the horrors of civil war."[43]

Prior to Vicksburg the spontaneous resistance meetings across the state normally had not specified the mode of secession. Typical was a meeting in Macon on November 17. A committee on resolutions was formed, and speakers took turns condemning the North and announcing their readiness to fight for Southern rights. Judge Ruff "thought the time for argument was passed; men were apt to talk too much and act too little." Judge Beauchamp concluded his speech by reading his slaveholding audience some inflammatory passages from Helper's *The Impending Crisis*. Others admitted being committed to disunion for some time or pronounced that the

---

Manly to Basil Manly, Nov. 29, Manly Collection, UA; *ibid.*, Nov. 29 and Dec. 2; S. C. Oldshue, "The Secession Movement in Tuscaloosa County, Alabama," unpublished master's essay (University of Alabama, 1961), 36–37.

[43] *Daily Mississippian*, Dec. 1. A fifth county, Madison, did have one representative.

Union was already dissolved. H. W. Foote, the largest slave-holder at the meeting, was one of the few who advised caution. General resolutions in favor of withdrawal were passed.[44]

Few accounts of the county campaigns in Mississippi have survived. However, the circumstances surrounding the elections were the same as those in Alabama and what accounts we do have closely paralleled the Alabama pattern. In most areas the secessionists were in the majority and pressed their advantages by maximizing the sense of crisis. In doubtful areas they concentrated on exacerbating racist fears and confusing the issues. J.A.P. Campbell and E. M. Wells, the two secessionist candidates from Attala County, stated the Republicans were "*in favor of abolishing all distinctions in social position and in civil and political rights between negroes and white men and women.*" The same candidates were accused by the cooperationist *Kosciusko Chronicle* of disguising their position in an obvious attempt "to suit the feeling of each particular locality."[45] Where conservatives did have some popular support, they frequently ruined their chances through the same indecision and political naïveté which characterized their Alabama counterparts.

In Lowndes County a bipartisan meeting on November 19, chaired by a Whig planter, took a conservative position. Secession was not to take effect until March 4 unless before then the North guaranteed Southern security and repealed "all their odious, offensive and unconstitutional legislation" on the rendition of fugitive slaves. Within a few weeks the Breckinridge men could no longer stand on such a platform. The Whigs had appropriated this position for themselves at Vicksburg and Pettus' Jackson meeting on November 24 had decided that the Democrats were to run on immediate secession. Apparently the Lowndes Democrats were in a bind. On the one hand, the resolutions passed on the nineteenth

[44] *Macon Beacon*, Nov. 21.

[45] *Kosciusko Chronicle*, undated December, 1860, clipping in the Jason Niles Books, Vol. 41, SHC; *ibid.*, Dec. 15.

were unacceptable, but at the same time they wanted to continue the common front with the Whigs which had evolved at the meeting. This was the practical value of the platform; it was one "upon which both [parties] could stand without too great a sacrifice of party pride."[46]

The Whigs, with their strong organization based in Columbus, had to be respected. They had the potential to defeat an immediate secessionist candidate. For this reason, the Democrats were willing to let Judge Clayton, a top ranking Whig, write a conciliatory platform which united the parties. They also agreed to Clayton as a candidate, along with their own leader, William S. Barry. This ticket could face no serious opposition. A Columbus merchant and an ex-Democrat who had broken with his party in 1859 did run against it but polled only 14% of the vote. In return for unity and an assured victory, the Democrats in reality had sacrificed little. As for the resolutions, the Democrats simply deciphered them to their own ends. "The general interpretation among their supporters was, that they contemplated, in effect, *operation upon the part of Mississippi first, and co-operation afterwards.*" The *Mississippi Democrat* felt compelled to offer this explanation on the eve of the election because the resolutions "appear to be misunderstood in some localities."[47] It is unlikely Democratic leaders ever misunderstood them; instead they cleverly used the resolutions as a compromise device which neutralized the Whig opposition.

Madison County conservatives, though not as openly disarmed, still reacted too slowly. At the first resistance meeting in Canton on November 19, the conservatives, led by three wealthy old Whigs, mustered enough support to force the passage of noncommittal secessionist resolutions. In commenting on the Canton meeting, the *Citizen* unwittingly revealed the root of the conservatives' weakness. The paper pointed out that many Union men went to the meeting determined not to vote on any resolutions. Identifying the call

[46] *Daily Mississippian*, Nov. 27; *Mississippi Democrat*, Dec. 20.
[47] *Mississippi Democrat*, Dec. 20.

for the meeting with the secessionists, these men attended with the vague hope of exerting a moderating influence but did not want to be party to any blatant disunionism. Even so, the *Citizen* felt that a referral back resolution would have carried were it not for the normal disinclination of a meeting to go against the wishes of the committee it had appointed. In addition, many believed that the candidates would eventually pledge themselves to referral back.[48] What the *Citizen* failed to stress was that it was this very passivity of the conservatives which enabled the secessionists to take the initiative and control events.

By early December the veneer of harmony which the meeting on the nineteenth had tried to impose had vanished. On December 3 the secessionists held their nominating convention in Canton. After hearing some cooperationist speeches which included the argument that neither Senator Jefferson Davis nor A. G. Brown favored separate state secession, the meeting got down to business. A motion was carried to exclude from balloting all who would not pledge to support and vote for whoever was nominated. This of course purged any cooperationists who were present. A small slaveholding Breckinridge lawyer, A. P. Hill, was nominated. Apparently some voted for Hill as a compromise candidate because he stood on the resolutions of the nineteenth. Criticizing such reasoning, John F. Bosworth of the *Citizen* argued "such persons are mistaken. These resolutions declare simply for 'resistance,' without pointing out the *mode* of resistance. Judge Hill may think—and, we have no doubt, does think—that the best way to *resist* is, to secede at once from the Union." Secessionist sentiment was so popular, however, that Bosworth found it necessary to be defensive about his response. "There is no factious spirit of opposition among the late supporters of Bell and Everett to anything that may be proposed by the late Breckinridge party; but they cannot and will not endorse the Yancey programme of precipitate

[48] *Semi-Weekly Mississippian*, Nov. 23; Canton *American Citizen*, Nov. 24, Dec. 1.

secession, and are driven, therefore, to the necessity of having a candidate to represent their own views." The conservatives lost a week's campaigning before they chose their candidate on December 10. Represented by C. C. Shackleford, a wealthy Whig lawyer-planter, they stood for referral back, a Southern Convention whose action should be ratified by the voters of the states represented therein, and keeping the state's Congressmen in Washington.[49] Though finally agreeing on a definite course of action, the cooperationists lost the county, winning just 37% of the vote.

Mississippi's conservatives made their best showing in the fertile river bottoms of the Delta and the rolling hills in the state's northern half. The Delta secessionists must rank among the state's boldest politicians. Even in the strongest Whig areas, they forcefully tried to push through their program. Counting on Whig apathy, they placed their hopes in controlling the county nominating conventions. This strategy can be seen in B. L. C. Wailes' account of a Natchez meeting on December 4. Wailes, far from an impartial observer, was a Whig of the old school who saw a demagogue in every Democratic politician and invariably read the worst into Democratic intentions. However, his account was corroborated by a briefer one appearing in the Breckinridge press.[50]

That an apolitical Whig such as Wailes even attended the Natchez meeting was a blow to the secessionists' strategy. After a brief and disappointing stint as a state representative in the 1820's he had eschewed politics for more than thirty years. The only exception came about in the late 1850's when he agreed to use his personal influence to block Demococratic inspired efforts to force Jefferson College, a Whiggish institution, to repay an old state loan of $10,000. He was successful but quickly returned to his plantation and intellectual pursuits. Nothing short of a distinct threat to the social order could ever push Wailes back into political action. He

[49] Canton *American Citizen*, Dec. 8, 15.
[50] Wailes Diary, Dec. 4, 1860, DU; *Mississippi Free Trader*, Dec. 10.

certainly saw such a threat after Lincoln's election. Lumping together "secession disunion violence and bloodshed" as "inevitable," Wailes was disheartened by the crisis. Instinctively he knew whom to blame: "the desperate demagogues are inflaming and exciting the populace to precipitate our country into a state of lawless violence & terror."[51] Pessimistic, but holding out a faint hope, he was both a cynical and astute observer at the Natchez meeting.

Breckinridge leaders, those referred to by Wailes as "the Free trader clique," were in charge of the meeting. The key man was the chairman, G. Malin Davis, a young slaveholding lawyer. Wailes had no doubts that Davis and one of the two vice-presidents, Dr. Walter Smith, were "ultra *fire-eaters* and separate and immediate secessionists." Three sets of resolutions were introduced. Two Whigs presented the usual conservative demands for a Southern convention and referral back; in direct opposition were the resolutions of Douglas Walworth, another young Breckinridge lawyer. A committee of nine, appointed by the chairman and vice-presidents, then considered the resolutions. Dominated by Breckinridge men, the committee reported out the Walworth resolutions. This, stressed Wailes, in spite of the fact that three-fourths of those present felt that only the people, not the legislature, had the authority to call for a state convention in the first place. The conservatives fought back. Additional cooperationist resolutions were put forth and passed as an amendment to the majority Walworth report. After some cooperationist speeches, the meeting climaxed. "An attempt was then made by some of the wire pullers of the free-trader office to have a committee of nomination appointed by the Presiding officers but in this they were foiled by a vote of at least ten to one when Issiah Winchester & Alen K. Farrar were nominated by acclamation by the meeting which then adjourned."[52]

[51] Charles S. Sydnor, *A Gentleman of the Old Natchez Region, Benjamin L. C. Wailes* (Durham, 1928), 230–233; Wailes Diary, Nov. 21, DU.

[52] Wailes Diary, Dec. 4, DU.

Although their power play had failed, the secessionists did not panic. They bolted the meeting, immediately regrouped, and nominated their own slate. There was none of the procrastination which characterized the Whigs in other areas when faced with similar defeats. With a political effrontery foreign to most of the Whigs, the secessionists even attempted to make capital out of their defeat. The Natchez *Free Trader* labeled the secessionists' meeting as the "People's Meeting." By a tortuous logic the paper argued that the people's will had been subverted at the original meeting since "the submissionists voted down the resolutions reported by the committee, and adopted another set by way of substitute that virtually yields to Black Republican Rule."[53]

Confronted with vigorous conservative opposition in Adams and Warren, the two traditional Whig counties of the lower Delta, the secessionists resorted to one last ploy. Since the cities of Natchez and Vicksburg were each entitled to separate representation in the lower house of the state legislature, the secessionists insisted that they likewise should vote separately for convention delegates. By this demand the secessionists hoped to concentrate on either the city or county nominee and thus win one of the two seats. They referred to the December 1 ruling of the state attorney general, Thomas J. Wharton, that the elections should be conducted separately in Adams and Warren. However, Wharton was a rabid secessionist, and the conservatives ignored his ruling. They claimed it was only a personal opinion with no legal backing. There were some rumblings from the secessionists that their tickets were the only legally elected ones in Adams and Warren since only they had run separately, but in the end they accepted defeat.[54] The state convention was safely secessionist. Disputing the two elections would serve no function and would smack of political greed. It would anger the

---

[53] *Mississippi Free Trader*, Dec. 10.

[54] *Ibid.*, Dec. 17; Natchez *Daily Courier*, Jan. 4, 1861; Vicksburg *Daily Evening Citizen*, Dec. 21. The cooperationists did have the

conservatives and weaken the secessionists' claim as the state's nonpartisan defenders.

In northern Mississippi the two parties fought to a standoff. Where the conservatives lacked the strength to carry cooperationist tickets, they frequently were able to force the creation of coalition slates, evenly divided between both factions. However, in agreeing to coalition tickets, the conservatives struck a bad bargain for themselves. Three of these slates—those in Carroll, Chickasaw, and Tippah—voted straight-out secessionist at the convention. Five others divided on at least one of the three conservative resolutions offered at the convention, but without voting for any one. In voting for the cooperationist Alcorn resolution, the Itawamba slate was the only one where the conservatives succeeded in getting better than a stalemate.[55] On the other hand, running on a coalition ticket enabled the secessionists to more than offset conservative strength in the North. The voter turnout in these elections was light and little excitement was generated. Since debates over the issues were minimized, conservative opposition was deprived of an effective voice.

On December 29 a Douglas Democrat from Corinth wrote Andrew Johnson that opposition to secession in northern Mississippi, combined with outside pressure, would soon force the decision on secession back to the people "where it will be as signally rebuked as it was in 1851 in this state."[56] By this late date, though, such hopes were a delusion. The conservatives had been neutralized in the north and crushed in the traditionally Democratic areas of the south. They soon would have no choice but to accept secession.

---

best of the argument since a precedent of no separate representation had been set in the elections for the state convention of 1851.

[55] The votes of individual delegates on the three main conservative resolutions offered at the convention can be followed in the *Journal of the State Convention and Ordinances and Resolutions Adopted in January, 1861, With an Appendix* (Jackson, 1861), 14–16.

[56] J. M. Jones to Johnson, Dec. 29, Andrew Johnson Papers, LC.

SEVEN

OLD FACES IN A NEW CAMPAIGN

THE secession campaigns were shorter but more intense versions of the same politics of fear which had marked the presidential election. Although this fear resulted in a nearly universal belief that Lincoln's election somehow had to be resisted, the contrasting social characteristics of both the leadership and mass support for the secessionists and cooperationists revealed that Southerners were once again divided by their status aspirations and roles in slave society.

I

The voting for the convention delegates provides the best approximation of mass sentiment on secession. Valuable as these returns are, they did not constitute a referendum and must be used with caution. As the conservatives frequently complained, some candidates ran on intentionally vague platforms. Bipartisan slates running as a united ticket left some voters with no clear-cut choice; they could vote for secession or not vote at all. Local considerations also influenced the results. In Jasper County, Mississippi, the cooperationist candidate swelled his vote by exploiting the resentment in the county's western half over the location of the courthouse. For these reasons the Vicksburg *Whig* was uncertain as how to assess the Mississippi vote. "In a majority of the counties but one ticket was running, and in others, the position of the candidates was so 'jumbled up', that we can form no opinion at this time of the probable proportion of co-operationists who will be in the Convention." The same was true in Alabama. Resolutions passed in Choctaw County were cited by

267

the Mobile *Advertiser* as an example of a posture that could be interpreted for or against immediate action.[1]

Despite calls from the secessionist press for "a vote so overwhelming that it will forever settle the issues which are agitating the public mind," many abstained from voting in the secession elections. Measured against the presidential vote, 20% of the Alabama voters and 40% of those in Mississippi did not bother to vote in December.[2] In both states only five counties registered a higher turnout for the secession elections —Franklin in Mississippi's southwestern corner and four mountain counties in Alabama. A light turnout reflected secessionist strength. Whereas all five of the above counties went cooperationist, those areas with the sharpest drop in voter participation were solidly secessionist. In these counties, centered in southeastern Mississippi and southern Alabama, the conservatives were too weak to mount any opposition, and the secessionists ran unopposed.

In addition to the uncontested races, other factors which accounted for the voters' apathy were the short time allotted for campaigning, confusion among the citizenry as to how the issues personally affected them, a general resignation that events had passed beyond individual control, and the intimidation of conservatives. Concerning this last point, the element of fear should not be overlooked. The campaign aroused intense emotions. Conservatives were exposed to undisguised contempt. Joseph Henderson of Camden, Alabama, wrote his brother, John, savagely denouncing his cooperationist stand. "I am in hopes that some of you will vomit up some of this dirty dirt you have been eating and vote right yet—Secession is now the religion of politics." After John sent back the letter unanswered, Joseph made it public. At a citizens' meeting in Camden on December 27 resolutions were passed urging

[1] Paulding *Eastern Clarion*, Dec. 26; *Weekly Vicksburg Whig*, Dec. 26; *Mobile Daily Advertiser*, Dec. 20. Secessionist papers, of course, interpreted the elections as unmistakable referendums.

[2] *Semi-Weekly Mississippian*, Dec. 18; these percentages were measured as the median decline in the county vote.

John and other cooperationists to "repent soon and turn from the error of their ways." Though reprimanded for his choice of such insulting words as "dirt-eating," Joseph was a hero.[3] The anger and scorn of a Joseph Henderson were extended on a massive scale as the secessionist newspapers and community leaders encouraged coercive measures against dissidents.

To vote for a cooperationist in this atmosphere frequently required personal courage. The ballot was theoretically secret, but the mechanics of voting made it difficult for one to conceal his politics. Nearly everyone knew everybody else at the polls. At small rural beats dissidents would be conspicuous, particularly during a time of great crisis with pressure for conformity at its peak. Some polling places did not even stock cooperationist ballots. When John Aughey asked for a Union ticket at an election precinct in Choctaw County, Mississippi, he was told that none had been printed and was advised to vote secessionist.

> I thought otherwise, and going to a desk, wrote out a Union ticket, and voted it amidst the frowns, murmurs, and threats of the judges and bystanders, and, as the result proved, I had the honor of depositing the only vote in favor of the Union which was polled in that precinct. I knew of many who were in favor of the Union, who were intimidated by threats, and by the odium attending it, from voting at all.[4]

Even with these limitations the results of the convention elections did disclose a clear pattern of allegiances. (See the

[3] Joseph Henderson to his brother, John, Dec. 16, John Henderson Papers, ADAH.

[4] John A. Aughey, *Tupelo* (Lincoln, Nebr., 1888), 46. For the electoral procedure see *The Code of Alabama*, Ormond, Bagby, and Goldthwarte (Montgomery, 1852), Sections 206–210, and *The Revised Code of the Statute Laws of the State of Mississippi* (Jackson, 1857), 90–94. One's vote could be checked since the written ballot was marked with a number which corresponded to the number of a list of all the voters, the poll list, which was made up by the election clerk in the order in which individuals voted.

maps on pp. 272–273.) The polarization in the Alabama returns was unmistakable. From the mountains north to the Tennessee Valley the cooperationists carried every county except Calhoun. South of the mountains they won only one county, Conecuh. The crisis snapped the traditional Democratic alliance which had linked the voting power of the yeoman farmers in the north with the leadership of the planters in the south.

The cooperationist victories in northern Alabama were attributable to two basic factors. They succeeded in holding onto the majority Bell-Douglas vote in the Valley and in winning over sizeable numbers of the Breckinridge farmers in the mountains. Common to both regions was the absence of a growing plantation economy. The river bottoms of the Valley did support plantation agriculture, but, as noted above, it was a decaying institution by the 1850's experiencing the same problems faced by Virginia planters in the 1820's and 1830's. The cooperationists reminded the slaveholders that their cotton markets were in Tennessee. If Tennessee stayed in the Union, not only would these markets be closed off but also slaveholders would find it difficult to secure the return of slaves who had fled into that state. Hence, hasty action must be avoided.

Slavery had barely taken hold in the mountains. The yeomanry practiced a subsistence agriculture based on family labor. Olmsted even believed that most of the slaveholders in this region were professionals, small businessmen, and politicians who were not exclusively engaged in agriculture. He was told that slaves were "unprofitable property" except insofar as the general rise in slave prices elsewhere increased their saleable value.[5] The mountain yeomanry switched from

[5] Frederick Law Olmsted, *A Journey in the Back Country* (London, 1860), 226; in his study of Burke County, a mountainous region in western North Carolina, Edward Phifer noted that 13 out of the 20 largest slaveholders in the county were engaged in occupations unrelated to agriculture. Phifer, "Slavery in Microcosm: Burke County, North Carolina," reprinted in *American Negro Slavery*, ed. Allen Weinstein and Frank Otto Gatell (New York, 1968), 81.

Breckinridge to cooperationism.[6] Of the thirteen northern counties which did switch, slaveholders comprised less than 25% of the family units in all but two. In losing this region the secessionists ran weakest in the poorest and most isolated counties.

There was no contradiction in the yeomanry's apparent political reversal. Their politics remained constant; it was the manner in which they were expressed that had changed. The mountain whites, deeply resentful of the planters' wealth and privileges, did not hate slavery so much as they did the second-class citizenship to which it relegated them. As Olmsted expressed it, "it is not slavery that they detest; it is simply the negro competition, and the monopoly of the opportunities to make money by negro owners, which they feel and but dimly comprehend."[7] This resentment was the foundation of the Democrats' popularity. When the region's political attitudes crystallized in the 1830's, they were expressed in the egalitarian rhetoric of Jacksonian Democracy. The seeming paradox of such a rhetoric in a slave society was handled with ease. The Whigs, with their commercial ties and infusion of Virginia planters, were identified as the party of privilege and snobbery. Although the Democrats in southern Alabama were also a planters' party, the mountain yeomanry related only to symbols grounded in their immediate environment. The inherent sectional conflict of interests built into the Alabama Democracy withstood all strains until 1860 when the

[6] Seymour M. Lipset, "The Emergence of the One-Party South— The Election of 1860," in his *Political Man* (New York, 1960), 344– 354, reasons that party lines held for the presidential election, but that class and economic factors were the key variables affecting voting in the secession election. This is a useful but overstated hypothesis. It is true that the Breckinridge yeomanry in the mountains broke party lines by taking a pro-Union position in the secession crisis, but the intrusion of class and economic factors was nothing new. What had changed was the political symbol of planter rule—now it was the Breckinridge secessionist and not the Whig aristocrat. Moreover, as we shall see, the Whigs as a group never did actively support secession.

[7] Olmsted, *Journey*, 265.

271

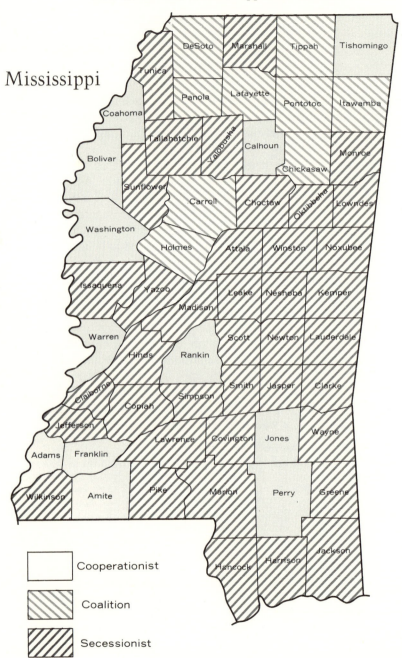

Secessionist Vote in Mississippi and Alabama

Mississippi

Cooperationist

Coalition

Secessionist

Alabama

first inroads were made by the Douglasites in the Tennessee Valley. Frightened by the aggressive demands of the party's southern wing, many Valley Democrats supported Douglas as a compromise candidate. In the remote mountain areas, there was too much inertia and indifference to shake party lines. But once the issue was reduced to Union or secession, the cement of party loyalty crumbled.

A Breckinridge man who now voted cooperationist was still consistent with his former political attitudes. The enemy was the same—the planter who lived off his slaves' labor. Only now, instead of being focused on the Whig party, his antiplanter antipathies were represented by the secessionists in the south. Why should he fight a rich man's war? Eking out a hard existence on inferior soil, he was independent and beholden to no one. Though a Negrophobe, he was not as security conscious as the residents of planting areas since there were too few blacks in the mountains for him to fear a slave revolt. Hardy and self-sufficient, having survived the drought better than the rest of the state, these farmers probably had no greater wish than to be left alone. Symbolic of this desire was the choice of Elder Robert Guttery as the cooperationist candidate in Walker County. Guttery, a minister of the Primitive Baptist Church for nearly forty years, was apolitical.[8] He stood for the simple and reassuring religious values of a folk drawn into the crisis despite themselves.

Bordering the mountains on the north and south was a group of cooperationist counties whose economies fell in between plantation agriculture and subsistence farming. In these counties slaveholders comprised 25% to 49% of the population. Six out of these eight had been lost by Breckinridge. Ten secessionist Breckinridge counties in southern Alabama on the fringes of the Black Belt had the same relative percentages of slaveholders. Comparing the economic development between these two sets uncovered the same pattern which held for the presidential election. As a whole, the cooperationist

---

[8] John M. Dombhart, *History of Walker County: Its Towns and Its People* (Thornton, Ark., 1937), 45.

group was expanding in popualtion and cotton production but at a much slower rate than the secessionist counties.

TABLE 11

Secession Vote and Growth Rates in Alabama
Medium Slaveholder Density Counties

	Median % White Pop. Change	Median % Slave Pop. Change	% Change Cotton Output
Secessionist[a]	+42	+62	+117
Cooperationist	+23	+12	+ 52[b]

SOURCES: See Appendix A.

[a] Bibb County was not included among the secessionist counties. Its delegate, James W. Crawford, a Whig physician, did vote secessionist at the convention but whether he ran as a secessionist is unclear. Conservative papers claimed Crawford as a cooperationist (*Mobile Daily Advertiser*, Dec. 30; *Weekly Montgomery Confederation*, Dec. 28) and on November 9 he had signed a call for a Union meeting (*Ala. State Sentinel*, Nov. 21).

[b] Tuscaloosa omitted from cotton statistics because of inconsistency in 1850 figures.

The dynamism of politics and the economy was mutually reinforcing; the energy of one fed that of the other. When expansion within the Union was apparently denied by Breckinridge's defeat, his supporters were more prone than the Bell and Douglas men to favor a secessionist policy which at least offered the chance of acquiring more slave territory. Conversely, slower economic growth did not create similar expectations for more expansion. A rising slaveholding class was not moving into these cooperationist counties nor had such a class been produced within them. The result was a politics of moderation.

Support for this hypothesis can be found by examining the election returns in Tuscaloosa, a county with distinct regions of plantation agriculture and small scale farming, and by looking at the economic characteristics of the politically devi-

275

ant counties. Breckinridge won a narrow victory in Tusca-loosa. His strength was in the county's southeastern portion, a fertile area watered by the Black Warrior River where the planters had enjoyed a mild boom in the 1850's. Bell ran strongly in the larger towns and among the hill farmers in the northwest. With one exception these cleavages held during the secession election. The planters voted secessionist but what backing Breckinridge had among the yeomanry either went cooperationist or did not vote. For example, in the two northwestern beats of Moore's Bridge and New Lexington where Breckinridge won 48% of the vote, the secessionists could garner only 18%. As a result of these defections in the hill country, the secessionists lost the election.[9]

Calhoun and Cherokee counties were in the northern Coosa River Valley. The former was the only secessionist county in northern Alabama and the latter came within a handful of votes of being the second. Aside from some older counties in the Tennessee Valley with stagnant economies, Calhoun and Cherokee were the leading cotton producing counties in the mountains of northern Alabama. Furthermore, they easily outranked all other northern counties in their cotton output increases during the 1850's. Conecuh, the deviant cooperationist county in the south, was a region of small farmers which was also the only southern agricultural county experiencing an increase in white population significantly greater than the influx of slaves. It was moving away from a slave-based economy.[10]

A continuity in leadership and mass support existed between the presidential and secession elections. The relationship in the voting between the two elections can be specified

[9] J. C. Oldshue, "The Secession Movement in Tuscaloosa County, Alabama," unpublished master's essay (University of Alabama, 1961), 97–98. The beat returns for the two elections were found in the Tuscaloosa *Independent Monitor*, Nov. 9, 1860; and Jan. 11, 1861.

[10] One of Cherokee's four delegates was a straight-out secessionist; Clarence P. Denman, *The Secession Movement in Alabama* (Montgomery, 1933), 162. In Conecuh during the 1850's the whites increased by 30%, the slaves by only 11%.

by employing the Spearman coefficient of rank-order correlation.[11] If election precincts are ranked by their politics, a correlation between Breckinridge and secessionist strength of +0.61, +0.58, and +0.57 respectively existed in the three Tennessee Valley counties of Madison, Marshall, and Lauderdale. In the hill county of Tallapoosa this correlation was +0.66. Extant beat returns from one other northern county, Tuscaloosa, revealed a correlation of +0.74 between Bell and cooperationist strength.[12]

The leadership of the secessionists and cooperationists can be identified in Madison and Franklin counties. Table 12 reveals their former politics.

TABLE 12

Party Affiliation of Secessionist and Cooperationist
Leaders in Northern Alabama

	Breck.	Bell or Doug.	Unknown
Madison County			
Secessionists	17	5	34
Cooperationists	0	31	22
Franklin County			
Secessionists	7	1	7
Cooperationists	0	12	15

SOURCES: See Appendix B.

Since party lines held so tightly, it is no surprise that the rival organizations exhibited the same socioeconomic char-

[11] This is a mathematical formula which measures the correlation between two ranked variables in such a way that perfect positive correlation will equal +1.0, a perfect negative correlation —1.0, and no correlation at all 0. The equation and its uses are explained in Hubert M. Blalock, *Social Statistics* (New York, 1960), 317–319.

[12] With the exception of Lauderdale, these correlations were taken from Peggy Jane Duckworth, "The Role of Alabama Black Belt Whigs in the Election of Delegates to the Secession Convention," unpublished master's essay (University of Alabama, 1961), 40–42, 44, 50, and 56.

acteristics which had differentiated the presidential parties. For example, in Madison the cooperationists were considerably older than their opponents. Of the former, 49% were age fifty and over, as opposed to 16% of the secessionists. Comparable in their property holdings and extent of slave ownership, the parties split along occupational and age lines. Professionals favored the secessionists and in every major occupational category—professionals, businessmen, planters, and farmers—there was a greater tendency toward cooperationism as the age was increased. In addition, the large cotton producers were strongly secessionist.[13] In summary, the wealthy old citizens, many of whom had been born in Virginia, rallied to the Union; the young wealth, including more natives of the Deep South, made up the backbone of the secessionists. J. C. Oldshue's study of Tuscaloosa County revealed an equally sharp contrast between the parties. However, in Tuscaloosa the key variable was involvement in planting. A majority of the secessionists were Breckinridge planters. The Whiggish cooperationists were drawn primarily from small slaveholding farmers. Rounding out the party structure, ministers and slaveholding professionals were secessionist; merchants and nonslaveholding professionals cooperationists.[14]

In other northern counties only much smaller lists of activists could be located. Direct comparison between the parties was possible in St. Clair and Franklin. In the former county, the secessionists were younger and wealthier and drew heavily on professionals and local leaders such as the sheriff and editor. The bulk of the cooperationists were the older non- and small-slaveholding farmers. In Franklin the two groups were about the same age, but the secessionists were twice as wealthy. They attracted more professionals and large slaveholders, the cooperationists more non- and small-holders. Only cooperationists were found in Talladega and Lauder-

---

[13] For example, seven of the nine secessionist planters produced over 100 bales; only one out of six cooperationist planters did so.

[14] Oldshue, "Secession Movement," 34–50.

dale. Each group was based on a similar coalition which aligned town businessmen with the older farmers in the countryside.

South of the mountains the most puzzling aspect of secession was the lack of any serious opposition from the Whigs. What cooperationist strength did exist was centered in counties where the growth of the plantation had slowed, such as Greene, Autauga, and Chambers, but the cooperationists ran a close race only in Autauga. Historians generally have interpreted the secessionists' near sweep as evidence of active Whig support for secession. Recently this view has been effectively rebutted by Peggy Jane Duckworth who utilized beat returns to show that the usual Whig response was to vote cooperationist or, when faced with only secessionist candidates, to abstain from voting as a political protest.[15]

Although most Whigs did not abandon their traditional conservatism, they did conspicuously fail in creating a political instrument for its expression. The handicaps were insurmountable. Too many top ranking Whigs had announced for withdrawal and were quickly put up as candidates by the secessionists. Key spokesmen and communications' leaders were lost when conservative editors resigned or were silenced. Most importantly, fear gripped public opinion with a pervasiveness uncommon in northern Alabama. Slaves were much more prevalent in the south, and their mere presence was always unsettling in a time of crisis. However unfounded most of the slave revolt stories turned out to be, they were widely circulated and exploited by the Breckinridge-secessionist press. The ensuing qualms and anxieties, which, in turn, were nurtured by the economic uncertainties and food shortages, frequently spilled over into terrorism. The political result was a closed system. Dissent was immediately suspect, and the honest doubter had to be concerned lest he be labeled a public enemy. In the words of Joseph Henderson, secession had become the religion of politics and it was a proselytizing religion.

---

[15] Duckworth, "Role of Alabama Black Belt Whigs," 61–133.

Who can blame the Whigs for not being more vocal or effective in their opposition? For at least a decade they had worked to temper the politics of intensity which they rightfully feared would rupture the Union. But now the strain of one crisis after another had sapped their will to do battle once more. Some assumed a defeatist attitude, sold their slaves, and invested the proceeds in an effort to ride out the storm. Others talked of leaving the South.[16] Those who did have the energy to resist by voting cooperationist were chiefly the Whig yeomanry. Black Belt Whigs usually refrained from voting or occasionally voted secessionist; those in the hill country more commonly voted cooperationist. These yeomen, as their cultural kinfolk in northern Alabama, were part of an environment and life-style not as intimately involved with slavery as the Black Belt society. Since these areas did not feel as directly threatened by the Republicans, they could support a more openly cooperationist movement. The most consistent secessionist Whigs appear to have been those in the Black Belt towns.[17] Small as most of these towns were, they were nevertheless the nerve centers for the rural society around them. It was here that the county resistance meetings were usually held and here that the wild rumors from the telegraph dispatches would first be heard. The citizenry reacted by milling around on the streets and anxiously awaiting the latest news. The excitement was contagious and conservatives must have found it difficult to remain uncommitted.

For political reasons the secessionists liked to portray their

[16] Thomas B. Carroll, *Historical Sketches of Oktibbeha County* (Gulfport, Miss., 1931), 101. Thomas Dabney's initial impulse was to sell everything and move with his family to England. He decided to remain after being reminded of his paternalistic responsibility to his slaves. Susan Dabney Smedes, *Memorials of a Southern Planter*, ed. Fletcher M. Green (New York, 1965), 172.

[17] Duckworth, "Role of Alabama Black Belt Whigs," 112, 118, 119, 151. The towns of Greensboro and Eutaw in Greene County, both of which had been lost by Breckinridge, voted 61% and 75% respectively for immediate secession. In contrast, secession polled only a 58% vote in the countryside.

movement as bipartisan. In some areas they tried to use this claim as a justification for participating in cooperationist meetings. Such an attempt in Gainesville, Alabama, elicited an indignant retort from a conservative. "Would a Democrat have a right to go into a meeting called to nominate a Whig, and claim a hearing; and then raise the cry of persecution and wrong, if his modest request was refused? Would a Whig have such a right?"[18] This conservative was acknowledging what the secessionists hoped to mask—party lines did not break over the secession issue in southern Alabama. Despite the prevalence of bipartisan convention slates, the typical secessionist was a Breckinridge supporter and the typical cooperationist was a Whig or Douglas Democrat. The available data on the party activists is in Table 13.

TABLE 13

Party Affiliation of Secessionist and Cooperationist
Leaders in Southern Alabama

County	Secessionists			Cooperationists		
	Breck./ S.R.O.	Bell/ Doug.	Not Known	Breck./ S.R.O.	Bell/ Doug.	Not Known
Autauga	17	1	15	2	18	12
Clarke	8	–	14	1	3	16
Greene	6	2	1	–	4	–
Mobile	20	14	30	6	49	83
Pickens	13	2	20	1	3	8
Dallas	–	–	–	1	20	25
Lowndes	27	1	13	–	–	–
Monroe	11	3	6	–	–	–
Montgomery	32	6	23	–	–	–
Total	134	29	122	11	97	144

SOURCES: See Appendix B.

Within the Black Belt no representative sample of both parties was found for the same county. A direct comparison

[18] Gainesville *Independent*, Dec. 22.

281

can be approximated by contrasting the Dallas cooperationists with the secessionists in Lowndes, Montgomery, and Sumter. All four groups were dominated by wealthy slaveholders but the cooperationists were the oldest with the bulk of this age differential deriving from those worth under $25,000. Combining age, occupation, and slaveholding, sharp cleavages consistently emerged between the parties. Whereas young slaveholding professionals accounted for 13% to 21% of the secessionists' strength, they constituted less than 3% of the cooperationists. An equally strong counterattraction was evidenced among small slaveholding farmers over the age of forty. Twenty-two percent of the cooperationists fell into this category, only 4% to 7% of the secessionists. Planters of comparable age tended to be secessionists. No conclusions can be drawn concerning the town middle class. They were insignificant in Lowndes and Sumter but comprised about 20% of the Montgomery secessionists. In Dallas they made up 10% of the cooperationists.

Both parties were identified in Autauga and Clarke counties, to the north and south respectively of the Black Belt. Although the Autauga cooperationists claimed they had cornered "nearly all of the wealthy, influential and prominent men in the county," their organization was not wealthier than the secessionists'. If influence and community standing are equated with both age and wealth, as conservatives were prone to do, then the cooperationists' self-appraisal was essentially correct. The county's old wealth was strongly cooperationist, its young wealth strongly secessionist.[19] Compared to their cooperationist counterparts, the secessionist planters and slaveholding farmers were more likely to be not only younger but also more involved in cotton agriculture, expressed either in absolute terms or as a ratio of corn to cotton production. Slaveholding professionals also split along

[19] *Autauga Citizen*, Nov. 29. Those age forty and over worth at least $25,000 comprised 39% of the cooperationists, 19% of the secessionists. Those in the same wealth bracket but under the age of forty constituted 36% of the secessionists, 13% of the cooperationists.

these same age lines, but businessmen divided their support regardless of age. All four Northern born activists were co-operationists. In Clarke County the same model emerged. The secessionists were easily the younger of the two parties with 45% of its membership under the age of forty as opposed to 21% of the cooperationists. The secessionist coalition was one of professionals and young slaveholding farmers; the co-operationists relied more on the older slaveholding farmers and merchants.

At first glance party distinctions appear blurred in Mobile. Although the secessionists were slightly younger and wealthier, the pattern was not as distinct as found elsewhere. The occupational make-up of the parties was also quite similar. However, examination of birthplaces revealed that whether or not one was born into slave society was an important variable affecting political behavior. Mobile was a great port city and had a heterogeneous population second only to that of New Orleans in its polyglot nature. The city was growing in the 1850's and attracting Yankees and foreigners eager to work in her commercial houses and on her teeming docks. These groups continued to support the cooperationists, as they had Bell and Douglas. For example, nonslaveholders born in the North or abroad comprised 20% of the cooperationists, only 2% of the secessionists. The same group, if natives of the Deep South, tended to be secessionists, 19% of whom fell into this category as opposed to 12% of the cooperationists. A comparable correlation between nativities and politics also held for the major occupations, especially among the upper middle class of merchants and lawyers. Northerners and the foreign-born who achieved slaveholding status accounted for an equal share of both parties, 24%. Among this group the merchants, those who maintained the closest business contacts with the North, were the most consistent cooperationists. Mobile's urban politics presented one dominant theme. Those born outside the slave system, and particularly nonslaveholders who did not yet share in its benefits and merchants whose interests depended on peace with the North, were the activists

283

least likely to back secession. Though prepared to defend slave society, they had not yet internalized its values to the point of demanding immediate separation from the North.

The party organizations in Pike, a southeastern county on Alabama's coastal plain, were unusual in being dominated by nonslaveholders. Although all three of the county's delegates owned slaves, nonslaveholders comprised about 65% of both factions. The secession crisis had politicized those elements who normally did not participate in politics—the very young (under the age of thirty) and the poor. Both presidential parties which were found in Pike, the States' Rights Opposition and the Douglasites, were much older and controlled by slaveholders. The county had undergone rapid changes in the 1850's when it was developed as a cotton producing region. Total farm acreage doubled and the cotton output nearly tripled, but the yeomanry did not have an equal share in this development. Slaves increased four times as fast as the whites and their owners were buying out the small farmers. Land ownership, measured by the ratio of farms to families, dropped from 78% to 62%. The expansion of the planters at the expense of the yeomanry made it more difficult for the latter to maintain their social position. Under such pressure and dissatisfied with the status quo, the yeomanry eagerly responded to secession as a program which at least held out a hope for change. Nearly half of the active secessionists in Pike were nonslaveholding farmers or farm laborers. Within this group 40% were landless. On the other hand, the bulk of the nonslaveholding cooperationists were small businessmen and artisans. Thirty-eight per cent of their support was in this category. These groups were not hurt by the expansion in the countryside, as were the yeomanry, but they received no direct benefit from it. Only one cooperationist was a landless yeoman.

Secessionist organizations alone were identified in Barbour, Macon, Monroe, and Pickens. The four groups shared the same characteristics. Wealthy slaveholders, the majority of whom were in their thirties or forties, constituted from 84%

to 95% of the membership and about one in three owned thirty or more slaves. The leading occupation was agriculture, followed by the professions, and then business. Professionals exercised the greatest influence in Pickens and Barbour, the two strongest Breckinridge counties.[20] In both cases young Breckinridge lawyers maintained their political activity from the presidential through the secession election.

Two small samples of ten Pickens cooperationists and sixteen Barbour residents who cancelled their subscriptions to the *Clayton Banner* because of its overly rabid prosecessionism represent the only index of cooperationist leadership in these counties. Though conclusions must be tentative, these groups were drawn from different social strata than the secessionists. The Pickens cooperationists were older and much less wealthy than the secessionists. They included only one lawyer, a New York born Whig, and one large slaveholder, an elderly Whig physician-planter. Whereas three cooperationists were yeoman farmers, none of the secessionists were. The Barbour residents who accused the *Banner* of advocating opinions "dishonorable to our country, and dangerous to our safety" were primarily small- and non-slaveholding farmers and businessmen.[21] Conspicuously absent were the planters and planter-lawyers who had been the core of Breckinridge and secessionist leadership.

II

The secessionists had an easier victory in Mississippi since there was no north-south division of yeomanry versus planters for the cooperationists to exploit. Mississippi's yeomanry voted cooperationist as did those in Alabama but there were far fewer of them. Discounting the three coastal counties where farming was not the citizenry's primary livelihood, Mississippi had four farming counties where nonslaveholders

---

[20] Forty-five per cent of the Pickens secessionists and 21% of the Barbour group were professionals.

[21] *Clayton Banner*, Dec. 6.

comprised 75% or better of the population (as opposed to sixteen such counties in Alabama). Three of these four sent cooperationist slates to the convention.

Tishomingo and Itawamba in the northeast highlands had economies based on subsistence farming. Aside from good soils along creek bottoms, the land was poor and hilly. Grain crops and livestock were the agricultural mainstays. The conservatives had to settle for a coalition ticket in Itawamba but all four delegates did vote for the cooperationist Alcorn resolution at the convention. The piney woods county of Jones was one of the poorest and most isolated farming areas in the state. Less than half of the farmers planted cotton and the largest crop was twenty-two bales. What market economy there was consisted of driving surplus cattle or carting garden vegetables to Mobile, 125 miles to the southeast. Though the sandy soil was of very poor quality, the yeomanry continued to move in looking for cheap land.[22] After casting its usual Democratic ballots, the county went strongly cooperationist. Wayne, directly to the east of Jones, went secessionist and was the politically deviant yeomanry county. Contrary to the three cooperationist counties, Wayne had tracts of good prairie land. Her agriculture was more commercially oriented and could support much greater concentrations of slaves.[23] In an unusually marked political shift, the county reversed its politics in the 1850's, Whig in 1852 and strongly Democratic in 1860. This was related to a change in the pattern of land ownership. Resident slaveholders and those coming in were buying up parcels of land with the result that the farm to family ratio dropped from 58% to 38% during the decade. Thus, rather than supporting a broadly based landowning

[22] DBR, XXIII (1857), 645; John K. Bettersworth, Confederate Mississippi: The People and Policies of a Cotton State in Wartime (Baton Rouge, 1943), 242; Suzanne Spell, "A History of Jones County, Mississippi," unpublished master's essay (Mississippi College, 1961), 23.

[23] While slaves comprised 53% of Wayne's total population, their highest percentage in the three cooperationist counties was 21% in Tishomingo.

yeomanry, the county had sharply concentrated its productive means. The secessionists had little opposition in the three seashore counties. With soil unsuited for farming except for a few shell hummocks, the region was dependent on the coastal trade with New Orleans and Mobile for its food supplies.[24] Its politics were as lethargic as its forest-based economy. For years the Democrats had monopolized the political offices and only one-third of the electorate bothered to vote for the secessionist tickets.

The secessionists carried by two to one those counties in which slaveholders made up 25% to 49% of the population. Their victories were in the strongly Breckinridge east central region which, as shown in Table 14, had experienced very high growth rates in its slave economies during the 1850's. The cooperationists won or were part of coalition states in seven counties, six of which were in north central Mississippi.[25] All of these counties had voted for Breckinridge. Not only were their natural trade outlets north into Tennessee, but their economies were more stable than those of the secessionist counties. Both factors influenced their more moderate response.

Secessionists were elected in eighteen out of the thirty-one counties where slaveholders were in a majority.[26] The cooperationists won nine counties and shared in coalition tickets

[24] Bettersworth, *Confederate Mississippi*, 242.

[25] The southern county was Perry, a piney woods area very similar to Jones. The cooperationist delegate, Porter J. Myers, was outpolled by the combined vote of two secessionists, 55% to 45%. Such disorganization was very unusual for the secessionists and accordingly the county has been placed in the cooperationist camp.

[26] Included here was Tallahatchie, a northern county described by Rainwater as having been carried uncontested by the cooperationists. However, the Vicksburg *Whig* on January 9 credited the county to the secessionists and the Democratic delegate did vote straight secessionist at the convention. Also included is Yalobusha. The county's two delegates voted against the conditional unionist and cooperationist resolutions at the convention, but did support the resolution calling for referral back to the people.

TABLE 14[a]

Secession Vote and Growth Rates in Mississippi, Medium Slaveholder Density Counties

	% Change White Population	% Change Slave Population	% Change Cotton Output
Secessionist	+46	+79	+272
Cooperationist/ Coalition	+19	+44	+140

SOURCES: See Appendix A.

[a] Median % changes could not be analyzed since portions of Chickasaw and Lafayette were used in the creation of Calhoun in 1852.

from four others. With the exception of Issaquena, the extremely wealthy river counties north of Vicksburg went cooperationist. Although the Vicksburg *Whig* claimed "but few sympathizers" for secession in these counties, the elections were very close.[27] Elsewhere, in areas where a less heavily capitalized plantation agriculture was expanding most rapidly, as in the prairies of eastern Mississippi, the secessionists ran strongest. The old planting counties whose economies were more mature were closely contested and often resulted in coalition slates. (See Table 15.)

The remaining three cooperationist counties were in southwestern Mississippi.[28] Common to all three was an exceptionally high percentage of land ownership, 72% to 76% as measured by the farm to family ratio. Moreover, this ratio had held or increased during the 1850's. On the other hand, the five secessionist counties where farms were comparable in size had a medium farm-to-family ratio of 61%. More significantly the small farmers in these counties were either

[27] *Weekly Vicksburg Whig*, Dec. 26. The delegate from Tunica, elected as a cooperationist, switched and voted secessionist.
[28] Franklin, Amite, and Rankin.

TABLE 15

Secession Vote and Growth Rates in Mississippi,
High Slaveholder Density, Plantation[a] Counties

	Median % White Pop. Change	Median % Slave Pop. Change	% Change Cotton Output
Secession Vote 60% & Greater[b]	+ 8.5	+30.0	+177
Secession Vote 50–59%[c]	−20.0	+13.0	+ 82
Coalition[d]	+ 1.5	+37.0	+151
Cooperation[e]	+ 8.5[f]	+ 7.0	+ 87

SOURCES: See Appendix A.

[a] A plantation county was defined as one in which a majority of the farms were in excess of 100 acres with an average valuation greater than $5,000. Omitted because of their disproportionately great wealth were the five submerged river counties.

[b] Claiborne, Jefferson, Yazoo, Lowndes, Madison, and Noxubee.

[c] Hinds, Marshall, and Wilkinson.

[d] Carroll, Holmes, DeSoto, and Panola.

[e] Adams and Warren.

[f] The white pop. change refers only to rural growth patterns; Natchez and Vicksburg were omitted.

leaving or being bought out. Kemper and Monroe showed a net loss of whites. In Copiah, Oktibbeha, and Pike, whites did increase but only about half as fast as slaves; the ratio of farm ownership dropped in all three counties.[29] The farmers in these counties seemed to have been receptive to political radicalism since they were having difficulty in holding onto their land.

After Lincoln's election, Mississippi conservatives in planting areas held their strength better than did their counterparts

[29] The decrease in Copiah and Pike was 24% and 23% respectively; in Oktibbeha it was 5%.

289

in Alabama. Of thirteen counties lost by Breckinridge the secessionists won outright only four.[30] Mississippi Whigs benefited from a stronger initial party organization which was based on greater concentrations of wealth than prevailed in Alabama and had not been sapped by defections to a State Rights Opposition type movement. In addition, the Whigs had two well-defined centers of support in Adams and Warren. The businessmen of Natchez and Vicksburg and the older planter aristocracy in the countryside were as staunchly Whiggish as any groups in the South. But by 1860 Alabama Whiggism had no bloc of supporters comparable in size, influence, or tradition to lead a concerted drive against secession. Their Black Belt vote had been slipping in the 1850's and with it went their control of the planting regions.

Had the Mississippi conservatives been able to carry the northern part of the state as they did in 1851, they might well have succeeded in blocking immediate secession. In the intervening decade, this area's economy had become more enmeshed in slavery and cotton. It was still a growing economy with the bulk of its fortunes not extending beyond the present generation. As one resident told Olmsted: "Most of the plantations in this vicinity, indeed, belonged to men who had come into the country with nothing within twenty years. Once a man got a good start with negroes, unless the luck was much against him, nothing but his own folly could prevent his becoming rich.[31] Thus, while the region did not enthusiastically back secession in 1860, the commitment to slavery was stronger than in 1851. The conservatives were either defeated or had to settle for coalition.

The party affiliations of the Mississippi secessionists and cooperationists disclosed no surprises. In seven counties where beat returns are extant for both elections the rank

[30] In addition the delegate from Tunica, elected as a cooperationist, switched at the convention and voted secessionist.

[31] Ralph A. Wooster, *The People in Power: Courthouse and Statehouse in the Lower South, 1850–1860* (Knoxville, 1969), 45; Olmsted, *Journey*, 130.

correlation between the Breckinridge and secessionist vote ranged from +0.33 to +0.91.[32] C. D. Fontaine, a Breckinridge secessionist from Pontotoc, explained this relationship and why some conservatives could be expected to support secession.

> I sincerely believe that 9 out of every 10 who voted for Breckinridge will vote for direct Secession. And I know that most of the Douglas men, to repel the free soil suspicion their late conduct has subjected them to, are already earnest advocates of Secession. Many good men besides who voted for Bell did so in an honest effort to defeat Lincoln, and thus avoid a cause which they think sufficient to justify Secession. So that I am satisfied that for every timid Breckinridge man who will vote for acquiescence we will gain two from the ranks of Bell and Douglas, who will vote for Secession.

Naturalized foreigners were the one normally Democratic voting bloc who solidly backed cooperation. After the Natchez *Courier* claimed that foreigners favored the Adams County cooperationists by three to one, its rival paper, the *Free Trader*, could do little except dredge up the Know-Nothing past of the *Courier*.[33]

The party identities of the leaders are more difficult to pin down since few membership lists of activists have survived. Those that have, however, point to the same continuity as in Alabama.

The delegates at the cooperationist Vicksburg convention on November 29 were primarily old-line Whigs. They were unceremoniously described by the Mississippian as "lame,

[32] These counties were Adams, Amite, Claiborne, Hinds, Jefferson, Madison, and Warren. For the returns, see Secretary of State Papers, Series F, Vols. 83 and 85, MDAH; *Mississippi Free Trader*, Nov. 12, for the presidential returns in Adams; and the *Daily Vicksburg Whig*, Nov. 9 and Dec. 25, for both returns in Warren.

[33] Fontaine to Gov. Pettus, Nov. 12, Governors' Records, MDAH; *Mississippi Free Trader*, Dec. 24; *Natchez Courier*, Dec. 21, quoted in *ibid.*, Dec. 24.

TABLE 16

Party Affiliation of Secessionist and Cooperationist
Leaders in Mississippi

County	Secessionists			Cooperationists		
	Breck.	Bell/ Doug.	Not Known	Breck.	Bell/ Doug.	Not Known
Adams	17	–	6	–	7	1
Clarke	9	–	11	–	–	–
Hinds	21	2	7	–	5	–
Madison	8	1	9	–	9	9
Rankin	–	–	–	–	5	–
Scott	6	1	3	–	–	–
Warren	–	–	–	2	35	91
Total	61	4	36	2	61	101

SOURCES: See Appendix B.

spavined, wind-broken, blind-staggered old hacks that were
long ago turned out to grass, and that now stand neighing and
braying on the commons waiting for some sudden gust to
blow a dry shuck or blade of fodder within their reach." This
sarcasm was not wide of the mark. More than a third of the
delegates were in their fifties or older; none of the state's
newer plantation areas was represented. Presided over by a
small slaveholding farmer from Rankin, Patrick Henry, the
convention rested on an extremely narrow base. Vicksburg
businessmen comprised the largest bloc of delegates, followed
by older farmers and lawyers.[34] A typically Whig alignment in
that it was largely devoid of the aggressive, young planting
and professional support which characterized the Breckinridge and secessionist parties, the delegates could shape a program suitable only to Whig needs. These needs were real
enough but they were those of the minority party in Mississippi. There was no reason to expect that their articula-

[34] *Semi-Weekly Mississippian*, Dec. 7; the *Weekly Vicksburg Whig*,
Dec. 5, carried a list of the delegates.

tion would attract a larger electorate in December than in November.

The same inability to escape the limitations of their class base plagued the conservatives in Madison County. The *American Citizen* called the secessionist candidate, Judge Hill, a demagogue for claiming that the *Citizen*'s characterization of a cooperationist meeting as being composed of the "solid men" of Madison was meant as an invidious comparison between the rich and the poor. The paper went on to attack Hill's assertion that all Southerners were equally interested in the institution of slavery. Obviously one's interest increased in proportion to the number of slaves owned. "Hence, we used the term 'solid men' to characterize *slaveholders* and landholders—those *most deeply* interested in the institution. They are clearly the '*solid men*' of Madison."[35]

This standard conservative argument must have delighted the secessionists. It performed the double function of pinning the politically disadvantageous label of rich man's party on the cooperationists and of drawing attention from the secessionists' wealth. In fact, the Madison secessionists were wealthier than the cooperationists.[36] However, their political rhetoric, as did that of the Breckinridge Democrats, never emphasized this. This was simply good politics, but more fundamentally it reflected the preponderance of young wealth which favored both Breckinridge and the secessionists. About one-third of the secessionists were under the age of forty and worth $25,000 or more; 6% of the cooperationists were in this category. But 40% of the latter, aged fifty and over, were this weathy, as opposed to 19% of the secessionists. The young weath in the secessionist camp aspired to be the county's "solid men," but they were quite willing to defer that title to those who appropriated it because of their longer community standing and who were prepared to pay the political price for so doing.

[35] Canton *American Citizen*, Dec. 22.
[36] The median property holdings of 16 secessionist leaders were $71,970; for 17 cooperationist leaders the median was $43,600.

Comparison of the parties in the same county was possible only for Madison. Elsewhere either just one party was located or the samples were greatly unequal in size.[37] Piecing this information together reveals a breakdown analogous to that discovered in Alabama. The secessionists in Adams and Hinds were younger than the Warren County cooperationists, with those aged fifty and over having roughly twice as much influence among the cooperationists. Those in their twenties and thirties broke evenly unless holding $25,000 and more in property; in that case they favored the secessionists by two to one. The old wealth was cooperationist but not as strongly as those over the age of fifty worth under $25,000. The sharpest division within the slaveholders, who constituted about 80% of all three groups, was between the professional and business groups. The former were strongly secessionist, the latter cooperationist. Reflecting their Whiggish ties with the upper South and the North, the cooperationists were more likely to be Virginians or natives of the free states.[38]

The remaining secessionist samples were from the Democratic regions of eastern Mississippi. Party chairmen identified in seven counties typically were young slaveholders, either farmers or professionals. The yeomanry played a large role in Jones County, but small-to-medium sized slaveholders easily dominated the organizations in Clarke, Scott, Greene, and Wayne. The influence of businessmen was minimal. Aside from Clarke, where lawyers were in control, most of the activists were farmers in their thirties and forties. These farming groups, slavery's small entrepreneurs, traditionally voted Democratic. They provided the leadership for seces-

[37] Several accounts of resistance meetings were found but the members could not be classified since they met before the issues of immediate secession and cooperation were defined and did not specify the mode of resistance in their resolutions. All of these meetings were controlled by slaveholders and uniformly declared for secession.

[38] A small group of 8 cooperationists was found in Adams. They were extremely wealthy old Whigs with a median property holding of $148,000.

294

sion within their communities and sponsored the vigilante committees for "ferreting out and removing from among us, all persons opposed to the institution of slavery, as it exists with us."[39]

In the midst of the Montgomery Convention, Robert Jemison privately described the secessionists as "restless, rash, reckless politicians."[40] This statement, when contrasted with the conservatives' own self-appraisal of being calm and mature statesmen, epitomizes the outstanding features of the secessionists and cooperationists. The former inherited the machinery, leadership, and voters of the dominant Breckinridge party. They were rash and reckless because of their willingness to gamble with the South's destiny. From their perspective secession was a gamble well worth taking. Enlisting the South's emerging wealth, the young slaveholding farmers, planters, and professionals, the secessionists clearly saw that any national administration, by morally stigmatizing slavery as sin and promising to restrict its growth, was also stigmatizing their own self-esteem and restricting their own ambitions. The cooperationists, drawn from the Whigs and Douglas Democrats, stood for the conservatism of these two parties. In broad terms they represented the South's old wealth and more specifically the yeomanry of northern Alabama, the very wealthy planters of the Mississippi-Yazoo Delta, slaveholders in the previously developed plantation areas, and the Northern and Virginia born business groups in the towns.[41] The plantation, as the focal point for energy and aspirations, was less of an immediate concern for this coalition than it was for the Breckinridge secessionists. Cooperationist planters feared and despised the Republicans but

[39] From resolutions passed in Hillsboro, Scott County, on November 24; *Eastern Clarion*, Dec. 5.

[40] Jemison to his daughter, Jan. 10, 1861, Jemison Collection, UA.

[41] The conservative town vote for cooperation held more strongly in Mississippi than in Alabama. In Vicksburg and Natchez the cooperationist candidates polled about a 10% greater share of the vote than had Bell and Douglas combined.

would, if at all possible, stop short of immediate secession. Enjoying the security and detachment of those accustomed to wealth, they could afford to be moderates. For the young slaveholders the picture was reversed. Their status was more recent and thus more exposed to external threats. Viewing themselves more as entrepreneurs than as paternalistic masters, they were still creating their wealth rather than resting upon it, and they demanded that the option of slavery's expansion into the territories be at the very least kept open.

Above all, the program of immediate secession won acceptance since it was grounded in needs which nonslaveholders desirous of achieving slaveholding status could readily understand. These groups, concentrated in the newer cotton regions, were not leaders of secession but their support was indispensable. To be a slaveholder was their greatest ambition; to be thrown into social and economic competition with blacks was their greatest fear. Secession promised to keep the South a white man's country, to expel abolitionist emissaries, and to remove the North as a drag upon Southern progress. The ambitious nonslaveholder, already faced with rising prices for slaves and land, was further squeezed in the fall of 1860 by short crops and tight money. He had little to lose by backing secession.

III

After the excitement of November and December, the secession conventions were nearly anticlimactic. From the beginning conservatives realized they were outnumbered and had next to no chance of stopping immediate secession. There were, of course, debates over the proper means of resistance, but in the main the conventions were not deliberative bodies in the sense of carefully assessing various alternatives and then hammering out compromises. The secessionists knew what they wanted and had the voting strength to push across their program regardless of what the cooperationists said. Moreover, as the secessionists constantly emphasized, time was of the essence. The South had already gone too far to recede. Withdrawal from the Union had to be quick and final and the process of creating a new Confederacy begun at once.

The Alabama convention assembled in Montgomery on January 7. Of the two sets of delegates the cooperationists were older and less wealthy. Occupationally, the chief contrast was among lawyers, who had twice as much influence in the secessionist camp. Comprising 40% of all the secessionists, lawyers played a role commensurate with the consistent support they had rendered the Breckinridge and secessionist parties on the county level. Both groups were dominated by slaveholders, but the holdings of the secessionists were larger. Reflecting their strength in the mountainous regions, the cooperationists included more nonslaveholders.[42]

The city was tense with anticipation. Excited crowds milled around the State House and troops were everywhere. "There is more excitement here than was ever seen in the country before," wrote Thomas J. McClellan, a cooperationist from Limestone. "There are 8 or 10 military companies organized in this place and a portion of them, as they say here, are in actual service, but I don't know what duties they are performing except parading the streets and guarding the Capitol." Another cooperationist, Robert Jemison, complained over what he felt were excessive precautions. After twilight, whether a convention member or not, one could enter the capitol only by giving a countersign to the guards. The "pretense," explained Jemison, was the necessity to protect public property in light of a recent attempt to burn the capitol. The crowds and troops, a visible embodiment of the secessionist spirit, impressed the cooperationists with their zeal. McClellan noted they were more rabid than their leaders. The enthusiasm in the streets spilled over into the convention as the packed galleries hung on to every word and wildly cheered

[42] Wooster, *People in Power*, 54–56.

prosecession utterances. Despite a resolution passed on the first day prohibiting applause from the galleries, the noise did not abate. So tumultuous was the reaction on the second day to the speech from the South Carolina commissioner, that one delegate cuttingly suggested that "unless the galleries shall be immediately cleared, the Convention should certainly adjourn to the Theatre. . . ."[43] The convention then decided to conduct most of their transactions in closed session.

On the eve of the convention McClellan rated the two parties' strength as about even. Any hopes for a cooperationist victory, however, were quickly dispelled by the events of the first day when the secessionists padded their majority by refusing to seat the two cooperationist candidates from Shelby County. The election there had been contested after returns from Bear Creek precinct had given the cooperationists an apparent victory. Arguing that these returns were illegal since they had not been filed with the sheriff within the legally designated time, the secessionists at the convention did not acknowledge them and honored the election certificates of the two straight-outs, Shortridge and McClanahan. In the vote for a permanent president, the convention first revealed the party lines which would hold for its subsequent key decisions. William M. Brooks, a young lawyer and Breckinridge secessionist from Perry, out-polled by eight votes the cooperationist nominee, Robert Jemison, an old Whig planter-manufacturer from Tuscaloosa.[44]

[43] John W. Inzer, "Alabama's Secession Convention," *Confederate Veteran*, XXXI (Jan., 1923), 7–9; Thomas Joyce McClellan to John Beattie McClellan, Jan. 7, 1861, Robert Anderson McClellan Papers, DU; Jemison to his daughter, Jan. 10, 1861, Jemison Collection, UA; William R. Smith, *The History and Debates of the Convention of the People of Alabama, Begun and held in the City of Montgomery, on the seventh Day of January, 1861* (Montgomery, 1861), 22, 45. Compiled by a cooperationist delegate from Tuscaloosa, this is the fullest and most accessible account of the convention.

[44] T. J. McClellan to his wife, Jan. 6, 1861, Thomas Joyce McClellan Letters, ADAH; T. J. McClellan to J. B. McClellan, Jan. 7,

Having won the first test of strength, the secessionists immediately took the offensive. G. C. Whatley introduced resolutions openly designed to force the cooperationists to choose between resistance or submission. In the heated debate which followed, the conservatives objected to the resolutions' intimation of force to prevent Lincoln's inauguration. In particular though, they deeply resented having their loyalty to the South called into question. "Now, sir, the proposition to make a test on such a subject," lectured Jeremiah Clemans, "necessarily implies suspicion, and suspicion is always more or less offensive." Amended to a simple declaration that Alabama would not submit to a Republican administration, the resolution satisfied all and passed unanimously.[45]

After the convention went into secret session on the second day, the secessionists continued to undermine the rationale of the cooperationist position. A resolution praising Governor Moore for seizing the federal forts in Alabama was amended by Yancey to authorize Moore to accept 500 volunteers for service under Florida's governor. An appropriation of $10,000 was requested to cover expenses. As justification for these measures, the secessionists cited the need to take possession of the federal forts at Pensacola before they were reinforced by a strong federal garrison. The cooperationists retorted that such troop deployments constituted "unnecessary aggression" and would destroy any hopes for a peaceful solution of sectional differences. In the middle of the debate, Brooks read a communication from Governor Moore. Asked by the convention to make known his information regarding the Florida forts, Moore replied that Alabama troops had been requested by Governor Perry of Florida who needed these troops since he lacked the forces in the Florida panhandle to take and hold the Pensacola forts. Unless Alabama came to his assistance, Perry feared that too much time would

1861, Robert A. McClellan Papers, DU; Denman, *Secession Movement*, 130; Smith, *Convention*, 23.
[45] Smith, *Convention*, 24, 25, 28, 30.

be lost while additional Florida troops were brought in from the rest of the state. After stressing that Alabama could be invaded as easily from Pensacola as could Florida, Moore capped his argument by passing on ominous information he had received from purportedly well-placed sources. "It is not only the policy of the Federal Government to coerce the seceding States, but as soon as possible to put herself in position by reinforcing all the Forts in the States where secession is expected." Despite further cooperationist protests, the amended resolution passed by a strict party vote of 52 to 45.[46]

The first conservative resolutions were introduced on the third day. Nicholas Davis' proposal for referral back to the people of any action taken by the convention was tabled by another party vote, and the Bulger resolutions calling for a Southern convention were referred to the hostile committee on federal relations. After these conservative moves were thwarted, the convention spent most of the day debating the Coleman resolution which pledged Alabama to assist any coerced state. Alluding to a similar declaration recently passed by the Virginia legislature, the secessionists reasoned it was only proper for Alabama to do the same. The cooperationists had no doubts that Alabama would rush aid to any sister state actually under federal attack, but they added that no such invasion had yet occurred. Technically the state was still in the Union and those who voted for this resolution would be liable to the charge of treason. Jemison, at the beginning of his speech, pointed out the convention had no reliable information on which to base its action, but he was interrupted by J. F. Dowdell who read a dispatch claiming that hostilities had already commenced.[47] This was a favorite technique of the secessionists. On the previous day telegrams had been read which told of the rejection of compromise by the Republicans in Washington and which announced the imminence of secession in Mississippi and Florida. Alabama's

[46] *Ibid.*, 50–55.   [47] *Ibid.*, 55–57.

commissioners to Virginia reported that this crucial border state was rallying to the cause. "What has your Convention done? Go out promptly and all will be right." These communications naturally favored the secessionist cause and with this in mind Jemison responded to Dowdell's action with a sharp denunciation. "Yes, we have various telegrams, the authenticity and reliability of which seem to be confided in, and are fully satisfactory to gentlemen of the majority." Admitting that he himself was no "wire-worker," Jemison accused the secessionists of using the telegrams "to tell whatever is most appropriate for effect. They keep the public mind in a continued state of excitement; and, for whatever matter under consideration here, we have a telegram suited to the occasion."[48]

As the debate continued, the secessionists committed one of their few blunders. Overreacting to a cooperationist request for a day's delay on the Coleman proposal, Yancey delivered a fiery speech. In a perfect example of the rash language and intemperate action which had left him personally unpopular even among secessionists, he flayed away at those who might oppose secession.[49] "There is a law of Treason, defining treason against the State; and, those who shall dare oppose the action of Alabama, when she assumes her independence of the Union, will become traitors—rebels against its authority, and will be dealt with as such." Yancey's speech was unprovoked and politically stupid. His Whig colleague from Montgomery, Thomas H. Watts, apologized and tried to assuage the conservatives' anger. Yancey got up again and stressed that his remarks had not been directed against any members of the convention but only against those in certain areas of the state who reportedly would resist an ordinance of seces-

[48] *Ibid.*, 34, 42, 63–64.
[49] J. Bragg wrote from the convention that "It is not to be disguised that Y—is personally unpopular—he has great talent in some things but his temper is impracticable & he makes few personal friends." J. Bragg to Gen. [McRae.], Jan. 12, 1861, Colin J. McRae Papers, ADAH.

sion. Yancey's effort was a clumsy one, for the cooperationists now responded that he was branding as traitors the gallant citizenry of northern Alabama. Before the convention was further divided, the secessionists wisely agreed to adjourn and no action was taken on the resolution.[50]

By January 10 the skirmishings were over. The proceedings began with the reading of dispatches from Jackson and Charleston which announced respectively the secession of Mississippi and the firing on a Northern relief ship in Charleston harbor. The thirteen-man committee on federal relations, chaired by Yancey, then issued majority and minority reports. As expected, the majority declared for immediate and separate state secession, with the other seceding states to meet Alabama in a provisional congress at Montgomery on February 4. The six members of the minority called for a general Southern convention before secession and the referral back to the people of any ordinance of secession. In rapid succession the cooperationist resolutions were rejected by identical votes of 53 to 45. With victory assured the secessionists permitted the cooperationists to take up the remainder of the session with speeches stating for the record their opposition to separate state secession.[51]

On January 11, after hearing that Florida had just seceded, the convention adopted the ordinance of secession by a vote of 61 to 39. This action touched off a wild celebration highlighted by the presentation of a new state flag hand sewn by the daughters of Alabama. A large crowd, which had waited six hours outside of the meeting room for news of secession, exploded with patriotic jubilation. As described by a participant, "bells were ringing—cannons firing[,] a steam boat whistling. Take it altogether it was one of the most stirring[,] enthusiastic & thrilling scenes I ever witnessed."[52]

Cooperationists were resigned but bitter. "Here I sit and from my window see the nasty little thing flaunting in the

---

[50] Smith, *Convention*, 69–74.   [51] *Ibid.*, 75–93.

[52] *Ibid.*, 118–122; Rev. Wm. H. Mitchell to his wife, Jan. 11, 1861, Reverend William H. Mitchell Letters, ADAH.

breeze which has taken the place of that glorious banner which has been the pride of millions of Americans and the boast of freemen the wide world over," wrote Lawrence R. Davis to John B. McClellan. He expected open hostilities to break out at any time and blamed it on "these gents of the tribe of Precipitators" who preached that secession would be peaceful. Northern Alabama could do nothing but "remain quiet." Vowing that he and thirty to thirty-five others would never sign the secession ordinance, he closed by damning the secessionists. "Praying God with my last breath that those who brought this on our country may meet their just award." Thomas J. McClellan spoke for many of the cooperationists when he explained his sense of futility to his wife.

> I have opposed this rash action of the Convention in every way I could and while I feel greatly outraged at the Convention for not submitting its action to the people for their ratification or rejection, I see no other course left but to submit to it. We must not do anything that would look like willingness on our part to submit to the policy of the black Republican party.[53]

Although cooperationism had crested and failed, the secessionists were still leery. They realized that the unpopularity of their actions remained a potent political force in northern Alabama. From Huntsville came reports "that there will be a successful attempt made to excite the people of N. Ala. to rebellion *vs.* the State & that we will have civil war in our midst." Cooperationist leaders there were supposedly planning to secede from the rest of Alabama and create a new state, Nickajack. Under these circumstances the secessionists had to guard against any pretense which would allow another set of elections around which the opposition might coalesce. Thus, on January 17 the convention tabled the Bulger motion

[53] Davis to McClellan, Jan. 13, 1861, Robert A. McClellan Papers, DU; McClellan to his wife, Jan. 14, 1861, Robert A. McClellan Papers, DU.

which provided for the popular election of delegates to the Montgomery Provisional Congress.[54]

The secessionists' great fear now was that lingering hopes for a reconstruction of the Union would yet scuttle their plans. "I am oppressed by the apprehension that we are in great danger from the reconstructionists," confided Alabama Congressman Pugh to Miles of South Carolina on January 24. The source of Pugh's concern was the famous Crittenden Compromise. Introduced in the Senate on December 18, the compromise consisted of six proposed constitutional amendments. The crucial amendment would have guaranteed the existence and protection of slavery south of the old Missouri Compromise line of 36°30' in all federal territories then held *and* "hereafter acquired." The border states pushed hard for Crittenden's plan since it was the only proposal with the least chance of acceptance in the lower South. However, for this very reason, the compromise was anathema to Republicans. They had not won a great victory based on the future restriction of slavery only to throw it away because the South could not countenance defeat.[55] When Pugh wrote Miles, the Crittenden plan was still officially alive. What worried Pugh was that the Republicans might change their minds and support the compromise, then "the border states will present an unbroken front & my fear is we shall be overwhelmed." If this did happen, Pugh saw one last alternative. "There is another way of avoiding the calamity of reconstruction and that is war. . . . Now pardon me for suggesting that South Carolina has the power of putting us beyond the reach of re-

[54] Hugh Lawson Clay to C. C. Clay, Jan. 11, 1861, Clay Papers, DU; Smith, *Convention*, 147–148. Elbert J. Watson, "The Story of Nickajack," *AR*, xx (Jan., 1967), 34–44, stressed that the chances of creating a new state were always remote.

[55] J. L. Pugh to Miles, Jan. 24, 1861, Miles Papers, SHC; Kenneth M. Stampp, *And the War Came: The North and the Secession Crisis, 1860–61* (Chicago, 1964), 129–141 and 167–170. The Crittenden plan was bottled up in the Senate in January, rejected by the House in February and by the Senate in March. Not one Republican representative or senator voted for it.

construction by taking Fort Sumter at any cost." There was no hurry, added Pugh. The South could afford to wait at least until a provisional government had been organized and then "let the question of time be settled by the apparent strength or weakness of the reconstruction movement."[56]

The secessionists in the Alabama convention shared Pugh's fears, if not necessarily his prescription of forcing war if worse came to worse. Even after the Provisional Congress had met and submitted a constitution for the new government back to the states, the cooperationists made one last effort. In editorials and public meetings, they demanded that the constitution should be subject to a vote of the people. "We have been precipitated out of the Union without this reference. If it is done again in so important a measure as this, the people may inquire, if they have no rights outside of the Convention."[57]

At the Montgomery convention, which had remained in session except for a brief recess, this demand was expressed in the Jemison resolution. In the ensuing debate, the secessionists accused their opponents of using the election as a subterfuge to rekindle party feelings and "to introduce the destructing elements of reconstruction, and other kindred questions." Why delay any longer? asked L. M. Stone. The convention had full authority to ratify the constitution and would be remiss in its duty if it failed to exercise this authority. The permanent government must be installed as soon as possible. Not only would it protect the South, but it "will

[56] Roy F. Nichols in *Blueprints For Leviathan: American Style* (New York, 1963), 146, argues that the real aim of many secessionists was the use of a new government as a bargaining agent for the winning of Southern rights within a reconstructed Union. The point is intriguing but overstated. The desire for a reconstructed Union was strongest among the reluctant secessionists, not the leaders of the movement.

[57] Tuscaloosa *Independent Monitor*, Feb. 1, 1861. Edward Dorr Tracy to C. C. Clay, March 6, 1861, Clay Papers, DU, has a vivid account of a Huntsville meeting in which Tracy claimed major credit for blocking the passage of reconstructionist resolutions.

put to flight, now and forever, all hopes of Reconstruction, and would prove to the world that our separation from the North is 'final, complete, and perpetual.' " Aided by the defection of a few cooperationists who believed by now that the best chance of averting war lay in strict unity, the secessionists won this last battle. The constitution, described by B. H. Baker as "this great magna-charta of the rights of white men," was adopted without referral to the people.[58]

The Mississippi convention met in Jackson on January 7. Its opening was a stirring occasion which captured all the romanticism and aggrieved sensibilities of the slaveholding class.

> When the President took his seat & the man of God addressed that Power which controls the destiny of nations, and invoked his blessings upon the proceedings of the day, the awful stillness was broken by sobs in every quarter of the apartment. Men and women were on their knees in prayer; tears streamed from many eyes, and every countenance evinced profound sorrow.

After the Reverend C. K. Marshall in his convocation had reminded those present that the South was the maligned party, forced to look outside of the Union for the safety of "the institution which Thy Providence has solemnly bound us to uphold, defend and protect," the convention got down to business. On the third ballot William S. Barry, a Breckinridge lawyer-planter from Lowndes, was chosen as permanent president. Alcorn, the conservatives' candidate, finished a distant second.[59]

Although the secessionists were clearly in command, they took pains to placate the conservatives. D. C. Glenn, a Breck-

[58] Smith, Convention, 323–325, 334–341, 361–363.

[59] Alexander M. Clayton and J. F. H. Claiborne, "The Secession Convention," Claiborne Papers, Folder 35, p. 4, SHC; *Journal of the State Convention and Ordinances and Resolutions Adopted in January, 1861, With an Appendix* (Jackson, 1861), 4, 7.

inridge lawyer and one of the more forceful secessionist leaders, declined a position on the committee to draft a secession ordinance. He privately explained to the president that placing another old-line Whig on the committee, such as Orlando Davis of Tippah, would better ensure harmony. In addition, Glenn was angling for the chairmanship of the committee on a Southern Confederacy, the post he considered as the most important in the entire convention. He received his wish on January 10. Another seemingly minor tactic revealed the secessionists' skill at soothing conservatives' feelings. On the first day all judges of the state's Circuit Courts and the High Court of Errors and Appeals were invited to take seats within the convention. Three days later the invitation was extended to all past judges of the High Court. These courtesies had an air of nonpartisan magnanimity and exhibited proper respect for the courts, the institution most venerated by conservatives.[60]

The second day, which was taken up in organizational details, presented an example of the feedback which existed between events on the floor and the participation of the galleries. Barry read a telegram announcing that immediate secession in Georgia was a certainty. This created such "great excitement" that Barry warned the galleries would be cleared unless order was restored. Glenn, basking in the limelight, announced that he also had joined in the applause. "Laughter —the ladies in the galleries looked smilingly in the direction of Mr. Glenn."[61] The convention would go into secret session for the crucial deliberations, but the crowd-pleasing tactics of a Glenn had already highlighted how outside pressure

[60] D. C. Glenn, "Memoranda," Claiborne Papers, Folder 39, p. 1, SHC; *Journal of the State Convention*, 12.

[61] J. L. Power's account of the convention, Claiborne Papers, Folder 51, Jan. 8, 1861, SHC. Power was a convention reporter and this manuscript account, interspersed with newspaper clippings, was a valuable supplement to his published work, *Proceedings of the Mississippi State Convention, Held January 7th to 26th, A.D. 1861* (Jackson, 1861).

307

could influence the behavior of the delegates. This pressure was an integral part of the convention, and few delegates could afford to ignore it.

L. Q. C. Lamar reported out the secession ordinance on January 9. For twelve hours behind closed doors, the convention debated the ordinance and three amendments proposed by the conservatives. The first amendment, a substitute for the entire ordinance, was offered by J. S. Yerger, a Whig lawyer from Washington County. A conditional unionist plan, it called for a convention of slaveholding states at Lexington, Kentucky, on February 10. This convention was charged with the twofold task of framing constitutional amendments which would guarantee Southern rights and of finding a formula "to finally settle and adjust all questions relating to the subject of slavery in such a manner as will relieve the South from the further agitation of that question." If the North rejected such compromise measures, the Lexington convention should immediately organize a Southern Confederacy. Utopian in its hopes and impractical in its operation, the Yerger amendment was rejected, 78 to 20. Support for the measure came from old Whig river counties and scattered counties in the north and southwest. The cooperationist Alcorn amendment, delaying Mississippi's secession until four neighboring states should secede, fared a little better, picking up 25 votes. A third Whig, Walker Brooke of Vicksburg, offered the last conservative amendment. His proposal for an election on the secession ordinance to be held the first Monday in February lost by a similar vote of 70 to 29.[62]

The conservatives had accomplished nothing except to place their opposition on the record. They had no reason to expect any differently since the secessionists were obviously in command from the first day. A Whig physician from Cal-

[62] Power, *Proceedings*, 10–12. Although the straight-out secessionists were younger than the conservatives, in the main there were no outstanding socioeconomic differences between those who voted for or against these three amendments. See Wooster, *People in Power*, 38–40.

houn, M. D. L. Stephens, who had voted for all three conservative amendments, explained why he was now for secession. "Amendment after amendment has been proposed to the
Ordinance from this side of the house, and each in turn have
been voted down by an overwhelming majority, until the
proposition has now narrowed down to *submission* or secession, and as between the two, I am for secession." Other conservatives agreed with Stephens' rationalization, and only fifteen members were bold enough to refuse to sign the secession
ordinance. Those who balked at the majority had uncommon
courage. As Alcorn told H. S. Fulkerson, the convention's
intolerance grew daily. Alcorn was well aware of the intense
zeal for secession and was a bit frightened by it.

Should we fail to commit ourselves, it will be charged
that we intend to desert the South. The people will be urged
to deny us a hearing. The epithet of coward and submissionist will be everywhere applied to us. We shall be
scouted by the masses! . . . I and others agreeing with me
determined to seize the wild and maddened steed by the
mane and run with him *for a time*. We voted for secession
and signed the ordinance.[63]

In a preview of the debate which would emerge at the Alabama convention in March, the convention now argued
whether it had the authority to ratify the constitution which
would be drafted by the Montgomery Provisional Congress.
Glenn, with the same fears of reconstruction that Pugh had
so forcefully expressed, played a pivotal role in the debate.
He later wrote J. F. H. Claiborne that the issue of ratification
"was *the* great question of the body & elicited all its talents
and much of its violence." Although in part magnifying his
own sense of importance, Glenn did have a valid point. Under

[63] Thomas H. Woods, "A Sketch of the Mississippi Secession Convention of 1861,—Its Membership and Work," *PMHS*, VI (1902),
93; Power, *Proceedings*, 13–15; H. S. Fulkerson, *A Civilian's Recollections of the War between the States*, ed. Percy Lee Rainwater
(Baton Rouge, 1939), 8.

no circumstances did the secessionists want to re-open the Pandora's box of another election since they had nothing to gain and, potentially, everything to lose. In his autobiography Wiley P. Harris was quite specific on this point. "When we brought back from Montgomery the Constitution which had been formed there, I opposed its submission to the people, because it involved delay and imperiled the whole undertaking. I felt that the defection of one state would be fatal."[64]

Glenn's committee on a Southern Confederacy issued its report on January 15. Its fifth resolution stipulated that any constitution and plan "for a permanent Government" adopted by the Montgomery Congress "shall be referred back to this Convention for its ratification or rejection." Various amendments from the floor proposed that the governor, legislature, or the Montgomery Congress, should call for a newly elected state convention for the purpose of ratification. Leading the fight for the original report, Glenn argued that the present convention had full authority in the matter. "Are the people to refer back to the people what the people have done? The Convention is the people or we are usurpers." He added that withdrawing Mississippi from the Union, a task already accomplished, entailed the equally vital responsibility of creating a new government for the protection of the state's sovereignty and institutions. Lamar professed as much faith in the people as any man but stated the ballot box was no place for the ratification of organic law. President Barry was more blunt and frankly admitted: "It is wiser and safer, in times like these, not to have too many elections—the people do not desire to be summoned from their homes to participate in a political crisis. At this time there ought to be complete unanimity for defence; old party strifes and jealousies would be renewed."[65]

[64] Glenn "Memoranda," SHC; "Autobiography of Wiley P. Harris," in Dunbar Rowland, *Courts, Judges, and Lawyers in Mississippi, 1798–1935* (Jackson, 1935), 325.

[65] Power's account of the convention, Jan. 15–17 and Jan. 22, 1861, SHC.

The proponents of a new convention put up a good fight. They failed to carry the crucial Fontaine amendment, but the vote was close, 49 to 43. The role of Fontaine, a straight-out secessionist from Pontotoc in northern Mississippi, was illustrative of the divisions over the ratification question. Delegates from the north and poorer farming counties in the south generally favored the submission back to the people of a permanent constitution. Fearing that a new government might yield too much power to the planters, they wanted a veto on the process. On the other hand, the votes to defeat the Fontaine amendment came from the Whiggish river counties and the Democratic plantation regions of central and eastern Mississippi. The vacillation of five Whigs was crucial in the defeat of any plan for a new convention. The five had voted for at least one of the three conservative amendments lost on January 9, but then voted against the Fontaine measure.[66] This refusal to support the call for an election on a permanent constitution had cost the Whig planters their best chance of introducing any uncertainty into Mississippi's secession and had given Glenn the victory he so earnestly desired.

The other extended debate concerned the question of raising revenue for the state's defense. A formula of a 50% increase in state taxes was finally agreed upon, but only after repeated charges that this plan perpetuated the present inequitous tax rates on land and slaves. Slaves under the age of sixty were taxed 75¢ per capita. Based on an average value of $600, this rate was 12½¢ per $100 or half that of the land tax of 25¢ per $100 valuation. This was obvious discrimination in favor of slave property, pointed out Joel Berry of Tippah, and he warned "that it is a storm *without*, against this species of property, that is the source of all our troubles, and we should be careful to give no just cause of complaint, *within*, against it."[67] Despite similar arguments from other

[66] For the individual voting, see *ibid.*, Jan. 22. The five were: Alcorn, Aldridge, Brooke, Isom, and McGehee of Bolivar.

[67] *Journal of the State Convention*, 42–43, 64–70; Power, *Proceedings*, 88.

northern delegates, the members from planting counties held firm and rejected all proposals to equalize the tax structure. Whig planters may have been forced to give up the Union, but they were not about to sacrifice the preferred tax status of their slave property. The revolution was to be as conservative as possible.

Mississippi's convention had been, in the words of a delegate from Kemper, "adorned, inspired, and largely controlled by its lawyer-members."[68] Since the legal profession traditionally had been ambitious Southerners' main entry into the planting class, it was no coincidence that lawyers should have led in this, the most ambitious undertaking in the state's history.

There was no talk of civil war or open resistance to secession in any parts of the state. The *Natchez Daily Courier* reported that the city greeted the news with gloom and sadness and that the delegate from Jones County was burned in effigy by his irate constituency for signing the secession ordinance. But far more typical was the response noted by Reuben Davis as he traveled through northern Mississippi on his way home from Washington. "I was scarcely out of the sound of cannon all the way." Where cannons could not be found for the celebration, anvils were substituted.[69] The yeomanry abided by the decision. Significant resistance would emerge only later, when the war effort began to disintegrate. Then, the yeomanry of eastern Mississippi, from the hill country in the northeast down through the piney woods in the southeast, would harbor Confederate deserters and become increasingly disloyal to what they viewed as a war fought for the rich by the poor.[70]

---

[68] Woods, "Sketch," 94.

[69] *Natchez Daily Courier*, Jan. 11, 1861; Bettersworth, *op.cit.*, 16; Reuben Davis, *Recollections of Mississippi and Mississippians* (Boston, 1891), 402.

[70] Bettersworth, *Confederate Mississippi*, 213–245. Bettersworth emphasized that not all this disloyalty was pro-Unionism; much of it was anti-authoritarianism. The disloyal regions in Alabama, also areas of poor land and small farms, can be traced in Wm. Stanley Hoole, *Alabama Tories* (Tuscaloosa, 1960), 5–14, and in Hugh C.

EPILOGUE

The exuberance and confidence with which the South seceded were unmistakable. This was not so much a fool's courage as it was a boldness spawned by desperation. Secession had to succeed if slavery, the core of the Southern reality, were to survive. The crisis involved her whole being—the legitimacy of her values and the continued existence of slavery, not only as an economic institution but also as a pattern of racial accommodations and the basis of society.

The young slaveholding planters, farmers, and lawyers of the Breckinridge Democrats, the most ambitious and dynamic elements in the South's political economy, were the first to perceive the crisis and they reacted most intensely to it. Southerners responded to their leadership because a majority had concluded that the victory of the Republicans in 1860 would eventually be as fatal to the perpetuation of slavery as any triumph of outright abolitionism. "The latter," wrote J. F. H. Claiborne in 1860, "would expel slavery, wherever it be found, by compulsory laws, or by fire and sword if necessary. The former would merely confine it where it is, exclude it from all territories, in whatever latitude, hereafter acquired by the common blood and treasure, and thus slowly but surely accomplish its destruction. Both aim at the same end."[71] Secession, by giving the South complete home rule and control over her own foreign policy, was a logical, though ultimately suicidal, outcome. It did not resolve the dilemma but offered the illusion of room for maneuver.

Southerners were certain that the most vital function of their society—its ability to assimilate and control slaves—would be destroyed by the confinement of slavery. As long as Southern racism lost none of its virulence and the demands of internal security remained so critical, the South would

---

Bailey, "Disloyalty in Early Confederate Alabama," *JSH*, XXIII (Nov., 1957), 522–528.

[71] John F. H. Claiborne, *Life and Correspondence of John A. Quitman* (New York, 1860), II, 265.

need ever more room for slavery. Southerners were incapable of accepting emancipation or viewing slavery as a flexible and progressive institution. Fearful of the racial and class consequences of shifting increasingly large numbers of slaves from the countryside and a soil-exhaustive agriculture into trades, industry, and the cities, they were captives of their own doubts and anxieties. Yancey rationalized that an independent South would have no need to expand since she would no longer require additional slave states to regain political parity within the Union, but others knew better. "Did we need more territory before secession, for the expansion of our peculiar institution? We yet have the same need for more territory," declared S. C. Posey at the Alabama secession convention. Ever concerned with the social effects of slavery's restriction, Posey asked: "When we look at the extent of our territory, the number and the increase of slaves upon our soil, which do we need most, more slaves, or more land for those we now have? Mr. President, the fierce strife we have had with the Northern States, which has led to the disruption of the Government, is a trumpet tongued answer to this question."[72]

For L. M. Stone, another delegate at the Alabama convention, "expansion seems to be the law and destiny and necessity of our institutions. To remain healthful and prosperous within, and to make sure our development and power, it seems essential that we should grow without." He talked of adding Arizona, Mexico, Cuba, and Central America to the Southern republic, and A. M. Clayton of Mississippi hoped that the "gold mines of California may be potent auxiliaries to the cotton fields of the South." A political union with the Pacific states, Clayton enthused, would give the South a direct route to the riches of the East Indies and China. "With the great valley of the Mississippi thus united with the Pacific, we could feed the world, we could clothe the world, and if assailed we could resist the world."[73]

[72] Smith, *Convention*, 251, 209.

[73] *Ibid.*, 236; Power's account of the Mississippi convention, Jan. 16, 1861, SHC.

These expansionist dreams were never realized by the Confederacy, but they furnished the impetus for its military campaigns into the Southwest. Possession of the New Mexico territory, which then included the present states of Arizona and New Mexico, would have given the Confederacy a gateway to all the western territories and the gold of California. Southern arms did succeed initially in gaining control over Arizona and the southern half of New Mexico but Union counterattacks pushed them out by the summer of 1862. Efforts to detach portions of northern Mexico and bring them into the Confederacy were also abortive.[74]

The failure of the Confederacy to expand has been overshadowed by its failure to survive. Some, of course, had foreseen the consequences and predicted the end of slavery. George F. Sallé, a Mobile Unionist, wrote Crittenden that "a civil war will as inevitably result in the abolishment of Slavery, as one event can possibly follow from another. This proposition, I think, needs no argument. The days of Slavery are numbered." But how much easier it was to give in to race chauvinism, to agree with the Southerner who, in speaking of his son, wrote: "he is *my Boy* and I *shall* endever [sic] to teach him not to love such a union as this has got to be. Better than his rights and neve [sic] to *submit* to the rule of a negro Presadent [sic]. I wish I had twelve Boyes [sic] to give there surves [sic] to there coutry [sic]."[75]

---

[74] W. H. Watford, "Confederate Western Ambitions," *SWHQ*, XLIV (Oct., 1940), 186–187; Clement Eaton, *History of the Southern Confederacy* (New York, 1954), 49–50; J. Fred Rippy, "Mexican Projects of the Confederacy," *SWHQ*, XXII (April, 1919), 291–317. Interest in Mexico would have been higher had it not been for Southern racism. At Alabama's secession convention Yancey warned that the annexation of any Mexican territory would bring with it "a mass of ignorant and superstitious and demoralized population." Earlier, Smith of Tuscaloosa had sneeringly remarked: "Even the slave would degenerate in Mexico." Smith, *Convention*, 251, 207.

[75] Sallé to Crittenden, Jan. 15, 1861, Crittenden Papers, LC; Frank A. Thert to his brother, Dec. 29, 1860, Crutchfield—Fearn—Steele Family Papers, MDAH.

The passion with which Southerners embraced secession was best expressed by Charles D. Fontaine. Writing his wife just after Mississippi had seceded, he proclaimed: "Our cause is holy, and we fear not the arbitrament forced upon us of the Sword." That was the crux of the Southern tragedy. Her highest ideals had become inseparable from the preservation of slavery. She would indeed defend slavery to the bitter end and welcome Northern armies "with bloody hands and hospitable graves."[76]

[76] Fontaine to his wife, Sally Ann, Jan. 13, 1861, Fontaine and Family Papers, MDAH.

POLITICS, SLAVEHOLDER (S. H.) DENSITIES
AND POPULATION GROWTH RATES (1850–1860)
IN ALABAMA AND MISSISSIPPI COUNTIES

Since many of the tables in the text were based on county units, the key variables for the individual counties are listed below.

Alabama

County	% Breck. Vote	% Secession Vote[a]	% S. H./ Families	% Change White Pop.	% Change Slave Pop.
Calhoun	85	74	18	+ 28	+ 15
Dale	82	84	18	+ 85	+139
Marion	79	24	12	+ 43	+ 41
Henry	78	100	26	+ 54	+ 98
Fayette	77	28	16	+ 32	+ 39
Clarke	74	81	34	+ 55	+ 54
Barbour	72	100	42	+ 14	+ 50
Jackson	72	45	18	+ 26	+ 49
Jefferson	72	46	19	+ 35	+ 17
St. Clair	70	40	15	+ 68	+ 34
Cherokee	69	49	19	+ 26	+ 78
Coffee	68	67	17	+ 52	+154
DeKalb	68	Cooperationist	10	+ 27	+ 68
Pickens	66	77	59	− 8	+ 16
Randolph	66	46	13	+ 71	+103
Wilcox	64	96	77	+ 23	+ 50
Lowndes	61	100	68	+ 15	+ 32
Marengo	59	100	68	− 5	+ 18
Montgomery	57	89	57	+ 19	+ 22
Pike	55	100	36	+ 29	+131
Tuscaloosa	54	36	30	+ 23	+ 33
Talladega	53	46	31	+ 26	+ 27
Sumter	53	96	77	− 20	+ 22
Shelby	53	52	29	+ 25	+ 57
Blount	52	39	7	+ 47	+ 56
Walker	52	15	8	+ 54	+ 95

Alabama

(*continued*)

County	% Breck. Vote	% Secession Vote[a]	% S. H./ Families	% Change White Pop.	% Change Slave Pop.
Russell	52	100	49	+ 30	+ 40
Perry	52	98	62	+ 14	+ 31
Winston	52	0	2	+133	+ 97
Washington	49	91	45	+ 77	+ 67
Chambers	49	60	65	− 11	+ 6
Covington	49	60	14	+ 83	+ 71
Autauga	49	51	45	+ 12	+ 10
Macon	48	86	63	− 24	+ 17
Tallapoosa	48	38	26	+ 49	+ 64
Choctaw	46	68	50	+ 46	+ 88
Dallas	46	74	85	+ 4	+ 16
Bibb	45	?[b]	33	+ 13	+ 34
Morgan	44	45	28	+ 14	+ 8
Monroe	44	53	55	+ 22	+ 38
Butler	44	100	37	+ 57	+ 87
Limestone	43	29	51	− 14	+ 1
Franklin	43	20	29	− 11	+ 4
Greene	43	61	78	− 22	+ 7
Conecuh	39	48	36	+ 30	+ 11
Coosa	37	44	26	+ 32	+ 27
Lauderdale	36	30	32	− 4	+ 12
Marshall	32	27	13	+ 21	+110
Mobile	31	65	30	+ 65	+ 22
Baldwin	28	99	44	+ 71	+ 67
Madison	27	21	51	− 2	+ 2
Lawrence	25	Cooperationist	30	− 14	− 1

[a] The % of the secession vote, here as in Mississippi, is often only an estimate since some voters split their ballot when faced with a multiple slate. In some counties candidates whose position could not be determined received a scattering of votes.

[b] As mentioned in the text, it is unclear what stand was taken by Bibb's unopposed candidate.

Mississippi

County	% Breck. Vote	% Secession Vote	% S. H./ Families	% Change White Pop.	% Change Slave Pop.
Jackson	95	100	24	+ 30	+ 32
Hancock	85	64	N. R.[c]	N. R.	N. R.
Lawrence	85	100[a]	48	+ 55	+ 40
Harrison	84	100	23	+ 11	− 30
Greene	82	100	38	+ 11	+ 11
Neshoba	81	91	35	+ 81	+ 66
Pike	79	62	51	+ 46	+ 59
Covington	77	71	43	+ 28	+ 40
Newton	74	73	39	+ 83	+227
Jones	73	35	24	+ 55	+ 49
Oktibbeha	73	100	57	+ 24	+ 58
Simpson	73	85	43	+ 17	+ 51
Winston	73	Secession	49	+ 8	+ 53
Scott	69	92	41	+ 86	+150
Clarke	68	84	45	+ 49	+208
Franklin	68	47	57	+ 38	+ 42
Itawamba	68	Coalition	22	+ 24	+ 67
Smith	68	68	38	+ 77	+120
Attala	66	48	38	+ 21	+ 47
Calhoun	66	44	27	−	−
Choctaw	66	61	30	+ 37	+ 41
Lauderdale	66	64	40	+ 36	+ 91
Monroe	66	65	55	− 9	+ 9
Chickasaw	65	Coalition	49	−	−
Copiah	65	80	56	+ 18	+ 45
Jasper	65	67	47	+ 50	+141
Leake	65	100	45	+ 57	+ 97
Perry	64	Cooperationist[b]	30	+ 11	− 1
Wayne	62	61	24	+ 16	+ 40
Carroll	60	Coalition	64	− 5	+ 41
Claiborne	59	69	56	− 3	+ 7
Madison	59	63	102	+ 22	+ 31
Noxubee	58	98	76	+ 4	+ 37
Lowndes	57	86	79	+ 6	+ 29
Rankin	57	44	60	+ 66	+117
Sunflower	57	73	N. R.	N. R.	N. R.
Tippah	57	Coalition	29	+ 3	+ 28
Marion	56	92	48	+ 13	− 1
Pontotoc	56	Coalition	35	+ 20	+ 53

Mississippi
(*continued*)

County	% Breck. Vote	% Secession Vote	% S. H./ Families	% Change White Pop.	% Change Slave Pop.
Holmes	55	Coalition	76	+ 5	+ 43
Kemper	55	82	51	− 17	+ 7
Lafayette	55	Coalition	46	−	−
Amite	53	41	81	+ 22	+ 31
Wilkinson	53	52	80	− 23	− 1
Jefferson	51	70	75	+ 11	+ 18
Yalobusha	51	Secession^d	54	−	−
Tishomingo	50+	27	22	+ 42	+154
Tallahatchie	48	Secession	73	+ 35	+ 98
Yazoo	48	63	66	+ 39	+ 62
Hinds	47	58	91	+ 3	+ 34
Washington	47	49	N. R.	N. R.	N. R.
Marshall	46	52	64	− 20	+ 13
Tunica	45	Secession	65	+123	+280
Bolivar	43	47	126	+253	+316
Issaquena	42	51	76	+ 60	+ 76
Warren	39	19	58	+ 15	+ 14
Adams	38	23	63	+ 43	− 1
Coahoma	38	26	76	+ 10	+266
Panola	38	Coalition	66	+ 4	+ 33
DeSoto	37	Coalition	65	− 1	+ 46

[a] It was assumed that both Breckinridge candidates stood for immediate secession.

[b] As noted in the text, a cooperationist won the election since the secessionists split their vote between two candidates.

[c] No returns.

[d] Voted conservative only on the first Brooke amendment.

A NOTE ON METHODOLOGY

FOR the number of the politicians who were traced in the census returns, their location by counties, and the newspapers in which they were identified, the interested reader is referred to Appendix B of my Ph.D. dissertation, "Road to Revolution: The Social Basis of Disunion in Alabama and Mississippi" (Columbia University, 1971).

The criterion used in the selection of politicians was whether an individual performed a specific role in the presidential campaign or in the election for secession delegates. This role was interpreted in an organizational sense and included a wide range of party service, whether as an officeholder, committee member, presidential elector, county delegate to a state convention, participant in a ratification meeting, member of a political club, or planner of a party function, such as a political barbecue. Identification of the politicians then permitted use of Schedule No. 1 of the 1860 census returns (which lists by counties all free persons) to learn the age, occupation, and place of birth of the politicians and the amount of real and personal property owned by them. Schedule No. 2, the slave schedule, revealed how many of the activists owned slaves and the size of their holdings. The relationships between these variables were presented either in tabular form or as part of the discussion in the text.

Certain methodological problems arose. Since the census takers were inconsistent in their use of the terms farmer and planter, it was decided that planter would be applied only to those agriculturists, whether labeled in the census as farmer or planter, who owned thirty or more slaves (see Charles S. Sydnor, *Slavery in Mississippi* [New York, 1933], 67, 68, for a discussion on the distinction between a farmer and planter). In order to simplify the categories, occasional multiple occupations, such as lawyer-farmers, were listed under that occupation which most seemed to have shaped the individual's formative outlook, in this case, lawyer. Clerks and artisans, as well as businessmen and shopkeepers, were categorized together under the term town middle class. This group was normally a very small part of the party samples and to have subdivided them further would not have been helpful.

Comparable sets of party organizations were isolated by the politics and extent of slaveholding within their respective counties. This classification had two advantages. It allowed meaningful comparisons to be drawn between organizations operating within similar socioeconomic milieus. It would be palpably misleading, for example, to compare the characteristics of politicians from a mountainous or pine barrens area with those from a cotton region. A small slaveholder in the former areas would have a social status and degree of wealth above that of his neighbors; in the cotton belt he would be overshadowed in wealth and status by the planter. Mixing party samples from both areas would have clouded the distinctive features of each set. Second, this classification revealed whether party allegiances varied with the strength of the party in comparable regions. That is, did a party, in say the Black Belt, attract the same sort of adherents in counties where it was in the majority as in those where it was in the minority?

The limitations of the census returns should be noted. Their reliability was a function both of the diligence of the census takers and the extent to which individuals would divulge all their property holdings. Complete accuracy is out of the question. However, since large samples were taken and since the primary concern was with the emergence of broad and consistent patterns, the effect of individual errors in the returns would tend to be canceled out.

BIBLIOGRAPHY

Manuscript Collections

Alabama Department of Archives and History
    Henry H. Armstrong Correspondence
    Alonzo B. Cohen Letters
    Sarah R. Espy Diary
    William P. Gould Diary
    Bolling Hall Letters
    Rev. Francis Hanson Diary
    John Henderson Papers
    Samuel Henderson Letters
    Henry W. Hilliard Papers
    Rev. William H. Mitchell Letters
    Governor A. B. Moore Correspondence
    John Tyler Morgan Papers
    Thomas Joyce McClellan Letters
    Colin J. McRae Papers
    Lewis Parsons Letters
    John B. Todd Papers
    Samuel Alexander Martin Wood Papers
    Michael Leonard Woods Papers
    William Lowndes Yancey Correspondence
    Election Returns—Secretary of State Files

University of Alabama
    Lewy Dorman Manuscript
    Jemison Collection
    Manly Collection

Duke University
    Benson-Thompson Family Letters
    John Cantey Papers

323

Duke University (*cont.*)
Clement C. Clay Papers
Edward Crenshaw Papers
George Smith Houston Papers
Robert Anderson McClellan Papers
Duncan McLaurin Papers
Nathaniel Niles Papers
B.L.C. Wailes Diary
Henry Watson, Jr. Papers
Thomas B. Webber Diary

Library of Congress
John Jordan Crittenden Papers
Andrew Johnson Papers

Mississippi Department of Archives and History
Simeon Roe Adams Papers
James L. Alcorn Papers
William R. Barksdale Letters
Crutchfield-Fearn-Steele Papers
Dr. Holden Garthur Evans Diary
W. S. Featherston Paper
Charles D. Fontaine Papers
Governors' Records—Series E, Vol. 49: Administration
of Governor John J. Pettus, Correspondence for the
year 1860
William Burr Howell Papers
T. N. Martin Manuscript
Mayes-Dimitry-Stuart Papers
Samuel M. Meek Papers
Flavellus G. Nicholson Diary-Journal
William L. Nugent Letters
J. A. Orr Papers
Walter Alexander Overton Diary
John J. Pettus Papers
Rucks-Valliant Papers

Oscar J. E. Stuart Papers (Diary of Ann L. Hardeman)
William T. Walthall Papers
William N. Whitehurst Papers
Election Returns—Series F, Vols. 83 & 85, Secretary of
    State Records

Southern Historical Collection: University of North Carolina
    Samuel Andrew Agnew Diary
    James Lusk Alcorn Papers
    James B. Bailey Papers
    Buchanan-McClellan Papers
    Edward C. Bullock Paper
    Campbell-Colston Papers
    J.F.H. Claiborne Papers
    Benjamin Fitzpatrick Papers
    Gordon-Hackett Papers
    John Gideon Harris Diary
    James Henry Joiner Papers
    Francis Terry Leak Diary
    Levert Papers
    James Mallory Diary(microfilm)
    William Porcher Miles Papers
    Niles Books
    P. H. Pitts Paper, Diary
    James Roach Diary
    William F. Samford Papers(microfilm)
    Emma Maria Service Papers
    Frank F. Steel Papers
    Robert Tweed Papers(microfilm)
    Wyche-Otey Papers
    Benjamin C. Yancey Papers

The bulk of these manuscripts were useful chiefly in gaug-
ing the reaction to a particular event—such as the drought,
rumors of abolitionist outrages, Lincoln's election, and secession. No single collection allowed the activities of the radicals

to be traced over an extended period of time. Particularly disappointing were the Yancey collections. The William Lowndes Yancey folders at the Ala. Dept. of Archives and History are an excellent source for the key public speeches Yancey delivered in 1860 but add little to our knowledge of political developments within Alabama. The two most useful letters were those from Yancey to Beverly Mathews, Aug. 6, 1860, wherein he revealed his sense of persecution at being labeled a disunionist by the Whigs, and Yancey to his brother, Benjamin, May 17, 1860, which spelled out his position on slavery in the territories. The Benjamin Cudsworth Yancey papers are invaluable for a study of Southern agriculture or Alabama politics in the mid-1850's, but have little on events leading up to secession. Noteworthy were the letters from William in December of 1856 in which he expressed his disappointment over not being offered a cabinet post under Buchanan.

Most valuable were the correspondence of Governors Moore and Pettus during the secession crisis. These incoming letters provided a wide sampling of prosecession sentiment. The Claiborne and Miles collections in the Southern Historical Collection should be mentioned. The former is a massive compilation dealing with many aspects of ante-bellum Mississippi history. The material on Mississipi's secession convention was an indispensable supplement to the official records published by the convention. The Miles collection is one of the finest depositories of the fire-eaters' correspondence. Although of primary value for South Carolina politics, the letters touched upon problems and tactics common to all the fire-eaters.

Of the diaries those of Gould, Mallory, and Wailes were most useful. All three men were conservative Whigs who accepted secession with great reluctance. Their diaries are a prime source for the dilemmas faced by the conservatives. Unfortunately, the diaries of rabid secessionists, such as Francis Terry Leak and John Gideon Harris, were either incomplete or thin on politics.

United States Census Bureau
1860 Census: Schedules No. 1(Free), No. 2(Slave), and No. 4(Agriculture) for Alabama and Mississippi.

Originals of the free and slave schedules are deposited at the National Archives, Washington, D.C.; the agricultural schedules are distributed among the individual states. Microfilm copies of all these schedules can be consulted at various libraries, such as the University of North Carolina in Chapel Hill, or may be purchased from the Census Bureau. Valuable as an introduction to the scope and use of these census manuscripts are: Joseph A. Hill, "The Historical Value of the Census Records," American Historical Association, *Annual Report* (1903), I, 197–208, and Barnes F. Lathrop, "History from the Census Returns," *Southwestern Historical Quarterly*, LI (April, 1948), 293–312.

Printed Primary Sources

Published Letters, Speeches, Writings, Editorials,
and Election Returns

Bassett, John Spencer, ed., *The Southern Plantation Overseer As Revealed in His Letters* (Northampton, 1925).

Burnham, W. Dean, *Presidential Ballots 1836–1892* (Baltimore, 1955).

Cluskey, M. W., *Speeches, Messages, and Other Writings of the Honorable Albert Gallatin Brown* (Philadelphia, 1859).

Dumond, Dwight L., *Southern Editorials on Secession* (New York, 1931).

Howard, Milo B., Jr., ed., "A. B. Moore Correspondence Relating to Secession," *Alabama Historical Quarterly*, 23 (Spring, 1961), 1–28.

Perkins, Howard C., ed., *Northern Editorials on Secession*, 2 Vols. (New York, 1942).

Rowland, Dunbar, ed., *Jefferson Davis, Constitutionalist: His Letters, Papers, and Speeches*, 10 Vols. (Jackson, 1923).

BIBLIOGRAPHY

Wish, Harvey, ed., *Ante-Bellum: Writings of George Fitzhugh and Hinton Rowan Helper on Slavery* (New York: Capricorn Books, 1960).

Burnham's work is the most complete and accessible documentation of county voting returns for nineteenth century presidential elections. Perkins and Dumond provide excellent samplings of editorial opinions on secession. Among the published correspondences Howard and Rowland were most valuable. Included within the Howard collection were letters from four of Alabama's secession commissioners and the extremely interesting Cabiness letter of Oct. 29 which described political sentiment in northern Alabama. Use of the multi-volumed Rowland collection saves the researcher from searching through the many Southern depositories which house Davis letters.

Government Publications and Documents

FEDERAL

Compendium of the Seventh Census, comp. J.D.B. DeBow (Washington, 1854).
The Seventh Census of the United States . . . , J.D.B. DeBow, supt. (Washington, 1853).
Eighth Census of the United States, 1860: Agriculture (Washington, 1864).
The Eighth Census: Population of the United States in 1860, comp. Joseph C. G. Kennedy (Washington, 1864).
Statistics of the United States (Including Mortality, Property, & C.) in 1860 (Washington, 1866).
Tenth Census of the United States: Report on Cotton Production in the United States, Eugene W. Hilgard, special agent in charge (Washington, 1884).

ALABAMA

Acts of the Seventh Biennial Session of the General Assembly of Alabama (Montgomery, 1860).

328

The Code of Alabama, prepared by John J. Ormond, Arthur P. Bagley, George Goldthwaite, with head notes and index by Henry C. Semple (Montgomery, 1852).
Senate and House Journal, 1859-'60 (Montgomery, 1860).

MISSISSIPPI

Journal of the House of Representatives of the State of Mississippi, Called Session, January, 1861 (Jackson, 1861).
Journal of the Senate of the State of Mississippi: Called Session (Jackson, 1860).
Laws of the State of Mississippi, Passed at a Called Session of the Mississippi Legislature held, in the City of Jackson, November, 1860 (Jackson, 1860).
Laws of the State of Mississippi, Passed at a Regular Session of the Mississippi Legislature held, in the City of Jackson, November, 1859 (Jackson, 1860).
The Revised Code of the Statute Laws of the State of Mississippi (Jackson, 1857).

The published federal census returns were of prime importance. Grouped around the county as the basic unit, these returns supplied the raw data necessary for compiling population, slaveholding, and agricultural growth patterns. The state publications were helpful in understanding the legal framework of slave society, as well as the prosecession pressure exerted by the legislatures.

Contemporary Speeches, Writings, Convention Accounts, Pamphlets, and Periodicals

DeBow's Review

DeBow, J.D.B., *The Industrial Resources, Etc., of the Southern and Western States . . . ,* 3 Vols. (New Orleans, 1852).
Hundley, Daniel R., *Social Relations in Our Southern States* (New York, 1860).
Important Political Pamphlet, for the Campaign of 1860 (Montgomery, 1860).

Journal of the State Convention and Ordinances and Resolutions Adopted in January, 1861, With an Appendix (Jackson, 1861).

Letters of Hon. John Forsyth, of Alabama, Late Minister to Mexico, to Wm. F. Samford, Esq., in Defence of Stephen A. Douglas (Washington, 1859).

Smith, William R., *The History and Debates of the Convention of the People of Alabama, Begun and held in the City of Montgomery, on the seventh Day of January, 1861; in which is preserved the Speeches of the Secret Sessions, and Many Valuable State Papers* (Montgomery, 1861).

Speech of Hon. Albert G. Brown, delivered at Crystal Springs, Copiah Co., Miss., September 6th, 1860 (Jackson, 1860).

Speech of William C. Smedes, Esq., delivered at Appolo Hall, Vicksburg, Miss., On the 27th day of October, A.D. 1860, Upon the Right of a State to Secede from the Union. And other Political Topics (Vicksburg, 1860).

The articles in *DeBow's Review* constitute one of the finest single sources for the politico-economic views of the South. Based in New Orleans and enjoying the largest circulation of any Southern periodical, the magazine was the leading spokesman for the Lower South. Its essays, supplemented by the material in DeBow's *Industrial Resources*, touch upon all the problems and their proposed solutions which faced the South in the 1850's. Hundley's sociological work is a classic. Writing with the confidence and detachment of an aristocrat, he describes the major classes and pinpoints social cleavages and tensions. The Forsyth letters and the speeches of Brown and Smedes furnish a succinct summary of the three major parties' positions. The exact wording of the party platform in Alabama will be found in the *Important Political Pamphlet*. Of the two published accounts on the secession conventions, Smith's *History and Debates* is easily the more complete.

BIBLIOGRAPHY

NEWSPAPERS

Unless otherwise specified, all newspapers have nearly complete files for the year 1860.

Alabama Department of Archives and History
  Ashville *St. Clair Diamond*, Dec. 5, 26, 1860.
  Auburn *Sketch Book*, Nov., Dec., 1860.
  Baptist Correspondent, Dec. 5, 1860.
  Benton Weekly Herald
  Cahaba Gazette, July 13, 27, 1860.
  Camden Republic, July 19, 1860.
  Carrollton *Pickens Republican*
  Carrollton *West Alabamian*
  Claiborne *Southern Champion*
  Eutaw *Independent Observer*, Jan. 11, 1861.
  Florence Gazette
  Gainesville *Independent*
  Greensboro *Alabama Beacon*
  Greenville *South Alabamian*
  Greenville *Southern Messenger*
  Grove Hill *Clarke County Democrat*
  Hayneville *Chronicle*
  Hayneville *Watchman*
  Huntsville *Southern Advocate*
  Jacksonville Republican
  Jacksonville *States' Rights Democrat*, Sept. 26, Nov. 14, 1860.
  Linden Jeffersonian, Oct. 10, 1860.
  Mobile Evening News, Sept. 27, 1860.
  Montgomery Weekly Advertiser
  Montgomery Weekly Mail
  Montgomery Weekly Post
  Weekly Montgomery Confederation
  Opelika *Southern Era*
  Pratteville *Autauga Citizen*

331

Pratteville *Southern Statesman*
Selma *Alabama State Sentinel*, Oct. 10–Dec. 19, 1860.
Selma *Issue*, Oct. 17, 1860.
Selma Morning Reporter, June 1, 1860.
Selma Weekly Reporter, Aug. 1, 12, 1860.
Southwestern Baptist
Talladega *Alabama Reporter*
Talladega *Democratic Watchtower*
Troy *Southern Advertiser*, Dec. 7, 1860–Jan., 1861.
Tuscaloosa *Independent Monitor*, Feb. 1, 1861.
Tuscumbia *States' Rights Democrat*, June 1–Dec. 21, 1860.

University of Alabama
    Huntsville *Weekly Democrat*, scattered.
    Tuscaloosa *Independent Monitor*

Clayton Courthouse
    Clayton Banner

Canton Courthouse
    Canton *American Citizen*

Columbia University
    Mobile Daily Register, Jan.–June, 1860.

Library of Congress
    Mobile Daily Advertiser
    Paulding *Eastern Clarion*
    Tuscaloosa *Independent Monitor*

Macon Courthouse
    Macon Beacon, scattered for 1860.

Mississippi Department of Archives and History
    Jackson *Semi-Weekly Mississippian*

Natchez Daily Courier
Natchez *Mississippi Free Trader*
Paulding *Eastern Clarion*, May, 1860.
Raymond *Hinds County Gazette*, scattered for 1860.
Weekly Vicksburg Whig

University of Mississippi
Yazoo Democrat, down through Aug., 1860.

University of North Carolina
Kosciusko Chronicle, Dec. 14, 1860.
Columbus *Mississippi Democrat*

Sardis Courthouse
Weekly Panola Star

Vicksburg Courthouse
Vicksburg Daily Evening Citizen, Dec., 1860.

Winifred Gregorie, ed., *American Newspapers, 1821–
1936: A Union List of Files Available in the United States
and Canada* (New York, 1937) is the best guide for locating
newspapers. Particularly helpful for this study were Rhoda
C. Ellison, *History and Bibliography of Alabama Newspapers
in the Nineteenth Century* (University, Ala., 1954) and The
Mississippi Historical Records Survey, *A Preliminary Union
List of Mississippi Newspaper Files Available in County
Archives, Offices of Publishers, Libraries, and Private Collections in Mississippi* (Jackson, 1942). Newspapers were
my source for the identification of political activists. In Alabama the four Montgomery papers, followed by those in
Huntsville and Mobile, were most useful in understanding
and following political events and ideology. Impressions
gathered from these newspapers were corroborated by the
editorials in the rural press. Far fewer Mississippi newspapers
have survived, but the Breckinridge and secessionist parties

are adequately represented by their chief spokesmen—the Jackson *Mississippian*, Natchez *Free Trader*, and the Paulding *Eastern Clarion*. The Whigs and cooperationists can be traced in the Vicksburg *Whig*, the *Natchez Daily Courier*, and the *American Citizen*.

SECONDARY LITERATURE

For an introduction to the ante-bellum South one may turn with profit to any of the writings of Clement Eaton. With a grace and polish that frequently underline his Whiggish proclivities, he has been the pre-eminent chronicler of the Old South. His *The Growth of Southern Civilization, 1790–1860* (New York: Harper Torchbook, 1963) summarizes much of the recent research and contains an excellent bibliography. For a short but well-balanced introduction see chapters 2 and 3 of James G. Randall and David Donald, *The Civil War and Reconstruction*, 2d ed. (Boston, 1961). Eugene D. Genovese, *The Political Economy of Slavery* (New York, 1965), is a provocative reinterpretation which stresses the South's need to expand. Of especial assistance in locating materials for this study were: Thomas M. Owen, "A Bibliography of Alabama," American Historical Association, *Annual Report* (1897), 777–1248; "Alabama Archives," *ibid.* (1904), 487–553; and "Bibliography of Mississippi," *ibid.* (1899), 633. Albert B. Moore, *History of Alabama and Her People*, 3 Vols. (Chicago, 1927) and Dunbar Rowland, *History of Mississippi: The Heart of the South*, 2 Vols. (Chicago, 1925) were helpful state studies.

Arthur C. Cole, *The Whig Party in the South* (Washington, 1913) and Charles G. Sellers, Jr., "Who Were the Southern Whigs?" *AHR*, LIX (Jan., 1954), 335–346, are the standard sources on that party. The Whigs' Know-Nothing phase is covered by W. Darrell Overdyke, *The Know-Nothing Party in the South* (Baton Rouge, 1950). There is no comprehensive history of the Democrats, the South's majority party by the 1850's. One must rely on the state studies or on general narrative works such as Avery O. Craven, *The Coming of the Civil War*, 1st ed. (Chicago: Phoenix, 1966) and *The Growth of Southern Nationalism, 1848–1861* (Baton Rouge, 1953). Little has been done on analyzing the composition of the Douglas and Breckinridge factions. Joel H. Silbey, "The Southern National Democrats, 1845–1861," *Mid-America*, 47 (July, 1965), 176–190, suggests what remains to be done. Avery Craven, Clement Eaton, and Ulrich B. Phillips, *The Course of the South to Secession*, ed. E. Merton Coulter (Gloucester, 1958) is valuable for Southern politics in the 1850's. Republican ideology is analyzed by Eric Foner in *Free Soil, Free Labor, Free Men* (New York, 1970). For Republican policy in 1860–61, see David M. Potter, *Lincoln and his Party in the Secession Crisis* (New Haven, 1962) and Kenneth M. Stampp, *And the War Came*, 1st ed. (Chicago: Phoenix, 1964). Of the two I found Stampp's emphasis on the near impossibility of compromise to be closer to my reading of the crisis.

A good beginning for an understanding of Alabama politics are Thomas P. Abernathy, *The Formative Period in Alabama, 1815–1828* (Montgomery, 1922) and Theodore H. Jack, *Sectionalism and Party Politics in Alabama, 1819–1842* (Menasha, Wisc., 1919). Lewy Dorman's *Party Politics in Alabama From 1850 Through 1860* (Montgomery, 1935) is both detailed and interpretative. Thomas B. Alexander's "The Basis of Alabama's Ante-Bellum Two-Party System," *AR*, XIX (Oct., 1966), 243–276, is superb for its conceptualization of how parties should be analyzed. Allen W. Jones, "Party Nominating Machinery in Ante-Bellum Alabama," *ibid.* XX (Jan., 1967), 34–44, looks at the evolution of the nominating process. More work needs to be done on the Alabama Democracy and the States' Rights Opposition party, but the Whigs have been well covered in: Alexander, Carter, Lister, Oldshue, and Sandlin, "Who Were the Alabama Whigs?" *AR*, XVI (Jan., 1963), 5–19; Thomas B. Alexander, "Persistent Whiggery in Alabama and the Lower South, 1860–1867," *ibid.*, XII (Jan., 1959), 5–34; Carlton Jackson, "A

History of the Whig Party in Alabama, 1828–1860," unpublished Ph.D. thesis (University of Georgia, 1962) and "The White Basis System and the Decline of Alabama Whiggery," *AHQ*, 25 (Fall and Winter, 1963), 246–253; Grady Mc-Whiney, "Were the Whigs a Class Party in Alabama?" *JSH*, XXIII (Nov., 1957), 510–522; and J.E.D. Yonge, "The Conservative Party in Alabama, 1848–1860," *TAHS*, IV (1904), 501–526. The role of Alabama's delegation at Charleston is surveyed in James L. Murphey, "Alabama and the Charleston Convention of 1860," *ibid.*, V (1905), 239–266, and Austin L. Venable, "The Conflict Between the Douglas and the Yancey Forces in the Charleston Convention," *JSH*, VIII (Feb.–Nov., 1942), 226–241. Although I strongly disagree with his conclusion that policy differences between the two parties were minimal, Durward Long's "Political Parties and Propaganda in Alabama in the Presidential Election of 1860," *AHQ*, 25 (Spring and Summer, 1963), 120–135, is the best study of the election in Alabama. Clanton W. Williams has collected election statistics measuring voter participation in "Presidential Election Returns and Related Data for Ante-Bellum Alabama," *AR*, I (Oct., 1948), 279–293, and *ibid.*, II (Jan., 1949), 63–73. Two accounts by Sutton S. Scott, "Recollections of the Alabama Democratic State Convention of 1860," *TAHS*, IV (1904), 313–320, and "The Alabama Legislatures of 1857–58 and 1859–60," *ibid.*, V (1905), 43–82, are valuable for a personal perspective on the state's politics. Data on legislators, governors, and county officials can be found in Ralph A. Wooster, *The People in Power: Courthouse and Statehouse in the Lower South, 1850–1860* (Knoxville, 1969).

Mississippi politics have not been as well canvassed by historians, but several good studies exist. For the earlier period, see Edwin A. Miles, *Jacksonian Democracy in Mississippi* (Chapel Hill, 1960). Cleo Hearon's "Mississippi and the Compromise of 1850," *PMHS*, XIV (Oxford, Miss., 1914), 7–230, is excellent. Percy Lee Rainwater, *Mississippi: Storm Center of Secession, 1856–1861* (Baton Rouge,

1938), and Donald M. Rawson, "Party Politics in Mississippi, 1850–1860," unpublished Ph.D. thesis (Vanderbilt University, 1964), cover the 1850's. Of the two, Rainwater is more interpretative. John K. Bettersworth, *Confederate Mississippi: The People and Policies of a Cotton State in Wartime* (Baton Rouge, 1943) includes material for 1860. Useful articles are Jack W. Gunn, "Mississippi in 1860 As Reflected in the Activities of the Governor's Office," *JMH*, xxii (July, 1960), 179–191, and R. H. Thompson, "Suffrage in Mississippi," *PMHS*, i (Oxford, Miss., 1898), 25–49. Other state studies which I found particularly helpful were Harold Schultz, *Nationalism and Sectionalism in South Carolina, 1852–1860* (Durham, 1950) and, for social analysis, Roger W. Shugg, *Origins of Class Struggle in Louisiana* (Baton Rouge, 1966).

For the election in the South one should begin with Ollinger Crenshaw, *The Slave States in the Presidential Election of 1860* (Baltimore, 1945). Crenshaw, in "Urban and Rural Voting in the Election of 1860," in *Historiography and Urbanization: Essays in American History in Honor of W. Stull Holt*, ed. Eric F. Goldman (Baltimore, 1941), 43–66, points out that the conservative candidates, Bell and Douglas, ran strongest in the urban areas of both the North and the South. Crenshaw, "The Psychological Background of the Election of 1860 in the South," *NCHR,* xix (July, 1942), 260–279, Donald B. Kelly, "Harper's Ferry: Prelude to Crisis in Mississippi," *JMH*, xxvii (Nov., 1965), 351–373, and Steven Channing, *Crisis of Fear, Secession in South Carolina* (New York, 1970), discuss the near hysteria over abolitionists and slave revolts which swept over the South. An analogous development in 1856, though not as intense, is covered by Harvey Wish, "The Slave Insurrection Panic of 1856," *JSH*, v (May, 1939), 206–222. Frank H. Heck, "John C. Breckinridge in the Crisis of 1860–1861," *ibid.*, xxi (Aug., 1955), 316–346, and Robert W. Johannsen, "Stephen A. Douglas and the South," *ibid.*, xxxiii (Feb.–Nov., 1967), 26–50, examine two of the leading protagonists. The entire problem of the election and secession is covered by the essays in George H. Knoles, *The Crisis of the Union: 1860–1861* (Baton Rouge, 1965). I found Arthur C. Cole, "Lincoln's Election an Immediate Menace to Slavery in the States?" *AHR*, XXVI (July, 1931), 740–767, which argued the negative, and the rebuttal by J. G. de Roulhac Hamilton in *ibid.*, XXVII (July, 1932), 700–711, to be disappointing. On the one hand, Cole states that slavery "was scarcely the crux of the sectional issue" and then paradoxically stresses that increasing class stratification and restlessness among nonslaveholders made unification around slavery all the more imperative for the South. Hamilton's essay is unbalanced and ill-tempered. It offers no more insight than a standard piece of Breckinridge campaign propaganda.

A satisfactory study of Southern expansionism has yet to be written. Parts of the story can be traced in Elmer LeRoy Craik, "Southern Interest in Territorial Kansas, 1854–1858," *Collections of the Kansas State Historical Society, 1919–1922*, XV (Topeka, 1923), 334–450, and Walter L. Fleming, "The Buford Expedition to Kansas," *TAHS*, IV (1904), 167–192. C. A. Bridges, "The Knights of the Golden Circle: A Filibustering Fantasy," *SWHQ*, XLIV (Jan., 1941), 287–302, and Ollinger Crenshaw, "The Knights of the Golden Circle," *AHR*, XLVII (Oct., 1941), 23–50, treat a well-known but little studied organization. J. Fred Rippy, "Mexican Projects of the Confederacy," *SWHQ*, XXII (April, 1919), 291–317, and W. H. Watford, "Confederate Western Ambitions," *ibid.*, XLIV (Oct., 1940), 161–187, detail the attempts of the Confederacy to expand. Genovese, *Political Economy*, 243–274, has the best discussion on the relationship between expansionism and the structure and exigencies of slave society. In particular, his analysis (251–254) of the famous Ramsdell article, "The National Limits of Slavery Expansion," *MVHR*, XVI (Sept., 1929), 151–171, seriously weakens one of the chief props of those who argue that slavery would have died a natural death if left alone. Chauncey S. Boucher, "*In Re* That Aggressive Slavocracy," *MVHR*, VIII (June–Sept.,

1921), 13–79, has shown how untenable is the concept of a united Southern conspiracy for aggressive expansion. However, the fact that the needs of various sections of the South differed, or were even contradictory, on expansion cannot be used to deny the central importance of the issue. In the 1850's Southern Democrats made unmistakable and increasingly shrill demands for an equal share in the federal territories. Such demands were, after all, the cornerstone of the Breckinridge ideology.

John Hope Franklin, *The Militant South, 1800–1861* (Boston, 1966), is the standard study on Southern militarism and violence. He tends to overstress the darker side of the Southern character and Charles S. Sydnor, "The Southerner and the Laws," *JSH*, VI (Feb. 1940), 3–23, is a welcome corrective. Southern legal attitudes are also treated in Clement Eaton, "Mob Violence in the Old South," *MVHR*, XXIX (Dec., 1942), 351–370. Foreigners were numerically insignificant but their concentration in towns and cities made them an important political force. Although it is clear that most foreigners were Democrats, their assimilation into the political process still requires more study. For their socio-economic role, see Ella Lonn, *Foreigners in the Confederacy* (Chapel Hill, 1940) and two articles by Herbert Weaver, "Foreigners in Ante-Bellum Towns of the Lower South," *JSH*, XIII (Feb., 1947), 62–73, and "Foreigners in Ante-Bellum Mississippi," *JSH*, XVI (July, 1954), 151–163.

My interpretation of the Southern economy was greatly influenced by Douglas C. North, *The Economic Growth of the United States, 1790–1860* (New York: Norton Library, 1966). Also helpful were Stuart Bruchey, *The Roots of American Economic Growth, 1607–1861* (New York, 1965) and Louis M. Hacker, *The Triumph of American Capitalism* (New York, 1940). William N. Parker, ed., "The Structure of the Cotton Economy of the Antebellum South," *AgH*, XLIV (Jan., 1970), contains the latest quantitative studies. Robert R. Russel, *Economic Aspects of Southern Sectionalism, 1840–1861* (Urbana, 1924) has yet to be superseded and is one of the few works which attempts to relate the economy with political developments. Touching upon this same problem are John Hebron Moore, "Economic Conditions in Mississippi on the Eve of the Civil War," *JMH*, XXII (July, 1960), 167–178, and Percy Lee Rainwater, "Economic Benefits of Secession: Opinions in Mississippi in the 1850's," *JSH*, I (Nov., 1935), 459–474.

Agriculture was the heart of the Southern economy and we are fortunate to have the masterful two volume study by Lewis C. Gray, *History of Agriculture in the Southern United States To 1860* (New York, 1941). Supplemental material is supplied by Paul W. Gates, *The Farmer's Age: Agriculture, 1815–1860* (New York, 1960) and Sam Bowers Hilliard, "Hog Meat and Hoecake: A Geographical View of Food Supply in the Heart of the Old South, 1840–1860," unpublished Ph.D. thesis (University of Wisconsin, 1966). Charles S. Davis, *The Cotton Kingdom in Alabama* (Montgomery, 1939) and John Hebron Moore, *Agriculture in Ante-Bellum Mississippi* (New York, 1958), are two fine state studies. Agricultural needs inexorably became politicized and this process is treated by James C. Bonner, "Advancing Trends in Southern Agriculture, 1840–1860," *AgH*, XXII (Oct., 1948), 248–259, and E. Merton Coulter, "Southern Agriculture and Southern Nationalism Before the Civil War," *ibid.*, IV (July, 1930), 77–91. Eugene D. Genovese, "Recent Contributions to the Economic Historiography of the Slave South," *Science and Society*, XXIV (Winter, 1960), 53–66. reviews some of this literature.

The pre-eminence of the plantation, the driving force of Southern agriculture, is explained by Lewis C. Gray, "Economic Efficiency and Competitive Advantages of Slavery Under the Plantation System," *AgH*, IV (April, 1930), 31–47, and Ulrich B. Phillips, "The Origin and Growth of the Southern Black Belts," *AHR*, XI (July, 1906), 798–816. Phillips was always most sensitive to the social consequences of the plantation's dominance. This can be seen in his *Life and Labor in the Old South* (Boston, 1963; reprint of the

1929 edition) and in his essays collected in Eugene D. Genovese, ed., *The Slavery Economy of the Old South* (Baton
Rouge, 1968). The first accurate measurement of the monopolization of wealth engendered by the plantation system was
Fabian Linden, "Economic Democracy in the Slave South:
An Appraisal of Some Recent Views," *JNH*, XXXI (1946),
140–189. Linden systematically revealed the flaws in the
methodology and conclusions of the Owsley school. The
yeomanry is shown to have had a much less significant economic role than postulated by Owsley and his followers. For
this school, which at least focuses on the too frequently overlooked yeomanry and makes use of manuscript census returns, see: Frank L. Owsley, *Plain Folk of the Old South*
(Chicago: Quadrangle Paperback, 1965); Frank L. and
Harriet C. Owsley, "The Economic Basis of Society in the
Late Ante-Bellum South," *JSH*, VI (Feb., 1940), 24–45;
Warren I. Smith, "Land Patterns in Ante-Bellum Montgomery County, Alabama," *AR*, VIII (July, 1955), 196–208;
and Herbert Weaver, *Mississippi Farmers, 1850–1860* (Nashville, 1945). Robert R. Russel, "The Effects of Slavery Upon
Nonslaveholders in the Ante-Bellum South," *AgH*, XV (April,
1941), 112–116, arrives at a conclusion similar to that of
the Owsley school—chiefly that the deleterious effects of
slavery upon nonholders have been greatly exaggerated.
Joseph Karl Mann, "The Large Slaveholders of the Deep
South, 1860," unpublished Ph.D. thesis (University of Texas,
1964), itemizes the control of the wealthy elite. Gavin
Wright, " 'Economic Democracy' and the Concentration of
Agricultural Wealth in the Cotton South, 1850–1860," *AgH*,
XLIV (Jan., 1970), 63–93, is very thorough and complements
the work of both Linden and Mann.

The cycle of migrations in the South and the resultant low
population density relative to the North cannot be separated
from the planters' monopolization of the best lands. W. H.
Yarbrough, *Economic Aspects of Slavery in Relation to
Southern and Southwestern Migration* (Nashville, 1932),
makes this connection clear. Barnes F. Lathrop, *Migration*

Into East Texas, 1835–1860 (Austin, 1949) is an exhaustive statistical study, based on census returns, of one phase of this pattern.

Although marred by the author's racism, Ulrich B. Phillips' *American Negro Slavery* (Baton Rouge, 1966; reprint of the 1918 edition) is still a good departure for an understanding of slavery. However, it should be read in conjunction with Kenneth M. Stampp, *The Peculiar Institution: Slavery in the Ante-Bellum South* (New York, 1956). Stampp does not necessarily offer greater insights into the workings of the institution, but he does document slavery's more brutal features which Phillips was prone to overlook. Slavery for each of the Southern states has been studied. James Benson Sellers, *Slavery in Alabama* (University, Ala., 1950), is a sound work, though not up to the standards set by Charles S. Sydnor, *Slavery in Mississippi* (New York, 1933). Thanks to Robert S. Starobin, *Industrial Slavery in the Old South* (New York, 1970) and Richard C. Wade, *Slavery in the Cities* (New York, 1964), we now have a balanced picture of slavery as it functioned in town and factory. The rising slave prices in the 1850's are documented by Ulrich B. Phillips, "The Economic Cost of Slave-Holding," *PSQ*, xx (June, 1905), 257–275. W. J. Carnathan, "The Proposal to Re-open the African Slave Trade in the South," *SAQ*, xxv (Oct., 1926), 410–429, and Harvey Wish, "The Revival of the African Slave Trade in the United States, 1856–1860," *MVHR*, xxvii (March, 1941), 569–588, look at the political consequences of this rise. The fullest treatment of the issue will be found in Ronald T. Takaki, *A Pro-Slavery Crusade* (New York, 1971). The interstate slave trade is covered by Frederic Bancroft, *Slave-Trading in the Old South* (Baltimore, 1931).

The issue of race has always been inseparable from that of slavery. Ulrich B. Phillips, "The Central Theme of Southern History," *AHR*, xxxiv (Oct., 1928), 30–43,—"that it [the South] shall be and remain a white man's country"—put the matter most bluntly. Invoking the very real fear of racial equality was the slaveholders' chief weapon in removing class and economic factors from politics and in winning the non-slaveholders' support. Wilbert E. Moore and Robin M. Williams, "Stratification in the Ante-Bellum South," *AR*, 7 (June, 1942), 343–351, and Edgar T. Thompson, "The Planter in the Pattern of Race Relations in the South," *Social Forces*, 19 (Dec., 1940), 244–252, analyze the effectiveness of this tactic. For the Negrophobia of the whites at the bottom of Southern society, see Paul H. Buck, "The Poor Whites of the Ante-Bellum South," *AHR*, xxxi (Oct., 1925), 41–54, and W. O. Brown, "Role of the Poor Whites in Race Contacts of the South," *Social Forces,* 19 (Dec., 1940), 258–268.

Several works dealing directly with secession proved helpful. The social and economic characteristics of the delegates and legislators who formally decided the question of secession have been compiled from census returns by Ralph A. Wooster, *The Secession Conventions of the South* (Princeton, 1962). Clarence P. Denman, *The Secession Movement in Alabama* (Montgomery, 1933), is a bit thin, but Percy Lee Rainwater's *Mississippi: Storm Center of Secession* ranks with the best of the state studies. J. C. Oldshue, "The Secession Movement in Tuscaloosa County, Alabama," unpublished master's essay (University of Alabama, 1961), examines an Alabama county and Peggy Jane Duckworth, "The Role of Alabama Black Belt Whigs in the Election of Delegates to the Secession Convention," unpublished master's essay (University of Alabama, 1961), reinterprets the Whigs' actions. The recollections of John W. Inzer, "Alabama's Secession Convention, 1861," *Confederate Veteran*, xxxi (Jan., 1923), 7–9, capture the mood of the convention. Also valuable are: William Brantley, Jr., "Alabama Secedes," *AR,* vii (July, 1954), 165–185; David L. Darden, "The Alabama Secession Convention," *AHQ*, 3 (Fall and Winter, 1941); and Durward Long, "Alabama's Secession Commissioners,"

CWH, ix (March, 1963), 55–66. The centers of resistance to secession are traced in: Wm. Stanley Hoole, *Alabama Tories* (Tuscaloosa, 1960); Hugh C. Bailey, "Disloyalty in Early Confederate Alabama," *JSH*, xxiii (Nov., 1957), 522–528; Durward Long, "Unanimity and Disloyalty in Secessionist Alabama," *CWH*, xi (Sept., 1965), 257–273; and Elbert L. Watson, "The Story of the Nickajack," *AR*, xx (Jan., 1967), 17—26. After Rainwater, I found Bettersworth's *Confederate Mississippi* and Winbourne M. Drake, "Constitutional Development in Mississippi, 1817–1865," unpublished Ph.D. thesis (University of North Carolina, 1954), to be most useful on Mississippi's secession. The convention itself is well described by a participant, Thomas H. Woods "A Sketch of the Mississippi Secession Convention of 1861. —Its Membership and Work," *PMHS*, vi (Oxford, Miss., 1902). The literature on the debate over the degree of popular support for secession is reviewed by Warren J. Donnelly, "Conspiracy or Popular Support: The Historiography of Southern Support for Secession," *NCHR*, xlii (Winter, 1965), 70–84, and Ralph A. Wooster, "The Secession of the Lower South: An Examination of Changing Interpretations," *CWH*, vii (June, 1961), 117–127.

In recounting the participant's perception of the past, memoirs provided some valuable insights. Reuben Davis, *Recollections of Mississippi and Mississippians* (Boston, 1891), has some essential political material. Accounts of two conservatives, Henry S. Foote, *War of the Rebellion; or, Scylla and Charybdis* (New York, 1866), and Henry W. Hilliard, *Politics and Pen Pictures at Home and Abroad* (New York, 1892), are disappointing on specific events but do present the standard Whig charge that secession should be blamed on overly ambitious Democratic politicians. Victoria V. Clayton, *White and Black Under the Old Regime* (New York, 1899), has an interesting chapter on the Clayton expedition to Kansas, 62–81. There is no better source for the flowering of Mississippi's antebellum culture than Susan

Dabney Smedes, *Memorials of a Southern Planter*, ed. by Fletcher M. Green (New York, 1965). Further material on Mississippi's culture and economy can be found in two works by H. S. Fulkerson, *A Civilian's Recollections of the War Between the States*, ed. Percy Lee Rainwater (Baton Rouge, 1939) and *Random Recollections of Early Days in Mississippi* (Baton Rouge, 1937); also see Frank A. Montgomery, *Reminiscences of a Mississippian in Peace and War* (Cincinnati, 1901). The life and economic problems of a Whig planter in the Delta are told in "The Autobiography of Benjamin Grubb Humphreys," ed. Percy Lee Rainwater, *MVHR*, XXI (Sept., 1934), 231–255. John A. Aughey, *Tupelo* (Lincoln, Neb., 1888), relates the tribulations of a Mississippi Unionist.

There are excellent biographical guides for Alabama and Mississippi. Thomas M. Owen's *History of Alabama and Dictionary of Alabama Biography*, 4 Vols. (Chicago, 1921) is a model of patient and thorough research. Despite some overlapping, one should also consult W. Brewer, *Alabama, Her History, Resources, War Record, And Public Men From 1540 to 1872* (Montgomery, 1872) and William Garrett, *Reminiscences of Public Men in Alabama for Thirty Years* (Atlanta, 1872). Goodspeed's *Biographical and Historical Memoirs of Mississippi*, 2 Vols. (Chicago, 1891), though bulky and poorly organized, contains a vast amount of material. Less thorough, but easier to use, are Robert Lowry and W. H. McCardle, *History of Mississippi* (Jackson, 1891), and Dunbar Rowland, *Encyclopedia of Mississippi History*, 2 Vols. (Madison, 1907).

For integrating their subjects with the politics and culture of the society in which they lived, James B. Ranck, *Albert Gallatin Brown, Radical Southern Nationalist* (New York, 1937) and Charles S. Sydnor, *A Gentleman of the Old Natchez Region, Benjamin L. C. Wailes* (Durham, 1928) are outstanding. Weymouth T. Jordan, *Hugh Davis and his Alabama Plantation* (University, Ala., 1948), combines biography with plantation management. Of two biographies on Lamar, Wirt Armistead Cate, *Lucius Q. C. Lamar: Secession and Reunion* (Chapel Hill, 1935), and Edward Mayes, *Lucius Q. C. Lamar: His Life, Times, and Speeches, 1825–1893* (Nashville, 1896), Mayes is more valuable for the antebellum period. There is no adequate study of Yancey. John DuBose, *The Life and Times of William Lowndes Yancey* (Birmingham, 1892), contains many of his speeches but as a critical biography is too verbose and fulsome in its praise. In a series of journal articles, which amplify points made in his *The Role of William L. Yancey in the Secession Movement* (Nashville, 1945), Austin L. Venable has examined Yancey's public career. However, his interpretation of Yancey as one who has constantly been maligned and misunderstood is overextended and leaves us with an image that blurs Yancey's significance rather than pinpointing it. Malcolm C. McMillan, "William L. Yancey and the Historians: One Hundred Years," *AR*, xx (July, 1967), 163–186, places the treatment of Yancey in historical perspective and stresses just how little is known of his motivations. Additional useful biographies are: Robert Wm. Dubay, "John Jones Pettus: A Study in Secession," unpublished master's essay (Southern Mississippi University, 1966); Paul A. Meigs, *The Life of Senator Robert Jemison Junior* (University, Ala., 1928); Ruth K. Nuermberger, *The Clays of Alabama, A Plantation-Lawyer-Politician Family* (Lexington, 1958); Lillian A. Pereyra, *James Lusk Alcorn, Persistent Whig* (Baton Rouge, 1966); Jessie P. Rice, *J. L. M. Curry, Southerner, Statesman, and Educator* (New York, 1949); and Hudson Strode, *Jefferson Davis, American Patriot, 1808–1861* (New York, 1955). The careers of several Alabama politicians have been treated in scholarly articles. Among these are included: Toccoa Cozart, "Henry W. Hilliard," *TAHS*, iv (1904), 277–299; Emma B. Culver, "Thomas Hill Watts, A Statesman of the Old Regime," *TAHS*, iv (1904), 415–439; George Petrie, "William F. Samford, Statesman and Man of Letters,"

TAHS, IV (1904), 465–486; Sutton S. Scott, "Personal Recollections of Thomas Hord Herndon, With Remarks Upon his Life and Character," *TAHS*, V (1905), 267–278; and Luther N. Steward, Jr., "John Forsyth," *AR*, XIV (April, 1961), 98–123.

County histories tend to be an open-ended melange of trivia interspersed with occasional bits of useful information for the historian. Welcome exceptions to this dreary generalization were: Rev. T. H. Ball, *A Glance into the Great South-East, or, Clarke County, Alabama, and its Surroundings, From 1540 to 1877* (Tuscaloosa, 1962; a reprint of the 1882 edition); Thomas B. Carroll, *Historical Sketches of Oktibbeha County* (Gulfport, Miss., 1931); John M. Dombhart, *History of Walker County: Its Towns and its People* (Thornton, Ark., 1937); and Benjamin F. Riley, *History of Conecuh County, Alabama* (Blue Hill, Maine, 1964; a reprint of the 1881 edition). One of the more imaginative county political histories is Kit C. Carter, "A Critical Analysis of the Basis of Party Alignment in Lowndes County, Alabama, 1836–1860," unpublished master's essay (University of Alabama, 1961). Useful, but less perspective, were: Mary F. Summers, "Politics in Tishomingo County, 1836–1860," *JMH*, XXVIII (May, 1966), 133–152; John W. Hadskey, "A History of Franklin County, Mississippi, to 1865," unpublished master's essay (Mississippi State College, 1954), and Suzanne Spell, "A History of Jones County, Mississippi," unpublished master's essay (Mississippi College, 1961). James C. Bonner, "A Profile of a Late Ante-Bellum Community," *AHR*, XLIX (July, 1944), 663–680, reveals how the careful use of census data for one county can be used to shed light on a whole range of socioeconomic questions. Unfortunately, few have followed Bonner's lead and we have too few similar studies to comprise a representative sampling of the Southern economy. Two articles by Harris G. Warren, "Agricultural Statistics of Claiborne County, 1850 and 1860," *JMH*, XV (Oct., 1953), 230–241, and "Population

Elements of Claiborne County, 1820–1860," *JMH*, IX (April, 1947), 75–87, and one by J. H. Jones, "Evolution of Wilkinson County," *PMHS*, XI (Oxford, Miss., 1910), 75–86, provide a detailed look at the society and concentrated wealth of two early settled river counties in Mississippi.

Inadequate attention has been paid Southern towns and cities. Ulrich Phillips pointed out the subservience of town to countryside in his brief essay, "Historical Notes of Milledgeville, Ga.," *Slave Economy*, ed. Genovese, 176–187, but his insight has not been built upon by historians. Weymouth T. Jordan has a fine chapter "The development of Marion, a Black Belt town," in *Ante-Bellum Alabama, Town and Country* (Tallahassee, 1957). For a sense of the pace and values of town life, see John Hardy, *Selma: Her Institutions and Her Men* (Selma, 1957; a reprint of the 1879 edition) and William L. Lipscomb, *A History of Columbus, Mississippi, During the 19th Century* (Birmingham, 1909). There is some useful material in William D. McCain, *The Story of Jackson: A History of the Capital of Mississippi, 1821–1951* (Jackson, 1953), Vol. I. Harris G. Warren, "People and Occupations in Port Gibson, 1860," *JMH*, X (April, 1948), 104–115, documents the foreign-born's dominance of business and trade activity in a Mississippi river town. Weymouth T. Jordan, "Ante-Bellum Mobile: Alabama's Agricultural Emporium," *AR*, I (July, 1948), 180–202, examines Mobile's economic growth. The state capitals are studied in Martha Boman, "A City of the Old South: Jackson, Mississippi, 1850–1860," *JMH*, XV (Jan., 1953), 1–32, and Clanton W. Williams, "Conservatism in Old Montgomery, 1817–1861," *AR*, X (April, 1957), 96–110. For alerting me to the contrasting roles played by the towns in the Old Southwest and Northwest, I am indebted to Stanley Elkins and McKitrick, "A Meaning for Turner's Frontier: Democracy in the Old Northwest," *PSQ*, LXIX (Sept., 1954), 321–353, and "A Meaning for Turner's Frontier: The Southwest Frontier and New England," *PSQ*, LXIX (Dec., 1954), 565–585.

The accounts of travelers have frequently been criticized as biased and unrepresentative descriptions of Southern life. Although all such literature necessarily suffers to some extent from these flaws, I found that many accounts held up surprisingly well when measured against later research. Of Frederick Law Olmsted's various works, *A Journey to the Back Country* (London, 1860) deals most extensively with Alabama and Mississippi. Often accused of ignoring the yeomanry, Olmsted simply denied that they played a major economic role and attributed this to the pernicious effects of slavery upon free labor. Fabian Linden has demonstrated the accuracy of this assessment. More biting than Olmsted, but less thorough, is James Stirling, *Letters From the Slave States* (London, 1857). Joseph Holt Ingraham, *The South-West. By a Yankee*, 2 Vols. (New York, 1835), conveys the energy of the Mississippi cotton frontier in the 1830's, and A. DePuy Van Buren, *Jottings of a Year's Sojourn in the South* (Battle Creek, Mich., 1859), describes the mores of a settled Mississippi plantation region in the 1850's. The common Southerner's jealousy of wealth, and especially ostentatious wealth, was noticed by Sir Charles Lyell, *A Second Visit to the United States of North America* (New York, 1849), Vol. 2. He also commented on how this jealousy engendered an egalitarian political rhetoric. Robert Russell, *North America, Its Agriculture and Climate* (Edinburgh, 1857), has a superb discussion on plantation agriculture and the manner in which it inhibited the growth of inland towns and severely curtailed rural consumption. Also useful were: Edmund Kirke (pseudonym of J. R. Gilmore), *Among the Pines: or, South in Secession Time* (New York, 1862); C. H. Rogers, *Incidents of Travel in the Southern States and Cuba* (New York, 1862); and William H. Russell, *My Diary North and South* (Boston, 1863). A few shorter accounts were of value. W. H. Venable, "Down South Before the War," *Ohio Archaeological and Historical Publications* (Columbus, 1893), Vol. ii, 488–513, touches upon the xenophobia of Mississippians in the late 1850's. F. N. Boney, ed., "Southern Sojourn: A

Yankee Salesman in Ante-Bellum America," *AR*, xx (April, 1967), 142–154, relates the business activities of a traveling salesman. Unsurpassed for a description of the loneliness and economic lethargy of the Mississippi pine barrens in the 1840's is J.F.H. Claiborne, "A Trip Through the Piney Woods," *PMHS*, ix (Oxford, Miss., 1906), 487–538.

Coffee County, Alabama, drought of 1860, 155–156

Columbus *Mississippi Democrat*, 205, 261

communications in South, controlled by slaveholders, 46–47

Compromise of 1850, 4, 92; Southern resistance to, 197

Concordia Parish, Louisiana, 29

conditional unionism, 193; arguments for, 238; definition of, 198–199; rejected by Mississippi convention, 308

Conecuh County, Alabama: anti-Breckinridge vote and the economy, 141; carried by cooperationists, 252, 270; cooperationist vote and economy, 276; excitement over election of 1860, 166, 190

Confederacy, 245, 297; as essential for maintenance of white supremacy, 227; military campaigns in the Southwest, 315

Confederate Provisional Congress, 245, 302, 304–305, 309–310

confinement of slavery, Southern anxieties over, 16–17, 23–24, 93, 101, 108–109, 111, 225, 313–314

Congress, power over slavery in the territories: and Crittenden Compromise, 304; Breckinridge Democrats' attitude on, 54–55, 106, 126, 151; Republicans' attitude on, 21

consumer demand, lack of in South, 30–33

Cook, John P., 247

cooperationists: advantages of, in northern Alabama, 257–258; bitterness over defeat in Alabama, 302–303; demands of, on North, 239; dilemma of, 240, 245; favor referendum on secession, 241; hesitancy of, 237; outmaneuvered in northern Mississippi, 266; public contempt for, 268–269, 279; success in northern Alabama, 270–272, 274; tactics of, 199–201; weakness of position, 238–239

cooperative secession, 193, 196, 231, 259; appeal to Southern conservatives, 242–245; arguments in favor of, 237–238, 240–241; as a brake on disunion in 1850, 197–198; definition of, 198–199; link with Union sentiment, 238; negative tone of, 238–239; opposition to, 196–197, 204, 208, 234–236; rejected by Alabama and Mississippi secession conventions, 302, 308; social basis of its appeal, 295–296; viewed as an alternative to anarchy, 241–242, 245, 259; vote for, in southern Alabama, 259. *See also* elections for secession conventions and secession

Coosa County, Alabama, anti-Breckinridge vote and economy, 141

Copiah County, Mississippi: and Minute Men, 208; drought of 1860, 155; secessionist vote and farm ownership, 289

cotton: output lowered by drought, 219n; prices, 5, 92; value to North and Britain, 235

cotton frontier: in Alabama, 139–140; in Mississippi, 148; link to ideology of Breckinridge Democrats, 151

surtax, 116; party affiliation and cotton production, 67

Greene County, Mississippi, socioeconomic background of secessionists, 294

Greensboro *Alabama Beacon*, 214, 250

Greenville (Ala.) *Southern Messenger*, 256

Grenada (Miss.) *Rural Gentleman*, 155

Guttery, Robert, 274

Hale, Stephen F., 204

Hall, Bolling, 207, 251; cooperationist nominee, 252

Hall, John, 207

Hamilton, D. H., 48

Hamlin, Hannibal, 205; Southern belief that he was a mulatto, 226

Hammond, James, 17

Hancock, J. B., 233

Hancock County, Georgia, 4

Hancock County, Mississippi, 144

Handsboro (Miss.) *Democrat*, 213

Hardy, John, 175

Hare, Willis V., 249

Harper, L., 146

Harrington, G., suspected abolitionist, 172

Harris, H. J., 104

Harris, Wiley P., 60; on arrogance of planters, 124; opposed to a popular election on Confederate constitution, 310; secessionist nominee, 209

Harrison, Benjamin, 248

Harrison, Edmund, 90

Harrison, G., 196

Harrison County, Mississippi, 144

Harvey, John G., opposition to

his conditional unionism, 214, 250

Hayneville (Ala.) *Chronicle*, 231

Hayneville (Ala.) *Watchman*, 105, 215

Hazel, Joseph Allen, 149

Helper, Hinton R., 48, 259

Henderson, John, 268–269

Henderson, Joseph, 268–269, 279

Henry, Andrew, 228

Henry, Patrick, 292

Henry County, Alabama, strong Breckinridge vote and expansion of cotton agriculture, 140

Hill, A. P., 262, 293

Hinds County Mississippi, 78, 85; and Vicksburg convention of cooperationists, 259; lost by Breckinridge, 146; slipping Whig majorities and expanding plantation economy, 147; socioeconomic background of secessionists, 294

Holcombe, Alexis E., 164

Holcombe, William H., 47

Holmes County, Mississippi, 79

Houston (Miss.) *Southern Patriot*, 82

Hudson, Thomas J., 114

Humphreys, Benjamin G., 96

Hundley, Daniel R., 42; on potential Southern abolitionists, 169

Huntsville (Ala.) *Southern Advocate*, 116, 162, 221–223

Illinois, 26; as a source of foodstuffs for the South, 159; importance of towns in development, 27

illiteracy: in mountains of Alabama, 143; in South, 47, 47n

359

and slaveholding status: in Alabama, 61–76; in Mississippi, 78–88; summary of, 88

party central executive committees: in Alabama, 60–61; in Mississippi, 78

party ideologies and voter support, summary of, 150–152

party profiles, summary of, 89–91

Paulding (Miss.) *Eastern Clarion*, 82, 234

Payne, Lem, suspected abolitionist, 172

Penick, Dr. W. C., 251

Pennsylvania, 243

Perry County, Alabama: election for secession convention, 248; moderate Breckinridge vote and expansion of plantation agriculture, 130–131; party affiliations and cotton production, 66

Pettigrew, James, 7

Pettus, E. W., 247

Pettus, John J., 82, 112, 115, 159, 175, 181, 196–197, 202, 205; and Minute Men, 208–209; and slave uprising scare in 1859, 166; career of, 53–54; issues call for secession convention, 194–195; on probability of war, 235; provides for arms purchases, 203

Phelan, John D., on threat of racial intermixture, 228–229

Phillips, Ulrich B., 9

Phillips, William S., 199, 208

physicians, in politics, 90

Pickens County, Alabama: election for secession convention, 249–250; food shortages within, 159, 162; socioeconomic background of secessionists and cooperationists, 284–285;

strong Breckinridge vote and expansion of cotton agriculture, 131

Pierce, Franklin, 215

Pike County, Alabama: election for secession convention, 249; moderate Breckinridge vote and expansion of cotton agriculture, 140; party affiliations and cotton production, 73; socioeconomic background of secessionists and cooperationists, 284

Pike County, Mississippi, secessionist vote and farm ownership, 289

piney woods of Mississippi: Democratic allegiances, 148–149; secessionist vote, 287; socioeconomic characteristics, 144, 148–149; voter apathy, 144, 145n

plantation agriculture: debate over self-sufficiency of, 33; dominance over Southern economy, 30–35, 43–44; higher costs in 1850's, 92–93, 96

plantation life, embodiment of Southern ambitions, 29, 36

planters: definition of, 63; fear of urbanization, 36–37; opposition to industrialization, 15–18

political parties: functions of in South, 50–54; structure of, 59–65

Pontotoc County, Mississippi, 79; and popularity of secession, 196; Douglas party within, 87

poor whites, 42; definition of, 39; racial pride appealed to, 43

Library of Congress Cataloging in Publication Data

Barney, William.
  The secessionist impulse: Alabama and
Mississippi in 1860.

    Bibliography: p.
    1. Secession. 2. Alabama—Politics and
government—To 1865. 3. Mississippi—Politics
and government—To 1865. 4. Alabama—Economic
conditions. 5. Mississippi—Economic conditions.
I. Title.
E440.5.B28   973.7'13   73-16769
ISBN 0-691-04622-0

كتب